ENCYCLOPEDIA OF GAY AND LESBIAN POPULAR CULTURE

ENCYCLOPEDIA OF GAY AND LESBIAN POPULAR CULTURE

LUCA PRONO

GREENWOOD PRESS
Westport, Connecticut • London

Library of Congress Cataloging-in-Publication Data

Prono, Luca.
  Encyclopedia of gay and lesbian popular culture / Luca Prono.
    p. cm.
  Includes bibliographical references and index.
  ISBN: 978–0–313–33599–0 (alk. paper)
  1. Homosexuality—North America—Encyclopedias. 2. Homosexuality—
Great Britain—Encyclopedias. 3. Popular culture—North America.
4. Popular culture—Great Britain. I. Title.
  HQ75.13.P76 2008
  306.76'603—dc22   2007032464

British Library Cataloguing in Publication Data is available.

Library of Congress Catalog Card Number: 2007032464
ISBN: 978–0–313–33599–0

First published in 2008

Greenwood Press, 88 Post Road West, Westport, CT 06881
An imprint of Greenwood Publishing Group, Inc.
www.greenwood.com

Printed in the United States of America

The paper used in this book complies with the
Permanent Paper Standard issued by the National
Information Standards Organization (Z39.48–1984).

10 9 8 7 6 5 4 3 2 1

CONTENTS

ENTRIES

PREFACE

The Encyclopedia of Gay and Lesbian Popular Culture provides both biographical and thematic entries that map out the presence of queer subjects within American popular culture in the twentieth and twenty-first centuries. The almost one hundred entries collected in this volume tell a double story. On the one hand, they attest to the pervasive presence of gays and lesbians in the worlds of film, television, theater, entertainment, popular literature, music, and sport. On the other hand, they also show the constant attempts to marginalize homosexual characters and themes within popular culture and to silence the same-sex desire and identities of many actors, writers, directors, singers, and athletes. This book aims to fight these attempts and to recover the queer legacy within popular culture. It documents the achievements of all those personalities who, with their examples, have started to smash the closet which seeks to render homosexuality invisible. While an increasing number of actors, artists, and singers do not conceal their sexual orientation any longer, popular culture and its institutions have not always been a welcoming place for queers. The biographical stories of Rock Hudson, Raymond Burr, and Cary Grant; the belated coming-outs of Dick Sargent and Richard Chamberlain; and Freddie Mercury's reluctance to discuss his sexual orientation, to quote but a few examples, attest to the pervasive force of what controversial journalist Michelangelo Signorile (1993, xviii) has called the "brilliantly orchestrated, massive conspiracy to keep all homosexuals locked in the closet." A view of the closet as simply repressing artistry would be reductive as the closet can also function as a source of inspiration. For example, directors such as George Cukor inscribed a coded gay sensibility in films like *Sylvia Scarlett* (1935), *The Women* (1939), and *Rich and Famous* (1983). Such works appealed to queers and, at the same time, reached a large audience who was unaware of their gay subtexts. Yet, it is undeniable that the power of the closet to destroy personal lives is well-documented. Popular culture figures that have stepped outside the closet have contributed to give homosexuality more visibility, which was denied for the best part of the twentieth century and that some institutions would like to continue to deny. Many entries in the book tell of the battle fought by gays and lesbians in popular culture to achieve such visibility against the power of the media and Hollywood industry. As Signorile points out, the media work to foster a sense of isolation and loneliness in homosexuals, creating the impression that very few public figures are gay and that homosexuality is a grotesque and largely unspeakable matter. For decades, the big popular culture center of Hollywood routinely represented celluloid homosexuals as unhappy and deviant individuals or made them completely invisible. It also forced many film-makers and actors to remain in the closet in return for a successful career.

In the last decades of the twentieth century, however, queer visibility within popular culture began to increase. As Alexander Doty and Ben Gove (1997) have pointed out, addressing the topic of lesbian, gay, and queer representation and presence in popular culture now implies challenging the identification of so-called mass and popular phenomena as only created and consumed by heterosexuals. They argue that since the 1970s, lesbians, gays, and queers have become active subjects in popular culture addressing increasingly larger audiences. Mass culture does not necessarily reinforce dominant ideology as it can also more or less explicitly challenge it. Many entries in the pages that follow document the ambiguous status of mass cultural products. Popular culture artifacts are inextricably linked to the social and political milieu in which they are produced, thus reflecting social stereotypes about lesbians, gays, and queers. Yet, some of them also work to subvert such stereotypes and provide a more affirmative vision of homosexuality. While popular culture is obviously informed by the predominant worldviews of the different historical periods, its authors possess the agency to challenge the social trends of their times. This ambiguity runs throughout the topics of the whole book. Works such as *Cruising* (1980), *Basic Instinct* (1992), and even *Philadelphia* (1993), to quote only film examples, have been praised as cinematographic milestones in the representation of queerness, or charged with concealing gay sexuality and same-sex desire, or reviled as demonizing. Mainstream popular culture has been conservatively described as reflecting the will of the majority and thus avoiding positive representations of what fails to support dominant ideology. Alternative media cultures, on the contrary, have been progressively defined as allowing for less censored representations, though reaching a more limited audience. Yet, since the mid-1990s, the boundaries between these two entities have become increasingly blurred as national networks were made more hospitable to programs produced by and for queers, including TV series such as *Will and Grace*, *Queer as Folk*, *The L Word*, and reality shows like *Queer Eye for the Straight Guy*. Films such as *Brokeback Mountain* (2005) and musicals such as *Rent* (1996) went on to become top-grossing hits. Contrary to the positive developments in the world of entertainment and showbiz, the world of sport has remained largely steeped in homophobia. The few athletes that have come out, including tennis legend Martina Navratilova and Olympic champions Greg Louganis and Mark Tewksbury, set important examples that, hopefully, will be of encouragement to many more.

Queer visibility within popular culture and within society as a whole increased dramatically also due to the spread of AIDS and the ensuing backlash against homosexuals. The media's representations of the virus and the description of the illness as a so-called gay plague prompted the need to speak openly about homosexuality. Since homosexual lifestyles were thrown into the limelight, it became increasingly important for gay people to offer their own representations of themselves to the larger society to counter the damning views of the media. While the media presented an image of homosexuals as marginal subjects whose deviant behavior generated the plague, many queers stressed the pride and solidarity surrounding their sexual orientation. The activism produced by the AIDS crisis battled to offer its own images of gayness to bring into straight homes. ACT-UP slogans, the AIDS Quilt, the Benetton advert with a Christ-like activist David Kirby bedridden with the illness, and the dramatization of gay life in the top-grossing film *Philadelphia* all became widely disseminated images in American culture. These images forcefully pointed out that American society was not simply multiracial and composed of different social classes, but also made up of different genders and sexualities. The debates surrounding popular culture representations of gayness became increasingly politicized. The need to reclaim gay and lesbian authors, texts, and subtexts from the past also became more urgent. The recovery of gay and lesbian personalities in popular culture and of homoeroticism in pop creations was instrumental in opposing a view of culture and society as solely heterosexual. Gay and lesbian celebrated queers as producers of culture, thus countering media representations of gays as producers of the plague.

By its very nature, a single-volume encyclopedia on such a vast topic must make a selection of those topics and people to include and of those to sadly leave out. Such selection tries to encompass the variety and diversity of strategies deployed by gays and lesbians in their resistance to stereotyping. Sharing Doty and Gove's identification of the 1970s as the decade in which queers started to become more active in popular culture, the book focuses mainly on well-known North American and British individuals whose contributions have helped to redefine and shape contemporary modes of queer representation. It also addresses the themes and debates that queer popular works have produced. Considerable attention is also paid to personalities, cultural movements, and issues dating back to the 1960s as the decade's championing of countercultural values paved the way for the more inclusive popular forms of the subsequent years. Some entries, such as Djuna Barnes and Gertrude Stein, are devoted to foundational figures in lesbian and gay popular culture who were mainly active before World War II. Explicitly out gay personalities and popular characters are not the only ones included in the following pages. Queer figures such as Paul Reubens's Pee-Wee Herman have been analyzed too as they can be read as gay by many viewers. In addition, icons such as Judy Garland, Barbara Stanwyck, and Barbra Streisand also deserve close scrutiny for their enduring appeal and influence on queer audiences. Entries are arranged alphabetically and are followed by a further reading section. This generally points the reader to secondary rather than primary material. These sources mainly include critical studies about a given topic, biographies of individuals, and books placing a particular personality and popular culture artifacts such as films, novels, plays, or songs within gay and lesbian popular culture and the larger American culture. Of course, it is hoped that this encyclopedia as a whole will deserve the reader's attention. Yet, the book does not need to be read from cover to cover and browsers who wish to find information on a particular topic or personality will be able to consult the encyclopedia smoothly thanks to the alphabetical order. In addition, the frequent cross-references will help them to find related topics or figures. The first time that the subject of another entry is mentioned, it is given in bold, indicating that more information on those particular topics or people can be found in their own entries.

The volume strives to avoid the elitism and the complex critical jargon that sometimes characterize critical studies. By keeping the entries as reader-friendly as possible, the book aims to reach not only scholars and students in the field of gay, lesbian, and queer studies, but also general readers who may be curious to know more about queer aspects of popular culture. Throughout the book, I employ the terms *gay*, *lesbian*, and *queer* in their most inclusive meanings. Although the terms gay and lesbian have become somewhat unfashionable in academic circles, I still believe, following Sally R. Munt (1997, xi) that they "have historically appealed across class and racial differences" and that they stand for an inclusive agenda. Although the terms gay and lesbian to some critics have come to represent outmoded and essentialist identity politics, Simon Watney (1997, 380) has rightly pointed out that sexual identities are not simply restrictive, but "may also provide refuge and stability, whilst providing us with our most intimate sense of psychic and social belonging in the world." Queer subjects active in popular culture can foster this sense of social belonging and an increased awareness of one's gayness beyond the stereotypes common in our society. Popular culture can provide encouragement and reassurance to overcome the isolation and loneliness that many gays may feel at the realization of their difference. Several stories in the volume document this power of popular culture, from John Waters's definition of Tennessee Williams as a virtual "childhood friend" to the enthusiastic reception of lesbians for the strong and independent female roles played by Barbara Stanwyck. The discovery of a vast and varied gay and lesbian tradition in popular culture provides homosexuals with a large body of works that speak directly to their own experiences. From the different entries collected in this volume, however, what emerges is not a single sensibility, but various manifestations of gayness that resist generalizations. The *Encyclopedia of Gay and Lesbian Popular Culture* tries to represent the many popular traditions that have co-existed throughout the twentieth century and at the beginning of the twenty-first, encouraging the social transition of homosexuality from a social problem to an identity at once personal and collective.

References

Bristow, Joseph, ed. *Sexual Sameness: Textual Difference in Lesbian and Gay Writing*. London: Routledge, 1992.

Doty, Alexander, and Ben Gove. "Queer Representation in the Mass Media." Sally Munt and Andy Medhurst, eds. *Lesbian and Gay Studies. A Critical Introduction*. London: Cassell, 1997. 84–98.

Munt, Sally. "Mapping the Field." Sally Munt and Andy Medhurst, eds. *Lesbian and Gay Studies. A Critical Introduction*. London: Cassell, 1997. xi–xvii.

Munt, Sally, and Andy Medhurst, eds. *Lesbian and Gay Studies. A Critical Introduction*. London: Cassell, 1997.

Signorile, Michelangelo. *Queer in America: Sex, the Media and the Closets of Power*. New York: Random House, 1993.

Watney, Simon. "Lesbian and Gay Studies in the Age of AIDS." Sally Munt and Andy Medhurst, eds. *Lesbian and Gay Studies. A Critical Introduction*. London: Cassell, 1997. 369–384.

ACKNOWLEDGMENTS

I am grateful first and foremost to Debra Adams, my editor at Greenwood Press, for her constant support, enthusiasm, and encouragement during the long process of writing this encyclopedia.

My parents, Sergio Prono and Carolina Magnani, were the first ones to introduce me to popular culture and to stimulate my interest in cinema, theater, and literature. Rather than leaving me with a babysitter, they would take me with them to the cinema and the theater from a very young age. I still remember with fondness our weekly trips to the cinema and the theater and the discussions and explanations that always followed. My parents have also been a source of constant support throughout my life. With different parents, this book would probably never have been written.

I am particularly thankful to the following people who expressed constant interest in the book or provided support with their friendship, taking me out and listening calmly to my ideas and worries about the project: Stefania Atti, Anna Baldisserri and Stefano Stefani, Luciano Bacci, Mario Billeci, Francesco Billeci and Marcel Van Ratingen, Davide Bisi and Cecilia Bertacchini, Sabrina Braghini, Marco Brasa, Antonio Carusillo, Nazaria Crisci, Bob Dodd, Roberto Garagnani, Patrizia Grandi, Eva Maietti, Gianluca Martino and Alessia Argenton, Anna Notaro, Paola Parisini, Cinzia Riguzzi, Alessandro Rioli, Mariarosaria Sorrentino, Caterina Taglioni and her wonderful bear partner Marco. In particular, Eva was very close to me during the writing of this book and was always very excited to hear its latest developments. Antonio was also always willing to offer his encouragement and he provided his IT expertise for the choice of a new laptop with which most of this book was written. I also wish to thank the two headmasters that I have encountered in my brief career as an English language teacher in Italy, Fortunato Morleo and Filomena Massaro.

During our 11 years of life together, my partner Domenico Colombari and I have built a strong union based on mutual respect, shared interest, and common passions, one of them, of course, being popular culture itself. Although there is not a definition in Italian legislation for our union, I feel that we form a strong and happy family. I would like to thank Domenico for his love and tolerance during the writing of this book, which is dedicated to him and to my parents.

A

ADVOCATE, THE

Since the late 1960s, the *Advocate* has grown from an underground newsletter into the largest gay and lesbian magazine in the world. It has recorded the developments of the queer community in the United States and worldwide, thus giving visibility to gay and lesbian identity. The magazine has both contributed to the dissemination of positive images for the creation of an affirmative homosexual consciousness and to the presentation of this new emerging community to the heterosexual majority. Over the years, the *Advocate* strengthened the confidence and pride of its readers, showing that they were not alone in their fight for recognition. It stimulated social change in the larger society and debate within the gay community. It also served as a springboard for the careers of many gay and lesbian writers such as Randy Shilts and **Pat Califia.**

The first issue of the bi-monthly *Los Angeles Advocate*, as it was first called, was dated September 1967. The magazine had its origin in the newsletter of the homophile organization Personal Rights in Defense and Education (PRIDE). PRIDE members Dick Michaels, Bill Rand, and Sam Winston collaborated on the initial project, which was catalyzed by several police raids and arrests in Los Angeles gay bars in 1967. These events, together with the radical politics and sexual revolution of the 1960s, persuaded Michaels, Rand, and Winston that the assimilationist policies pursued by homophiles had failed to address the discriminations homosexuals had to bear for a long time. The *Advocate* would adopt a new style in dealing with what was happening in and impacting on the world of gays and lesbians. The first issue, assembled in the basement of ABC's Television Los Angeles headquarters where Rand worked, consisted of 12 pages and was sold for 25 cents in gay bars and shops in the Los Angeles area. The first run was of only 500 copies, but the publication grew steadily from the very first months.

The following year, Michaels, Rand, and Winston purchased the publishing rights for the *Advocate* for one dollar from PRIDE as the organization was falling apart, torn by internal disagreements. By its first year, the magazine had grown to 32 pages and, with its 5,500 copies, it circulated throughout Southern California. Soon the founding trio set the ambitious goal of making the *Advocate* the first nationally distributed publication of the gay liberation era. Within two years the magazine had captured enough readers to become a monthly. In April 1970, the title was shortened from the *Los Angeles Advocate* to the *Advocate*, to reflect its expanding national focus.

It was under the leadership of gay businessman David B. Goodstein, however controversial and, at times, openly contested, that the *Advocate* achieved the status of national newsmagazine. Goodstein purchased the *Advocate* in 1975 and controlled it until his death 10 years later. Goodstein's wealth allowed unprecedented financial investments which supported the development of the magazine. Reporters and editors were suspicious of the many changes introduced by Goodstein such as moving the magazine's headquarters from Los Angeles to San Francisco and restyling the publication in a more commercial tabloid format. The *Advocate* was accused of having lost its political edge in favor of wider appeal. However, the *Advocate* soon emerged as a veritable point of reference for the gay community, cited also by many mainstream publications. When Goodstein died of cancer in 1985, the *Advocate* had a circulation of 65,000 copies per issue and had been once again reinvented as a glossy news magazine. During the next 10 years, the difficult period of the AIDS onslaught, the magazine changed numerous editors, including Niles Merton, Lenny Giteck, Stuart Kellogg, Richard Rouilard, and Jeff Yarborough. In 1992, Sam Watters became the new publisher and the magazine was changed to the more mainstream glossy format, separating the sexually explicit personals and classifieds (the so-called pink pages) into a different publication.

Throughout its history, the *Advocate* has not been immune to criticism. It has been argued that its focus has predominately been on urban gay white males, leaving out stories on lesbians, African Americans, and homosexual belonging to other ethnic groups. The word *lesbian* was added to the cover only in 1990. Many, including former *Advocate* journalist Randy Shilts, considered that the *Advocate*'s response to the AIDS crisis during the 1980s was dramatically late, treating the subject at some length only after it had been widely discussed in the mainstream press. However, as Shilts himself concludes in his foreword to *Long Road to Freedom*, a collection of the most significant articles from the *Advocate*, this criticism does not diminish the importance of the magazine in the history of the American lesbian and gay movement. The magazine has had a central role in defining the American gay and lesbian community and setting its agenda.

Further Reading

Bull, Chris, ed. *Witness to the Revolution: The Advocate Reports on Gay and Lesbian Politics, 1967–1999.* Los Angeles: Alyson Books, 1999; Ridinger, Robert B. Marks. *An Index to the Advocate: The National Gay Newsmagazine, 1967–1982.* Los Angeles: Liberation Publications, 1987; Thompson, Mark, ed. *Long Road to Freedom: The Advocate History of the Gay and Lesbian Movement.* New York: St. Martin's Press, 1994.

AIDS

When the HIV virus made its first appearance in the late 1970s, it was considered only a Western phenomenon and limited to definite risk categories. The rapid spread of HIV through all social strata and all sexual orientations has proved that the initial risk categories and the identification of the virus with gay men made little sense. Although the virus spread rapidly through developing countries right from its discovery, no links were made between the Western victims of AIDS and those who died from it in Africa. AIDS had a massive impact on gay life and, consequently, on queer popular culture and on how it is produced and interpreted. Homosexual artists have struggled in their various fields to assert their own representation of the virus and narrate their experiences of living with HIV either as patients or as partners and friends of people with AIDS. Gay men, in their double roles of authors and subjects, have been at the center of written, oral, or film representations of the virus. Their voices often tried to break the silence which surrounded the epidemic. They struggled to subvert the popular imagery and vocabulary which indissolubly linked sexual difference with danger and disease, pointing to gays as threats to national health. Novels, plays, songs, films, and public displays and demonstrations produced by queer subjects have sought to dispel the triple equation of homosexuality, illness, and death.

In the late 1970s, the then-unidentified virus made its appearance. It was quickly labeled as a disease of the gay community when a group of gay men from San Francisco and Los Angeles showed constant signs of rare opportunistic infections. The very name initially given to the virus, GRID (Gay Related Immunodeficiency), points to the first definition of the virus as a new so-called gay plague. From 1982, however, the presence of the virus in women and children even in Western countries could no longer be ignored. So, the name of the disease was changed into AIDS (acquired immunodeficiency syndrome). The following year the virus which caused the disease was isolated. Yet, until the late 1980s, AIDS largely remained a disease of intravenous drug users and homosexuals.

AIDS is caused by the human immunodeficiency virus (HIV). The virus can show no symptoms of its presence in the body for a phase as long as 10–15 years and damages the immune system by destroying the helper T-cells. The absence of these cells and the consequent lack of activation of the immune system cause the body to become prey to multiple infections. As the immune system deteriorates, these infections become increasingly serious and can cause pneumonia, pulmonary tuberculosis, musculoskeletal pain and neuropathy. HIV is transmitted between individuals through seminal or vaginal fluids, contact with infected blood (including blood transfusions) and between mother and child during pregnancy, childbirth, and breastfeeding. People usually become infected after a few weeks from the primary contact with the virus. Yet, the infection is difficult to diagnose in its early stage as its symptoms are very similar to other common illnesses. The progression of the disease varies greatly between individuals. The most effective prevention against AIDS is condom use. Yet, while the adoption of condoms and of screenings in blood transfusion have proved effective in Europe and North America, in other regions of the world these have proved more controversial. Conservatives and church members oppose the use of condoms and argue that the best way to prevent AIDS is through abstinence from sexual intercourse and faithfulness to the partner. In turn, progressives criticize abstinence promotion for denying young people, especially in poorer countries, information about HIV prevention.

Figures about AIDS make it impossible to deny its global reach. After more than 20 years of AIDS, there is still no vaccine for the disease or a cure for those who have been infected. Yet, the so-called cocktails of drugs, which combine at least three medicines based on two different classes of anti-retroviral agents, have proved to be extremely effective in inhibiting the development of AIDS. During the 1990s, the life spans and the living conditions of people living with HIV have considerably improved in spite of the many side effects of the cocktails. The combinations of different drugs and anti-retroviral agents, however, are extremely costly and this has reduced the access to the treatment for patients in developing countries.

Artistic representations of AIDS are unmistakably political. American artists challenged the lack of governmental action in the early years of the epidemic with popular forms of resistance by producing works that made the virus visible. In 1988, the gay activist group ACT UP (Aids Coalition to Unleash Power) encouraged the formation of Grand Fury, the first artists' collective which was to serve as the organization's agit-prop branch. As such, their artworks were not so much intended for galleries as for the streets. Their graphics, which combined words and imagery to a gripping effect, confronted the general public with images of the disease and provided AIDS activism with compelling slogans. The year before the formal foundation of Grand Fury a group of six gay men who were members of ACT UP invented the famous phrase *silence = death* written under a pink triangle (the symbol which branded homosexuals in Nazi concentration camps). This graphic was soon reproduced on T-shirts, posters, and buttons for fund-raising events and demonstrations. Grand Fury was fundamental in the early stages of the disease to subvert the most common stereotypes about AIDS, particularly the notion that there were two categories of patients: the guilty gays and drug-users and the innocent children and hemophiliacs. "All people with AIDS are innocent," proclaimed one of the collective's most famous campaign. Parallel to their attack on the received conceptualization of the epidemic, these artists also defied the silence of the Reagan Administration. A 1988 poster by Donald Moffett showed a picture of the President next to a target with the caption "He kills me." In 1990, the collective reached the zenith of its polemical campaign when it exhibited its "Pope Piece" at the Venice Biennale, one of the most prestigious art exhibitions in the world. The artwork juxtaposed a picture of the Pope and a text on the Catholic Church's position on AIDS and safe sex with an image of an erect penis. It obviously caused a heated debate and threats of censure and arrest for the collective.

A year after the Biennale hullabaloo, another powerful AIDS symbol appeared during the television broadcast of the Tony Awards: the red ribbon, signifying commitment to people with AIDS and to the raising of general awareness of the disease. The red ribbon was originally created by the Visual AIDS Artists' Caucus and, since its adoption by AIDS activists, many other movements have displayed their own ribbons to raise awareness about their causes. With the years, the red ribbon has become a widespread popular icon of the struggle against the virus and the prejudices that surround it. The NAMES Project AIDS Memorial Quilt, a more ambitious visual project, was started in 1985 by San Francisco activist Cleve Jones. The Quilt is an ever-growing memorial formed by more than 40,000 panels, honoring the lives of people who died of AIDS. The initial display took place on October 11, 1987, on the National Mall in Washington, DC, during the National March on Washington for Lesbian and Gay Rights. At the time, it included 1,920 panels, covering a space larger than a football field. This inaugural display was so successful that the Quilt embarked on a national tour and enriched itself with thousands of new panels. The project quickly became the largest work of art in the world and was the subject of the Academy-Award winning documentary *Common Threads: Stories from the Quilt* (1989).

Because of its universal reach, music has been used as a powerful tool to raise funds for research on the illness. One of the earliest example was the cover of the Bacharach and Sager's song "That's What Friends Are For," which, in 1985, was performed by Dionne Warwick, Stevie Wonder, Gladys Knight, and **Elton John** as a charity single for the American Foundation for AIDS Research. Major popular artists from Madonna and Patti Smith to Prince and Janet Jackson have confronted the public with the issue of the virus with their songs. These usually take the point of view of those who survive partners or friends lost to AIDS. Openly out gay singers and groups such as Jimmy Sommerville and the **Pet Shop Boys** have devoted many pieces to AIDS. These performers have focused their songs not only on the surviving individuals, but have also sought to capture the climate of the gay community and the changes in its lifestyles in response to the epidemic. For example, in "Dreaming of the Queen" from the album *Very* (1993), the Pet Shop Boys imagine a tea party with the Queen and Lady Di. When the Queen asks why love does not seem to last these days, the voices of Diana and Pet Shop Boy singer Neil Tennant reply in unison: "There are no more lovers left alive, no one has survived....So that's why love has died." The song effectively plays the surreal background in which the conversation takes place against the very real effects of the epidemic on gay men's lives. The same album also contains a cover of **The Village People**'s "Go West," which reverses the original vision of utopia into a reflection on how that utopia has been changed by AIDS. Musicals such as William Finn's *Falsettoland* (1990), John Greyson's *Zero Patience* (1994), and Jonathan Larson's *Rent* (1996) all feature plots and characters struggling with the disease. *Rent*, which went on to win the Pulitzer Prize for Drama and four Tony Awards, is particularly innovative in its update of Puccini's opera *La Bohème* to the late 1990s, substituting tuberculosis with AIDS.

Films and TV movies such as *Longtime Companion* (1990), ***Philadelphia*** (1993), *An Early Frost* (1985), *Our Sons* (1991), *And the Band Played On* (1993), and *Angels in America* (2003) have reached millions of people worldwide with their stories of the epidemic. These films also led to a less stereotypical representation of gay people on celluloid, although many of them were still timid in showing affection between same-sex partners. For example, scenes which showed the male lovers played by Tom Hanks and Antonio Banderas in bed together were cut from the final version of *Philadelphia*. From its very title, *Longtime Companion* denounced the hypocrisy of mainstream media whose definition of surviving same-sex partners as so-called longtime companions failed to explicitly acknowledge homosexuality. Yet, the film was accused of focusing exclusively on white gay males, leaving people of color out of the picture. *An Early Frost* and *Our Sons* were praised for their solid scripts and acting. Yet, as Paula A. Treichler has pointed out, they fail to represent the activism sparked by the AIDS crisis within the gay community (1993, 188). Even more so than *Philadelphia*, they also neglect same-sex relationships preferring to focus on the larger (heterosexual) family network. *Our Sons*, in particular, seems more interested in the relationship developing between the mothers of the two gay lovers than in that of the two lovers themselves.

Novels, memoirs, testimonies, poems, and essays about AIDS and living with the virus soon became central to gay and lesbian literature. Joseph Cady (1993) has divided the literary response to the epidemic into two types of writing. "Immersive" writing takes issue directly with the denial which surrounds the virus, plunging readers face to face with the tragedy of AIDS and requiring them to deal with the horrors of the plague without any relief or buffer provided by the writer. "Counterimmersive" literature, on the other hand, still recognizes the devastation caused by the disease, but protects its readers from too harsh a confrontation with the matter through a variety of distancing techniques. Counterimmersive literature about AIDS eventually proves to be "deferential" to the problem of denial, focusing, as it does, on characters or speakers who are going through various degrees of denial about AIDS themselves. Cady cites *Love Alone* (1988), Paul Monette's collection of elegies for his dead lover of 12 years, Roger Horwitz, as an example of immersive writing. Andrew Holleran's 1986 short story "Friends at Evening" provides a paradigm of counterimmersive narrative strategies such as camp or humor. Several gay critics have argued that the protection of the reader in these counterimmersive texts can go too far and risks cooperating with the larger social denial that still surrounds AIDS.

Whether immersive or counterimmersive, AIDS literature has adopted war as a central metaphor. Although Susan Sontag has charged mainstream media with the creation of what she considers as a pernicious imagery, Michael S. Sherry has pointed out that the metaphor of the armed conflict, using, in particular, World War II and the Holocaust, has also been widely adopted by gay writers from the very titles of their books such as *Reports from the Holocaust* (1989) by **Larry Kramer** and *Ground Zero* (1988) by Andrew Holleran. Most AIDS writing is testimonial and elegiac in nature, reconstructing the lives of those lost to the disease and trying to recreate their presence through literature. AIDS has also entered more popular genres such as science fiction and fantasy. In 1985, Samuel Delaney published the third part of his *Nevèrÿon* saga, "The Tale of Plagues and Carnival," which chronicles the spreading of a deadly plague on Nevèrÿon, inserting the writer's reflections on the AIDS crisis of the 1980s. The last three volumes of **Armistead Maupin**'s popular *Tales of the City* series devote increasingly larger space to AIDS and a number of anthologies have finally brought to light the usually neglected testimonies of men and women of color.

AIDS discourse has forcefully entered the many artistic expressions that constitute popular culture. The numerous contributions of gay artists to such discourse have started to remove the shroud of embarrassed silence which surrounded the virus in the early years of the crisis. They have constantly challenged the stereotypical understandings and representations of the epidemic. The works of popular gay artists encouraged millions of people to stand up to the virus, fighting it so that it does not defeat love and hope.

Further Reading

ACT UP—AIDS: Coalition to Unleash Power. www.actupny.org; Avena, Thomas, ed. *Life Sentences: Writers, Artists, and AIDS.* San Francisco: Mercury House, 1994; Baker, Rob. *The Art of AIDS.* New York: Continuum, 1994; Cady, Joseph. "Immersive and Counterimmersive Writing about AIDS: The Achievement of Paul Monette's *Love Alone.*" *Writing AIDS: Gay Literature, Language and Analysis.* Timothy F. Murphy and Suzanne Poirier, eds. New York: Columbia University Press, 1993. 244–264; Crimp, Douglas, ed. *AIDS: Cultural Analysis/Cultural Activism.* Cambridge, MA: MIT Press, 1988; Jones, Wendell, and David Stanley. "AIDS! The Musical!" *Sharing the Delirium: Second Generation AIDS Plays and Performances.* Therese Jones, ed. Portsmouth, NH: Heinemann, 1994. 207–221; Meyer, Richard. "This Is to Enrage You: Grand Fury and the Graphics of AIDS Activism." *But Is It Art? The Spirit of Art as Activism.* Nina Felshin, ed. Seattle: Bay Press, 1995; Miller, James, ed. *Fluid Exchanges: Artists and Critics in the AIDS Crisis.* Toronto: University of Toronto Press, 1992; Murphy, Timothy F., and Suzanne Poirier, eds. *Writing AIDS: Gay Literature, Language and Analysis.* New York: Columbia University Press, 1993; The NAMES Project AIDS Memorial Quilt. www.aidsquilt.org; Nelson, Emmanuel S., ed. *AIDS: The Literary Response.* Boston: Twayne Publishers, 1992; Pastore, Judith Laurence, ed. *Confronting AIDS through Literature: The Responsibilities of Representation.* Urbana: University of Illinois Press, 1993; Roman, David. *Acts of Intervention: Performance, Gay Culture, and AIDS.* Bloomington: Indiana University Press, 1998; Treichler, Paula A. "AIDS Narratives on Television: Whose Story?" *Writing AIDS: Gay Literature, Language and Analysis.* Timothy F. Murphy and Suzanne Poirier, eds. New York: Columbia University Press, 1993. 161–199; Ward, Keith. "Musical Responses to HIV and AIDS." *Perspectives on American Music since 1950.* James Heintze, ed. New York: Garland, 1999. 323–351.

ALBEE, EDWARD FRANKLIN (1928–)

Edward Albee is a Pulitzer Prize–winning playwright whose controversial plays often have gay subtexts and show the inextricable link between love and violence. Albee's career has covered six decades from the 1950s to the present, although with uneven critical fortune. His most successful years were the 1960s when his independent hits *The Zoo Story* (1958), *The American Dream* (1960), and *The Death of Bessie Smith* (1961) paved the way for his critically acclaimed Broadway debut with *Who's Afraid of Virginia Woolf?* (1962). By the mid-1960s, Albee was the most celebrated young playwright in the United States and was hailed as the veritable heir to Eugene O'Neil, Tennessee Williams, and Arthur Miller. Yet, from the late 1960s through to the 1980s, Albee's fame declined, although he won two Pulitzers for *A Delicate Balance* (1966) and *Seascape* (1975). This decline was partly due to his own attacks against the New York drama critics and their resentment for Albee's frank treatment of homoerotic situations. During the 1990s, however, even his most hostile critics acknowledged his major comeback with the highly personal *Three Tall Women* (1994), for which he received his third Pulitzer, about the troubled relationship between a mother and her gay son.

Albee was born on March 12, 1928, in Virginia. Abandoned by his biological parents, Edward was adopted by the upper-class Reed and Frances Albee who owned the Keith-Albee chain of vaudeville theaters. Albee was brought up in Westchester County, New York, mainly by a governess and his maternal grandmother. His parents were distant and cold, and they would later serve as models for the recurrent character types in Albee's plays of the domineering mother and the uncommunicative father. Albee's encounters with theater date back to an early age as Edward and his nanny often attended Broadway matinees. His first play, a sex farce, was written when he was only 12 years old. His schooling suffered from his parents' winter trips to the South, and Albee was expelled from several private boarding schools until he enrolled at Choate School in Wallingford, Connecticut. There he found supportive teachers who encouraged his literary aspirations and he successfully graduated

Arthur Hill and Uta Hagen as George and Martha in *Who's Afraid of Virginia Woolf,* Albee's scathing portrayal of heterosexual marriage. Courtesy of Photofest.

in 1948. His latent conflicts with his family exploded when he was expelled from Trinity College in Hartford, Connecticut. Albee was able to leave his parents' home thanks to a small trust fund left to him by his grandmother. In the early 1950s, Albee traveled to Europe and lived in New York's Greenwich Village where he settled down with the composer William Flanagan. During these years, Albee met famous literary figures such as the gay poet W. H. Auden and the playwright Thornton Wilder. Encouraged by them, Edward wrote relentlessly although many of these early plays, where his personal life features strongly in the plots, were never published or produced.

The one-act *The Zoo Story*, written in only three weeks, was Albee's first success. It initially premiered in Berlin in 1959 given its rejection from American producers. Similar to his subsequent early works *The American Dream, The Death of Bessie Smith*, and *The Sandbox, The Zoo Story* is clearly influenced by Eugene Ionesco, Samuel Beckett, and the Theater of the Absurd. The scenes seem pointless and this apparent lack of meaningful plot development hints at the isolation and frustration of humankind. When performed in Berlin, *The Zoo Story* was significantly paired with Beckett's *Krapp's Last Tapes*. The play, which finally had an off-Broadway run and earned Albee a Obie Award in 1960, has strong homoerotic overtones and depicts with dark humor the exchanges between a disturbed drop-out, Jerry, and a traditional middle-class family man, Peter. The dialogues between Jerry and Peter are tinged with gay and camp references which lead the narrative to a shocking climax, as Jerry is telling his life story to drive his listener to murder him. Love and violence are inextricably intertwined, as Jerry is sacrificed to rescue Peter's life from its inanity and boredom. It is only thanks to Jerry's death that Peter is emotionally revived from his meaningless suburban existence. Like much of Albee's future productions, *The Zoo Story* satirizes American society and its myths of wealth and middle-class success.

Albee's first Broadway hit was his full-length play *Who's Afraid of Virginia Woolf?* (1962). It focuses on two heterosexual couples, the older and more abusive George and Martha and the younger and apparently more reserved Nick and Honey. Both have built their marriages on illusions. The couples will witness the mutual crumbling of their illusions during an all-night confrontation made of abuse, drinking, and swearing at George and Martha's house. The play comments on the failure to face reality and on the fabrication of lies to make existence more palatable. George and Martha have created an imaginary child to revive their childless and emotionally sterile marriage. Nick and Honey are younger, but they are no alternative to George and Martha. They married because they thought that Honey was pregnant which, in fact, turned out to be untrue. Their marriage would have probably never taken place had it not been for Honey's supposed pregnancy. As in *The Zoo Story*, Albee targets American middle-class institutions: *Who's Afraid of Virginia Woolf?* is a scathing portrayal of heterosexual marriage. The play was denied a Pulitzer Prize for its harsh language and so-called filthy scenes, but it proved immensely popular with critics and audiences alike. It ran for more than 600 performances, won five Tony Awards, and the New York Drama Critics Prize. Hollywood also bought the screen rights for the play which was adapted into an Academy Award-winning film by director Mike Nichols with unforgettable performances from Richard Burton, Elizabeth

Taylor, George Segal, and Sandy Dennis. With the money earned from *Who's Afraid of Virginia Woolf?*, Albee was able to establish an artists' colony in Long Island. He also set up his own producing company together with Richard Barr and Clinton Wilder, The Playwright's Unit, which helped to stage the plays of emergent young writers such as Sam Shepard and Amiri Baraka. Albee's relationship with William Flanagan ended as the playwright became involved with the young actor and writer Terrence McNally, who would later write successful plays about homosexual themes.

None of Albee's subsequent plays repeated the commercial and critical success of *The Zoo Story* and *Who's Afraid of Virginia Woolf?* His adaptations for Broadway of Carson McCuller's *The Ballad of the Sad Café* (1963) and James Purdy's *Malcolm* (1966) were negatively reviewed as was his second full-length original play *Tiny Alice* (1964), which features a couple of former lovers composed of a cardinal and a lawyer. Albee's frank depiction of homoerotic attraction between the two males angered the most conservative critics who panned the play. Philip Roth vulgarly described it as "ghastly pansy rhetoric." The comedy of manners *A Delicate Balance* (1966) was a critical success, earning Albee his first Pulitzer, but had only a limited Broadway run. The unsuccessful return to one-act plays with the interrelated *Box* and *Quotations from Chairman Mao Tse-Tung* (1968) prompted Albee to adopt a more conventional and realistic style in *All Over* (1971), *Seascape* (1975), *The Lady from Dubuque* (1980), his adaptation of Nabokov's novel *Lolita* (1981), and his last Broadway production for 15 years, *The Man Who Had Three Arms* (1983). Albee's personal life proved a refuge from this series of flops. In the early 1970s, Albee met the Canadian sculptor Jonathan Thomas, and their relationship lasted until Thomas's death in 2005.

Ostracized by Broadway, Albee continued to write and produce plays far from New York. His long one-act *Finding the Sun* (1983) contains an explicit depiction of gay life. Yet, the death of his adoptive mother, with whom Albee had reconciled himself in her later years, was to provide the playwright with the material for his major critical and commercial comeback, *Three Tall Women* (1994). The play focuses on a woman who has rejected her gay son and depicts her in three different moments of her life: her twenties, fifties, and nineties. Although it premiered in Vienna, *Three Tall Women* had a successful off-Broadway production which sparked an Albee revival in New York, including a year-long festival of his works. The play reconciled the author with critics and audiences alike, earning him his third Pulitzer, the New York Drama Critics Circle Award, and running for more than 500 performances. Albee's later plays *The Play about the Baby* (2001) and *The Goat, or Who Is Sylvia?* (2002) received mixed reviews, but *The Goat* got Albee his first Tony Award for Best Play since *Who's Afraid of Virginia Woolf?*

In his plays, Albee forces us to confront the harsher side of American society and challenges America's most cherished traditional institutions such as the conventional heterosexual family, the all-American boy and the church. Gay critics have lamented that Albee is not concerned enough with the gay community. These remarks are not entirely fair to the playwright. While explicitly gay characters are absent from his early and more successful plays, a gay subtext is always detectable. In addition, his later plays offer more explicit descriptions of gay characters which deserve careful scrutiny.

Further Reading

Bigsby, C.W.E. *Modern American Drama, 1945–200.* New York: Cambridge University Press, 2000; Bigsby, C.W.E., ed. *Edward Albee, A Collection of Critical Essays.* Englewood Cliffs, NJ: Prentice-Hall, 1987; Bigsby, C.W.E. *A Critical Introduction to Twentieth Century American Drama, II: Williams, Miller, Albee.* Cambridge: Cambridge University Press, 1982; Clum, John M. *Acting Gay: Male Homosexuality in Modern Drama.* New York: Columbia, 1992; Sarotte, Georges-Michel. *Like a Brother, Like a Lover: Male Homosexuality in the American Novel and Theater from Herman Melville to James Baldwin.* Garden City, NY: Doubleday, 1978.

ALLEN, CHAD (1974–)

Openly gay actor Chad Allen is one of the very few TV child stars to have developed a successful career as an adult performer. After the tabloid *Globe* ran a story on Allen pictured with another man in a hot bath in 1996, the actor decided to come out as gay five years later with an article in the ***Advocate***. Proving wrong all those who were convinced of the likely negative impact of his coming out on his profession, Allen has continued acting portraying both gay and straight characters on screen and on stage. At the same time, he has become an outspoken supporter of queer causes. Allen serves as a member of the Honorary Board of Directors for the Matthew Shepard Foundation, and he sustains several **AIDS** charities.

Chad Allen was born Chad Allen Lazzari on June 5, 1974, in Cerritos, California. He is the youngest of four boys and has a twin sister, Charity. Allen grew up in Long Beach and was introduced to the world of show business when his mother started to enter the twins in competitions at fairs. Chad and Charity won several of these and their parents were persuaded to allow them to go into acting. Contrary to his sister, Allen loved it and had his first part at the age of four in a McDonald's television advertisement. At this time, it was decided to drop Lazzari from his name as the Italian surname did not suit his physical appearance. At the age of six, Allen got his first dramatic part in a pilot episode of the series *Cutter to Huston.* The series, however, never went into production.

The role that made the child a star was that of an autistic boy, Tommy Westphall, in the series *St. Elsewhere.* Allen's sensitive performance won unanimous praise, and he was on the series until its very last episode in 1988. The 1980s were definitely a busy decade for the actor and marked his development into a teen idol. In addition to *St. Elsewhere,* Allen appeared in popular shows such as *Webster* (1985–1986), *Our House* (1986–1988), and *My Two Dads* (1989–1990). He also guest-starred in *Hunter, Star Trek: The Next Generation, In the Heat of the Night,* and *Simon and Simon.* During these years, Allen was often on the pages of teen magazines, where he was portrayed as an ideal teenager. As fans started to stop him wherever he went, it became difficult for him to cope with such popularity. The price of fame was becoming too much for Allen, who had only attended primary school at a public institution and was then educated by private tutors. He also resented the characterization of a perfect teenager. In reality, Allen said later, he was just "A 13-year-old who's as fucked up as every other 13-year-old across the country" (The *Advocate* Online, October 2001). The star increasingly felt the need for a normal life away from the sets.

When *My Two Dads* ended in 1990, Allen decided to leave acting and went to high school with the main ambition of being a "normal teenager." Upon his graduation, he was accepted by New York University, but was offered, at the same time, the part of Matthew Cooper on CBS series *Dr. Quinn: Medicine Woman*. Allen was on the show for its whole six seasons and this role marked his transition from child star to mature actor. It was also while filming *Dr. Quinn*, a family-oriented program, that Allen was outed by the tabloid *Globe*. As he later told the *Advocate* in his coming out interview, "I was 21 years old when a guy that I was seeing sold photos of us kissing in a swimming pool to a magazine, a tabloid. I was 21 and working on a family-oriented TV series. All of a sudden I get this phone call from a publicist saying the *Globe* is doing this thing and running this picture, and they're going to claim I was with a prostitute and all these things that weren't true. So I was scared. Just scared" (The *Advocate* Online, October 2001). Allen decided not to reply to the outing, although he was happy of the support he received from his co-stars on the series and from letters by gay fans. The *Globe* story did not attract much media attention and the issue of Allen's sexuality was not brought up again until five years later. In 2001, Allen decided to come out with an interview for the *Advocate* where he also acknowledged past problems with drugs and alcohol. Since then, he has taken part in several events for queer rights. He also spoke openly in support of gay marriages on *Larry King Live* in February 2004.

The same year of his coming out Allen starred in three movies: *A Mother's Testimony*, *Do You Wanna Know a Secret*, and the independent *What Matters Most*, which was positively reviewed. After his coming out, Allen has also been keen to play more gay characters not only on the television screen but also on the theater stage. Theater, the actor has maintained, was his first love and he has starred in important works for gay and lesbian culture. These include Mike Ambrose's *Dearboy's War*, on the issue of gays in the military, and Terence McNally's award-winning *Corpus Christi*, which attracted particular controversy for its depiction of Christ and the disciples as gays living in contemporary Texas.

As the next step in his commitment to queer culture, Allen formed his own production company, Mythgarden, together with fellow actor Robert Gant and producer Christopher Racster. Mythgarden "is entirely dedicated to turning the page on gay and lesbian storytelling in film, television, and theater. We believe that it's time that our stories can be told fully: good relationships, real relationships, honest characters, in all of the genres of storytelling-fantasy, fiction, fairy tales, great mysteries, adventure films, and honest drama" (Chad Allen Official Fan Site). As part of this project to revise gay and lesbian depictions in the arts, Allen has been involved with the queer networks *Logo*, *Q Television*, and *Here! TV*. In particular, *Here! TV* will produce six films based on Donald Strachey, the gay detective created by Richard Stevenson. Allen has also continued to guest-star in mainstream TV series as *NYPD Blues* and *Cold Case*. He played the leading role in *End of the Spear* (2006), a film mainly addressed to the Christian community centering on the true story of the murder of five American missionaries in Ecuador in the 1950s. Although some Christian groups expressed reservations that an openly homosexual actor should portray a missionary, Allen's performance was generally well received, even among the Christian community. The son of the murdered missionary also expressed his appreciation. Allen is an example of how media homophobia about gay actors can be successfully defeated.

Further Reading

Vilanch, Bruce. "Chad Allen: His Own Story." The *Advocate* Online, http://www.advocate.com/currentstory1_w_ektid20034.asp, October 9, 2001 (accessed on September 5, 2007); Chad Allen Official Fan Site. http://www.chadallenonline.com. (accessed on September 5, 2007).

ARAKI, GREGG (1959–)

Along with **Rose Troche** and **Todd Haynes**, Gregg Araki is one of the central figures in the New Queer Cinema, a loose group of directors whose independent films of the early 1990s openly dealt with queer politics and identity. Although Araki has rejected the label of gay filmmaker, which he finds restrictive, he shares with the directors of the New Queer Cinema an aggressive stance against homophobia and the fears spurred by the **AIDS** crisis. Araki's films have been both praised and berated for their unconventional representations of homosexuals. To some, his films are refreshingly new in their departures from hypocritical media stereotypes of queers and their reversal of Hollywood models. Others are offended by the negative representations of gays and lesbians.

Born on December 17, 1959, in Los Angeles to Japanese-American parents, Araki obtained a B.A. in film history and criticism from the University of California and subsequently completed an M.F.A. in film production at the University of Southern California. During his studies, he developed a particular predilection for the irrational narratives of the American screwball comedies of the 1930s and 1940s. "For me," Araki states, "movies like *Bringing up Baby* are incredibly profound and provocative—more interesting than *Citizen Kane.* There is such a deconstruction of manners and social structure" (Filmmaker Magazine Online, 1999). He also admired the films of Jean-Luc Godard, one of the founders of the 1960s French New Wave, an innovative movement of filmmakers who subverted the received cinematic standards. Araki consciously paid homage to his French master with *Totally F***ed Up* (1993), modeled on Godard's *Masculine-Feminine* (1966), and with *The Doom Generation* (1994), which recalls the French director's *Weekend* (1967). Punk culture and music, with their emphasis on anarchy and confrontational style, were also important influences on Araki's beginning as a filmmaker. His early films were characterized by spontaneous filming, often without legal permits and with only basic equipment. The first of his films to enjoy a wider circulation and which made the name of Araki known in the festival circuits were *Three Bewildered People in the Night* (1987), which won the Bronze Leopard at Locarno Film Festival, and *The Long Weekend (O' Despair)* (1989). Araki's polemical stance against the conservatism embodied by Hollywood is clear in his definition of the latter film as an antithesis to the typically regressive Hollywood stories that Araki finds best represented by such movies as *The Big Chill*. His 1989 film *The Long Weekend* in many ways subverts *The Big Chill:* in both movies, young college graduates discuss their future and their anxieties. Yet, Araki's movie graphically depicts the characters' polymorphous sexuality in stark contrast with its polemical target.

The radical and anarchic vein of Araki's imagination is clear in the subtitle to his next production, *The Living End* (1991), subtitled "An irresponsible film." The director further contributed to heat the debate surrounding his movie, one of the first films to deal with AIDS, dedicating it to the "the hundreds of thousands who've died and the hundreds of thousands more who will die because of a big, white house full of Republican fuckheads." Starting from a *Thelma and Louise* situation, Araki chronicles the tragic on-the-road romance of a queer couple made up by a disruptive drop-out and an intellectual, a film critic. Both men are HIV-positive and flee from Los Angeles after they accidentally kill a policeman. The film aggressively entered AIDS discourse, which, until then, had been dominated by the reassuring gay images of movies such as *Longtime Companion* (1990). There is nothing reassuring about the characters of *The Living End* who react to society's homophobia with violent and irrational behavior. The critics of Araki's first movies did not come only from the conservative cohorts of "Republican fuckheads," but also within the gay community, and both sets of critics were angered by the director's political incorrectness.

*Totally F***ed Up* (1993), subtitled "Another Homo Movie," *The Doom Generation* (1994), "A Heterosexual Movie," and *Nowhere* (1997) form the "teen apocalypse trilogy," which focuses on adolescent struggles to come to terms with identity, sexuality, and social norms. Using a fragmented narrative made up of video interviews, *Totally F***ed Up* centers on six gay characters trying to build up an alternative family unit, while *The Doom Generation* explores a ménage à trois between two boys and a girl on the run from the police and skinheads groups. *Nowhere* was marketed as *"Beverly Hills 90210* on acid," and its cast included Kathleen Robinson, who played Claire on the television series. It follows the stories of a bisexual teen couple and their friends as they prepare for a party made of excess, sex, and drugs. All three films feature romantic naive teenagers whose idealism about love is destroyed by a cynical society. Araki's use of green, red, and orange filters in all three films gives them a surreal character which is heightened by the sudden shift in tone from comic to tragic, from sentimental to violent. Araki's postmodern mixing of film genres is apparent in his description of *Totally F***ed Up* as "a rag-tag story of the fag-and-dyke teen underground.... A kinda cross between avant-garde experimental cinema and a queer John Hughes flick" (Slant Magazine Online). Some critics strongly reacted to what they perceived as the gratuitous violence and graphic sexual acts of the trilogy, particularly in *The Doom Generation*. In it, limbs and heads are torn apart from bodies; horror and love-making scenes are juxtaposed in a disturbing way; and characters are seen masturbating and then licking their own semen.

During the shooting of *Nowhere*, the media sensationally reported that Araki was having a relationship with Kathleen Robinson. Although the dynamics of the relationship were summarized as "Gay filmmaker falls for *Beverly Hills 90210* babe" in the press, Araki used the publicity surrounding this alleged relationship to strongly reject the label of "gay filmmaker": "I like to be thought of without any kind of adjective attached to it. A gay filmmaker, a Gen-X filmmaker, an Asian-American filmmaker—I'd just like to be thought of as a filmmaker. I don't make films to be thought of as a spokesperson or to toe any politically correct line" (*Montreal Mirror Online*, July 1997). Robinson also starred in Araki's next project, his most apparent homage to the screwball comedies he admires, *Splendor* (1999). The film came as a surprise since it does not share the apocalyptic tones of Araki's previous movies. The story of *Splendor* adapts the situations of the romantic comedy genre to Araki's predilection for three-ways and queer undertones: Veronica (Kathleen Robertson) is unable to choose between her two boyfriends Abel and Zed and decides to live with both of them. In one scene, the two men are led to kiss in front of the woman, reversing the usual stereotype of lesbians kissing for a man's sexual excitement. The film ends with the optimistic beginning of the characters' ménage-à-trois. Araki has repeatedly stated his dissatisfaction for the "couple thing," "the Boy meets Girl, or Boy meets Boy" situation: "In the threeway there is confusion and the element of unpredictability. The dynamic is much more interesting because it is just not a part of what we perceive as Western civilization." To him "*Splendor* is ultimately about…being outside of that pairing." The film premiered at the Sundance Film Festival and Araki underlined the continuity with its previous works: "there is a connection with my other films in that there is a romantic core to the work. It has been part of my films since 1989—a romanticism bordering on the naive." At the same time, the director recognized that *Splendor* represented a development of his style, from the anger of *The Doom Generation* to a more "groovy, ecstasy, peaceful type of movie" (*Filmmaker Magazine* Online, 1999).

In 2000, Araki embarked on a TV series for MTV, *How the World Ends*, an ambitious project, which, in Araki's intentions, was to represent a "Twin Peaks for the MTV generation." The director rejoiced at the possibility that his radicalism would reach a large audience through the television medium. Yet, the series never materialized: only its pilot was shot and it was never shown on TV. After this disappointing experience, Araki made a major comeback with *Mysterious Skin* (2004) which was shown to critical acclaim at the prestigious Venice and London Film Festivals. Based on the homonymous novel by Scott Heim, the film chronicles the lives of Neil, a teenage hustler, and Brian, a shy adolescent obsessed with aliens, who were both abused by their baseball coach when they were kids. Brian has completely blanketed out the abuse, while Neil remembers it all too well and his urge to please men is certainly a factor in his hustling. The two characters will finally start to find a balance by sharing their own experiences in an ending, which Araki describes as "a perfect blend of light and dark, a sense of the beginning of the healing" (indieWIRE). This story of sexual abuse is mainly set in the quiet American heartland of Hutchinson, Kansas, continuing the director's challenge to middle America. *Mysterious Skin*, however, is not an act of accusation as much as an investigation in the lives of its characters as they grow up and have to come to terms with their past experiences.

Further Reading

Bowen, Peter. "Designed for Living." *Filmmaker* 7.4 (Summer 1999) http://www.filmmakermagazine.com/summer1999/splendor.php (accessed on September 9, 2007); Chang, Chris. "Absorbing Alternative." *Film Comment* 30.5

(September/October 1994): 47–48, 50, 53; Cole, C. Bard. "Out on the Lam." *New York Native* 11.35 (August 17, 1992): 20–21; Croce, Fernardo. "Review of *Totally F***ed Up*." *Slant Magazine* http://www.slantmagazine.com/dvd/dvd_review.asp?ID=694 (accessed on September 5, 2007); Gever, M., J. Greyson, and P. Parmar, eds. *Queer Looks: Perspectives on Lesbian and Gay Film and Video.* New York: Routledge, 1993; Hays, Matthew. "Make Art, Not Politics: Gregg Araki on Going *Nowhere*." *Montreal Mirror*, July 17, 1997. http://www.montrealmirror.com/ARCHIVES/1997/071797/film1.html (accessed on September 5, 2007); Hernandez, Eugene. "Dispatch from Toronto: American Auteurs Araki, Kerrigan, and Solondz Stir Festival." *indieWIRE*. http://www.indiewire.com/ots/onthescene_040917toro.html; Wu, Harmony H. "Queering L.A.: Gregg Araki's Homo-pomo Cinema City." *Spectator* 18.1 (1997): 58–69; Yutani, Kimberly. "Gregg Araki and the Queer New Wave." Leong, Russell, ed. *Asian American Sexualities: Dimensions of the Gay and Lesbian Experience.* New York: Routledge, 1996. 175–180.

B

Baldwin, James (1924–1987)

The African American novelist, playwright, essayist, and social critic James Baldwin rose from humble origins to international literary success. He was one of the first African American writers to include homosexuality in his novels, although he was more reluctant to treat the theme in his non-fiction writings and he resisted the labels of *gay* and *queer*. His analysis of gender and racial discrimination and his agenda for liberation gave him a leading role in debates over the meaning of American democracy and citizenship, particularly during the 1960s. Art and activism are inextricably interwoven in Baldwin's works, although he repeatedly claimed that artists should not subscribe to ideology or write for propaganda. Baldwin's writings explain homophobia and racism on grounds of heterosexual and white panic and as consequences of the inability to acknowledge the humanity of difference. His literary production articulates a strong rejection of compulsive heterosexuality and explicitly revises the straightjacket of black virility which made any black man "a kind of walking phallic symbol" (Baldwin 1985, 190). Bitterly criticized during his lifetime by influential African Americans such as Richard Wright, Eldridge Cleaver, and LeRoi Jones, Baldwin celebrated homosexuality as an instrument of social change and criticized his contemporaries' sexism. Love between men, graphically portrayed in its exchange of bodily odors and fluids, represented, in Baldwin's view, what could keep society united. Contrary to his prominent contemporaries Richard Wright and Ralph Ellison, in his writings, Baldwin conceptualized the fundamental link between racial and sexual oppression in American society. As African American gay writers such as Melvin Dixon and Essex Hemphill became more visible during the 1980s and 1990s, James Baldwin was an increasingly acknowledged influence in queer popular culture.

Baldwin was born in New York on August 2, 1924, from Emma Berdis Jones, a domestic worker, who gave birth to him out of wedlock. Emma married David Baldwin, Sr., a clergyman and factory worker, three years later. The couple had nine children. Baldwin never knew his biological father and his childhood was a difficult one. The relationship with his stepfather was characterized by abuse and intimidation: David Baldwin proved a strict and violent parent who undermined his son's self-esteem. Outside his home, Baldwin had to face the adverse economic conditions of the Great Depression and the oppression of white racism. The young Baldwin found solace from such difficult circumstances in the educational and religious institutions which he attended. His intellectual abilities became apparent from a very early age. After attending Public School 24 and the Frederick Douglass Middle School, Baldwin was admitted to Dewitt Clinton High School in the Bronx, one of the city's most distinguished schools, from where he graduated in 1942. Throughout his school years, Baldwin was taught by New York's most innovative intellectuals, including the gay poet Countee Cullen, one of the chief animators of the **Harlem Renaissance**. The black church was also crucial for Baldwin's youth and proved a refuge from the violence of his stepfather. At the age of 14, Baldwin became a boy preacher at the Pentecostal Mount Calvary Church, a role he kept for over two years. The atmosphere of black churches is vividly recreated in many fictional and non-fictional passages of his works, particularly in the semi-autobiographical novel *Go Tell It on the Mountain* (1953) and in the play *The Amen Corner*, first performed in 1965.

The cultural milieu in which Baldwin grew up was that of the Harlem Renaissance, an artistic and literary movement which was led by many gay and lesbian artists. Intellectuals such as Countee Cullen, Langston Hughes, and Claude McKay viewed literature and the arts as tools for social change. Although he is often considered as the heir of the Harlem literati, Baldwin soon found that Harlem was constraining for his creativity and, in 1948, he left America for France where he settled down in Paris. His move to France was also motivated by his growing awareness of racial discrimination and sexual difference; in America, Baldwin felt doubly targeted for his skin and for his sexual orientation. Once in Paris, Baldwin's literary career suddenly flourished and his personal life was enriched by his meeting with Lucien Happersburger, who became Baldwin's lifetime partner. His literary output of the 1950s included an important polemical essay against Richard Wright and those African American writers who were taking him as a model, "Everybody's Protest Novel" (1949), a collection of essays, *Notes of a Native Son* (1955), as well as his early novels *Go Tell It on the Mountain* (1953) and *Giovanni's Room* (1955). *Go Tell It on the Mountain* portrays the efforts of the 14 year old John Grimes to come to terms with both his African American cultural inheritance and his homosexuality. The young protagonist in Baldwin's first, and to many critics his best, novel struggles to forge his own identity. As the novel unfolds, John is increasingly attracted to his Sunday School teacher Elisha, a feeling which both excites and scares him. The novel provides a rare insight into adolescent gay sexuality and it effectively weaves the characters' narratives into the social and racial contexts of America, starting from the turn of the century and leading up to the 1930s. While the setting of *Go Tell It on the Mountain* is the black community, *Giovanni's Room* is a so-called white novel set in Paris. It portrays the homosexual relationship between David, an American who is exploring his sexuality while his fiancée Hella is in Spain, and the handsome Italian Giovanni. The central tension in the novel derives from David's inability to accept his own homosexuality. In denying his own desire, David abandons Giovanni, who in turn, deserted by David and jobless for his rejection of his employer Guillaume, joins the Parisian street boys and eventually kills Guillaume. Giovanni is then arrested, tried, and sentenced to death. David's eventual betrayal of his lover represents the collapse of love within American society, which imposes compulsive heterosexuality on its citizens. *Giovanni's Room* also provides an homosexual alternative to Western heterosexual romances where mythical lovers such as Romeo and Juliet are united in love and death. Although it is Giovanni who dies, David's inability to accept his homosexuality as well as his awareness of having caused his lover's death constitute a metaphorical death sentence. The novel was initially rejected by American publishers who felt that an African American author writing on white homosexuals may alienate his readers. Yet, after it was accepted by a British publisher, the Dial Press published it to good reviews, and the novel has since become a central text for gay and lesbian studies.

Baldwin's writings of the 1950s anticipate the tone of the civil rights movement that will fully develop in the United States in the following decade. Baldwin became increasingly involved in race conflict as he wanted to show his compatriots that he had not left America to live a raceless existence in Europe. In 1957, he was commissioned a series of journalistic assignments which brought him back to the American South where he interviewed Martin Luther King and witnessed the birth of the civil rights movement. In the 1960s, Baldwin found himself thrown into the role he loathed: that of spokesperson for the rights of his own race in America. Race and sexual difference continued to proceed simultaneously in Baldwin's career. The collection of essays *Nobody Knows My Name: More Notes of a Native Son* (1961) contained Baldwin's reflections on race and denounced the violence of white racism in America. Baldwin's third novel *Another Country* (1962) was based on his bohemian years in the Village and became an instant bestseller, although the critical reception was less enthusiastic than that of his two previous novels. *Another Country* depicts the lives of eight diverse individuals who all engage in bisexual and interracial relationships, transgressing the fixed boundaries imposed by American society. In their intimate encounters, the characters attempt to bridge the gaps between races, genders, and social orientations. *Another Country* is a parable on reconciliation, and its multiethnic cast constitutes a microcosm for America, representing the country's tensions and crises. In a radical move for the times, Baldwin endowed homosexuality with an ability for healing: it is Eric, the gay character, who is able to resolve many of the conflicts in which the other protagonists of the novel find themselves involved.

The growth of the civil rights movement and, consequently, of violence against African Americans at the hands of white racists encouraged Baldwin to speak with more conviction against the pervasive white supremacy in the United States. The writer became one of the best-known African American intellectuals and the media started to give him an increasing visibility unusual for a gay black man. *Time* magazine devoted its cover to him; newspapers and television networks asked for interviews. Baldwin's engagement with the civil rights movement is witnessed by the essays in the form of letters to his nephew collected in *The Fire Next Time* (1963) and by his play *Blues for Mr. Charlie* (1964). Both works warned middle-class white Americans not to underestimate the discontent brewing in the African American community. This growing discontent could lead to unprecedented violence. Baldwin reiterated his concerns in the meeting between Civil Rights activists and the

Kennedy administration which took place in May 1963, just before the march on Washington. Baldwin did not have such a visible role in the march which prefigured the writer's distancing from the movement and his growing radicalism. In *Blues for Mr. Charlie*, Baldwin seems to dramatize his position within the struggle for African American rights as the play is equally unhappy about both Martin Luther King's strategy of nonviolent resistance and Malcolm X's racial pride and his separation from whites. In particular, the play challenges the effective commitment of white liberals to the civil rights movement.

Baldwin's fourth novel, *Tell Me How Long the Train Has Been Gone* (1968), is a strong rejoinder to those black militants who had questioned Baldwin's role in the civil rights movement because of his homosexuality. Baldwin's critics were led by Eldridge Cleaver who, in his controversial collection *Soul on Ice* (1968, 102), condemned Baldwin's homosexuality as race hatred and dismissed all black homosexuals as "outraged and frustrated because in their sickness they are unable to have a baby by a white man. The cross they have to bear is that, already touching their toes for the white man, the fruit of their miscegenation is not the little half white offspring of their dreams." In *Tell Me How Long the Train Has Been Gone*, Baldwin reacted to these attacks by portraying the relationship between Leo Proudhammer, a successful black actor who has risen to stardom from poverty, and Christopher, a gay black militant. The character of Christopher, whose very name recalls the theme of redemption through homosexuality explored in *Another Country*, denies that there is a contradiction between gay sexuality and black militancy.

Baldwin's separation from the civil rights movement became more apparent in the 1970s and was precipitated by the assassinations of Medgar Evers, Malcolm X, and Martin Luther King, as well as by his growing disillusionment with American politics. Baldwin also resented the instrumental use of his works by militant groups such as the Black Panthers to promote their own revolutionary agenda. He decided to give up his status of transatlantic commuter and settled down in an old Provençal farmhouse in Saint-Paul-de-Vence, an artist's colony on the Côte d'Azur in southern France. In the early 1970s, Baldwin's writings focused more on race rather than sexuality. His fifth novel, *If Beal Street Could Talk* (1974), has no homosexual characters while it continues the exploration of the dynamics of black urban families and communities which had marked his literary debut. *A Rap on Race* (1971) and *James Baldwin Nikki Giovanni: A Dialogue* (1973) collect a series of Baldwin's conversations with the prominent anthropologist Margaret Mead and with the young black poet and activist Nikki Giovanni. *No Name in the Street* (1972) documents Baldwin's search for a meaningful identity to counter American racism. Baldwin describes the defining moments in his life: his Harlem childhood, his encounters with Martin Luther King and Malcolm X, and his divided existence between France and the United States. In 1972 Baldwin also published the screenplay *One Day When I Was Lost*, which he had initially written for a biographical film on Malcolm X to be produced in Hollywood. The project never materialized due to disagreements between Baldwin and the producers. In the early 1970s Baldwin received several awards and honorary degrees by literary institutions, although critics were less enthusiastic about the writer's later works, which they found to be simple reiterations of Baldwin's original stances against racism.

Homosexuality reappeared as a major theme in Baldwin's sixth and last novel, *Just Above My Head* (1979), which tells the life of Arthur Montana, an African American gay gospel singer, who has recently died. The story is told by Arthur's surviving brother, Hall, who, through his narration, attempts to understand Arthur's life and his tragic death. Like many of Baldwin's previous works, the novel continues the depiction of family and religious institutions in African American communities, celebrating some of their members while criticizing others for their hypocrisy and conservatism. The treatment of homosexuality in *Just Above My Head* is less sensational than in Baldwin's early fiction: sexuality is merely one aspect of Arthur's search for a meaningful existence. The novel did not receive good reviews and, during the 1980s, Baldwin concentrated on non-fiction writings, which culminated with the publication of the monumental *The Price of the Ticket: Collected Nonfiction, 1948–1985* to celebrate the author's sixtieth birthday. He also taught African American literary and history courses at the Five Colleges in Massachusetts. In 1986 French President François Mitterrand awarded Baldwin the French Legion of Honor. The following year, Baldwin received treatment for stomach cancer, but his health continued to deteriorate throughout the year. He died on December 1, 1987, at his home in Saint-Paul-de-Vence. After the funeral at the Cathedral of St. John the Divine in New York City, which was attended by several thousand people, James Baldwin was buried in Ferncliff Cemetery in Hartsdale, New York.

Baldwin occupies a ground-breaking and central position in American and African American gay writing. His oeuvre challenged both the racism and the compulsive heterosexuality dominant in American society and culture. His plea for an open and direct exploration of homosexual and bisexual themes in literature also broke away with previous African American literary depictions of black masculinity. Thus, in spite of his reluctance to embrace the role of spokesperson, James Baldwin has become a model for entire generations of African American gay writers.

Further Reading

Adams, Stephen. *The Homosexual as Hero in Contemporary Fiction*. London: Vision Press, 1980; Baldwin, James. *The Price of the Ticket*. New York: St. Martin's/Marek, 1985; Bergman, David. *Gaiety Transfigured: Gay Self-Representation in American Literature*. Madison: University of Wisconsin Press, 1991; Bigsby, C.W.E. "The Divided Mind of James Baldwin." *Journal of American Studies* 14 (1980): 325–342; Bloom, Harold, ed. *James Baldwin*. New York: Chelsea House, 1986; Campbell, James. *Talking at the Gates: A Life of James Baldwin*. New York: Viking, 1991; Cederstrom, Lorelei. "Love, Race and Sex in the Novels of James Baldwin." *Mosaic* 17.2 (1984): 175–188; Cleaver, Eldridge. "Notes of a Native Son." *Soul on Ice*. New York: Ramparts, 1968. 97–111; Cohen, William A. "Liberalism, Libido, Liberation: Baldwin's Another Country." *Genders* 12 (Winter 1991): 1–21; Giles, James R. "Religious Alienation and 'Homosexual Consciousness' in *City of Night* and *Go Tell It on the Mountain*." *College English* 36 (November 1974): 369–380; Harris, Trudier. *Black Women in the Fiction of James Baldwin*. Knoxville: University of Tennessee Press, 1985; Harris, Trudier, ed. *New Essays on "Go Tell It on the Mountain"*. New York: Cambridge University Press, 1999; Leeming, David. *James Baldwin: A Biography*. New York: Knopf, 1994; McBride, Dwight, ed.

James Baldwin Now. New York: New York University Press, 1994; Miller, Quentin, ed. *Reviewing James Baldwin: Things Not Seen.* Philadelphia: Temple University Press, 2000; Sarotte, Georges-Michel. *Like a Brother, Like a Lover: Male Homosexuality in the American Novel and Theater from Herman Melville to James Baldwin.* Garden City, NY: Anchor Press/Doubleday, 1978; Scott, Lynn Orilla. *James Baldwin's Later Fiction: Witness to the Journey.* East Lansing: Michigan State University Press, 2002; Summers, Claude J. *Gay Fictions: Wilde to Stonewall.* New York: Continuum, 1990; Trope, Quincey, ed. *James Baldwin: The Legacy.* New York: Simon & Schuster, 1989.

BARNES, DJUNA (1892–1982)

American poet, novelist, and playwright Djuna Barnes contributed to the development of modernist literature in the first half of the twentieth century first in New York's bohemian Greenwich Village and later in Paris, the capital of American modernist expatriates. She introduced lesbian themes and characters in the modernist tradition and protested against society's compulsive heterosexuality, although in her later years, which were plagued by alcoholism and depression, she refused to be identified as a lesbian.

Barnes was born on June 12, 1892, in Cornwall-on-Hudson near New York, the daughter of a failed artist, Wald Barnes, and the Englishwoman Elizabeth Chappell. Djuna had an unconventional and, at times, painful childhood. Her father kept both his wife and mistress together with respective children in the same household, and Barnes later hinted in her books that she had been abused by him with the tacit consent of her mother and grandmother. The trauma of childhood abuse emerges throughout her writings, particularly in her novel *Ryder* (1928) and in the play *The Antiphon* (1958). The Barneses separated in 1912, when Elizabeth Chappell moved to New York with her children. Djuna attended the Pratt Institute in Brooklyn and, in 1913, she started to work as a reporter for the *Brooklyn Daily Eagle* and *New York World* to help her mother support the family. Barnes quickly became a successful and self-supporting journalist and went to live in the Greenwich Village, the bohemian center of New York's modernism, where she became friends with many avant-garde artists such as the painter Marcel Duchamp, the playwright Eugene O'Neill, the poets Williams Carlos Williams and Mina Loy.

Although Barnes later dismissed her early journalist writings as mere commercial pieces to pay her rent, these already exhibit her characteristic experimentation with form and content. They are witty and camp observations of New York's society at the turn of the century which often contain, under their frivolous surface, sharp remarks on ethnicity, race, and gender. They also include references to same-sex relationships in their depiction of the eccentric population of the Greenwich Village. Barnes's love for women is also apparent in her early poems and short stories such as *The Book of Repulsive Women: 8 Rhythms and 5 Drawings* (1915) and "Paprika Johnson" (1915). While in New York, Barnes contributed to the founding of the drama association The Provincetown Players for which she wrote a series of highly experimental one-act plays. In her personal life, Barnes had many lovers including the poet Mary Pyne, the photographer Bernice Abbott, the writer and collector Peggy Guggenheim, Natalie Barney, the Dada artist Baroness Elsa von Freytag-Loringhoven, and, most importantly, sculptress Thelma Ellen Wood.

Barnes lived with Wood in Paris where she was sent in 1921 on an assignment for *McCall's*. As Paris was becoming the international capital of modernism, Barnes was only too glad to accept. She lived in the French capital and in Europe for the next 15 years, establishing contacts with modernist personalities such as **Gertrude Stein**, Ezra Pound, Kaye Boyle, and James Joyce, whom she interviewed for *Vanity Fair*. In Paris, Barnes also encountered a thriving lesbian community, which inspired her most successful works. From the early 1920s, Barnes started to be a regular contributor of short stories to *The Little Review* and *The Transatlantic Review*. However, it was her novel *Ryder* that established her reputation within the modernist circles. The book, clearly semi-autobiographical in nature and based on the author's childhood, focuses on the eccentric lifestyle of Wendell Ryder who keeps both his wife's and his mistress's families in the same household. Barnes depicts her father in an ambivalent fashion, admiring his non-conformism and his rejection of conventional Puritan morality, but also taking him to task for his constant adultery and belittling of women. Wendell Ryder both represents an alternative to the hypocritical middle-class sexual repression and an extension of it in his neglecting of the sexual gratification of women, whose main purpose he considers as a vehicle for procreation. To Ryder, women's sexuality is simply a tool to celebrate his own masculinity. His conceiving of sexual intercourse primarily for procreative aims makes Ryder an unsympathetic character, given Barnes's description of pregnancy as weakening the female body and of childbirth as destructive and painful. American authorities censured the book, and Barnes had to rewrite passages where she had made too explicit references to sexual intercourse or where she challenged religious institutions. However, the debate around the book did not harm its good sales, which allowed Barnes to take a break from her journalistic writing.

The same year of *Ryder* Barnes also privately published the *Ladies Almanack*, a satire of the Parisian lesbian community written upon Natalie Barney's request. The book, divided according to different phases of female sexuality, illustrates the life of Dame Evangeline Musset, a character clearly based on the aristocratic and wealthy Barney, and the construction of her lesbian identity. Musset's life, however, is simply the pretext for digressions on philosophical, religious, social, and sexual matters. In its repetition of medical, popular, and literary views about female sexuality, however playful and ironic, the book runs the risk of replicating those very stereotypes. Some scholars have argued that Barnes was never able to free herself from normative heterosexual perceptions of lesbian bodies and sexualities. Lillian Faderman (1981, 365), for examples, writes that even though Barnes criticized the representations of lesbianism in the works of Proust, her own "treatment...was not much different. It attests to the power of literary images over lesbian writers that, even after criticizing Proust's lies, Barnes called on her knowledge of lesbians in literature rather than in life in order to write her own novel." Others stress instead that her mocking and detached style gives her the position of a distant observer of the lesbian community she writes about, rather than claiming her membership in it.

In the early 1930s, trying to overcome the painful breaking up of her relationship with Thelma, Barnes went to England, where, surrounded by her friends Peggy Guggenheim, Emily Coleman, and Antonia White, she wrote her last significant work, the novel *Nightwood* (1936). Set between Berlin and the Parisian Left Bank on the backdrop of rising totalitarianisms, the plot revolves around the American heiress Nora Flood and her relationship with Robin Vote, the enigmatic wife of the Jew Felix Volkbein. The story is mainly narrated through the conversations between Nora and transvestite gynecologist Matthew O'Connor. Robin is the object of desire within the narrative, and she eludes the attempts of other characters to control and possess her. *Nightwood* is populated entirely by people marginalized for their social and sexual positions. However, within the universe of the novel, there is nothing marginal about them as they are the reader's only guides to the topographies of desire designed by Barnes. The world of *Nightwood* is only made up of characters who deviate from the received norms, with the result that they are not perceived as deviating at all. Significantly for the years in which it was written, the novel strongly condemns the establishment of social norms based on gender and racial distinctions. Because of its radical content, *Nightwood* was rejected by all the American publishers it had been submitted to. It was the modernist author T. S. Eliot, at the time editor at the British publishing house Faber, who accepted the manuscript asking, however, substantial revisions. In particular, Eliot demanded the attenuation of the book's sexual descriptions and its harsh tones against religion. *Nightwood*, published with an influential introduction by Eliot himself, quickly became a cult work within modernist literary salons which praised it for its formal experimentation and its innovative style.

Barnes's literary career, however, did not continue to flourish. In 1940, beset by ill health caused by her heavy drinking and debts, she moved back to New York where she again settled down in the Village. She lived the rest of her life as a recluse, in poverty, and did not publish anything of note, except for the surreal family drama *The Antiphon*, which, as her previous autobiographical writings, strongly features an incest story. She died on June 18, 1982.

Her constant later refusal to be identified as a lesbian, "I am not a lesbian, I just loved Thelma," has been explained by feminist critic Monique Wittig with Barnes's fear of being made a spokesperson for a movement. This, she felt, would have reduced her status as a writer. After a period of obscurity and neglect, Barnes's writings are being reassessed by feminist and lesbian scholars who find them powerful articulations of lesbian sexuality.

Further Reading

Allen, Carolyn. *Following Djuna: Women Lovers and the Erotics of Loss*. Bloomington: Indiana University Press, 1996; Benstock, Shari. *Women of the Left Bank: Paris, 1900–1940*. Austin: University of Texas Press, 1986; Broe, Mary Lynn. "Djuna Barnes." *The Gender of Modernism*. Bonnie Kime Scott, ed. Bloomington: Indiana University Press, 1990. 1–45; Broe, Mary Lynn, ed. *Silence and Power: A Reevaluation of Djuna Barnes*. Carbondale: Southern Illinois University Press, 1991; Brossard, Nicole. "Djuna Barnes: De Profil Moderne." *Mon héroine*. Montréal: Remue-ménage, 1981. 189–214; Faderman, Lillian. *Surpassing the Love of Men: Romantic Friendship and Love between Women from the Renaissance to the Present.* New York: William Morrow, 1981; Field, Andrew. *Djuna: The Life and Times of Djuna Barnes.* New York: G. P. Putnam's Sons, 1983; Meese, Elizabeth. *(sem)erotics theorizing lesbian: writing.* New York: New York University Press, 1992; Wittig, Monique. *The Straight Mind and Other Essays.* Boston: Beacon, 1992.

BASIC INSTINCT

Written by Joe Eszterhas and directed by Paul Verhoeven, the erotic thriller *Basic Instinct* (1992) was one of the top-grossing films of the 1990s and crucially contributed to the fame of its stars, propelling the then relative unknown Sharon Stone into stardom and confirming Michael Douglas's ability in his portrayal of flawed heroes. Yet, the film's position within queer popular culture remains problematic. Even before it was released, *Basic Instinct* stirred the reactions of gay and lesbian communities worldwide, sparking debates on the politics of queer representations in popular culture. The openly bisexual characters of Catherine Tramell (Stone) and her female partners were considered offensive by many gays and lesbians, leading to a global boycott of the film. Others found the narrative of the film empowering and pointed out how Catherine easily manipulates the male hero played by Douglas. The outspoken lesbian academic Camille Paglia went as far as declaring *Basic Instinct* her favorite film and provided commentaries for its DVD edition.

The plot follows the investigation of troubled San Francisco detective Nick Curran (Michael Douglas) into the murder of rock-and-roll musician Johnny Boz. Boz was repeatedly stabbed with an ice-pick and the prime suspect is his openly bisexual girlfriend Catherine Tramell, a psychologist and a best-selling thriller author. Curran immediately becomes suspicious of Tramell, yet he is also attracted to her because of her explicit sexuality. Catherine does not show signs of grief for her boyfriend's death, and she readily admits to have used him for her sexual pleasures. Curran, whose psychological balance is unstable due to stress and drug abuse, is further suspicious because of Catherine's exact description of the dynamics of Boz's murder in one of her books. As the investigation continues and more murders are committed, Curran and Tramell start a dangerous sexual liaison.

Basic Instinct takes to the extreme Paul Verhoeven's inclination for the graphic representation of violence and sexuality. Gay rights activists felt that the movie followed the usual Hollywood pattern of describing homosexuals as predatory, insatiable, and homicidal. In the spring 1991, the beginning of the shooting in San Francisco, which has one of the largest gay communities in the United States, provoked anger against the film. The first day ended with large demonstrations and arrests by the police. Demonstrations continued to disturb the crew for the rest of the shooting. Negative as well as positive reactions to *Basic Instinct* have hinged on Stone's role as an independent, sexually threatening woman. The film was marketed upon Stone's predatory character and promise of forbidden sexuality. These two features make Catherine Tramell a direct descendant of the femme fatales of the noir tradition of the 1940s and 1950s from **Barbara Stanwyck**'s Phyllis in *Double*

A brutal murder.

A brilliant killer.

A cop who can't

resist the danger.

Putting the predatory lesbian on the film poster: Catherine Tramell (Sharon Stone) clawing detective Nick Curran (Michael Douglas) on the infamous poster of Paul Verhoeven's *Basic Instinct*. Courtesy of Tristar Pictures/Photofest.

Indemnity (1944) to Kim Novak's Madeleine in *Vertigo* (1958). "Flesh seduces, passion kills" was the line used on the film's poster over a naked Douglas clawed by Stone. Once *Basic Instinct* was released, its main selling point became the few seconds of female crotch gazing during the police interrogation scene. Catherine Tramell is able to manipulate both the male hero, the gaze of her audience, and the film narrative itself, through the novel she writes in the course of the movie.

In her commentary for the DVD edition, lesbian theorist Camille Paglia praises *Basic Instinct* as perfectly capturing the tension between the sexes that contemporary society has destroyed. In a 1995 interview with Owen Keehnen published in the online encyclopedia *GLBTQ*, she declared herself shocked by the protests. "Those protests show the complete disintegration of gay politics. It was a pornographic film receiving national distribution. It should have been rightly hailed as extreme and beautiful and bizarre." To Paglia, criticism of the film in gay and lesbian constituencies demonstrated that gay activism "had completely lost touch with the people. The more you get in groups, the more you lose your instincts. . . . It was a revolutionary film that pushed a porn style and language into Middle America. It makes me sick that instead of being seen as revolutionary, it was seen as reactionary."

Other critics have suggested readings of the films that go beyond the for/against debate and take into account the postmodern cultural milieu in which *Basic Instinct* was made. As Kate Stables has argued, popular culture expresses and reproduces the ideologies necessary for the existence of social configurations. Because of their polysemic nature, however, postmodern films can accommodate radically diverging discourses at the same time. They self-consciously bring out, rather than conceal, the social contradictions built into their narratives and exploit them for largely conflicting interpretations of the same text. Thus, Stables explains (1998, 166), "*Basic Instinct* could be variously reviled as a misogynistic fantasy and celebrated as a feminist *tour-de-force*, condemned for blatant homophobia and celebrated as the ultimate cult lesbian movie."

Further Reading

Finch, Mark. "Gays and Lesbians in Cinema." *Cineaste's Political Companion to American Film.* Gary Crowdus, ed. Chicago: Lake View Press, 1994; Keehnen, Owen. "Coffee with Camille: Chatting with the Incomparable Camille Paglia." *Encyclopedia of Gay, Lesbian, Bisexual, Transgender and Queer Culture.* 1995 http://www.glbtq.com/sfeatures/interviewcpaglia.html (accessed on September 5, 2007); Stables, Kate. "The Postmodern Always Rings Twice: Constructing the *Femme Fatale* in 90s Cinema." *Women in Film Noir.* E. Ann Kaplan, ed. London: BFI Publishing, 1998. 164–182.

BEAN, BILLY (1964–)

Former baseball player Billy Bean documented, with his moving testimony *Going the Other Way: Lessons from a Life in and out of Major League Baseball* (2003), the impact of homophobia on his career as a player and on his personal life. Although Bean has been out since 1999, he remained closeted throughout his baseball years. The fact that he had to keep secret his private life was painful, particularly when his partner Sam Madani died of **AIDS** in 1995. Bean felt he could not talk about his loss to anyone, and, for fear of being questioned, he did not ask for days off to attend Madani's funeral. The stress accumulated during all those years in the closet led Bean to leave baseball in 1996. Since his coming out, Bean is a staunch supporter of queer rights and has hosted the revival of the 1950s panel game show *I Have Got a Secret* on the Game Show Network. Bean was the second baseball player to openly talk about his homosexuality, and, after the death of **Glenn Burke** in 1995, he is the only surviving player to have acknowledged his sexuality.

William Daro Bean was born on May 11, 1964, in Santa Ana, California, the son of William Joseph Bean and Linda Robertson. The marriage between the couple was arranged in haste when they discovered Linda's pregnancy. William's paternal family was strictly religious and they never fully approved of the marriage, although they saw it as the lesser evil. After less than a year into the marriage, William was persuaded to go on a two-year Mormon mission and left his wife and child alone. After his divorce, Billy did not see his father again until the late 1980s, a few months before he died of a heart attack. Linda married two more times and she finally found happiness with her third marriage to policeman Ed Kovac.

Bean was a sports fan since his childhood and, during his high school years, he became a strong athlete, playing both in his school's baseball and football teams. In his senior year, he was chosen as athlete of the year of Santa Ana High School. Due to his academic and athletic skills, Bean received several scholarship offers from different university and finally chose the Jesuit Loyola Marymount University in Los Angeles. Although he made friends quickly, in his autobiography, Bean describes how he constantly felt an outsider in the erotic world of his university teammates.

He was embarrassed by their continuous boasting of sexual conquests with women. Already in his junior year, Bean was named to the Division I All America team and attracted the attention of talent scouts. After tearing a quadriceps muscle during a game, however, Bean saw his career prospects as a professional player diminish. Yet, he was not to be discouraged and continued to play for the Marymount team in his senior year. His coach also arranged for him to play minor league baseball with the Fairbanks Goldpanners of the Alaska League and Bean gave strong performances which led to his choice as the team's player of the year. In the 1986 championship, the Marymount team succeeded in entering the College World Series, but was eliminated by the Arizona team. Bean graduated from Marymount the same year with a degree in business administration.

Due to Bean's strong performances in his senior year, the player was selected by the Detroit Tigers and he started his professional career in 1987. Bean did well in his debut match, tying the major league record for most hits by a player in his first game. The Tigers employed Bean as long as their star outfielder Kirk Gibson was on the disabled list. When Gibson came back, Bean had less chances of playing and, at mid-season, he was sent to the Tigers' minor league associated team, the Toledo Mud Hens so that he could play more regularly and perfect his talent. Bean remained with the Tigers for two years, alternating matches in Toledo and Detroit, but his status as utility, rather than position player, seriously damaged his hopes of career within the team. In July 1989 Bean was traded to the Los Angeles Dodgers. Moving to California was significant also for his developing consciousness as a gay man. Although Bean married his college fiancée Anna Maria Amato that same year, he started to befriend several gay men he had met at the local gym. Bean's apartment was located in West Hollywood, the so-called gayest neighborhood in L.A. The player felt attracted by the gay world that he was discovering.

During his time with the Dodgers, Bean was coached by baseball legend Tommy Lasorda, while the manager's gay son was dying of AIDS, a circumstance that Lasorda has still not acknowledged. In spite of Lasorda's appreciation, Bean felt uncomfortable because of his homophobic remarks. After nine unhappy months in Japan with the Kenetsu Buffaloes in 1992, Bean came back to the United States where he got a minor league contract with the San Diego Padres for the 1993 season. Here he also had his first homosexual intercourse. While visiting his wife's parents in Washington D.C. the athlete met his first partner Sam Madani. Bean and his wife soon divorced and, when the Padres called him again for the next season, Madani moved in the new house Bean had bought in California. Yet, their relationship remained secret to Bean's teammates, and, when Madani tested HIV-positive in 1994, Bean could not get from them the support he needed. He was not even able to attend Madani's funeral in Washington a year later for fears of being asked questions about the nature of their relationship. At the same time, the Padres decided to use Bean, much to his disappointment, in their triple-A club in Las Vegas.

In 1996, Bean, who by then had started a relationship with his present partner Efraìn Veiga, was told by his agent that the Padres would not offer him more than a minor league contract. Frustrated by the prospect of remaining in the closet to play in a minor team, Bean quit baseball and became a partner in Veiga's restaurant business. The couple later started a partnership in real estate. Bean also came out to his parents, who were supportive. In 1999, the former player publicly acknowledged his homosexuality in an interview with the *Miami Herald.* The news was picked up by the national press and the *New York Times* ran a front-page article on it. Bean and Veiga were also interviewed for ABC's program *20/20.* In the spring 2006, the former-player turned into a TV personality joining the all-gay panel of the Game Show Network's *I Have Got a Secret.*

After his coming out, Bean became an outspoken supporter of queer struggles for equal rights. His autobiography *Going the Other Way* constructs Bean as a role model for other closeted homosexuals to follow, learning from, rather than sharing, his mistakes.

Further Reading

Bean, Billy. www.billybean.com (accessed on April 9, 2007); Bean, Billy, with Chris Bull. *Going the Other Way: Lessons Learned from a Life in and out of Baseball.* New York: Marlowe & Company, 2003; Bull, Chris. "Safe at Home." *The Advocate* 801 (December 21, 1999): 34; Lipsyte, Robert. "A Major League Player's Life of Isolation and Secret Fear." *New York Times* (September 6, 1999): A1.

BEAT GENERATION

The so-called Beat Generation was the most significant literary movement of the second half of the twentieth century. The founding figures of the movement, Jack Kerouac (1922–1969), Allen Ginsberg (1926–1997), and William Burroughs (1914–1997), as well as lesser known writers such as Neal Cassidy, Herbert Huncke, Peter Orlovsky (Ginsberg's partner), and Carl Solomon were all gays or bisexuals. Most of them explicitly talked about homosexuality in their works, challenging the censors of the Eisenhower years and becoming inspirational icons for the counterculture of the 1960s. Throughout their literary careers, they rejected the conformism of the 1950s in the name of political, social, and spiritual reforms, including gay liberation. Beat writers, or, as they were disparagingly called, *beatniks,* defied middle-class values in their explorations of an openly unconventional sexuality, drug-use, and Eastern spirituality.

Kerouac, Burroughs, and Ginsberg met in New York in 1944, but the Beat phenomenon would not come to national prominence before the mid-1950s. Until then, Beat circles were restricted to New York and San Francisco, their writers were mostly unpublished enthusiasts for literary experimentation, drugs, and jazz. Their spontaneous and uncensored writing was primarily based on their own experiences among social outlaws. Kerouac explained that the term *beat* in the name of the movement did not mean only "exhausted," but also "beatific." Thus, he emphasized the key position of spiritualism in the group's philosophy, which championed the causes of those left behind by the American dream and the consumerist credo of the Cold War years. It was the obscenity trial against Allen Ginsberg's *Howl and Other Poems* (1956) which effectively launched the Beat movement, paving the way for the publication of such seminal works as Jack Kerouac's *On the Road* (1957) and Burroughs's *Naked Lunch* (1959).

Ginsberg, who had avoided the military draft in the World War II by declaring his homosexuality, first read his poem "Howl" in San Francisco in October 1955. The poet and publisher Lawrence Ferlinghetti was immediately impressed by it. His publishing house City Lights Books brought out Ginsberg's collection *Howl and Other Poems* in 1956, but the work was seized by the San Francisco police and U.S. customs. In the trial that ensued, however, Judge Clayton Horne ruled that the poems were not obscene and the collection soon became a bestseller. Censors were angered in particular by the strong sense of solidarity among the dispossessed and the explicit depiction of gay life and sexuality contained in the book. The poem "Howl" opens with a lamentation about the power of middle-class values to destroy the best minds of Ginsberg's generation. These opening lines became a common cry

Male bonding between Beats: Neal Cassidy (left) and Jack Kerouac (right). Courtesy of Photofest.

of protest for the 1960s counterculture which demanded more freedom of choice for individuals and less state control on personal lives. Many poems in the collection explicitly portray gay sex. This in itself already meant infringing a literary and social taboo. Ginsberg's crude language led many to brand the collection as pornography. In "Howl," for example, Ginsberg (1996, 9) celebrates "the best minds of my generation…who let themselves be fucked in the ass by saintly motorcyclists, and screamed with joy,…[and] who blew and were blown by those human seraphim, the sailors, caresses of Atlantic and Caribbean Love." In *Sexual Politics, Sexual Communities*, John D'Emilio (1998, 181) summarized the centrality of *Howl* in the development of gay literature. The collection's "description of gay male sexuality as joyous, delightful, and indeed even holy turned contemporary stereotypes of homosexuality upside down." Gay readers were finally offered "a self-affirming image of their sexual preference." Ginsberg became a crucial link between the literary avant-garde, which was becoming increasingly tolerant, and even supportive of homosexuality, and the emerging protest against the social and sexual conformism of the 1950s. "Howl" became the manifesto of the emergent counterculture, and Ginsberg the icon for many battles of the 1960s and beyond, including anti-War protests and queer rights.

Burroughs, too, was subjected to a trial for obscenity. Published first in Paris and then in the United States, his novel *Naked Lunch* represented an upfront attack against all forms of power and control. Burroughs had already focused on the world of social and sexual outlaws in his novels *Junkie* (1953) and the unfinished *Queer*, written in the 1950s but published only in 1985, which, from the very title, focuses on the gay world. With *Naked Lunch*, however, Burroughs relinquished the naturalistic mode of his previous works in favor of a more surrealist style. To Burroughs, sexuality and language were sites of social conflicts. Influenced by the theories of psychoanalyst Wilhelm Reich, Burroughs condemned sexual repression as a form of social control. As he later stated in an *Advocate* interview (Brent 1994, 203), to him, sex was "very definitely a political issue.…One of the most potent weapons in the hands of the people in control is sexual suppression." Praised by intellectuals such as poet Karl Shapiro and novelist and social critic Norman Mailer, *Naked Lunch* was considered pornography by the state of Massachusetts. As for *Howl*, the trial had a beneficial effect on the book, turning it into a bestseller. The several court cases concerning Burroughs's novel eventually ended with a landmark decision in the history of censorship by the Massachusetts Supreme Court in 1966. The novel was cleared from obscenity charges.

Burroughs's following novels were written in the genres of pulp literature such as science fiction, westerns, and detective stories. Yet, the writer twisted the conventions of genre literature to accommodate his subversive messages against social and sexual control. Burroughs's literary pulps do not endorse the hegemonic values of dominant groups, as genre literature often does. On the contrary, they incorporate the voices of those considered on the margins of society. The literary innovations of Burroughs's texts, with their fragmented postmodernist narrative and subversion of linear chronological development, mirror the plea for political reform. As Ginsberg, Burroughs too became a countercultural icon. His contempt for authority and his honest depiction of homosexuality and drug-taking made his appeal last well beyond the rebellious 1960s. In his later life, Burroughs metamorphosed from an outlaw into an pop symbol, taking part into a number of films, including Gus Van Sant's *Drugstore Cowboy* (1989), and collaborating with popular musicians such as Tom Waits, Kurt Cobain, and U2. This global celebrity did not lead Burroughs to sever his links with the movement for queer rights. In an interview to the *Advocate* (Brent 1994, 203), Burroughs defined the gay liberation movement as serving "a very useful purpose.... [G]ay has now become a household word and people realize that it is not all as sulphurous and evil and distressing as it was once thought to be."

Often considered as the central voice of the Beat Movement, the bisexual Jack Kerouac was more evasive than Ginsberg and Burroughs in representing his own homosexual experiences in his autobiographical writings. His most famous work is the novel *On the Road* which Kerouac wrote with the method of what he called spontaneous prose. It relied more on spontaneity rather than on revisions to create a more meaningful bond between the writer and his audience.

Although the Beat Generation was primarily white and male, the Beats embraced the causes of the subjects on the margins of American Cold War society. The movement influenced several gay writers such as Paul Bowles, Frank O'Hara, Robert Duncan, and John Rechy. As John D'Emilio (1998, 181) points out, the Beats altered the stereotype about homosexuals as dangerous and treacherous perverts that enjoyed such wide currency in the 1950s. Thanks to Beat writing, "gays could perceive themselves as nonconformists rather than deviates, as rebels against stultifying norms rather than immature, unstable personalities." Equally important for gay and lesbian popular culture was the Beats' rejection of self-censorship and their stress on the necessity to convey personal experiences in literary works. To many homosexual artists, this meant a call to represent without shame their sexual identity.

Further Reading

Charters, Ann, ed. *The Portable Beat Reader.* New York: Viking, 1992; Charters, Ann. *Kerouac: A Biography.* New York: St. Martin's Press, 1994; D'Emilio, John. *Sexual Politics, Sexual Communities.* Chicago: University of Chicago Press, 1998; George, Paul S., and Jerold M. Starr. "Beat Politics: New Left and Hippie Beginnings in the Postwar Counterculture." *Cultural Politics: Radical Movements in Modern History.* Jerold M. Starr, ed. New York: Praeger, 1985. 189–233; Ginsberg, Allen. *Howl and Other Poems.* San Francisco: City Lights Books, 1996; Harris, Brent. "William S. Burroughs." *Long Road to Freedom: The Advocate History of the Gay and Lesbian Movement.* Mark Thompson, ed. New York, St. Martin's Press, 1994. 202–203; Nicosia, Gerald. *Memory Babe: A Critical Biography of Jack Kerouac.* New York: Grove Press, 1983; Skerl, Jennie, ed. *Reconstructing the Beats.* New York: Palgrave Macmillan, 2004; Stimpson, Catherine R. "The Beat Generation and the Trials of Homosexual Liberation." *Salmagundi* 58–59 (1982–1983): 373–392; Theado, Matt, ed. *The Beats: A Literary Reference.* New York: Carroll & Graf Publishers, 2003; Tytell, John. *Naked Angels: The Lives and Literature of the Beat Generation.* New York: McGraw-Hill, 1976; Watson, Steven. *Birth of the Beat Generation: Visionaries, Rebels and Hipsters, 1944–1960.* New York: Pantheon, 1995.

BERNSTEIN, LEONARD (1918–1990)

Academy Award nominee Leonard Bernstein was the first American musician to receive worldwide acclaim for his skills as a conductor and composer. He was music director of the New York Philharmonic from 1958 to 1969, leading more concerts than any other conductor. His compositions, the musical *West Side Story* (1957) above all, were both critical and commercial successes. In spite of his classical music background, the conductor was eager to explore popular culture and frequently appeared on television, displaying his flamboyant style of conducting to the delight of vast audiences. As his popularity grew in the 1960s, Bernstein also lent his support to radical causes, such as anti-Vietnam War demonstrations and the civil rights movement. Yet, throughout his life, he was unable to fully come out of the closet and declare openly his homosexuality. Commenting on his death, journalist Paul Moor ("Klassik in Berlin," 1990) wrote: "Over and over, Leonard Bernstein gave the appearance of a profoundly troubled man desperately trying to come out. But if he never came out in the customary sense, he did everything just short of it.... if he had, it would have made him a far less unhappy man."

Bernstein was born into a Jewish family of Ukrainian origins in Lawrence, Massachusetts, on August 25, 1918. His original name was Louis, but his parents always called him Leonard and the name was officially changed when he was 16. From a very early age, Bernstein developed an intense interest in music and started to take piano lessons, much to his father's disapproval. Sam Bernstein wanted his son to become a businessman like him and he initially opposed Leonard's passion for the piano. Bernstein first attended the Garrison and Boston Latin Schools, and, upon his graduation in 1935, he went on to Harvard University where he pursued his music studies with Walter Piston, Edward Burlingame-Hill, and A. Tillman Merritt. His attention for radical causes was apparent also during his university years as he directed Marc Blitzstein's radical opera *The Cradle Will Rock* (1937) before graduating in 1939. Bernstein continued his studies in Philadelphia at the Curtis Institute of Music, where he was taught piano by Isabella Vengerova, conducting by Fritz Reiner, and orchestration by Randall Thompson.

In 1943, Bernstein was appointed to his first conducting post as Assistant Conductor of the New York Philharmonic. In November of that same year, he stepped in for Bruno Walter at a Carnegie Hall concert. Broadcast on the radio, the performance was an immediate success and launched Bernstein's international career. European and American orchestras demanded him as guest director and important music schools sought him as a teacher. From 1945 to 1947, Bernstein was music director of the New York City Symphony Orchestra and, in 1951, he started teaching at Tanglewood, the prestigious Massachusetts music institution. In the immediate post-war years, Bernstein directed in London, Prague, and Tel Aviv, establishing a lifelong relationship with the state of Israel. His growing fame did not make him more timid about his radical commitments. In November 1947, a month after the Hollywood Ten hearings and in the midst of the mounting anti-Communist hysteria, Bernstein conducted a revival of *The Cradle Will Rock*. Music critic Virgil Thomson praised it as an effort to counter the attacks on the left and the labor movement.

More threatening for the musician's career than his radical associations was his homosexuality. Bernstein's biographers agree that during his New York years, the musician was involved sexually with different male partners. It was Dimitri Mitropulos, the music director of the New York Philharmonic and one of Bernstein's mentors and his probable lover, who advised him to marry to respond to the gossip about his sexual life. After an intermittent engagement, in 1951, a doubtful Bernstein married Chilean actress Felicia Montealegre Cohn from whom he had three children. However, Bernstein continued to have homosexual relationships throughout his married life, probably with his wife's full knowledge.

In the 1950s, the musician's celebrity skyrocketed as he performed in the most prestigious theaters of Europe and the United States. He also started to conduct operas and was the first American conductor to perform at La Scala in Milan, where he directed Maria Callas in what was to become one of her classic roles, that of Cherubini's *Medea*. In 1958 he was appointed music director of the New York Philharmonic, a position that he held until 11 years later when he was awarded with the lifetime title of Laureate Conductor. Bernstein paralleled his conducting career with that as a composer of both highbrow pieces such as symphonies and ballets and more popular Broadway musicals including his best-known work *West Side Story*. While *West Side Story* is primarily a heterosexual love story, Charles Kaiser has pointed out its centrality in queer popular culture. The musical was, after all, the

Romance, violence, danger, and mystery in the streets: the queer appeal of Leonard Bernstein's *West Side Story*. Courtesy of United Artists/Photofest.

product of four gay men, Leonard Bernstein, Jerome Robbins, Arthur Laurents, and **Stephen Sondheim**. "Thousands of gay Americans fell in love with *West Side Story* when they were children in the fifties," writes Kaiser (1998, 85) in his account of New York homosexual life, "To many gay adults coming of age in the sixties, the romance, violence, danger, and mystery so audible on the original cast album all felt like integral parts of the gay life they had embraced. The lyrics of 'Somewhere' in particular seemed to speak directly to the gay experience before the age of liberation."

Popular culture enhanced Bernstein's fame. His soundtrack for Elia Kazan's movie *On the Waterfront* (1955) received a nomination for an Academy Award. Although reared in classical music, Bernstein was highly appreciative of popular music and scholars have noted his efforts to infuse jazz and pop motifs even in his more classical compositions. With his albums Bernstein won 11 Grammy Awards throughout his career. The conductor's association with popular culture was further strengthened by his extensive use of television. From 1958 Bernstein directed 53 *Young People's Concerts*, which were broadcast by CBS and sold to foreign networks throughout the 1960s. In this educational program, the musician explained how classical music could become alive and constitute an exciting experience for everybody regardless of their education. His distinctive approach to conducting received wide publicity, to the enchantment of television audiences and the irritation of purists. Bernstein's eccentricity was not limited to his stage mannerism. As an outspoken supporter of civil rights, the musician invited members of the Black Panthers, the revolutionary African American organization, to his cocktail parties. Conservative satirist Tom Wolfe (1970, 2) lambasted him as the quintessential so-called radical chic who organized parties where the revolutionary Panthers eat "little Roquefort cheese morsels rolled in crushed nuts…, and asparagus tips in mayonnaise dabs, and *meatballs petites au Coq Hardi*, … offered to them on gadrooned silver platters by maids in black uniforms with hand-ironed white aprons."

In spite of his championing of unpopular causes, Bernstein, a dominant figure in New York post-war society and a close friend of the Kennedy family, still remained reticent about his own sexuality. Yet, in the mid-1970s, as the movement for gay liberation became more visible, the musician decided to leave his wife to live with his partner Tom Cochran. In December 1976, before conducting Shostakovich's Fourteenth Symphony with the New York Philharmonic, Bernstein came as close to a public coming out as he would ever do confessing to a startled audience that he had come to understand, with the approach of death, "that an artist must cast off everything that may be restraining him and create in complete freedom. I decided that I had to this for myself, to live the rest of my life as I want." This decision, however, was short-lived as Bernstein soon returned to his dying wife, who had been diagnosed with cancer. After the death of his wife, Bernstein was more open about his homosexuality, but without officially coming out. In his opera *A Quiet Place* (1983), the composer reworked material from his previous work, *Trouble in Tahiti* (1952), explicitly treating the themes of homosexuality and suburban hypocrisy.

Bernstein continued to perform until his death on October 14, 1990. Of particular note throughout the 1980s were his Christmas Day concert in 1989 as part of the celebrations for the fall of the Berlin Wall, broadcast live in more than

20 countries, and his PBS series on Beethoven's music. In 1985, he was awarded the Lifetime Achievement Grammy Award by the National Academy of Recording Arts and Sciences and he was named honorary president of the London Symphony Orchestra two years later. Bernstein's repertoire was vast and complex. He was considered especially accomplished with the works of Gustav Mahler, Aaron Copland, Johannes Brahms, Dmitri Shostakovich, and George Gershwin.

Further Reading

Burton, Humphrey. *Leonard Bernstein*. New York: Doubleday, 1994; Burton, Willi Westbrook, ed. *Conversations about Bernstein*. New York: Oxford University Press, 1995; Keiser, Charles. *The Gay Metropolis*. Fort Washington, PA: Harvest Books, 1998; Moor, Paul. "Remembering Lenny." 1990. *Klassik in Berlin.* http://www.berlinerklassik.de/seiten/frames-paulmoor-en.html?artikel/paulmoor/pm-bernstein-90.html (accessed on September 5, 2007); Myers, Paul. *Leonard Bernstein*. London: Phaidon, 1998; Peyser, Joan. *Bernstein: A Biography*. Rev. ed. New York: Billboard Books, 1998; Secrest, Meryle. *Leonard Bernstein: A Life*. New York: Knopf, 1994; Thompson, Mark, ed. *Long Road to Freedom: The Advocate History of the Gay and Lesbian Movement*. New York, St. Martin's Press, 1994; Wolfe, Tom. *Radical Chic and Mau-Mauing the Flak Catchers*. New York: Farrar, Straus and Giroux, 1970.

BOWIE, DAVID (1947–)

English singer, songwriter, and actor, David Bowie has become, over a 40 year career, an international pop music icon. The artist has been widely celebrated for his accomplishments, ranking among the 10 best-selling singers in British pop history and reaching number 29 in the 2002 BBC poll on the 100 most famous Britons. His records have sold over one hundred million copies. His significance for queer popular culture, however, is a matter of dispute. Bowie's claims in the 1970s to be gay or bisexual seem to have been discredited as mere publicity scams, which the artist himself has later retracted. The lyrics of his songs also show little gay pride. However, the different so-called glam-rock personae that he came to embody, especially at the beginning of his career, all share drag and androgynous elements which bring Bowie close to a queer sensibility.

Bowie was born David Robert Jones on January 8, 1947, in Brixton, London, to a working-class family. His parents soon moved to Kent, where David grew up. His interest for music was encouraged by his parents, who bought him a saxophone when he was 12. Throughout his school years, Bowie performed with several small bands. After his graduation in 1963, Bowie formed his first serious group, *Davie Jones and the King Bees*. Both this group and his next one, *The Manish Boys*, did not gain any commercial success. In 1965 the artist changed his name into Bowie to avoid confusion with Davy Jones of *The Monkees*. He chose the name out of admiration for the Alamo hero Jim Bowie and his homonymous knife. In the late 1960s, Bowie played in *Lower Third* and *Buzz*. Although these bands were short-lived, Bowie had acquired a certain fame on the London music scene and Deram Records offered him a solo contract. His first album, *David Bowie* (1967), was a mixture of psychedelic and folk-influenced rock that failed to attract audiences. Bowie then studied mime with gay artist Lindsay Kemp, who has had a constant influence on the singer's career.

"Space Oddity" (1969) was the artist's first top-ten hit, produced by Mercury Records. It was a single taken from Bowie's second album, which, in the United Kingdom, was released with the same title as Bowie's first work, while its American title was *Man of Words, Man of Music*. The single proved so popular, also thanks to the coincidental first landing on the moon, that it gave the title to the album as a whole when it was re-released in 1972. "Space Oddity" also introduced Bowie's first persona, Major Tom, an astronaut stranded in space, who was also featured in Bowie's number 1 single "Ashes to Ashes" (1980).

In 1970 Bowie married Mary Angela Barnett, from whom he had a son, Zowie. In the same year, he released *The Man Who Sold the*

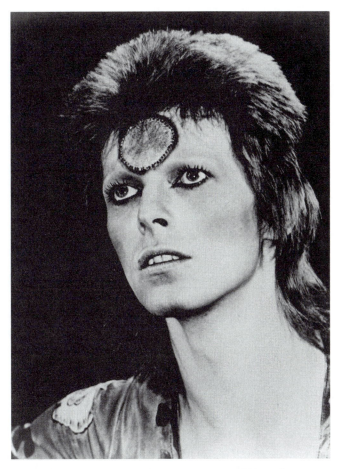

David Bowie as a glam-rock icon. Courtesy of Photofest.

World. The limited success of the album led Mercury to separate from Bowie, who was signed by RCA Records. The label produced Bowie's fourth album, *Hunky Dory* (1972), which featured the single "Changes," often taken as a manifesto for the singer's frequent changes in outlook. One such change took place with the release of the hit album *Ziggy Stardust and the Spiders from Mars* (1972), which was promoted exploiting Bowie's androgynous appearance. The persona of Ziggy and his extraterrestrial band served as the basis for Bowie's glam-rock world tour, in which Bowie performed with flaming red hair and outrageous outfits. The tour helped the album, unanimously considered as one of the most influential of the 1970s, to reach number five in the U.K. chart. Sales were also helped by public interest in Bowie's much-publicized sexual life. Though married, Bowie declared he was gay, and was the first major rock star to talk openly about his homosexuality. In September 1972 the tour premiered in the United States at Carnegie Hall where Bowie had a standing ovation from his audience, but shocked critics with his blatantly homosexual conduct. During the concert, Bowie kissed his handsome guitarist and faked a blow-job. These may seem rather tame actions today, but, at the time, they caused a furor. Bowie further banked on his ambiguous image with the non-album single "John, I Am Only Dancing" which became a U.K. hit and was banned in the states for its allusive lyrics.

Already a rock star, Bowie also started to produce the songs of Lou Reed and Iggy Pop. He followed up *Ziggy* with *Aladdin Sane* (1973) which punned with the words "a lad insane." The album continued to exploit the commercial success of the Ziggy persona and, on the tour stage as well as at press conferences, Bowie maintained the same outrageous make-up and clothes that had propelled him into stardom. At the peak of their success, Bowie announced at London's Hammersmith Odeon in 1973 the demise of Ziggy and the Spiders from Mars: "Not only is it the last show of the tour, but it's the last show that we'll ever do." Bowie was clearly trying not to become hostage of the Ziggy character that had made him famous. His next U.K. number-one album, *Pin Ups* (1973), a collection of British covers from the 1960s, clearly explored new directions for the artist. It is this first part of Bowie's career where his contribution to, and, to a certain extent, exploitation of queer popular culture are more apparent. Bowie's heavy make-up and glittery outfits, no matter how commercially constructed, proved liberating for gay men. As his fame grew, however, Bowie progressively distanced himself from a homosexual identity. In January 1970, the artist was eager to give an interview for *Jeremy*, the only gay publication in Britain at the time. Two years later, he was interviewed for *Melody Maker* and unmistakably declared that he was gay and had always been. Yet, in 1976, *Playboy* published an interview in which Bowie described himself as bisexual, rather than gay.

Diamond Dog (1974) represented a shift from glam-rock to disco/soul music and was Bowie's homage to George Orwell's *1984* (1949). It reached number one in the United Kingdom, making Bowie the best-selling British artist for two consecutive years. Encouraged by the success of the album in the United States, where it arrived at number five, Bowie launched a major North American tour with lavish sets and elaborate special effects. *Young Americans* (1975) further distanced Bowie from glam rock and closely linked him to the smoother Philadelphia soul, which the artist appropriated, renaming it "plastic rock." *Young Americans* contained "Fame"; co-written with John Lennon, it was Bowie's only single to reach number one in the U.S. chart. At the top of his fame, the artist also began his career as an actor, giving a critically praised performance in Nicholas Roeg's *The Man Who Fell on Earth* (1976). Subsequent roles included a vampire in *The Hunger* (1983), Pontius Pilate in Martin Scorsese's *The Last Temptation of Christ* (1988), a mysterious FBI agent in David Lynch's *Twin Peaks* (1992), and **Andy Warhol** in *Basquiat* (1996). Bowie also starred in the highly praised Nagisa Oshima's film *Merry Christmas, Mr. Lawrence* (1983) and took part in Julian Temple's musical *Absolute Beginners* (1986), which was panned by critics, but soon acquired cult status. It is often claimed that Slade in Todd Haynes's *Velvet Goldmine* (1998) is based on Bowie, who resented Slade's manipulative personality and legally fought against the film's release.

The character in *The Man Who Fell on Earth* also provided Bowie with his next music persona, that of the Thin White Duke. Relinquishing altogether the glamorous look that had propelled him into fame, Bowie adopted a sober and formal fashion. After a turbulent period at the end of the 1970s, characterized by his divorce from Angela Barnett, increasing dependence on drugs and controversial comments on Hitler and fascism, Bowie nourished his superstar fame through the 1980s and 1990s, joining rather than resisting the commercial dance scene. *Let's Dance* (1983), *Tonight* (1984), and *Never Let Me Down* (1987) are clearly in that vein. Following his divorce, the artist remarried with Somali-born model Iman who bore him a daughter, Alexandria. After the brief interlude with the band Tin Machine in the early 1990s, Bowie returned to his solo career; his enduring appeal demonstrated by the bestselling 2004 *Reality Tour*. The long career of David Bowie is the result of a shrewd promotion, which was careful to sponsor not only the artist's vocal skills but also, more crucially, his sexual ambiguity. While the 1970s were increasingly failing to adapt the 1960s upheavals into viable social models, Bowie as Ziggy lingered on the nostalgia for a countercultural utopia of sexual and political liberation. The queer accents of his performances are part of this project, whose honesty, however, has been deeply questioned.

Further Readings

Gill, John. *Queer Noises: Male and Female Homosexuality in Twentieth-Century Music.* London: Cassell, 1995; Reynolds, Simon, and Joy Press. *The Sex Revolts: Gender, Rebellion and Rock'n'roll.* London: Serpent's Tail, 1995; Rock, Mick. *Ziggy Stardust: Bowie 1972/1973.* London: St. Martin's Press, 1984; Simpson, Mark. *It's a Queer World.* London: Vintage, 1996; Thompson, Mark, ed. *Long Road to Freedom: The Advocate History of the Gay and Lesbian Movement.* New York: St. Martin's Press, 1994.

BOY GEORGE (1961–)

British songwriter and disc jockey Boy George rose to international celebrity in the 1980s with his group *Culture Club*, producing several hits in the genre of blue-eyed soul (soul composed by white people). The *Culture Club* production was influenced by reggae and rhythm and blues. It had an unmistakably romantic and sensuous quality. Boy George's androgynous looks and flamboyant dresses made the singer a gay icon, although he initially denied being homosexual or bothered with sexuality at all. "I prefer a nice cup of tea to sex," he remarked once, a comment which he deemed totally untrue years later. As his career developed, the artist proved an accomplished performer rather than just an eccentric character. He also explicitly talked about his homosexuality and took a firm stand against homophobia, both in society and the world of music.

George Alan O'Down was born in London on June 14, 1961, from working-class parents of Irish origins. His father was a builder and a boxing coach while his mother worked in a nursing home. George was the third of six children. Barely in his twenties, George began to appear on London's New Romantic scene in clubs such as Billy's, Blitz, and Heaven and Hell. His flashy cross-dressing style attracted the attention of hip magazines and Malcolm McLaren, former Sex Pistols manager, who offered him to team up with Annabella Lwin in the band *Bow Wow Wow*. Their partnership was short-lived and George soon formed his own group with Jamaican bassist Mickey Craig, Jewish drummer Jon Moss (with whom George had a long and troubled relationship), and English keyboardist Roy Hay. After various names were dropped, the band was called *Culture Club* to reflect its members' diverse ethnic backgrounds.

Culture Club were contracted by Virgin Records in Britain and Epic Records in the states. Their first album, *Kissing to Be Clever*, was released in 1982. The first two singles went almost unnoticed, but the release of the third, "Do You Really Want to Hurt Me," made George and his band instant pop idols. The song reached number one in the charts of many countries and arrived at number two in the United States. The next two singles, "Time (Clock of the Heart)" and "I'll Tumble 4 Ya," also proved big hits, making *Culture Club* the only band since The Beatles to have three top-ten singles from a debut album. The group's second work, *Color By Numbers* (1983), also featured a string of hits, including U.S. number one hit "Karma Chameleon." In two years, Boy George and *Culture Club* had risen from anonymity to stardom, earning the Grammy Award for Best New Artist and selling millions of copies of their albums worldwide. George took part in the Band-Aid project to help Ethiopia and appeared in one episode of the cult TV series, *The A-Team*. Such immediate success and the pressure to keep George and Jon Moss's love affair secret took a toll on the band and its members. George, worldwide revered as an alternative teen icon, began to use drugs heavily, including heroin. *Culture Club*'s next two albums suffered from this tense atmosphere and only included two more hits, "The War Song" and "Move Away." The group disbanded in 1986.

Boy George. Courtesy of Photofest.

Battling against his heroin addiction was not easy for the singer. Following the death of American keyboardist Michael Rudetski of a heroin overdose at George's London home, George was arrested on a charge of drug possession. He was successfully treated for his dependence; however, George's arrest in October 2005 in Manhattan on suspected cocaine possession shows that the star's battle against drugs may still be in progress. In 1987, George launched his solo career with *Sold*. The album included many U.K. hit singles, but did not achieve the same success in America. Now completely comfortable with his gay identity, George used his music to fight against the decision of the British conservative government of introducing Clause 28, which imposed heavy restrictions on sexual education, practically forbidding any positive mention of homosexuality in state schools. In 1989, George formed his own label More Protein and fronted a new band, Jesus Loves You.

In the 1990s, George constructed a different persona, which was more sober and less in the spotlight of media attention than during his *Culture Club* years. He revived his pop career with a cover of the song "The Crying Game" in the 1995 film of the same title and reunited the *Culture Club* for the 1998 "Big Rewind Tour." The band also recorded a new album *Don't Mind If I Do* (1999), which contained the U.K. hit single "I just wanna be loved." Aside from his achievements as a DJ, Boy George's projects have been mainly autobiographical in nature. The first part of his autobiography, *Take It Like A Man*, was published by Harper Collins in 1995 and frankly portrayed George's homosexual relationships with Jon Moss and Kirk Brandon, the Spear of Destiny singer. Brandon claimed he had never had a relationship with George and sued him, but lost the court case. The second chapter of George's autobiography, *Straight*, came out in 2005. In 2002, the artist recreated the London New Romantic scene in the musical *Taboo*, for which he wrote the songs. The show had good reviews and a successful West End run in London. However, when it opened in the United States the following year with **Rosie O'Donnell** making her debut as a Broadway producer, it had much colder reactions from critics and audiences alike, closing after only 100 performances.

Further Reading

Bono, Chastity. "Boy's Life." *The Advocate* No. 694 (November 14, 1995): 68–75; Boy George. *Take It Like a Man*. New York: Harper, 1995; Boy George. *Straight*. London: Century, 2005; Collins, Nancy. "Boy George: He Wears the Pants in Culture Club." *Rolling Stone* (June 7, 1984): 13–17; Galvin, Peter. "Boy Will Be Boy." *The Advocate* No. 762 (June 23, 1998): 103–112; www.boygeorgeuk.com.

BROKEBACK MOUNTAIN

Directed by Taiwanese filmmaker Ang Lee, *Brokeback Mountain* was one of the most critically acclaimed and controversial movies released in 2005. Based on a 20-page short story by E. Annie Proulx, it portrays the romantic relationship of two men in the American West over 20 years, from the 1960s to the 1980s. An unexpected box office hit, the film was also the most critically honored feature of 2005, winning many prestigious awards including three Academy Awards (Best Director, Best Adapted Screenplay, and Best Score), four Golden Globes (Best Film, Best Director, Best Screenplay, and Best Song), and the Golden Lion for Best Film at Venice Film Festival. *Brokeback Mountain* lost the Oscar for Best Picture to *Crash*, a decision that sparked accusations of homophobia against Academy members. Proulx explicitly wrote that "heffalump academy voters" live "out of touch...with the shifting larger culture and the yeasty ferment that is America these days" (*The Guardian* Online, March 2006). Conservative commentators found the film simply thinly disguised propaganda to promote same-sex marriage. The film also caused debates within the queer community. While generally well received, it was faulted by some influential gay critics as a product of bland Hollywood liberalism whose radicalism is more apparent than real.

Rancher Joe Aguirre (Randy Quaid) hires Ennis Del Mar (Heath Ledger) and Jack Twist (Jake Gyllenhall) to work as sheepherders on Brokeback Mountain in Wyoming. Gradually, both the reserved Ennis and the more talkative Jack become friends and start to open up to each other. It is after one of their whiskey conversations around the campfire that they make love for the first time, starting their tormented 20-year relationship, which, at the beginning, neither of them wants to acknowledge. "I'm no queer," says Ennis the next morning and Jack replies, "Me neither. A one-shot thing. Nobody's business but ours." When their summer job comes to an abrupt end due to approaching storms, Ennis and Jack separate with no definite plans about their future. This uncertainty about their lives is lacerating to them both, although neither confesses this to the other. Ennis and Jack meet again four years later after they have married and have had kids. Yet, in spite of their heterosexual lives, they instantly feel the same passion that had marked their Brokeback days. Jack and Ennis spend the night together at a motel, the first of a sporadic strings of meetings in which the two lovers officially go on fishing trips together. Jack would like them to end their marriages and start a ranch together. Yet, to Ennis, the mere idea of two men living together is inconceivable. After a bitter argument during their last trip together, it is Ennis's turn to look for Jack, but he will only be able to find out that his lover has died. Lureen explains Jack's death as accidental, but Ennis, who will become the depositary of Jack's memory, is afraid the answer lies in the mutilated corpses of gay men that his father used to bring him to see when he was a child.

Although the screenplay inflates Proulx's short story into a full feature, it is very faithful to its source. *Brokeback Mountain* has the same mood of sharp desolation and longing which permeates Proulx's prose. It takes to its extremes the homoerotic vein of a number of westerns and buddy movies. These are genres where, de rigueur, male characters must be quintessentially heterosexual. Yet, the characters' bonding suggests there is a shadowy area of unexplored sexual attraction among them. Ang Lee's film is not afraid to explore this area, turning homoeroticism into a fully explicit sexual attraction and tragic love-story. Sustained by powerful performances by Heath Ledger and Jake Gyllenhall, whom reviewers compared favorably to actors such as Marlon Brando and Sean Penn, *Brokeback Mountain* has angered both conservative and progressive sectors of American society. While the official position of the Catholic Church was ambiguous, Christian fundamentalists and conservative commentators attacked the movie as a spot for legislation on same-sex marriages. At the same time, influential gay critics such as David Ehrenstein have faulted the film for being "utterly removed from the political movement whose success made it possible" (*Los Angeles Times* Online, February 2006). Ehrenstein complains that *Brokeback*'s ahistoricism leaves no room in the narrative for references to the gay and lesbian liberation movement. The movie prefers instead to play a universal card, making Ennis and Jack two tragic lovers in the tradition of Romeo and Juliet. While *Brokeback Mountain* does not set its gay love-story within a history of the liberation movement, it surely documents the effects of homophobia on its characters whose story takes place in the same state where Matthew Shepard was murdered in 1998.

Further Reading

Ehrenstein, David. "*Brokeback*'s Tasteful Appeal." *Los Angeles Times.* February 1, 2006. http://www.latimes.com/news/opinion/commentary/la-oe-ehrenstein 01feb01,0,2740219.story?coll=la-news-comment-opinions (accessed on August 6, 2007); Proulx, Anne. "Blood on the Carpet." *The Guardian.* March 11, 2006. http://books.guardian.co.uk/comment/story/0,1727309,00.html (accessed on August 6, 2007).

BURKE, GLENN (1952–1995)

African American outfielder Glenn Burke was the first major league baseball player to reveal his homosexuality publicly. Although he waited until his retirement at 27 years of age to discuss his sexuality, he felt that rumors about it still damaged his career. The rampant homophobia of the baseball world finally won over his determination to play. As he told Jennifer Frey (1994, B15), who interviewed him for the *New York Times* one year before his death from **AIDS**-related complications, "Prejudice drove me out of baseball sooner than I should have. But I wasn't changing. And no-one can say I didn't make it. I played in the World Series. And I am in the book and they can't take that away from me. Not ever." Yet, the decision to leave baseball was lacerating for Burke, who started to make heavy use of drugs and to panhandle. As a result, he was imprisoned several times. Because of his precarious way of life, his health worsened fast.

Burke was born on November 16, 1952, in Oakland, California from Luther Burke, a sawmill worker, and Alice Burke, a nursing-home aide. Glenn and his large family, composed of seven other children, were deserted by Luther when Glenn was only a year old. His father had occasional contacts with his children, but the task of supporting the family was left entirely to Alice. As a student at Berkeley High School, Burke dreamed of a professional career in basketball. He earned praise for his performances in both the basketball and baseball school teams. His ability as a player made him the recipient of an athletic scholarship for the University of Denver, where he enrolled in 1970. After only a few months, however, he was back in California transferring to Merritt Junior College. As a baseball player in the college team, Burke impressed a Los Angeles Dodgers scout, who signed him for their minor league teams, where the player spent the following five seasons.

It was during this time that Burke became fully aware of his homosexuality and went to gay bars both in San Francisco and in the cities where he played. Yet, he kept his sexuality secret to his teammates fearing that such a revelation would hurt his chances for a major career. In 1976, Burke was finally promoted to the Dodgers with the high expectations of coach Jim Gilliam. His relationship with the Dodgers management, however, proved difficult. Burke repeatedly stressed that his sexuality was part of it. His friendship with the openly gay son of manager Tommy Lasorda, for example, made his relationship with the father constantly tense. Burke also stated that the Dodgers general manager Al Campanis put pressure on him to marry, although Campanis has denied the story.

Burke's career reached its highest point in 1977 when the player took part with the Dodgers in the World Series. Friends and his partner Michael Smith urged him to make his coming out, but Burke refused. After the World Series, Burke's career started, however, to decline. The following year, the Dodgers traded him to the Oakland Athletics. Since his coming out, Burke vigorously claimed that the move had been provoked by the management's aversion to his homosexuality. In spite of official denials, fellow Dodgers player Davey Lopes, interviewed by the *New York Times* in 1994, supported Burke's accusations. "I think everyone would agree with that except management," said Lopes.

Burke was unhappy with the Oakland Athletics, a minor team who was performing particularly badly when Burke was with them. In addition, the atmosphere was even more homophobic than with the Dodgers. He initially retired in the 1979 season, although he later changed his mind and reported for training in 1980. However, after he injured his knee, Burke was sent to a minor league team in Utah. This persuaded him to retire for good. Throughout his career, Burke hit 237 and stole 35 bases.

After his retirement, Burke became more active in the San Francisco gay athletic community playing in San Francisco's Gay Men's Softball League and in the 1982 and 1986 editions of the Gay Games. In 1982 Burke made his coming out through an article written by his partner and published in *Inside Sport*. His amateur activity came to an abrupt end when a speeding car ran him over in San Francisco, shattering his leg. After the incident, as Burke himself admitted, he started to take massive quantities of drugs. Unable to hold a steady job, he was arrested three times for possession of drugs, theft, and violation of parole. In 1994, after a series of bad colds, Burke was diagnosed with AIDS. His health deteriorated quickly and he became increasingly dependent on his sister, Lutha Davis, who took care of him until his death on May 30, 1995. Once nicknamed King Kong for his imposing body and strength, Burke spent his last days bedridden and in poverty, a promising young talent crushed by the force of prejudice and ignorance.

Further Reading

Burke, Glenn, and Erik Sherman. *Out at Home: The Glenn Burke Story*. New York: Excel Publishing, 1995; Crowe, Jerry. "When Glory Has Soured: Former Dodger Glenn Burke Battles AIDS as He Struggles to Survive Life on the Streets." *Los Angeles Times* (August 30, 1994): C 1; Frey, Jennifer. "A Boy of Summer's Long, Chilly Winter: Once a Promising Ballplayer, Glenn Burke Is Dying of AIDS." *New York Times* (October 18, 1994): B 15; Light, Jonathan Fraser. "Homosexuals." *The Cultural Encyclopedia of Baseball*. Jefferson, NC, and London: McFarland & Company, 1997. 346–347; "The Outfielder Who Came Out." *People*

Weekly 42. (November 21, 1994): 151; Smith, Michael J. "The Double Life of a Gay Dodger." *Inside Sports* (October 1982): 57–63; Szymcazk, Jerome. "Glenn Burke." *Gay & Lesbian Biography.* Michael J. Tyrkus, ed. Detroit: St. James Press, 1997. 94–95.

BURR, RAYMOND (1917–1993)

Due to his successful television personae of Perry Mason and Ironside, Raymond Burr is synonymous in the popular mind with American jurisprudence. Yet, to queer popular culture, Burr has become a symbol of the impact of institutionalized Hollywood and media homophobia on the lives of stars. Burr carefully crafted a heterosexual persona for the public, while living a gay private life with a longtime partner. As Michelangelo Signorile (1993) points out, the case of Burr is peculiar because, although many journalists and friends knew Burr was gay, the actor was kept in the closet even after his death. Hundreds of stories, rich in personal and intimate details, appeared after Burr died of cancer. Yet, all of them spoke of a heterosexual Burr, listing his relationships with women. Homosexuality has been constantly written out of Burr's biography both during the actor's life and after his death.

Raymond William Stacy Burr was born in New Westminster, British Columbia, Canada, on May 21, 1917. His father, William Burr, was a hardware dealer and his mother, Minerva Smith, was a pianist and music teacher. When Raymond was only six years old, the couple divorced and the child went to live with his mother in California. The Great Depression compromised his education as Burr dropped out from school to help his mother support the family. Thanks to his imposing build he worked at cattle and sheep ranches. In his late teens, Burr was able to return to school and, at the same time, work as singer and as radio and theater actor. He made appearances in Broadway in *Crazy with the Heat* in 1941 and *The Duke in Darkness* in 1944.

During World War II, Burr served in the U.S. Navy, fighting at the Battle of Okinawa. His debut in Hollywood took place in 1946 with Mervyn LeRoy's *Without Reservations.* Because of his physical appearance, Burr was often cast as a threatening villain, starring in such classics as George Stevens's *A Place in the Sun* (1951) and Alfred Hitchcock's *Rear Window* (1954). The turning point of Burr's career was the movie *Godzilla, King of the Monsters* (1956), the American re-editing of a Japanese movie. Unusually, Burr played a positive character, the heroic reporter Steve Martin who, together with a group of Japanese scientists, challenges and eventually defeats the sea-monster Godzilla. While panned by the influential *New York Times* critic Bosley Crowther as "a cheap cinematic horror-stuff," *Godzilla* was an international success. As a result of his newly found popularity, Burr was chosen for the role of Perry Mason, the defense attorney created by the pen of Erle Stanley Gardner, for the homonymous CBS series. The show proved a big hit and ran originally from 1957 to 1966. After the end of Perry Mason, Burr starred in *Ironside*, another popular TV series which ran on NBC from 1967 to 1975. Both the astute Mason and the paralyzed detective Ironside were positive characters, carrying on Burr's change of screen persona from his earlier films.

The success of the two series made the public identify Burr completely with the two characters. As a result, there was room for little else in his career. When he tried to portray a new character, such as the journalist R. B. Kingston in the NBC series *Kingston: Confidential* (1977), his efforts met with the public's cold reactions. In the late 1970s and early 1980s, Burr starred in a dozen TV films as well as in Dennis Hopper's contentious work, *Out of the Blue* (1980). In the spoof *Airplane II: The Sequel* (1982), he offered a parody of his role as Perry Mason, a character whom Burr started to play again in 1985. His comeback as the defense attorney for a series of NBC TV movies was widely appreciated by his fans and by the general audience. Ratings were so good that, from 1985 to a few weeks before the actor's death on September 12, 1993, a total of 26 movies were made.

The private life of Raymond Burr was carefully invented by the actor to comply with Hollywood heterosexual requirements for a successful film and TV star. In spite of being involved in a long-term relationship with actor Robert Benevides, Burr mentioned being married three times and having had a son from his first wife. According to the actor's reconstruction, his private life was indeed a tragic one. His first wife, British actress Annette Sutherland, married in 1941, died two years later, leaving Burr with a son, Michael Evan. Burr maintains Annette died on a plane shot down by the Germans during World War II. However, there is no mention of Sutherland on the passengers' list of the flight. His son allegedly died of leukemia when he was 10. The actor then married Isabella Ward in 1947, but their marriage was declared null a few months afterwards. Burr's third spouse was Laura Andrina Morgan. Again, the union was short-lived as the couple was married in 1953 and Laura succumbed to cancer in 1955. None of the actor's friends seem to have met his wives and son. On the contrary, Burr's life with Benevides was under everybody's eyes. The couple bought an island in Fiji in the 1960s where they started a profitable orchid-breeding business. They also jointly promoted many philanthropic actions and, in the 1980s, they began grape growing and wine production in California.

Raymond Burr is a clear example of how the Hollywood establishment and the media join forces to manipulate stars' memories, writing out homosexuality from their biographies as an aberrant orientation which cannot be voiced even after death.

Further Reading

Grimes, William. "Raymond Burr, Actor, 76, Dies." *The New York Times* (September 14, 1993): B9; Hill, Ona L. *Raymond Burr: A Film, Radio and Television Biography.* Jefferson: McFarland & Company, 1999; Mann, William J. *Behind the Screen: How Gays and Lesbians Shaped Hollywood 1910–1969.* New York: Viking, 2001; Signorile, Michelangelo. *Queer in America: Sex, the Media and the Closets of Power.* New York: Random House, 1993.

C

Originally written as play by Jean Poiret in 1973, *La Cage Aux Folles* has been successfully adapted both as a film and as a musical. The family intrigues of a St. Tropez gay club owner and his drag queen fiancé explicitly focused on homosexuality, rejecting allusions in favor of a frank, even excessive, depiction. Although it may seem dated in the new millennium and its characters little more than stereotypes, *La Cage Aux Folles* contributed to the visibility of queerness in popular culture. Through their emphasis on drag and performance, the different versions of *La Cage Aux Folles* challenge normative notions of gender, sexuality, and family.

The number of versions of Poiret's play testifies to the enduring appeal of the story. Edouard Molinaro's 1978 film adaptation of the story went on to become one of the top-grossing foreign films in the United States. It was nominated for three Oscars (Best Director, Best Adapted Screenplay, and Best Costume Design) and won a Golden Globe as Best Foreign Film. A Franco-Italian co-production, Molinaro's *La Cage Aux Folles* retained Michel Serrault from the original cast of the play and replaced Jean Poiret with Italian actor Ugo Tognazzi. The film's success led to two sequels, *La Cage Aux Folles II* (1980) and *La Cage Aux Folles III: The Wedding* (1985), but neither equaled the first in terms of audiences and critics' reception. In 1983, an all-gay group made up of composer Jerry Herman, playwright **Harvey Fierstein**, and director Arthur Laurents teamed up with producer Allan Carr to work on a musical version for Broadway. At a time when **AIDS** was still strictly identified with male homosexuals, a project based entirely on gay characters was a commercial risk. Yet, *La Cage Aux Folles* became the biggest hit of the 1980s running for 1761 performances over four years and winning a host of prestigious prizes including Tony Awards for Best Musical, Best Score, Best Book, Best Actor, Best Costumes, and Best Direction. Although it centered on gay characters, the musical was not radical. It did not show overt kissing between men and exhibited all the characteristics of a mainstream musical: a lyrical score, glitzy costumes, and elaborate sets. Yet, its mainstream character allowed all sorts of people to become acquainted with this

William Thomas (left) and Gene Barry (right) in the Broadway production of *La Cage Aux Folles*. Courtesy of Photofest.

homosexual story. As producer Allan Carr noted: "Fourteen-year-olds are going to see *La Cage* because they saw the 'I Am What I Am' number on the Grammy Awards" (Russo 1994, 264). The song "I Am What I Am" was indeed recorded by Gloria Gaynor, becoming one of her biggest hits. It was also adopted by the gay movement as an anthem of liberation. The musical was revived on Broadway in 2004.

The latest adaptation of the story was Mike Nichols's film *The Birdcage* (1996), starring Robin Williams, **Nathan Lane**, Gene Hackman, and Dianne Wiest, which takes the setting from St. Tropez to South Beach. However, little changes in terms of plot in the different versions. The life of Armand, a drag club owner, and his drag queen partner Albin (Albert in Nichols's film) is turned upside down when Armand's son, the consequence of a one-off heterosexual encounter, comes to visit them. He announces that he is engaged to be married to the daughter of a staunch conservative politician.

To avert media attention from a sex scandal that is threatening their organization's credibility, the bride's family announce a traditional white wedding for their daughter. They have obviously not yet met the groom's unconventional family. The plot revolves around the dinner party for the in-laws thrown by Armand and his partner, attempting to pass as straight, in their flat just upstairs from the club. In spite of all the obvious obstacles and setbacks, including the politician's escape in heavy drag from the paparazzi-besieged club, the couple will finally be able to get married.

All the different versions of *La Cage Aux Folles* rely considerably on stereotypes that call into question "normal" perceptions of sexuality and family relationships. The gay family seems to come out as the winner of the two models, as Armand and Albin/Albert display a selfless love for their son in stark contrast to their hetero in-laws who want to stage a traditional wedding for their own political ends. The plot also pits the affectionate relationship of the gay couple against the coldness of the straight couple. Yet, as Lucy Mazdon (2000) argues, because of their stereotypical qualities, the gay characters of *La Cage Aux Folles* cannot escape their farcical nature and remain confined to sympathetic caricatures. Sex is conspicuously absent from every version of the story and homosexuality ultimately results non-threatening to the dominant heterosexual ideology.

Further Reading

Clum, John M. *Something for the Boys: Musical Theater and Gay Culture*. New York: St. Martin's Press, 1999; Mazdon, Lucy. *Encore Hollywood: Remaking French Cinema*. London: BFI Publishing, 2000; Russo, Vito. *The Celluloid Closet: Homosexuality in the Movies*. Revised Edition. New York: Harper, 1987; Russo, Vito. "Allan Carr." *Long Road to Freedom: The Advocate History of the Gay and Lesbian Movement*. Mark Thompson, ed. New York: St. Martin's Press, 1994. 264.

CALIFIA, PATRICK (1954–)

A self-defined gender outlaw and sex anarchist, Patrick Califia, known as Pat before she started a sex change in the late 1990s, explores in his fictional and non-fictional writings the different forms of human sexuality. Throughout his career and genders, Califia has been particularly firm in defending both pornography and sadomasochism. Such stance provoked the criticism of many lesbians and feminists, but also earned Califia the reputation of being an advocate of individual rights. To Califia, an individual's gender identity is crucially shaped by how others perceive that person. "Socially conditioned behaviors that signal gender," writes Califia in his *Speaking Sex to Power* (2003), "are even more crucial than physical traits" (Alvear, *Salon.com*). Thus, gender is influenced by social notions on how a man or a woman should dress and behave, traits which society considers better markers of manliness or femaleness than sex chromosomes, secondary sex characteristics, or genitalia.

Califia was born in Corpus Christi, Texas, on March 8, 1954. Her father was an itinerant road-construction worker and the family followed him in his various jobs. Her mother was a housewife. Pat was the oldest of six children who all grew up within the rigid precepts of the Mormon community to which their parents belonged. Her fundamentalist parents and the abuse she was subjected in public school because of her difference made Califia's childhood an unhappy one. In 2000 Califia stated somewhat paradoxically and provocatively that one basic tenet of Mormon religion informed her oeuvre, the fact that if "the truth has been revealed to you and you don't speak out, you are culpable for any wrongs that are committed in those realms of life" (Marech, October 2000). Califia was constantly aware of her sexual difference throughout her childhood, an awareness that continues to plague the author nowadays and brings him to write about the truths he knows and which may be unsettling, even disturbing for most people. As he writes in *Speaking Sex to Power*, even after his sex change, he is unable to declare his allegiance to one gender paradigm and "to climb up on only one soapbox in the orator's park of sexuality.... There are days when it seems to me that I am tortured by my own perversity and willfulness, that if I had the right sort of subtle knife, I could sever the carping parts of my soul that will not shut up and could quit setting off the security alarms of normal people" (Alvear, *Salon.com*).

Califia started to write at a very early age and was a brilliant student at school. She began attending the University of Utah in 1971 where she met other lesbians and came out as such to her family. Her parents tried to confine her to a mental institution, provoking a nervous breakdown. In 1973, Califia moved to San Francisco where she joined lesbian separatist circles and regularly contributed to the lesbian magazine *Sister*. However, her nonconformist views on sadomasochism and pornography soon put her at odds with the movement. As many of her previous lesbian friends turned against her, Califia was increasingly drawn to sadomasochism. She founded the lesbian S-M organization Samois, but also started to move within gay male leather groups. Califia graphically described S-M practices in her sex manual *Sapphistry* (1980), which popularized the butch and femme figures in lesbian popular culture, and repeatedly attacked feminists and lesbians who were active in the anti-porn crusade. In the late 1970s, Califia started to contribute regularly to gay publications such as the ***Advocate***, where she wrote a sex advice column for 10 years, and *The Journal of Homosexuality*. Since then, her articles have appeared in important magazines including *Out*, *POZ*, and the *Village Voice*. In 1981, Califia graduated from San Francisco State University with a bachelor's degree in psychology and went on to pursue graduate studies in counseling.

Replying to those radical feminists who charged that lesbian sadomasochism simply mirrored the power imbalance implicit in patriarchy, Califia contended that an explicit debate on sadomasochism could also address many other traces of inequality in the feminist and lesbian movement such as the marginalization of non-white and working-class women. S-M practices and the leather subculture prominently feature in her fictional writings, including the short story collections *Macho Sluts* (1988), *Melting Point* (1993), and *No Mercy*, and the novel, *Doc and Fluff: The Dystopian Tale of a Girl and Her Biker* (1990). Califia also continued to publish collections of essays on sex such as *Public Sex* and *Sensuous Magic*. These writings embrace sexual diversity in all its forms and are not afraid of portraying S-M sexuality graphically and without making apologies for those who practice it. Califia's outspoken defense of sadomasochism has sparked controversy even within the gay community where her detractors have argued that her representation of S-M sex might have a negative impact on the image of gay people. Califia has found herself at the center of censorship trial cases such as the one which opposed her against the Canadian customs in the 1990s. Yet, the author always defended her right to represent all kinds of human sexualities whose legitimacy she firmly believes in. Califia's stories deconstruct the boundaries between *erotica* and *pornography*, rejecting the usual privileging of the former on the latter term.

Her study *Sex Changes: The Politics of Transgenderism* (1997) signaled Califia's new interest in transgender sexuality. The book collects interviews and life-stories to examine how the awareness of transgender people and their social status have evolved throughout the years. *Sex Changes* views gender as a personal choice instrumental to self-expression rather than a biologically and socially imposed category. Two years later, Califia herself started gender reassignment, first with testosterone injections and then with surgery. He became a Female-To-Male transgender and changed his first name to Patrick. Since Califia's books had always been identified as lesbian literature, the author was afraid that gender reassignment might cost him his readers. Yet, Califia's literary career has continued to flourish and lesbian magazines for which Califia used to work before her sex change retained him even after the operation. In spite of the painful effects of fibromyalgia, an auto-immune disease which has been affecting him for several years, he has continued his literary career, publishing the collection of essays *Speaking Sex to Power*, the vampire novel *Mortal Companion* (2004), and the gay male porn *Hard Male*. He has also planned a fantasy saga entitled *The Circle of Life*.

Whether vilified or praised, Califia has given visibility to the controversial issues of sadomasochism and pornography within queer popular culture. He conceives his literary production and his public statements as a fight against sexual oppression, which he considers the base of class and gender oppression. A frank discussion of all sexualities, including sadomasochism, can counter the hatred of the body instilled in the individual by the state's interest in controlling people's pleasures. Pornography absolves a similar form of resistance and is equaled by Califia to the "seditious rhetoric" of political dissidents: "Political dissidents voice their discontent with business-as-usual; they say out loud that the emperor has no clothes. Pornography is the great brawling voice of sexual frustration and panic" (Cusac 1996, 35). Through his writings, Califia has suggested different ways to envision sadomasochism and pornography. For example, he has described sadomasochists as intent in teaching each other safe ways to produce intense physical sensations without endangering health. Rather than an abusive form of sexuality, sadomasochism prevents sexual abuse. S-M practices involve a careful negotiation about people's desires and limits. Thus, they imply "high standards of consent and consideration." Califia stands as a critical voice within the queer movement, constantly reiterating the need to address "heterosexuality as an institution" to counter its oppressive norms.

Further Reading

Alvear, Michael. "Gender Bending." *Salon.com*. http://dir.salon.com/story/sex/feature/2003/02/19/califia/index.html (accessed on August 9, 2007); Austin, Bryn. "Pat Califia." *Contemporary Lesbian Writers of the United States: A Bio-Bibliographical Critical Sourcebook*. Sandra Pollack and Denise D. Knight, eds. Westport, CT: Greenwood Press, 1993. 106–110; Barnard, Ian. "Macho Sluts: Genre-Fuck, S/M Fantasy, and the Reconfiguration of Political Action." *Genders* 19 (June 30, 1994): 265–291; Califia, Pat. "Pat Califia's Book *Sex Changes*." 1997. Society for Human Sexuality. http://www.sexuality.org/l/transgen/scpc.html (accessed on September 8, 2007); Califia-Rice, Patrick. "Family Values." *Village Voice* 45 (June 27, 2000): 46–47; Cusac, Anne-Marie. "Profile of a Sex Radical." *The Progressive* 60 (October 1996): 34–37; Herren, Greg. "The Author Formerly Known as Pat: An Interview with Patrick Califia-Rice." *Lambda Book Report* 8 (June 2000): 13–14; Marech, Rona. "Radical Transformation." *San Francisco Chronicle* Online. October 27, 2000. http://sfgate.com/cgi-bin/article.cgi?file=/chronicle/archive/2000/10/27/WB78665.DTL (accessed on September 8, 2007); "Patrick Califia." *Suspect Thoughts: A Journal of Subversive Writing*. http://www.suspectthoughtspress.com/califia.html (accessed on September 8, 2007).

CAMP

The vast body of critical literature on camp may appear as a contradiction in terms when one considers that the argument critics all seem to agree upon is the difficulty in pinning down exactly what camp is all about. After Susan Sontag introduced the term to mainstream cultural debates in the late 1960s, queer critics have appropriated camp as a distinctive form of gay sensibility and humor, building on excess, theatricality, irony, and kitsch. The coded discourses of camp have been used by gays and lesbians to subvert the homophobic assumptions of mainstream culture of which queer subjects are still an important part both as consumers and as producers. Defining camp as "gay culture's crucial contribution to modernism" (and, I would add, post-modernism), the editors of the volume *Out in Culture* (1995, 2) describe it as "an attitude at once casual and severe, affectionate and ironic," which "served to deflate the pretensions of mainstream culture while elevating what that same culture devalued or repressed." Camp thus gives queers the opportunity to rewrite and challenge their official representations in mainstream culture. It also helps uncover the ubiquity of gay sensibility within mainstream popular culture products. Dealing with mass culture through the lenses of camp has allowed gays and lesbians to uncover the queerness at the core of dominant culture. Under its glittery patina of decorations and excess, camp is, according to Philip Core's phrase that gives the title to his study, "the lie that tells the truth."

Camp is not only applicable to artistic expressions that are made by queers for the consumption of a queer audience, but it extends to mainstream texts whose images, ideologies, and readings qualify them as being about heterosexuality. For example, Steven Cohan (2005) has shown how the elaborate costumes and the sumptuous sets of the MGM musicals of the 1940s, together with their bright dance numbers and idolized stars, have come to embody the very notion of camp. While these films were made to appeal to a broad audience, Cohan demonstrates that the films' queerness and their popular success are not contradictory elements. On the contrary, the queerness, the incongruity, and the theatricality of the MGM musicals were instrumental in making them popular hits, and the studio's marketing strategies banked on these characteristics: "What MGM marketed," Cohan writes (2005, 43), "was the genre's oversized spectacle, achieved by a combination of oftentimes very diverse musical elements with the aim of dazzling the spectator's eyes and ears, not of advancing the story. The studio's reputation rested on its musicals' lavish production values." The incongruities in the narratives, the tension between the dazzling musical numbers, and the advancement of the plot "correspond with...the dialectical operation of camp as an ironic engagement with the incongruities of the dominant culture's representational systems and hierarchical value codings, particularly but not exclusively with respect to gender and sexuality" (Cohan 2005, 43). The defining MGM house style for its musicals "incites category dissonance, visualizes it as the juxtaposition of cultural binaries, emphasizes it through overadornment and exaggerated theatricality, and aims it with humor and wit" (Cohan 2005, 45)

The difficulty to define camp goes hand in hand with the location of the start of a camp sensibility and its practice. While Sontag dates this as far back as the Gothic novels and even mannerist art, a more obvious candidate is Oscar Wilde, although he never seems to have used the word. As with its definition, the origins of the word are widely debated. According to some critics, camp derives from the French verb *se camper*, meaning "to take a stand," "to flaunt," or "to pose." In *Gay Talk* (1972), Bruce Rodgers argues that camp was originally a slang word employed in sixteenth-century English theater to define a male actor dressed as a woman. Although Wilde did not use the word camp, one of his most famous epigrams from the play *An Ideal Husband* (1895) has come to embody the Victorian roots of the sensibility: "To be natural is such a very difficult pose to keep up." Being natural is here defined as a pose in itself and thus loses its more obvious meaning to be connected, instead, to aestheticism with which camp is also linked.

Well before Sontag recognized the increasing influence of camp on mainstream culture in the 1960s, camp was a coded form for many gays and lesbians in the first half of the twentieth century to signal their queerness. It was central to a discourse through which homosexuals could come out to other homosexuals and thus form larger groups of individuals who shared the same sexual orientation. Camp strategies such as the substitution of female pronouns for male ones, and the reliance on double-entendres and on covert meanings were ways of claiming an insider's status in gay culture. Camp is both situated within the constricting boundaries of the closet and, at the same time, opens them up by allowing queers to display strategies of resistance to read themselves into mainstream culture. One of the ways in which pre-Stonewall gay men referred to themselves to let other homosexuals know that they were part of the same group, that of being "friends of Dorothy," precisely built upon a camp reading of such mainstream cultural product as MGM's *The Wizard of Oz*. As Corey K. Creekmur and Alexander Doty (1995, 3) have pointed out, "MGM's wholesome children fantasy…and its child star, **Judy Garland**, could be elaborated in terms of their camp functions." The plot of *The Wizard of Oz* centers on characters that lead double lives in two different worlds, and its teenage heroine Dorothy, feeling oppressed, longs for a different existence where she can freely express her innermost feelings. Dorothy finally finds this existence in a Technicolor world peopled by a sissy lion, an artificial man prone to tears, and a couple of witches who recall the butch-femme paradigm. As Creekmur and Doty conclude (1995, 3), "This is a reading of the film that sees the film's fantastic excesses (color, costume, song, performance, etc.) as expressing the hidden lives of many of its devoted viewers." The nature of camp is a double one, as cultural objects that were not conceived as camp by their creators can assume camp features when they are consumed by audiences. At the same time, some artists may want to create camp objects deliberately. This may be the case of people as diverse as **Andy Warhol, John Waters, Tony Kushner, Liberace,** and drag performers. Camp is both in the eye of the beholder and a feature of the object beheld.

Such identification of camp as a political form of resistance, however, is disputed by Susan Sontag (1966, 277), who sees it as a form of mere aestheticism and thus "disengaged, depoliticized—or at least apolitical." Through camp, one can see the world in terms of artifice and style and take pleasure in its inability to be taken seriously: "Camp is art that proposes itself seriously, but cannot be taken altogether seriously because it is 'too much'" (1966, 284). Sontag also noted that "While it's not true that Camp taste *is* homosexual taste, there is no doubt a peculiar affinity and overlap. Not all liberals are Jews, but Jews have shown a peculiar affinity for liberal and reformist causes. So, not all homosexuals have Camp taste. But homosexuals, by and large, constitute the vanguard—and the most articulate audience—of Camp" (1966, 290). Although starting from a different political agenda than Sontag's, the militants of the gay liberation movement from the late 1960s and 1970s agreed that camp was not political. While earlier homosexuals had found in camp a liberating form of discourse that allowed them to live their lives without being exposed to social exclusion or, even, persecution, the militants of the 1970s found that camp was too coy in acknowledging its homosexual links. They described camp as a form of ghettoization, which is complicit with mainstream culture in the reinforcement of the sexual binaries of gay and straight. In the years that followed the Stonewall riots, the imperative for gays and lesbians was to be out and visible. Camp was perceived to be too closeted and self-oppressive to be of any use to the queer cause of visibility. Writing in the late 1980s, Andrew Ross (1988) still faulted camp for reconciling people with their own oppression. According to Ross, camp is part of the larger problem of popular culture, that of preventing the masses from becoming aware of their exploitation and thus fight for effective social change. Feminist critics also pointed out the misogynistic character of camp, which, in spite of its many female icons, is rooted in a troubling interest with waste and decay, relating them, in particular, to women's aging bodies.

More recently, however, queer critics have re-evaluated the possibilities of camp to function as an explicitly gay strategy of subversion. In particular, camp has been praised for its ability to unsettle gender distinctions, because it provides exaggerated forms of masculinity and femininity. Esther Newton (1979), among others, has linked camp to the performances of drag queens to highlight how incongruity, theatricality, and humor work to reverse social norms about sexuality and gender. Newton (1979, 22) finds that such effect depends on the "perception or creation of incongruous juxtapositions" such as a man dressing in women's clothes. Al LaValley (1995, 63) has given other examples of what he calls "the collision of two or more opposite sets of signals" that produces "a sudden self-consciousness in the viewer": Joan "Crawford's wide, masculine shoulders conflicting with her feminine image," Hollywood and Broadway musical choreographer and director "Busby Berkeley's straight-faced use of women for mechanical designs, even Carmen Miranda's tutti-frutti hat." Agreeing with Newton, LaValley (1995, 65) finds that "[i]n their less commercialized forms, drag and camp can be on the cutting edge of both sexual and social reality by their power to overturn images, to confuse and distort, and to make the ordinary surreal." The films by John Waters starring **Divine** are a clear example of this ability to confuse and distort. The Divine character in *Pink Flamingos*, for example, exhibits proudly her title of "the filthiest woman in the world." The alliance of camp and drag, moreover, illustrates the pioneering definition of gender given by queer theorist Judith Butler as a "performance" that creates the illusion of an essence or identity. Drawing attention to theatricality, excess, and incongruities, camp and drag define the concept of gender as a sustained performance. It is not a coincidence that Butler has reversed Andrew Ross's judgment on camp, finding it one of the most effective strategies for social and sexual change.

Decades after its first sketchy formulations in Susan Sontag's notes, camp and its applications continue to exude heated debates both within and outside the queer community. One of the most recent and controversial uses of camp is its employment in representations of **AIDS**. Drama, with Tony Kushner's *Angels in America* (1993–1994), **Paul Rudnick**'s *Jeffrey* (1993), and several plays by Terrence McNally, has been a particularly receptive genre to this use of camp. Several stand-up routines about AIDS also employ camp. These texts exploit the ability of camp to unsettle the rigidity of identity, thus healthily destabilizing the association between AIDS and homosexuality. Camp AIDS narratives call into question the stereotypical image of the depressed, lonely and promiscuous dying homosexual so firmly established by mainstream media. The violence of camp's incongruities challenges the apathy and the denial with which many react to the epidemic. Yet, not everyone, even within the gay and lesbian community, applauds to this new use of camp. For some, including a central figure in the queer movement such as writer **Edmund White**, the excesses of camp humor (such as "AIDS—God! I hope I never get that again!") are totally inappropriate to the tragedy represented by the virus. Whether exalted as a revolutionary form to change people's perception of gender and sexuality or reviled as a self-ghettoizing tactic, camp will continue to stand at the center of debates concerning gay and lesbian popular culture. Its different forms will also continue to belie unambiguous definitions.

Further Reading

Bergman, David, ed. *Camp Grounds: Style and Homosexuality.* Amherst: University of Massachusetts Press, 1993; Booth, Mark. *Camp.* New York: Quartet, 1983; Bronski, Michael. *Culture Clash: The Making of Gay Sensibility.* Boston: South End Press, 1984; Butler, Judith. *Gender Trouble: Feminism and the Subversion of Identity.* New York: Routledge, 1990; Chauncey, George. *Gay New York: Gender, Urban Culture, and the Makings of the Gay Male World, 1890–1940.* New York: Basic Books, 1994; Cleto, Fabio, ed. *Camp: Queer Aesthetics and the Performing Self—A Reader.* Edinburgh: Edinburgh University Press, 1999; Cohan, Steven. *Incongruous Entertainment: Camp, Cultural Value and the MGM Musical.* Durham, NC: Duke University Press, 2005; Core, Philip. *Camp: The Lie That Tells the Truth.* New York: Delilah Books, 1984; Creekmur, Corey K. and Alexander Doty, eds. *Out in Culture: Gay, Lesbian and Queer Essays on Popular Culture.* Durham, NC: Duke University Press, 1995; Dollimore, Jonathan. *Sexual Dissidence: Augustine to Wilde, Freud to Foucault.* New York: Oxford University Press, 1991; Dyer, Richard, ed. *Gays and Film.* London: British Film Institute, 1977; Dyer, Richard. *Now You See It: Studies on Lesbian and Gay Film.* London: Routledge, 1990; Halberstam, Judith. *Female Masculinity.* Durham, NC: Duke University Press, 1998; Harris, Daniel. *The Rise and Fall of Gay Culture.* New York: Hyperion, 1997; Kiernan, Robert F. *Frivolity Unbounded: Six Masters of the Camp Novel.* New York: Continuum, 1990; LaValley, Al. "The Great Escape." *Out in Culture: Gay, Lesbian and Queer Essays on Popular Culture.* Corey K. Creekmur and Alexander Doty, eds. Durham, NC: Duke University Press, 1995. 60–70; Meyer, Moe, ed. *The Politics and Poetics of Camp.* New York: Routledge, 1994; Newton, Esther. *Mother Camp: Female Impersonators in America.* Chicago: University of Chicago Press, 1979; Ross, Andrew. "Uses of Camp." *The Yale Journal of Criticism* 2.2 (1988): 1–24; Russo, Vito. *The Celluloid Closet: Homosexuality and the Movies*. New York: Harper and Row, 1981; Sontag, Susan. "Notes on Camp." *Against Interpretation and Other Essays*. New York: Dell, 1966. 275–292; Tinkcom, Matthew. *Working Like a Homosexual: Camp, Capital, Cinema*. Durham, NC: Duke University Press, 2002; Van Leer, David. *The Queening of America: Gay Culture in Straight Society*. New York: Routledge, 1995.

CAPOTE, TRUMAN (1924–1984)

The flamboyant novelist, journalist, and screenwriter Truman Capote successfully defeated homophobia, becoming a gay national icon and an omnipotent socialite whose organization and mere attendance of a social event made it fashionable. Capote set the standards of gay writing in the 1950s and 1960s and, with *Breakfast at Tiffany's* (1958), his screenplay for *The Innocents* (1961), and his pioneering nonfiction novel *In Cold Blood* (1966), Capote made visible the homosexual contribution to mainstream popular culture. Yet, his increasing dependence on alcohol and drugs proved his undoing and, during the 1970s and 1980s, he became a caricature of his previous witty and camp persona.

Born Truman Streckfus Persons on September 30, 1924, in New Orleans, Louisiana, Capote was neglected by his parents during his early years. His biological father, Archulus Persons was too intent to pursue vain plans to improve his economic conditions to look after his son. Truman's mother Lillie Mae Faulk was also often away to achieve a better social status and used to leave the child with her relatives in Monroeville, Alabama. There Truman became friends with the future writer Harper Lee, the author of the acclaimed *To Kill a Mockingbird* (1960). In 1931, Lillie Mae divorced her husband and moved to New York to live with the successful businessman Joseph Garcia Capote. She changed her name into Nina Capote and, in 1932, she took Truman to New York to live with her and her new husband, who formally adopted the child in 1935. Capote did not show much interest for education, although he was convinced that he wanted to be a writer. He soon left school at the age of 17 to work for two years as a copyboy for the *New Yorker*. In his twenties, he started to publish short-stories in quality magazines such as *Harper's Bazaar* and *Mademoiselle*. When he was merely 22 years old, Capote won his first literary prize, the prestigious O. Henry Memorial Award, for his short story "Miriam."

Already well established in New York's literary circles, where he was admired for his witty talent, Capote published his first novel, *Other Voices, Other Rooms* in 1948. The book chronicles a young gay boy's search for his father and his roots in the South. When his mother dies, 13-year-old Joel Knox is sent to live with his father who abandoned him at the time of his birth. Arriving in the family's decaying mansion in rural Alabama, Joel meets his gloomy stepmother Amy, the effeminate Randolph and rebellious Idabel, a girl who becomes his friend. He also repeatedly sees a spectral "queer lady" with "fat dribbling curls" watching him from a window. When Joel is finally allowed to see his father, he finds him paralyzed and near speechless. Traumatized, he runs away with Idabel but falls ill with pneumonia. Upon his return to the family home, he is cured by Randolph. The "queer lady" turns out to be Randolph himself in drag. As Capote's acute biographer Gerald

Clarke writes (1988, 136), the conclusion of the novel points out that
"when he goes to join the queer
lady in the window, Joel accepts his
destiny, which is to be homosexual,
to always hear other voices and live
in other rooms. Yet acceptance is
not a surrender; it is a liberation. 'I
am me,' he whoops. 'I am Joel, we
are the same people.' So, in a sense,
had Truman rejoiced when he
made peace with his own identity."
The same year of the novel's publication, Capote met the writer Jack
Dunphy with whom he remained
in an open relationship until his
death.

The novel has often been linked
to the tradition of the Southern
Gothic for the many references
to ghostly presences, supernatural
tales, and weird dreams. The setting of the story is, significantly, a
secluded Southern mansion named
Skully's Landing, which people call
simply "The Skulls." Yet, Capote
also employs a sentimental style
which encourages the reader's sympathy towards his main character

Truman Capote in 1967. Courtesy of Photofest.

and, thus, towards his homosexuality. All the characters in the novel defy conventional gender roles: Joel is "too pretty" and "too delicate" with a "girlish tenderness"; Idabel has masculine ways and attires; Cousin Randolph, on the contrary, is
effeminate, "smooth and hairless," and has "wide-set womanly eyes." These coded
descriptions made the characters of the novel gays and lesbians. Skully's Landing
serves as a place outside the patriarchal and hetero-normative American society
where both Joel and Cousin Randolph can accept their own homosexuality and
support each other. As Randolph puts it at the end of the novel: "The brain may
take advice, but not the heart, and love, having no geography, knows no boundaries: weight and sink it deep, no matter, it will rise and find the surface: and why
not? any love is natural and beautiful that lies within a person's nature" (Clarke
1988, 135).

When *Other Voices, Other Rooms* was published, it became an instant bestseller staying on the *New York Times* list for nine weeks and selling more than
26,000 copies. The promotion and controversy surrounding this novel catapulted
Capote to fame. A photograph of Capote by Harold Halma was used to promote
the book and was printed on its dust jacket. As Clarke concludes (1988, 124), the
photograph, portraying the author in a suggestive pose, "caused as much comment

and controversy as the prose inside." It created the author's literary and public persona for many years to come.

Acclaimed by critics as a promising young writer, Capote continued to publish successful fiction such as the short story collection of lone individuals *A Tree of Night* (1949), the autobiographical novel *The Grass Harp* (1951), and the novella *Breakfast at Tiffany's* (1958). He also worked with internationally respected directors such as John Huston and Vittorio De Sica, and contributed to the screenplay for *The Innocents*, starring Deborah Kerr and Michael Redgrave, a fine adaptation of Henry James's *The Turn of the Screw*. Capote's fiction established a homosexual writing style that would be adopted by many gay writers in the 1950s and 1960s. The characters in his fictional writings were rarely described explicitly as homosexuals, yet their coded description resulted obvious to readers. Capote contributed to the identification of his literature as gay with his bitchy comments uttered in his characteristic high-pitched voice and his camp mannerism, which he displayed ostentatiously on television shows and interviews. Holly Golightly, the heroine of *Breakfast at Tiffany's*, best represents Capote's gay sensibility. In her move from her desolate provincial life to New York, Holly mirrors every gay man's ambition to escape constraining surroundings and reach freedom in the impersonal metropolis. Capote's women, however, are not merely men in drag, but point to a possible intersection between female and homosexual desires and needs. The film adaptation of *Breakfast at Tiffany's* (1961), directed by Blake Edwards and starring Audrey Hepburn and George Peppard, contributed to enhance Capote's fame, although he was not directly involved in the production process. Capote himself declared *Breakfast at Tiffany's* a turning point in his career.

Capote was increasingly drawn to journalism and this interest resulted in his most successful and critically praised work, *In Cold Blood* (1966), which was unanimously defined as a masterpiece upon its publication. The book was originally conceived as a short article for the *New Yorker*. Its topic was the murder of a farmer and his family which took place in 1959 in Holcomb, Kansas, where Capote went with his friend Harper Lee to gather information. Yet, as he was researching the small-town community of Holcomb and its culture, the events began to haunt the writer and the project expanded. When the murderers were arrested, Capote added their life stories to the work, which eventually grew into a full-length book. He invented the term *non-fiction* to define his masterpiece, which he considered part of a new literary genre. Although critics disagreed that it was a new literary form, they raved about it. Audiences matched the critics' enthusiasm and Capote obtained the critical and commercial success that he had started to pursue at a very early age. The *New York Times* described the book as "the hottest property since the invention of the wheel." The controversial director Otto Preminger wanted to buy film rights to turn *In Cold Blood* into a Frank Sinatra's vehicle, but the film version was eventually adapted and directed by Richard Brooks.

Openly gay at a time when homosexuality was rarely talked about, Capote apparently moved with ease through the literary and social circles of New York's rich and famous. His public life was just as important as his literary achievements to give him his legendary status. In November 1966, Capote hosted the most important social event of the 1960s, the Black and White Ball in honor of Katherine

Graham, the *Washington Post* publisher, at the Plaza Hotel in New York. Deborah Davis has gone so far as to argue that it was the party of the century, as evident in her 2006 book *The Party of the Century: The Fabulous Story of Truman Capote and His Black and White Ball.* The event attracted so much attention that the *New York Times* printed the guest list on its front page. The masked ball proved to be a defining moment in American social history and popular culture: Capote was among the first to mix the wealthy families of American capitalism such as the Vanderbilts and the Rockefeller with pop artists, writers, actors, and models. Many gay, lesbian, and bisexual artists took part in the event such as Noel Coward, **James Baldwin**, **Edward Albee**, **Tennessee Williams**, and Tallulah Bankhead. After this great success, Capote became the center of New York's social life; the *New York Times* wrote that his "name on an invitation…[was] as potent as a Rockefeller signature on a check."

During the early 1970s, Capote's fame started to decline both literary and socially. He was unable to match the achievements of *Breakfast at Tiffany's* and *In Cold Blood.* Frustrated, he turned to an increasingly bitter style and personal attacks that made him alienated from many of his previous influential friends. Capote's biggest literary project of his later years was a novel he had been working on since the 1950s, *Answered Prayers.* In his plans, the book was conceived as a Proustian epic about America's rich and famous for which Random House offered a generous advance. Yet, *Answered Prayers* was never completed and was published as an unfinished novel after Capote's death. The publication of large excerpts in *Esquire* in 1975 provoked angered reactions from the writer's acquaintances, who found thinly disguised references to themselves and their most intimate secrets in the various characters of the story.

As a reaction to the ostracism of the many social circles that had welcomed him in the 1950s and 1960s, Capote turned increasingly into a recluse in his later years. He also tried to find solace from his loneliness in drugs and alcohol, and, in spite of attempts at rehabilitation, he was never able to overcome his dependence. His public appearances were marked by eccentric behavior, insult, and self-hatred, making him a caricature of his previous self, which had so successfully battled against homophobia. His role as so-called cultural darling, the witty camp entertainer, the persona he had been willing to take on to attend New York's glittering circles as an open homosexual, finally became constraining for Capote. His rebellion became his destruction, as he was unable to channel his rage in a productive way and turned it against himself as well as against his enemies. He died of cardiac and liver complications induced by drug overload on August 25, 1984, in Los Angeles, just a few days before his sixtieth birthday. The critical and commercial success of Bennett Miller's biopic film *Capote* (2005) and the Academy Award–winning performance by Philip Seymour Hoffman have revived popular interest in Truman Capote's personal life and literary achievements.

An assessment of Capote's contribution to gay and lesbian popular culture should not restrictively focus on his later life, but should carefully consider how his early successes were shaped by his sexuality and his refusal to accept heteronormative standards of behavior. His final capitulation to homophobia should not obscure his achievements towards gay liberation in the mid-twentieth century.

Further Reading

Clarke, Gerald. *Capote*. New York: Ballantine, 1988; Davis, Deborah. *Party of the Century: The Fabulous Story of Truman Capote and His Black and White Ball*. Hoboken, NJ: Wiley, 2006; Garson, Helen. *Truman Capote*. New York: Ungar, 1980; Garson, Helen. *Truman Capote: A Study of the Short Fiction*. New York: Twayne Publishers, 1992; Nance, William L. *The Worlds of Truman Capote*. New York: Stein and Day, 1970; Nelson, Emmanuel. *Contemporary American Novelists*. Westport, CT: Greenwood Press, 1993; Plimpton, George. *Truman Capote*. New York: Doubleday, 1997; Pugh, William. "Boundless Hearts in a Nightmare World: Queer Sentimentalism and Southern Gothicism in Truman Capote's Other Voices, Other Rooms." *The Mississippi Quarterly* 51: 4, September 1998. 663–682; Reed, Terry. *Truman Capote*. Boston: Twayne Publishers, 1981.

CELLULOID CLOSET, THE

The Celluloid Closet is both a 1981 book by gay activist and film scholar Vito Russo and a 1995 documentary film directed by Academy Award winners Rob Epstein and by Jeffrey Friedman based on Russo's study and lectures. Both the book and the film focus on the celluloid depictions of gays, lesbians, and transgenders, and they represent a defining moment in the popularization of gay studies. While Russo's study also includes sections on silent films and European cinema, Epstein and Friedman's documentary mainly centers on Hollywood's mainstream productions. Yet, common to both works is the exploration of how the film medium can reflect as well as help to produce social attitudes towards homosexuality, gender roles, and sexual orientations.

Russo first conceived the idea for his book in the early 1970s when he was working as an archivist in the film department of the Museum of Modern Art in New York. After extensive researches both in the United States and in Great Britain, *The Celluloid Closet* was published in 1981 by Harper and Row and then reissued in 1987 with a new chapter on the films of the 1980s. Russo's strategy to expose the sexual clichés of the different eras innovatively interwove close readings of film texts with an analysis of contemporary reviews and critical reception. Highly acclaimed, the book combined scholarly accuracy with an entertaining style and has been hailed as a pioneering work in the intersecting areas of queer, film, and popular culture studies. *The Celluloid Closet* is a crucial point of reference for anyone interested in the film representation of queer subjects. Film scholar Richard Dyer (1990, 7) has described it as "by far the most comprehensive survey of images of gays in films." Russo was one of the first gay activists to convince the GLBTQ movement of the need to take issue with the images of gays and lesbians produced by popular culture. As Russo (1981, xii) stated in the book, "We have cooperated for a very long time in the maintenance of our own invisibility. And now the party is over."

In the mid-1980s, Russo was working for Epstein as the national publicist for his documentary *The Times of Harvey Milk* (1984). Russo, Epstein, and Friedman began talking about the film adaptation of *The Celluloid Closet* and a first version of the script was drafted by Russo himself in 1986. The film was to be the first produced by Epstein and Friedman's new company, Telling Pictures, which was formed in 1987. However, both the filmmakers and Russo agreed that the impact of the **AIDS** epidemic on American society was a more pressing project. Thus, they went on to realize *Common Threads: Stories from the Quilt* (1989) where Russo acted as one of the storytellers narrating the outbreak of the illness in his life and in that of his partner Jeffrey Sevcik.

It was not until after Russo's death from AIDS-related complications in 1991 that the British Channel 4 approached Epstein and Friedman, providing the necessary funds to start the project. The directors relied on researcher Michael Lumpkin and editor Arnold Glassman to choose the clips that would go into the documentary, obviously making a selection among the hundreds of examples given by Russo. Executive Producer Howard Rosenman worked to ensure the cooperation of every motion picture studio and to persuade dozens of actors, actresses, screenwriters, and directors to comment on their own work. Raising the necessary funds for such a broad and ambitious project proved difficult and took several years. Friends of Russo's such as actress **Lily Tomlin**, public institutions, and cable networks made fundamental contributions. HBO eventually supplied the money needed to start shooting and author **Armistead Maupin** provided the final text for the documentary. *The Celluloid Closet* proved a critical and a commercial success, although some reviewers regretted the film's diminished political dimension and its restricted focus on the Hollywood mainstream. The documentary highlighted, like the book, how the Production Code (the set of censorship rules adopted by Hollywood studios in the early 1930s to avoid external control) prohibited only in theory the portrayal of queers on screen. In actual fact, the Code encouraged filmmakers to create coded homosexual characters and events to con the censors and reach the smarter viewers. The abolition of the Code in the 1960s did not encourage more liberating depictions of gays and lesbians, who were often described as maladjusted at best and suicidal at worst. The documentary ends on a more optimistic note than Russo's books as it remarks some positive developments within the Hollywood of the 1990s.

Further Reading

Dyer, Richard. *Now You See It. Studies on Lesbian and Gay Film*. London: Routledge, 1990; Greco, Stephen. "Secret History: An Interview with Film Producer Howard Rosenman." *Interview*. January 4, 1996; Russo, Vito. *The Celluloid Closet: Homosexuality in the Movies*. New York: Harper and Row, 1981.

CHAMBERLAIN, RICHARD (1935–)

For most of his acting career, Richard Chamberlain epitomized the quintessentially heterosexual romantic male lead. The American actor, who was propelled into television stardom when he was 26 years old by the popular NBC series *Dr. Kildare*, did not openly reveal his homosexuality until 2003 when his autobiography *Shattered Love* came out. In the book, Chamberlain discusses the tension he experienced between his increasing need to live his sexuality openly and his fears that a more out lifestyle might harm his acting career. Although he did not comment on his personal life until 2003, Chamberlain was outed in 1990. His outing was based on an interview which the actor had supposedly given to the French magazine *Nous Deux* in December 1989 and which was later denied by Annette Wolf, the actor's publicist. Michelangelo Signorile has given a pivotal role to Chamberlain's outing in the debate that raged in the 1990s about that practice. Before Chamberlain, tabloids were reluctant to name Hollywood celebrities believed to be gay. However, the Chamberlain story was picked up by the popular press forcing the mainstream press to devote more attention to outing and to consider it as an important cultural, social, and political phenomenon.

Richard Chamberlain was born in Los Angeles on March 31, 1935, and grew up in Beverly Hills although in his memoir the actor points out that his family did not live in the fashionable side of the area. Chamberlain's childhood was marked by his father's abusive behavior. Due to his alcoholism, Charles Chamberlain was a constant threat for his family whom he subdued by instilling in its members a sense of inadequacy. In Richard's case, this sense of inferiority was increased by the young boy's awareness of his homosexuality. As he states in his memoir (2003, 191), "I learned to dislike gay people, myself included, from my family." His peers were no better. They "were frantic to prove their normalcy by quite viciously rejecting anything 'abnormal' in themselves and, by extension, in other children" (2003, 191). Chamberlain vividly remembers walking home from school one day swearing to himself that he would have never revealed his "loathsome" secret to anyone. This sense of self-hatred would plague the actor for most of his life, and writing honestly about his homosexuality in his autobiography acquired for him a liberating dimension.

It was while majoring in art at Pomona College that Chamberlain decided to pursue an acting career encouraged by his personal success in college plays. Although his plans were delayed for two years because of his drafting to serve in the army, Chamberlain began taking acting classes upon his return to civilian life. In one of these classes, the actor also fell in love with a fellow student, but, because of the widespread homophobia of the 1950s, the couple was forced to keep the affair secret. Chamberlain (2003, 20) writes of how difficult it is for people nowadays to understand "how deeply terrifying it was to imagine to be labeled a faggot, a pansy, a pervert" in the 1940s and 1950s. "It seemed to me," Chamberlain (2003, 20) goes on, "that even traitors and murderers were generally held in higher esteem than I would be if anyone found out the truth about me."

After a disappointing debut in William Witney's *The Secret of the Purple Reef* (1960) and the filming of a pilot for a TV series that never followed, Chamberlain enjoyed a meteoric rise to stardom thanks to the title role in the NBC's *Dr. Kildare*. The series was a huge hit and ran from 1961 for five years, launching Chamberlain as a TV star and an handsome male lead. More TV roles were offered to the actor when *Kildare* ended, yet he declined, joining instead the cast of the Broadway musical adaptation of **Truman Capote**'s *Breakfast at Tiffany's*. The show had the largest advance ticket sale of the 1966 season, but, due to disagreements between director, producer, script-writers, and the cast, the musical never opened. Chamberlain then decided to pursue his career on the stage and on the big screen in England. Chamberlain lived in the United Kingdom for more than four years, starring in Shakespearian plays at the theater and playing in two of his finest films, Bryan Forbes's *The Madwoman of Chaillot* (1969) and Ken Russell's *The Music Lovers* (1971). Russell's film, an unconventional biopic of Tchaikovsky stressing the composer's homosexuality, offered Chamberlain the chance of playing a gay role.

In the 1970s, however, Chamberlain starred in more commercial features with all-star casts such as Richard Lester's adaptations of Alexandre Dumas's work *The Three Musketeers* (1973) and *The Four Musketeers* (1974), and John Guillermin's disaster film *Towering Inferno* (1974). He also returned to television playing Edmond Dantes in *The Count of Monte Cristo* (1975) and the double role of King Louis XIV and his twin brother Philippe in *The Man with the Iron Mask* (1977). He was also the Prince in the musical *The Slipper and the Rose* (1976), which is considered one of the best film adaptations of the Cinderella story. The early 1980s saw the culmination of Chamberlain's career as *the* star of miniseries based on bestsellers thanks to his roles in *Shogun* (1980) and in the extraordinarily popular adaptation of Colleen McCullough's *The Thorn Birds* (1983). The latter, the story of the ill-fated affair between Father Ralph de Bricassart and the Australian sheep rancher Maggie, reinforced Chamberlain's image as an icon of heterosexual romance. The popularity he had achieved with these two miniseries finally allowed Chamberlain to star as leading actor, rather than being just a star in a cast of many, in *King's Solomon Mines* (1985) and its sequel *Allan Quatermain and the Lost City of Gold* (1987).

At the end of the 1980s, however, Chamberlain experienced a period of professional and personal upheaval. *Island Son* (1989), the TV series which he had planned with his partner Martin Rabbett about a doctor living in Hawaii, closed after only a season of 18 episodes due to poor ratings. In addition, American and European media were quick to seize upon a sentence that he had allegedly said in an interview with the French magazine *Nous Deux* (Signorile 1993, 295): "I have had enough pretending. I'm officially moving in with my friend, Martin Rabbett. We have been lovers for twelve years now and we have been building a house on the beach [in Hawaii] which will be our home. And too bad for people who are upset by it." Chamberlain's publicist issued a formal denial of the statement, but the news was already reaching beyond the gay press and appeared in popular and mainstream publications. In *Shattered Love*, Chamberlain recalls his confusion and his anxiety for his career. He feared that the revelation of his homosexuality would alienate his fans. His heterosexual image, which he had cultivated so carefully over a 40-year career, was suddenly shattered. To Michelangelo Signorile (1993, 299), the Chamberlain case "sent unprecedented fear through all of Hollywood, where image is money and where people make money off many gay stars' perceived heterosexuality." Outing, until then limited to the boring world of politicians and bureaucrats, suddenly became a popular culture phenomenon invading the glamorous Hollywood. Signorile (1993, 299) points out that, after Chamberlain's incident, "many mainstream papers were covering the outing phenomenon and using names." He quotes the *Los Angeles Times* opinion that "what began as a gay political tactic has heated up the tabloids and shifted into the mainstream press" (1993, 299).

Although Chamberlain writes disparagingly of outing in his autobiography, he also admits that the tabloid headlines forced him to come to terms with his repressed fears of being identified as a homosexual, a process which would last for a decade. Following the revelation of his homosexuality, Chamberlain did not work for an entire year. Yet, more successes were to mark his career such as the 1994 Broadway revival of *My Fair Lady* and a national tour of *The Sound of Music* in 1999. In his later appearances as a theater and film actor, Chamberlain has also starred as a gay man. In 2002 he was Maggie Wick in *The Drew Carey Show*, while the following year he was directed by Rabbett in Timothy Findley's play *The Stillborn Lover* where he portrayed an ambassador coming to terms with his homosexuality. In 2005 he appeared in an episode of the series *Will and Grace* and in 2006 he joined the cast of *Nip and Tuck* for the episode "Blue Mondae" as a gay man who forces his younger partner to undergo cosmetic surgery. These roles are part of Chamberlain's newly found confidence about his sexuality.

Further Reading

Bernstein, Fred A. "A Night Out with Richard Chamberlain; A Couple Makes a Debut." *New York Times* (July 13, 2003): Sec. 9, p. 4; Chamberlain, Richard. *Shattered Love: A Memoir*. New York: ReganBooks, 2003; Guthmann, Edward. "The Doctor Is Out; New Memoir, New Honesty from TV's *Dr. Kildare*." *San Francisco Chronicle* (June 18, 2003): D1; Levine, Bettijane. "Richard, Reconciled; In His New Book, Leading Man Chamberlain Reveals He Is Gay, and It's Liberated Him." *Los Angeles Times* (June 13, 2003): Part 5, p. 23; Signorile, Michelangelo. *Queer in America: Sex, the Media and the Closets of Power*. New York: Random House, 1993.

CONDON, WILLIAM "BILL" (1955–)

Bill Condon became a central figure in gay and lesbian popular culture with his 1998 film *Gods and Monsters* (1998), which earned him, among other prestigious prizes, an Academy Award for Best Screenplay. Together with his subsequent *Kinsey* (2004), *Gods and Monsters* challenges notions of so-called normal sexual behavior and blurs the boundaries between sexual orientations. For these two films the Gay and Lesbian Alliance against Defamation (GLAAD) has presented Condon with the Stephen F. Kolzak Award, a prize given to openly gay figures in the entertainment and media communities for their commitment against homophobia. In an interview with the ***Advocate*** (Steele 2004, 70), the director expressed his surprise for being described as "a homosexual activist": "I'm embarrassed by the fact that I've never really been a homosexual activist—I've been too busy writing movies. . . . I'm proud to wear those stripes. I just haven't done enough to earn them."

William Condon was born on October 22, 1955, in Queens, New York. He grew up in an Irish Catholic family and attended High Regis School, a Jesuit institute in Manhattan. Although his parents learned about the director's homosexuality at an early stage, they were highly embarrassed by any discussion of sex. In 1976, Condon graduated from Columbia University with a bachelor's degree in philosophy. He then moved to Los Angeles to take film studies at UCLA. Condon

Brendan Fraser as gardener Clayton Boone (left) and Sir Ian McKellen as homosexual horror director James Whale in Bill Condon's *Gods and Monsters*. Courtesy of Lions Gate Films Inc./Photofest. Photograph by Anne Fishbein.

made his debut in the film industry as a screenwriter of horror movies by British director/producer Michael Laughlin. He directed his first film, *Sister, Sister,* in 1987. A thriller starring Eric Stoltz and Jennifer Jason Leigh, the movie was a commercial failure relegating Condon to direct TV movies for almost a decade.

The director returned to the big screen with *Candyman II: Farewell to the Flesh* (1995), scripted, as the first movie, by leading horror author Clive Barker. In spite of initial difficulties in securing funds and actors, it was Condon's following film, *Gods and Monsters,* to establish the director as one of the most original filmmakers of the 1990s. It represented a transition between Condon's early horror films and his subsequent productions, which mainly investigate the multiple forms of human sexuality. The film, based on Christopher Bram's novel *Father of Frankenstein,* depicts the last days in the life of horror film director James Whale (played by **Ian McKellen**), focusing on his homosexuality. Whale was openly gay in the homophobic Hollywood of the first half of the twentieth century. He directed the horror cult-classics *Frankenstein* (1931), *The Invisible Man* (1933), and *The Bride of Frankenstein* (1935), which crucially contributed to the big earnings of Universal Pictures in the 1930s. Yet, his career declined by the end of the decade and most of his films after *The Man in the Iron Mask* (1939) were box office flops. His later life was plagued by bouts of depression and a debilitating stroke. He committed suicide in 1957. *Gods and Monsters* hinges on the director's loneliness and physical decline of the mid-1950s when he had turned to painting and had stopped directing. Through flashbacks, *Gods and Monsters* also shows details of Whale's previous life: his underprivileged childhood in England, the horror of the First World War, the success of his 1930s horror films, as well as Whale's liberated way of living his homosexuality. The film centers in particular on Whale's relationship with his new gardener and former Marine Clayton Boone (Brendan Fraser). Boone becomes an obsession for Whale who devises a plan to be killed by his gardener after provoking him sexually. The enactment of this plan represents the film's climax, ending, however, with Boone dutifully putting Whale to bed and refusing to kill him. The next morning he will discover that Whale has taken his own life. With Boone, Whale creates his last monster, who, turning on his creator, will free him from the burden of his past memoirs.

Gods and Monsters constantly subverts and challenges stable binary notions of hetero/homosexuality, director/actor, father/son. Significantly, the audience soon discovers that Whale is not so much attracted to Boone for his body, but for his ability to kill the director. With time, on the contrary, Boone is increasingly attracted to Whale and his elegant, even decadent, way of life. Homosexuality is not depicted as predatory, nor as negating masculinity. It is Whale, not former Marine Boone, who has fought in the trenches. The final suicide may resemble a rather long string of gay characters depicted as hopeless victims by Hollywood's celluloid closet. Yet, in this case, Whale's act becomes a self-affirming action. Whale cannot simply direct his own death, he has to take responsibility for it himself.

Condon's next project was the Oscar-nominated screenplay for the adaptation of the musical *Chicago* (2002), whose success and critical acclaim resurrected the genre of musicals after years of neglect. Condon returned behind the camera in 2004 with *Kinsey*, a highly personal biopic on the famous and controversial sex researcher Alfred Kinsey (played by Liam Neeson), who shocked the conformist society of the 1940s and 1950s with his honest discussion of American sexual mores. Americans were stunned to hear Kinsey state that 37 percent of Americans had at least one homosexual encounter. Condon's fascination with Kinsey stems from the close connection between the researcher's life and his study of sex. In the movie, Condon makes this clear by showing Kinsey's desire to study sex as a direct result of his own situation. The study of sex allowed him to liberate himself from the sexually repressed home where he had grown up. Condon wanted to stress the contemporary significance of Kinsey's legacy: "His emphasis on the complexity and importance of individual sexuality, and his fight against the oppressive notion of normality that produces such damaging aspects as peer pressure and ostracization of individual sexualities" (Grundmann, 2005 *Cineaste* online). *Kinsey* also speaks out against the conservative sexual politics that characterize the Bush Administration, whose main remedy for sexually transmitted diseases is abstinence. Although the director considers Kinsey as "one of the fathers of the gay movement," Condon did not want to make exclusively a gay film because "this would…have been very much against the spirit of Kinsey's own philosophy. He believed in a great variety of forms of sexuality" (Steele 2004, 70). However, an important part of the movie is devoted to the relationship between the researcher and his younger student Clyde Martin (Peter Sarsgaard), who was also Kinsey's wife's lover.

Throughout the years, Alfred Kinsey has remained a controversial subject. His bold challenges to the notion of a so-called normal sexual behavior made him the target of vicious attacks from conservatives. Such attacks have continued even after his death, as he is routinely accused of having practiced pseudo-science and legitimated pedophilia. Condon's *Kinsey* details the pressure that ultimately led to the researcher's downfall. Yet, the film closes on an hopeful note as a lesbian Kinsey is interviewing (a cameo appearance by Lynn Redgrave) thanks him for having improved her life, giving her the courage to come out. Although Condon portrays Kinsey as a sexual liberator, his is not a hagiography as the director is well-aware of the contradictions that make the scientist such a fascinating topic of study: "For example, he got a myriad of strangers to tell him their sex secrets, but was less than forthcoming about his own. And he attacked the regime of sexual categories by creating ever more such categories" (Grundmann, 2005 *Cineaste* online). To Condon, Kinsey is not so much a scientist as a social reformer and an artist, who made introspection one of the foundations for his own research.

In 2006 Condon returned to the musical genre with the international hit *Dreamgirls*, based on the Broadway musical of the same name on the successes and rivalries in a group of three female singers, modeled on The Supremes. Although Condon feels embarrassed by his lack of gay activism, his films so far have contributed to challenge the stereotypical depictions of homosexuals that proliferate in Hollywood. His work therefore has been of service to the queer community, offering different representations of homosexuality.

Further Reading

Arnold, Gary. "From Monster to Godlike Films? The Low-Budget Adventures of a Director." *Washington Times* (November 22, 1998): D3; Bronski, Mark. "*Gods and Monsters:* The Search for the Right Whale." *Cineaste.* (September 22, 1999); Grundmann, Roy. "Sex, Science and the Biopic: An Interview with Bill Condon." *Cineaste* (March 22, 2005). http://www.highbeam.com/doc/1G1-130932592.html (accessed on September 8, 2007); Hartl, John. "'Monsters' Brings Unlikely Success to Indie Director." *Seattle Times* (November 15, 1998): M1; Rosen, Steven. "'Gods' Gives Filmmaker His Just Due; 'Best Picture' Designation Puts Light on an Unknown." *Seattle Times* (December 13, 1998): H1, 6; Steele, Bruce C. "Bill & Al's Excellent Adventure." *The Advocate* 927 (November 23, 2004): 70; Vargas, Jose Antonio. "Naked Contradictions; 'Kinsey' Creator Analyzes the Famed Sex Researcher." *Washington Post* (November 20, 2004): C1.

CRISP, QUENTIN (1908–1999)

The British artist's model, actor, and writer Quentin Crisp became an icon of queer culture of the 1970s after the publication of his witty and defiant autobiography *The Naked Civil Servant* (1968), which was soon adapted into a successful award-winning film. He attracted worldwide attention for his nonconformist behavior, not merely refusing to conceal his homosexuality, but actually exhibiting it. According to his own definition, Crisp was "not merely a self-confessed homosexual, but a self-evident one," who was determined not to hide his effeminacy. On the contrary, he displayed and heightened it through his dandy persona who made use of make-up and high-heeled shoes. His uncompromising stance was the target of many homophobic attacks and Crisp was assaulted several times during his life. His books covered many areas of popular culture such as fashion, cinema, and lifestyles, all areas that Crisp treated with humor and wit comparable to those of Oscar Wilde. To many, Crisp's persona was a twentieth-century adaptation of Wilde.

Crisp was born Denis Charles Pratt in Sutton, a suburb south of London, on December 25, 1908. He was the youngest of four children. His family embodied the middle-class values that Crisp would so adamantly reject in the course of his life. "[K]eeping up with the Joneses," writes Crisp in his autobiography (1968, 3), "was a full-time job with my mother and father." His memoirs of childhood are not happy ones. As he wrote, he was sent "between the ages of fourteen and eighteen, to a school in Derbyshire which was like a cross between a monastery and a prison." In that school, he learnt nothing except "how to bear injustice." His effeminate behavior made him the object of teasing by his schoolmates. In his twenties, Denis Pratt changed his name into Quentin Crisp and moved out from home, starting to build that image of effeminate dandy which would make him a distinctive character on the London gay scene. In the city, Crisp held a variety of jobs such as book-cover designer, freelance commercial artist and, even, for a short period of time, male prostitute. Because of his homosexuality, Crisp was exempted from military service during the war. In the years of the Blitz, he worked as a nude model in a government-funded art school. Because the institution was state-subsidized, he considered himself akin to a civil servant, albeit a naked one. This situation provided the title for his autobiography.

The Naked Civil Servant was published by Jonathan Cape in 1968, just after male homosexual acts had been decriminalized in Britain. The book, unusual, at the time, for its unrepentant depiction of a homosexual life, sold well and had good reviews. The author's fame, however, was greatly enhanced by the success of the television adaptation of the memoir, starring John Hurt and directed by Jack Gold in 1975. *The Naked Civil Servant* chronicles Crisp's coming-of-age on the backdrop of the conservative English society of the 1940s and 1950s. It subjects discriminatory social norms to the author's witticism and corrosive humor. At the same time, the narrative of *The Naked Civil Servant* is informed by those very stereotypes that justified the discrimination of homosexuals. In the very first line of the book, Crisp (1968, 1) defines himself as "disfigured by the characteristics of a certain kind of homosexual person." His homosexual condition is a "predicament," a "disgrace" that dramatically restricted the opportunities in the life of the author. In spite of his internalization of dangerous stereotypes, Crisp deserves admiration for his relentless refusal to comply with heterosexual standards of behavior.

The television success of *The Naked Civil Servant* launched Crisp's career as an actor as he began to tour Britain with his one-man show, *An Evening with Quentin Crisp*, constituted by monologues and sharp answers to questions picked at random from the audience. In the late 1970s, Crisp brought his show to New York to immediate acclaim. Because he had always liked Americans, Crisp decided to settle down in New York in 1980. In his American years, he continued to tour with his show, which he periodically updated, and he also became a columnist and a film critic, contributing provocative pieces to such important publications as *Christopher Street* and *Native*. Crisp continued to play the role of social critic, observing, as he had done for Britain years before, the biases and ludicrousness of American public life. Yet, his American works, including *How to Become a Virgin* (1981) and *Manners from Heaven* (1985), suggest that the author had found a more hospitable home in the United States.

In the 1990s, Crisp also became a film actor, appearing as himself in important documentaries such as *Resident Alien* (1991) and *The Celluloid Closet* (1995). He also had cameo roles in Jonathan Demme's **Philadelphia** (1993), the romantic comedy *Naked in New York* (1994), and the Priscilla-inspired *To Wong Foo: Thanks for Everything, Julie Newmar* (1995). Director Sally Potter gave Crisp a more substantial role for her film *Orlando* (1993), based on Virginia Woolf's novel. Here Crisp played Queen Elizabeth I, in a performance that was highly praised by critics. He also co-starred in the farce *Homo Heights* (1996). His scene in the controversial thriller *Fatal Attraction* (1987) was cut from the final version of the movie.

While on the English tour of his show, Crisp died in Manchester on November 21, 1990, at the age of 90. His taste for controversy did not abate in his later years and was also partly directed against that very gay community of which he had unwillingly become a symbol. In interviews, Crisp repeatedly stressed that it was a great mistake for any minority to assume that they can demand equal rights. "I don't think anyone has any rights," he famously stated once. He did not believe in romantic love and considered homosexuality to be an illness. More problematic still was his stance on **AIDS**, the impact of which he completely failed to understand, describing the epidemic as a "fad." Yet, Crisp was hailed as a pioneer of the gay and lesbian movement in the obituary of the **Advocate**: "while he wasn't supportive of the gay movement, he was a relentless gay activist by virtue of his unrepentantly flamboyant appearance" (Kinser 2000, *Advocate* online). Crisp picked up Wilde's legacy in his refusal to compromise with discriminatory social norms and to give up his own identity. Most of his epigrammatic sentences emphasize the need for everyone to live according to their personalities regardless of how they are perceived by others. The British singer Sting devoted his 1987 song "Englishman in New York" to Crisp, celebrating his courage and summarizing effectively the author's philosophy of life: "It takes a man to suffer ignorance and smile, Be yourself no matter what they say."

Further Reading

Bailey, Paul, ed. *The Stately Homo: A Celebration of the Life of Quentin Crisp*. London: Bantam, 2000; Crisp, Quentin. *The Naked Civil Servant*. London: Jonathan Cape, 1968; Fountain, Tim. *Quentin Crisp*. London: Absolute Press, 2001; Kinser, Jeremy. "Crisp Wit." *The Advocate*. January 18, 2000. http://www.highbeam.com/doc/1G1-58435719.html (accessed on June 8, 2007); Official Quentin Crisp Web site: www.quentincrisp.com; Robinson, Paul. *Gay Lives: Homosexual*

Autobiography from John Addington Symonds to Paul Monette. Chicago: University of Chicago Press, 1999.

CROWLEY, MART (1935–)

Mart Crowley acquired overnight fame in gay and lesbian popular culture with his play *The Boys in the Band* (1968), which became an instant off-Broadway hit and was later adapted into a successful movie. With *The Boys in the Band*, Crowley smashed the closet of silence that surrounded gay life on stage. In the tumultuous year of Vietnam demonstrations and race riots, and the year before the Stonewall events, Crowley offered a whole play centering on a group of gay men at a cocktail party. The text was considered a groundbreaking work in American drama. Yet, Crowley's centrality in gay and lesbian popular culture has been successively challenged. The plays which followed *The Boys in the Band* have not kept the promise of that first work. With the years, even *The Boys in the Band* has come under critical attack from queer critics who argue that the advent of **AIDS** has made it anachronistic. In addition, many are not so sure any longer that Crowley's representation of homosexuality was so groundbreaking. They claim, on the contrary, that his play can be read as perpetrating the usual stereotypes of gay men as sad, depressed, and self-loathing people.

Crowley was born in Vicksburg, Mississippi, on August 21, 1935. His childhood was plagued by his parents' alcoholism and drug addiction. Crowley escaped the dreary reality of his family life with frequent trips to the cinema, a fact that acquainted him to the arts from an early age. After his graduation from high school, the playwright attended The Catholic University of America in Washington, DC. He obtained his degree in 1957 and then went on to work as an assistant for film director Elia Kazan who was adapting William Inge's play *Splendor in the Grass* for the screen. On the set, Crowley met gay-friendly actress Natalie Wood and the two became close friends. Wood encouraged Crowley to write, but his early attempts at screenwriting for the cinema and the television were unsuccessful. His projects were either rejected or canceled at the last minute. Wood then hired Crowley as a personal assistant, which gave him time to start writing what would eventually become *The Boys in the Band*. Originally produced by Richard Barr and **Edward Albee**'s Playwright Unit, the play opened off Broadway in April 1968 running for more than a thousand performances. Because of its success, it was turned into a film two years later. William Friedkin, who was later to be accused of homophobia for his thriller ***Cruising*** (1980), directed the movie version.

At a time when gay characters were rarely seen on stage or on the screen, *The Boys in the Band* presented an unusually exclusive focus on gay life. It portrays the interaction between a group of nine gay males during a birthday party on Manhattan's Upper East Side thrown by Michael for Harold. The title, the author explains, "was a catchword in the 40's Big Band era: 'Let's hear a big hand for the boys in the band.' The line is also in *A Star Is Born*. James Mason says to Judy Garland, 'It's three o'clock in the morning at the Downbeat Club and you're singing for yourself and for the boys in the band'" (Rickard 2001, 9). He also added that the title wanted to convey "a slightly outlaw quality; a band as a band of thieves" (Rickard 2001, 9). All the characters in the play except for Alan, who drops in unexpectedly to tell Michael something about his life, explicitly identify as homosexuals. *The Boys in the Band* is deliberately outrageous in its use of campy and bitchy humor and its sustained employment of four-letter words. While the play adopts the tone of the comedy in its first part, it shifts more decidedly towards melodrama in its second half. The turning point takes place when the host suggests his guests play "Affair of the Heart," a kind of truth game where they should phone the one person that they have truly loved. The game brings up stories of unrequited love. In addition, when Alan, the only one in the group who does not identify as gay, picks up the phone, the other boys think he will call a man and will thus out himself. Yet, he turns out to be calling his wife, a call that reasserts his own heterosexuality. The play never makes clear what Alan had planned on telling Michael in the first place. The audience is left wondering whether he might have wanted to confess his homosexuality but the disgust for the lifestyle that he has witnessed at the party eventually prevented him from doing so. There is no doubt that the characters in the play suffer from neuroses and loneliness, a trait that was already criticized by gay militants at the time. Writing an editorial in the **Advocate**, Dick Michaels commented: "Mart Crowley's *The Boys in the Band* may be one or two or three strictly gay plays to win rave notices from major theater critics. But in one way or another, the critics usually say the play depicts the true world of the homosexual. And by 'true world,' they mean the 'sad,' 'tragic,' or 'miserable' world of the homosexual. The critics may know about the theater, but as for knowing about homosexuals, we're afraid they've been cruising in the wrong places."

The self-loathing, flamboyance, and sexual promiscuity of the characters in the play have been major targets of successive generations of critics, who have denounced the play as dated and perpetrating the usual stereotypes about queers. The play, they argue, ultimately presents a depressing portrayal of gay life and of gay males who have internalized homophobia. It does not assert an alternative lifestyle. Tellingly, the most-often quoted line of the play is "You show me a happy homosexual, and I'll show you a gay corpse" (Crowley and Lambert 1996, 128), which is uttered by Michael, the character with whom Crowley most closely identifies. Michael also closes the play pondering, rather depressingly, "If we…if we could just…not hate ourselves so much. That's it, you know. If we could just learn not to hate ourselves quite so much." The author has defended his text as a period piece, which was written at a time of severe depression without "any politically militant stance or defiance of society in mind" (Crowley and Lambert 1996, 128). To Crowley, the mere showing of people who explicitly identified as homosexuals was a positive act. In addition, he also argued that the couple formed by Hank and Larry illustrated the power of long-term commitment and love among gays. This is debatable as the two are shown arguing for most of the play over how exclusive their relationship should be. However, Crowley is right to suggest that we consider *The Boys in the Band* as a reflection on the pervasive and pernicious effects of social homophobia on the lives of gay men before Stonewall and the advent of gay liberation.

Crowley's next plays failed to replicate the critical and commercial success of his debut. *Remote Asylum* opened in 1970 with high expectations, but quickly closed.

The autobiographical *A Breeze from the Gulf* (1973) reconciled Crowley with critics, earning him good reviews and even a nomination for Best Play by the Los Angeles Drama Critics Circle. Yet, the play closed after only six weeks. During the rest of the decade, Crowley survived on the money earned with *The Boys in the Band* until his friend Natalie Wood got him a job as script editor and then producer for the ABC series *Hart to Hart*, where her husband Robert Wagner starred. He also continued to write screenplays that were, however, never filmed.

In the early 1990s, Crowley returned to drama with *For Reasons That Remain Unclear*, focusing on the sexual abuse of young student by a Catholic priest. As with most writings by Crowley, the play has several autobiographical elements. Its original run was planned for a year, but the show closed well in advance. In 2002 the playwright presented *The Men from the Boys*, a sequel to *The Boys in the Band*, in San Francisco. Set in the same Manhattan apartment, the play gathers seven of the original characters at the wake of Larry, who has died of cancer. What is most disappointing about this sequel is its inability to show any evolution in the characters, who seem to have remained severed off from any political and social movement. In spite of his inability to reach the vast audiences and obtain the rave reviews of his debut play, Mart Crowley should still be credited with his pioneering role in opening up American theater to gay-themed texts.

Further Reading

Bilowit, Ira J. "Mart Crowley on *The Boys in the Band:* From Author's Anguish to NYC Revival." *Back Stage* 37 (June 14, 1996): 17; Crowley, Mart and Gavin Lambert. *Three Plays: The Boys in the Band; A Breeze from the Gulf; For Reasons That Remain Unclear*. Los Angeles: Alyson Publications, 1996; Harvey, Dennis. "The Men from the Boys." *Variety* (November 25–December 1, 2002): 32; Rickard, John. "The Boys in the Band, 30 Years Later." *The Gay & Lesbian Review Worldwide*. (March 2001): 9; Thompson, Mark, ed. *Long Road to Freedom: The Advocate History of the Gay and Lesbian Movement*. New York: St. Martin's Press, 1994.

CRUISING

Directed by William Friedkin and starring Al Pacino, *Cruising* (1980) provoked angry reactions and boycotts from gay and lesbian activists even before it was released. The film was condemned for its reinforcement of negative Hollywood depictions of homosexuals as predatory killers inhabiting a seamy underworld of vice and violence. As *Cruising* came out in the aftermath of Anita Bryant's campaign to repeal anti-discrimination legislation, many felt it would validate the backlash against the movement for gay rights. The gay community also feared that the film would encourage violence against homosexuals. Gay activists disrupted the filming of *Cruising* and organized boycotts against its theatrical release. Partially rehabilitated by successive generations of gay critics, *Cruising* made the gay and lesbian movement aware that street demonstrations were not enough. As James M. Saslow (1994, 177) summarizes, in the wake of Friedkin's movie, "many concluded that it was time to shift our battleground from the self and the streets to the corridors of power. Taking on political parties, media, and corporations would require large organizations, professional skills, and fund-raising."

The film follows undercover policeman Steve Burns (Al Pacino) through New York's S-M gay bars in his search for a serial killer who picks up unsuspecting homosexuals and then ritually kills them. As more dismembered bodies are found, Burns's investigation takes him deeper into the gay scene and his emotional balance is endangered. He breaks up with his girlfriend (Karen Allen) and becomes increasingly friendlier with his neighbor Ted, an aspiring gay writer, to the point of being jealous of him. Eventually, Burns manages to organize a trap for the murderer and kills him. The last scenes of the film portrays Burns happily returning to his girlfriend. However, we soon learn that Ted has been cruelly murdered and the film leaves open the possibility that Burns himself is the killer.

Probably because of the demonstrations during its filming, *Cruising* opens with the message: "The film is not intended as an indictment of the homosexual world. It is set in one small segment of that world which is not meant to be representative of the whole." In spite of this partial disclaimer, gay activists were obviously concerned that the scenes of fist fucking, S-M practices, and drug taking would be regarded by the larger society as characteristic features of gay life. A statement by producer Jerry Weintraub reinforced these concerns. Weintraub declared that he was not putting into the film anything that does not take place every night. *Cruising* was not simply fiction, but the truth. The fact that *Cruising* leaves open the possibility that Burns is Ted's killer also seemed to assert that when Burns finally recognized his homosexual desires he became a murderer. This equation of homosexual love and violence is recurrent throughout the film. A scene which portrays the serial killer stabbing one of his victims is alternated with images of anal penetration, thus linking the two acts. When the film was first released, gays were not alone in panning it. Critics generally disliked the film, finding a lack of coherent psychological development in the main character which harmed the narrative as a whole. The negative reviews affected the film's box office results for the worse, and *Cruising* was nominated for Worst Film, Director, and Screenplay at the Golden Raspberry Awards.

Some gay artists, including the novelist Felice Picano and playwright John Rechy, opposed disrupting the filming of *Cruising* since they argued that prior censorship was always wrong. Over the years, some gay critics have revaluated the film pointing to its frank depiction of the gay S-M subculture of the 1970s and to its indictment of the latent homophobia of American institutions. Before Pacino is introduced into the narrative, for example, we witness two policemen assaulting two gay prostitutes and forcing them to have oral intercourse. Gary Morris (1996, *Bright Lights Film Journal* online) further argues that "Friedkin contrasts the police officers' state-sanctioned sadism with the consensual, practically playful kind found in the bars." In a later scene, a black policeman only wearing a jockstrap physically assaults Burns and one his casual partners after they have been both taken to the police station. Morris (1996, *Bright Lights Film Journal* online) concludes that "If Friedkin…shows any sympathy in *Cruising*, it is for this and other gay victims of state-sponsored brutality." Whether reviled as homophobic or praised as a challenge to institutionalized gay-hatred, *Cruising* represents a central film in the battle over the representation of queer subjects within American popular culture.

Further Reading

Morris, Gary. "William Friedkin's *Cruising*." *Bright Lights Film Journal*. April 1996, Issue 16. http://www.brightlightsfilm.com/16/cruise.html (accessed on June 5, 2007); Russo, Vito. *The Celluloid Closet: Homosexuality in the Movies*. Revised Edition. New York: Harper, 1987; Saslow, James M. "Taking It to the Streets." *Long Road to Freedom: The Advocate History of the Gay and Lesbian Movement*. Mark Thompson, ed. New York: St. Martin's Press, 1994. 177–178.

Cukor, George (1899–1983)

Academy Award winner George Cukor was one of the most successful directors in Hollywood during its so-called Golden Age (1930–1950). Dubbed a woman's director, Cukor was part of a group of gay filmmakers, including James Whale and Vincente Minelli, whose career flourished within the studio system. Although Cukor disliked the label of woman's director, which he found restrictive, his films were indeed built around Hollywood's top female stars, including such gay icons as Greta

Joan Crawford (left) and Norma Shearer (right) in George Cukor's *The Women*, whose camp humor made it a gay cult classic. Courtesy of MGM/Photofest.

Garbo, Katharine Hepburn, Tallulah Bankhead, Joan Crawford, and **Judy Garland**. This was obviously no coincidence and reveals Cukor's fascination with strong female characters whose screen identities blur the boundaries between genders and fixed roles. The phrase may have also obliquely referred to the filmmaker's homosexuality which, as in many other cases, was a well-known secret in Hollywood.

Cukor was born in New York City on July 7, 1899, from Jewish-Hungarian immigrants. Theater was Cukor's first passion and, once he graduated from De Witt Clinton High School in 1916, he worked as an assistant stage manager for a Chicago company for three years. He then founded his own company in Rochester, working there for seven years before going to Broadway to work with such actresses as Ethel Barrymore and Dorothy Gish. When sound was introduced into Hollywood and the film industry started to recruit people from the theater to adapt to the new technological developments, Cukor was hired by Paramount as a dialog director in 1929. He co-directed three films before directing his first feature, *Tarnished Lady* (1931) with Tallulah Bankhead. His career moved fast, although he found himself embroiled in a legal battle with Paramount that led him to leave that studio for David O. Selznick's RKO. At RKO, Cukor directed a string of major hits including *A Bill of Divorcement* (1932), which marked Cukor's long-standing collaboration and friendship with Katharine Hepburn, *Dinner at Eight* (1933), *Little Women* (1933), *David Copperfield* (1935), *Romeo and Juliet* (1936), and *Camille* (1937). *Sylvia Scarlett* (1935) was far less successful than Cukor's other films of the decade and one which persuaded him not to be too daring with his challenges to gender difference. At a preview of the film attended by Cukor himself, people walked out in spite of the director's presence. In *Sylvia Scarlett*, Katharine Hepburn plays the title role, but her character masquerades for most of the film as a man in order to escape from the police. She also kisses a woman and makes another fall in love. Looking at her, a male artist, played by **Cary Grant**, exclaims, "I don't know what it is that gives me a queer feeling when I look at you." Grant also invites Sylvia, who is pretending to be Sidney, to keep him warm in bed. This suggests a double reading. On the one hand, it titillates the audience who is aware of Hepburn's gender as Grant is not. On the other hand, it also points out Grant's own double life and his real sexual interests. In spite of the disastrous box office results of *Sylvia Scarlett*, Hepburn was to star in many of Cukor's films, developing into an icon for the director. As Dan Callahan (*Senses of Cinema* online) puts it, "a butch but vulnerable actress became the seminal artistic creation of a sensitive but thrillingly earthy gay man."

Such impressive series of successes was abruptly interrupted when Cukor was dismissed from the set of *Gone With the Wind*, a film on which he had spent two years of his career for its pre-production. After only three weeks of shooting, Cukor was replaced by Victor Fleming and Sam Wood, although he continued to coach privately the female stars of the film. Clark Gable and Cukor, on the other hand, never got on particularly well and some accounts report that it was Gable's insistence not to be directed by a fairy that got the director sacked. Although he could not finish his work on *Gone With the Wind*, Cukor went on to direct two of the biggest successes of the late 1930s. *The Women* (1939), based on Clare Boothe Luce's allusive play, became renowned for its all-female cast of stars including Norma Shearer, Joan Crawford, Rosalind Russell, Paulette Goddard, and Joan Fontaine. Its camp humor soon proved the film a favorite for queer audiences, and the movie became a gay cult classic. *The Philadelphia Story* (1940) was a screwball comedy starring Katharine Hepburn, James Stewart, and Cary Grant. Its commercial success helped to rescue Hepburn's career after a series of flops that had caused her to be nicknamed "box-office poison."

Throughout the 1940s and 1950s, Cukor continued to direct highly theatrical and women-centered films that exercised a constant attraction for queer audiences. He consolidated his reputation as a director able to make his actors and actresses likely candidates for Oscars. In particular, the musical *A Star Is Born* (1954), his first film in color, an innovation that fascinated Cukor, represented a triumph for Judy Garland, who had not been able to work since her contract had been humiliatingly canceled by MGM. Cukor gave Garland the possibility of a major comeback with an Academy Award nomination for her performance. The fact that Garland lost to Grace Kelly was famously stigmatized as a robbery by Groucho Marx. Cukor himself won an Academy Award for Best Director in 1964 for *My Fair Lady*, starring Rex Harrison, who also won an Oscar, and Audrey Hepburn. The label of woman's director actually does not do full justice to Cukor, who, during the 1950s, also explored less theatrical and stylized techniques, giving some of his films, such as *The Marrying Kind* (1952), an almost neo-realist flavor.

Cukor's films are characterized by an attraction for impersonation, masquerading, and lying. The characters in the director's oeuvre often come from the world of showbiz and cinema itself, they are dreamers both on and off the stage. Yet, Cukor was aware that the relationships within such world could be fleeting and unstable at best. *A Star Is Born* illustrates Cukor's fascination with Hollywood and its dreams, and, at the same time, his awareness of the de-humanizing powers of the studio system. The relationship between two charismatic actors, played by Garland and James Mason, quickly becomes rivalry and ends in tragedy and death. The dreamers in Cukor's films have larger-than-life egos, but they often have to compromise with everyday reality. Only rarely, can two dreamers successfully team up to affirm their way of life, as the Cary Grant and Katharine Hepburn's characters do in *Holiday* (1938). As some critics have pointed out, Cukor's interest in this particular theme may stem from his queerness and his partially closeted existence. As many of the characters in his films, the filmmaker had to make compromises to reconcile his queer ego with the unwritten Hollywood rule of not openly talking about homosexuality.

In his private life and among his circle of friends, Cukor was well known for his love of a good life. He threw legendary pool parties and rivaled with Cole Porter for the title of "Queen of Hollywood." Cukor's parties became a distinctive feature of southern California gay life. Recent biographies of Cukor have, however, strongly emphasized the exploitative nature of these events, where rich and manipulative queens such as Cukor himself would meet young hustlers or aspiring artists, willing to trade sexual favors to gain entry into the world of Hollywood. The portrayal of the director emerging from these biographies is far from flattering, arguing that Cukor was perfectly able to separate his private and professional lives and was as skilful in directing actors as he was in manipulating people for his own ends. In the face of rampant homophobia that subjected gays and lesbians to the psychological pressure of having a public life based on falsehood, Cukor was instrumental in creating what historian John Loughery

(1998, 75) calls "a precious enclave, a world-within-the-world of Hollywood." This, Loughery continues (1998, 75), "was both a credible defensive measure and an unfortunate means of ensuring the system's control." As screenwriter Frank Mankiewicz remarks, "homosexuals would call George [Cukor] as soon as they arrived in Hollywood, and, if he liked them, he would introduce them to other members of the elite" (Loughery 1998, 75).

Cukor's last film, *Rich and Famous* (1983), was a remake of *Old Acquaintance* (1943). The original film starred Hollywood icon Bette Davis, while Cukor's remake banked on the strong performances and sex appeal of Jacqueline Bisset and Candice Bergen. The film focuses on the friendship between two women writers, the intellectual Liz Hamilton (Bisset) and the bestselling Merry Blake (Bergen), who become both literary and sentimental rivals. Under its heterosexual plot, *Rich and Famous* is, of all Cukor's films, that which best expresses a strong fascination with male bodies. It was famously attacked for expressing a gay sensibility by leading American film critic Pauline Kael, who strongly disliked it. The film, as Vito Russo (1987, 299) noted in his study *The Celluloid Closet* (1981), was one of the first to treat the male body as an object of desire. Bisset's love scenes with the young men she picks up are shown employing a point of view usually associated with a male gaze. Kael did not approve of the promiscuous behavior of the Bisset's character and wrote that "*Rich and Famous* isn't camp, exactly; it's more like a homosexual fantasy. Bisset's affairs, with their masochistic overtones, are creepy, because they don't seem like what a woman would get into" (Seligman 2005, *Salon.com*). Kael attributes Liz Hamilton's promiscuity to Cukor's gay sensibility "as though," as Vito Russo rebuts, "straight women have never been promiscuous or been given the permission to be promiscuous. So when George Cukor created one for the first time, Kael said they shouldn't be like that; it's homosexual; they're the ones who are promiscuous" (Seligman 2005, *Salon.com*). *Rich and Famous* has important connections with Cukor's homosexuality, not because of the creation of a promiscuous woman, but because of its reflections on "emotions associated with transient relationships, the role of friendships instead of family, sexual adventure, the privacy of intimate feelings and even the allure of young sex objects" (Russo 1987, 299). Because of the debate engendered by the movie, Cukor's own sexuality received some attention, although no explicit discussion was made. Cukor died safely in the closet on January 24, 1983, in Los Angeles, California.

Further Reading

Callahan, Dan. "George Cukor." *Senses of Cinema*. http://www.sensesofcinema. com/contents/directors/04/cukor.html#b1 (accessed on July 9, 2007); Ehrenstein, David. *Open Secret*. New York: Harper Perennial Library, 2000; Hadleigh, Boze. *Conversations with My Elders*. New York: St. Martin's Press, 1986; Lambert, Gavin. *On Cukor*. New York: Rizzoli, 2000; Levy, Emanuel. *George Cukor: Master of Elegance: Hollywood's Legendary Director and His Stars*. New York: William Morrow, 1994; Lippe, Richard. "Gender and Destiny: George Cukor's *A Star Is Born*." *CineAction* nos. 3–4 (January 1986): 46–57; Loughery, John. *The Other Side of Silence. Men's Lives and Identities: A Twentieth-Century History*. New York: Henry Holt & Company, 1998; McGilligan, Patrick. *George Cukor, a Double Life:*

A Biography of the Gentleman Director. New York: Harper Perennial, 1992; Russo, Vito. *The Celluloid Closet: Homosexuality in the Movies.* New York: Harper Paperbacks, 1987; Seligman, Craig. "The Gay Attacks on Pauline Kael." *Salon.com,* June 25, 2004. http://archive.salon.com/books/feature/2004/06/25/seligman/index_np.html (accessed on July 9, 2007).

CUNNINGHAM, MICHAEL (1952–)

In his fiction, Michael Cunningham has constantly challenged traditional views of gender roles, giving visibility to gay and lesbian alternatives to heterosexual families and relationships. Although his novels focus on themes of insecurity, isolation, death, and loss, they also show the power of the gay community to support its members. Cunningham always depicts homosexuals as part of the larger mainstream society and culture. Critical and public interest in Cunningham's work has soared since the publication of his Pulitzer Prize–winning novel *The Hours* (1998), which was on American and English bestseller lists for several weeks. It was also adapted into a successful film directed by Stephen Daldry in 2002, with an all-star cast including Meryl Streep, Nicole Kidman, Julianne Moore, and Ed Harris.

Michael Cunningham was born in Cincinnati, Ohio, in 1952 and grew up in La Canada, California. He attended Stanford University where he graduated with a B.A. in English in 1975. He got his M.F.A. in creative writing at the University of Iowa in 1980. He then moved to Provincetown, Massachusetts, to study at the Fine Arts Work Center. Since then, Cunningham has remained in Provincetown, a town to which he has also dedicated his non-fiction book *Land's End: A Walk through Provincetown* (2002). Cunningham's first short stories were published in the *Atlantic Monthly,* the *Paris Review,* and the *New Yorker.* Although Cunningham published a first novel, *Golden States,* in 1984, he has almost disowned it, preferring to remember his following work, *A Home at the End of the World* (1990), as his literary debut in the novel genre.

The book focuses on the love triangle between Jonathan, Bobby, and Clare, introducing the themes of loss and death which will become recurrent in Cunningham's fiction. As *A Home at the End of the World* centers on a triangle, it shows the different and unconventional forms that falling in love may take during the process of defining one's own identity. The narrative raises questions on how to interpret and use the legacy of the countercultural and liberated 1960s in our contemporary society. It is not perhaps a coincidence that the story starts just at the end of that decade, when Jonathan and Bobby meet in their Cleveland high school. The two are immediately drawn to each other, although their characters and social backgrounds could not be more different. As an adolescent, Jonathan is increasingly becoming aware of his homosexuality. He is finally getting to know that external world from which his loving parents have always sheltered him. Bobby, on the contrary, has never been sheltered by his family, but has been constantly scarred by it. He has already experienced the loss of his mother and his older brother. When his father dies too, Bob is virtually adopted by Jonathan's parents and the two boys begin to open up their isolated worlds to each other. Their friendship also becomes the occasion for experimenting sexually with each other. Their bond, however, does not develop into a romantic relationship. Jonathan moves to New York where he ends up living with the eccentric Clare, while Bobby remains with Jonathan's family. The two are reunited when Jonathan's parents retire to Arizona, and Bobby moves in with Clare and Jonathan. Although Jonathan is gay, Clare is the only person he has loved since leaving Cleveland. His encounters with other gay men have been limited to casual sex and he has avoided romantic involvement with them. The stability of the relationship between Clare and Jonathan is offset by Bobby's arrival as both of them feel attracted to the newcomer.

The balance between Bobby, Jonathan, and Clare is constantly precarious, but the book also emphasizes the constant commitment and devotion that temporarily reunite all the characters in a secluded home when Bobby and Clare have a baby. The extended family also includes Jonathan's former lover Erich, who has fallen ill with **AIDS**, and Alice, Jonathan's mother. *A Home at the End of the World* is told in the first person by Bobby, Jonathan, Clare, and Alice who, in turn, take the role of narrators, offering their perspectives on the events. The novel's title mirrors the ambiguous ending of Cunningham's narrative: the characters seem to find a home for themselves only under the shadow of death as Jonathan too may start soon to get sick with AIDS. While the male characters accept the presence of death in their lives, Clare rejects it and runs away with her baby from "the home at the end of the world" that she has helped to found. Thinking of Bobby's daughter, Clare wonders: "What if she came into her full consciousness as Erich died and Jonathan started to get sick? What would it do to her if her earliest memories revolved around the decline and the eventual disappearance of the people she most adored?" (Cunningham 2004, 322). On the contrary, Bobby muses that Jonathan and himself belong in the house at the end of the world, without Clare and without their daughter Rebecca: "Clare has taken Rebecca to the world of the living—its noises and surprises, its risk of disappointments.... We here are in the other world, a quieter place, more prone to forgiveness. I followed my brother into this world and I've never left it. Not really" (Cunningham 2004, 331).

The last section of the novel introduces the AIDS pandemic, showing not only the tragedy of the disease and the panic generated by it, but also the magnifying effects of homophobia on the crisis. As Erich puts it, his biological family has written him off. It is only thanks to his new extended and caring family made up of Jonathan and Bobby that he is able to face his death with dignity. *A Home at the End of the World* constantly challenges notions of what constitutes a family. It shows the flaws and the limitations of the traditional one but, at the same time, it depicts with honesty the instability that can affect an unconventional union such as the one between Jonathan, Bobby, and Clare. Cunningham has commented several times on the impact of AIDS into his life and also onto his writing. In an interview to the Italian gay monthly *Babilonia* (Gnerre 1999, 31), Cunningham has gone as far as saying that *A Home at the End of the World* and his subsequent novel *Flesh and Blood* (1995) were written for the people who were dying of AIDS and their caring friends. These people, Cunningham argues, were not interested in experimental literature, but in reading stories with which they could identify.

Flesh and Blood is a family saga which focuses on the lives of the Greek-American Constantine Stassos, his Italian-American wife Mary Cucci, and their three children: the beautiful Susan, the ambitious Billy, who is gay, and the rebel Zoe. As the conventional marriage of Constantine and Mary fails, their children find alternative families for themselves. Billy finds in Harry his life partner. Zoe raises her son, Jamal, with a transvestite until she dies of AIDS, and Jamal goes to live with Billy and Harry. Susan increasingly finds herself enmeshed into an improper relationship with her father and then trapped in a marriage which becomes as unsatisfactory as her parents'. Once again Cunningham challenges the standard notion of the family, showing two gay lovers bringing up a son more successfully than a traditional family. *Flesh and Blood* consolidated Cunningham's reputation as a novelist interested in bringing to life the complex psychological nuances of his characters. The novel received the Whiting Writers' Award and was later adapted for the stage by Peter Gaitens.

The comparatively traditional literary form of *A Home at the End of the World* and *Flesh and Blood* gives way to the more experimental postmodern narrative of Cunningham's third and most successful novel, *The Hours*. The book tells the stories of three women living in three different epochs, but whose existences are somehow deeply intertwined. Chronologically, the first narrative thread concerns Virginia Woolf while writing *Mrs. Dalloway*. The second portrays the life of Laura Brown, a depressed American housewife of the 1950s, whose existence is radically changed by her reading of Woolf's novel. The third story brings us to New York City in the 1990s, where Clarissa Vaughn, a lesbian who has a stable relationship with Sally, is organizing a party for her former lover, the gay poet Richard, Laura Brown's son. The poet has just received a major literary award and is dying of AIDS. *The Hours* evokes and pays homage to *Mrs. Dalloway* from its very title which Woolf had originally chosen for her own novel. The stories and characters of *The Hours* all mirror events and people in *Mrs. Dalloway* from the very start: both Clarissa Dalloway and Clarissa Vaughn are on an errand to buy flowers, and they are getting ready to host a party later in the day. While the female characters plunge into life in both novels, the poets, Septimus in *Mrs. Dalloway* and Richard in *The Hours*, both plunge towards death in the end. Both men have gone through catastrophic events: the First World War and AIDS (which Cunningham has, like many other writers, conceptualized through the metaphor of the war). True to Woolf, Cunningham also adopts the modernist technique of stream-of-consciousness narration, where the characters' thoughts seem apparently unfiltered and shift continuously as if in a mental flux. In addition, Cunningham's three stories take place during a single day, just like *Mrs. Dalloway*, because, the writer has argued in a *New York Times* article (2003, 22), "the whole human story is contained in every day of every life more or less the way the blueprint for an entire organism is present in every strand of its DNA." Cunningham appropriates Woolf's motifs such as flowers, mirrors, and kisses, as well as the themes of suicide, art, and identity to construct his own narrative.

As the rest of Michael Cunningham's oeuvre, *The Hours* prominently features gay and lesbian characters. Clarissa Vaughn is in a lesbian relationship with Sally, Richard Brown is gay. Virginia Woolf and Laura Brown cannot be strictly defined as lesbians, but they are attracted to other women. In the DVD commentary to the film based on *The Hours*, Cunningham states that if they had lived in a later period, both women would have identified as lesbians. The novel also blurs the boundaries between mental health and illness, as the readers are made to sympathize with Woolf's and Brown's plights.

Following the success of the movie version of *The Hours*, *A Home at the End of the World* was also adapted into a movie in 2004 scripted by Cunningham himself and directed by Michael Mayer in his film debut. Starring Colin Farrell (cast against type), Dallas Roberts, Robin Wright Penn, and Sissy Spacek, it failed to capture such a large audience as *The Hours*. The film was praised both for its subtle dialogues and for the actors' fine performances, although many pointed out that some of the novel's complexity had been lost due to the cuts necessary to reduce the almost four hundred pages of a story spanning four decades to a 90 minute film.

Cunningham's last literary effort to date, *Specimen Days* (2005), is again a triptych inspired by another literary figure, Walt Whitman. Employing the same set of characters in each novella (an older man, a young boy, and a young woman), Cunningham plays with the genre conventions of the ghost story, the noir thriller, and the sci-fi tale. All the stories take place in New York over a time span of several hundred years, beginning with the industrial revolution, continuing with the terrorist threats of the early twenty-first century and ending with an invasion of refugees from another planet in the future.

Further Reading

Cunningham, Michael. "The Hours Brought Elation, But Also Doubt." *New York Times*. Jan. 19, 2003. 22; Cunningham, Michael. *A Home at the End of the World*. New York: Picador, 2004; Gnerre, Francesco. *"Virginia Woolf, c'est moi. Intervista a Michael Cunningham." Babilonia*. November 1999. 30–31; Hughes, Mary Joe. "Michael Cunningham's *The Hours* and Postmodern Artistic Re-presentation." *Critique: Studies in Contemporary Fiction*. Summer 2004; Schiff, James. "Rewriting Woolf's Mrs. Dalloway: Homage, Sexual Identity, and the Single-day Novel by Cunningham, Lippincott, and Lanchester." *Critique: Studies in Contemporary Fiction*. Summer 2004; Woodhouse, Reed. "Michael Cunningham." *Contemporary Gay American Novelists: A Bio-Bibliographical Sourcebook*. Emmanuel S. Nelson, ed. Westport, CT: Greenwood Press, 1993. 83–88; Woodhouse, Reed. *Unlimited Embrace: A Canon of Gay Fiction, 1945–1995*. Amherst: University of Massachusetts Press, 1998.

D

DEAN, JAMES (1931–1955)

James Dean's premature death in a car crash after only three films made the enigmatic and androgynous actor a popular culture legend and icon, the subject of countless biographies, films, and plays. His delicate and brooding looks challenged predominant notions of masculinity in the conformist 1950s of the Eisenhower Presidency. In a political climate where individual rights were sacrificed in the name of the preservation of social standards, James Dean came to represent the rebellion against the status quo. He appealed to a whole generation of young men and women who took him as their hero and their model. Questions about Dean's sexual nonconformity have repeatedly surfaced through the decades. He was never explicitly identified as gay or bisexual, yet his relationships with several men are well documented. Whether or not Dean was aware of his queerness, he brought an unprecedented ambiguity to sex and sexuality. His masculine looks contrasted with the vulnerability of his screen and public persona, setting him apart from older stars such as John Wayne, Gary Cooper, and Clark Gable.

James Byron Dean was born February 8, 1931, in Marion, Indiana, to Winton and Mildred Dean. His father, a dental technician, moved with the family to Los Angeles when Jimmy was five. Dean returned to the Midwest after his mother passed away. He was only nine when his mother died and was then raised by his aunt and uncle on their Indiana farm. After high school, Dean returned to California enrolling at Santa Monica Junior College and UCLA. Throughout his school years, Dean took part successfully to talent contests and acting competitions. However, his mind remained set on his mother's death. In a short autobiographical sketch written in 1948, Dean wrote that he never knew the reason for his mother's death, a fact that continued to haunt him. The child had always felt rejected by his father, and his mother's death deprived him of the only person who cared for him. After returning to California, Dean started to pursue his acting career, joining James Whitmore's workshop and appearing in several TV commercials. He also obtained bit parts

James Dean as Jim Stark in *Rebel Without a Cause* (1955). Courtesy of Photofest.

in films and plays, mostly thanks to Rogers Brackett, an influential radio director for a prestigious advertising agency with whom Dean is rumored to have had an affair.

In 1951, Dean took Whitmore's advice and moved with Brackett to New York where he was admitted to Lee Strasberg's Actors Studio, the most prestigious and avant-garde acting school in the country. The actor wrote enthusiastically about his admission to the Actors Studio: "After months of auditioning, I am very proud to announce that I am a member of the Actors Studio. The greatest school of the theater. It houses great people like Marlon Brando, Julie Harris, Arthur Kennedy, Mildred Dunnock....Very few get into it, and it is absolutely free. It is the best thing that can happen to an actor. I am one of the youngest to belong. If I can keep this up and nothing interferes with my progress, one of these days I might be able to contribute something to the world" (Alexander 1997, 110). At Lee Strasberg's school, Dean learned method acting and his admission represented an important step forward in his career. The actor obtained a role in Richard Nash's *See the Jaguar* (1952), which had an unsuccessful run of only five performances, but allowed Dean to be noticed by critics and producers. He was then cast as an Arab boy who seduces an archeologist, Michel, during his honeymoon in the stage adaptation of André Gide's novel *The Immoralist*. When Elia Kazan, then the most respected director in Hollywood with his impressive string of commercial and critical hits, saw the actor's performance in the play, he decided that he wanted Dean in his next film. Warner Brothers were pleased with Dean's screen test for the adaptation of John Steinbeck's family drama *East of Eden* and signed him for the role of Cal Trask.

Dean could relate to the plot of *East of Eden*. One of the story lines concerns Cal's constant longing for his father's affection and approval. Such a quest is repeatedly frustrated given the man's stern and puritanical character. Dean's relationship with his own father was equally troubled, as Kazan felt after witnessing a father-son meeting: "Obviously, there was a strong tension between the two, and it was not friendly. I sensed the father disliked the son" (Alexander 1997, 153). The working relationship between Dean and Kazan was not devoid of serious arguments, but Dean managed to deliver an extremely mature performance that earned him a posthumous Academy Award nomination. The release of the film coincided with a Warner Brothers campaign to present its new leading star as virile and unmistakably heterosexual, the dream boyfriend American girls should aspire to. The up-and-coming Italian actress Anna Maria Pierangeli, usually billed and referred to as Pier Angeli, seemed the perfect date for Dean. Pictures of the couple began appearing in the popular press and the two rising stars stimulated media curiosity. A gossip column read: "James Dean has the lead in *East of Eden* and you'll be hearing of him soon. Pier Angeli, who isn't in the movie, has discovered him already" (Alexander 1997, 163). Another reporter asked Dean if they were planning on having kids together. Yet, one of Dean's biographers, Paul Alexander (1997), has pointed out that the extent to which Dean and Pier Angeli were involved with each other is unclear. He quotes an unnamed actor as saying that the relationship was a cover-up for Dean's homosexuality and thus entirely platonic. Dean himself described their relationship as "nothing complicated....Nothing messy, just an easy kind of friendly thing" (Alexander 1997, 163). In turn, he portrayed Pier Angeli as "a nice girl," someone with whom he could talk and who would understand his feelings. Yet, he also added: "I respect her. She's untouchable. We're members of totally different castes. She's the kind of girl you put on the shelf and look at" (Alexander 1997, 163). Pier Angeli herself qualified Dean as "different": "He loves music. He loves it from the heart the way I do. We have so much to talk about. It's wonderful to have such an understanding" (Alexander 1997, 163). This characterization clearly sets Dean apart from the rugged masculinity of his contemporary male leads. Whatever its nature, the relationship soon folded as Pier Angeli's mother, an influential and manipulating presence in the actress's life, disapproved of Dean. Pier Angeli abruptly broke off her relationship with Dean and hastily married singer Vic Damone.

Dean's second film, Nicholas Ray's *Rebel Without a Cause* (1955), established the actor as a Hollywood star and an enduring icon for the dissatisfied youth of 1950s American society. Released shortly after Dean's death, the film has since become a classic of teenage alienation, exploring the ever-widening rift between the younger and older generation. Dean plays Jim Stark, an adolescent unable to fit in the new Los Angeles neighborhood where his parents have moved to. In his attempts to do so, he gets into trouble with the local bully, Buzz. Although at the end of the film Jim falls in love with Judy (Natalie Wood), a girl who, like him, is looking for emotional stability, for most of the film he is involved in a tender and, in the end, tragic friendship with the younger Plato (Sal Mineo, himself a homosexual). The relationship between Jim and Plato, who adores his older friend and takes him as a role model, is clearly coded as a homosexual romance. Film critic Vito Russo (1987, 92) has taken the scene where Jim mourns over Plato's corpse as an example of gay sensibility, "a product of oppression, of the necessity to hide so well for so long....[a] ghetto sensibility, born of the need to develop and use a second sight that will translate silently what the world sees and what the actuality may be." Dean's muttering "Poor kid...he was always cold" over the dead body of his friend expresses "the unspoken, forbidden feelings that were always present, always denied" (Russo 1987, 92). Russo further elaborates that Jim Stark is torn between what society prescribes as masculine behavior and his attraction for men as well as for women. Jim, Plato, and Judy thus form a loving family relationship. Screenwriter Stewart Stern also detected a quest for affection in Jim and Buzz's antagonistic relationship. In *Rebel Without a Cause*, he wanted to show that "underneath all the bullshit macho defense, there was that pure drive for affection, and it didn't matter who the recipient might be. There was a longer time in those days for young men to be in the warrior phase, where a lot of romantic attachments were formed before heterosexual encounters" (Russo 1987, 110) Although the film exploits the stereotypical Hollywood solution of killing off the effeminate homosexual (the Mineo character), Stern's script pleaded for a redefinition of manhood: "I realize it was necessary to…redefine masculine behavior so that it was all right for a man to see tenderness as strength" (Russo 1987, 110). Stern concluded that, although Plato "would have been tagged as the faggot character" (Russo 1987, 110), Jim was willing to endanger his own popularity to protect his friend. Through his portrayal of Jim, Dean's screen persona challenged the rigid sexual and gender standards prescribed in 1950s America.

Dean's third and last screen role was in George Stevens's epic *Giant* (1955), co-starring Rock Hudson and Liz Taylor, and earned the actor his second consecutive posthumous Oscar nomination. Dean often disagreed with the choices of the director and disliked Hudson. As Paul Alexander (1997, 215) has pointed out, the feeling was mutual and probably due to the different ways of coping with their sexualities: "Dean and Hudson…were from opposite camps of the homosexual world. Jimmy would have hated Rock for his fey ways and his penchant for drag….Rock would have been threatened by Jimmy's edgy and unconventional personality even as he was attracted by his sweet boyish looks." While filming, Dean was romantically involved with actor Jack Simmons, but as the two kept a low profile, the studio did not have anything to complain about. Dean hated the shooting of *Giant* and, as soon as he finished filming, he left the set. Dean had always been a car race enthusiast and, shortly after finishing *Giant*, he decided to take part in a competition in Salinas. While driving there with his mechanic in his Silver Spyder Porsche, Dean had a car accident and died on September 30, 1955.

The international wave of emotion that followed Dean's untimely death made him an enduring symbol of American cinema. Dean soon developed a mass cult following and has remained one of the most visible pop culture icons throughout the decades. His appeal has remained untarnished by time. This is partly due to the mystery that still surrounds Dean's personality. Joe Hyams (1994), one of his biographers, has explained the star's lasting fame with his ability to express the hopes and fears that are a part of all young generations. According to Hyams (1994), Dean succeeded in dramatizing brilliantly the universal questions that young people must face. A fundamental part of his legacy was to begin to alter the prescribed notions of masculinity and the rigid distinctions in gender roles that characterized American society during the 1950s.

Further Reading

Alexander, Paul. *Boulevard of Broken Dreams: The Life, Times, and Legend of James Dean*. New York: Viking, 1997; Bast, William. *Surviving James Dean*. Fort Lee, NJ: Barricade Books, 2006; Dalton, David. *James Dean: American Icon*. New York: St. Martin's, 1984; Grant, Neil. *James Dean: In His Own Words*. London: Michelin House, 1991; Holley, Val. *James Dean: The Biography*. New York: St. Martin's Griffin, 1995; Hyams, Joe. *James Dean: Little Boy Lost*. New York: Random

House, 1994; Martinetti, Robert. *The James Dean Story*. New York: Pinnacle, 1975; Russo, Vito. *The Celluloid Closet: Homosexuality in the Movies*. New York: Harper and Row, 1981; Spoto, Donald. *Rebel: The Life and Legend of James Dean*. New York: Harper Collins, 1996.

DeGeneres, Ellen (1958–)

American comedian and TV host Ellen DeGeneres revolutionized the world of popular culture when she used an episode of her own sitcom *Ellen* to come out as a lesbian at the same time as her character on the show. She was the first openly gay person to play an openly gay character on TV, and she became an icon for the movement for gay and lesbian rights. Her highly publicized coming out made her political status as a militant activist for homosexual rights as significant as her screwball humor and her long monologues for the development of her career.

DeGeneres was born on January 26, 1958, in Metairie, Louisiana, and grew up in New Orleans together with her brother Vince and her middle-class parents who raised their children as Christian Scientists. When Ellen was 13, her parents divorced and she moved to Texas with her mother, who remarried. Ellen's stepfather abused her, an experience that her mother told in her book *Love, Ellen: A Mother/Daughter Journey* after obtaining her daughter's approval. In an interview with the ***Advocate*** (Wieder *Advocate* online, 2000), DeGeneres denied that being molested had anything to do with her being gay: "If you look at pictures of me when I'm 11 years old, wearing a tie when I'm playing, clearly I was gay. It had nothing to do with a bad experience with a man." While she was not too eager to talk about this painful memory, she also realized that it was important for a public person like her to address the issue: "the statistics are that one in three women have been molested in some way, and that's a pretty high statistic. And there should be more people talking about it; it shouldn't be a shameful thing. It never is your

Ellen DeGeneres hosting the 79th Annual Academy Awards. Courtesy of AMPAS/Photofest. Photography by Michael Yada.

fault. So I don't mind talking about it. He did horrible things to me and was a bad man" (Wieder *Advocate* online, 2000). It was also while living in Texas that the actress found she was attracted by women and had her first lesbian intercourse.

DeGeneres returned to New Orleans for university, majoring in communications. However, she dropped out after only one semester and held a variety of jobs including housepainter and waitress. She came to comedy almost by chance, starting to perform at friends' parties. DeGeneres was then asked to perform as a standup comedian at bars and coffee houses in the city and soon became the master of ceremonies of the then only comedy club in New Orleans, Clyde's Comedy Club. She began to tour throughout the country with her act and, in 1982, she won a cable television contest for the "Funniest Person in America." This allowed her to take part as a guest to several cable shows including *The Tonight Show* and *Arsenio Hall*. In the late 1980s and early 1990s, DeGeneres started her TV career, appearing in supporting roles in the sitcoms *Open House* (1989–1990) and *Laurie Hill* (1992), which ran for less than 10 episodes.

DeGeneres's chance to launch her career was provided by ABC which offered the comedian the leading role in the sitcom *These Friends of Mine*, partly inspired by the success of *Friends* and *Seinfeld*. Starting in 1994, the series changed its name to *Ellen* in its second season. As DeGeneres became a recognizable TV star, she felt disturbed by the widening gap between her public persona and her private lesbian life. Thus, in the third season of *Ellen*, DeGeneres took the decision to come out together with the character she played on the show. Contrary to most media personalities who decide to come out, DeGeneres took her step out of the closet using her own show and decided not to talk to the gay press about it. "The Puppy Episode," where Ellen came out to her therapist played by Oprah Winfrey, aired on April 30, 1997, and, thanks to a high-profile advertising campaign, it captured one of the largest TV audiences ever, almost 40 million watchers. Yet, after such peak, the ratings of the sitcom sank and viewers reacted badly to the increasing focus on Ellen's relationship with another woman. In spite of the Emmy Award for writing given to the coming out episode, ABC cancelled the show at the end of the following season.

"The Puppy Episode" had a decisive influence on DeGeneres's career and sparked debates on the presence of openly gay entertainers on prime-time television. In spite of her public coming out, some gay activists criticized DeGeneres for not being radical enough. In her first interview to the *Advocate* which took place only in March 2000, three years after her coming out, DeGeneres admitted that she did not give interviews to the gay press at that time because she was still unsure on how to identify: "I was still scared and feeling, Oh, do I want to just completely position myself as a gay person now? As much as I was labeling myself, I was afraid." DeGeneres also confessed that she did not intend to become an activist: "I really was just doing something I thought would be creative and also freeing for me" (Wieder *Advocate* online, 2000). Her coming out affected her family as well: her mother became one of her strongest supporters and a parent activist for queer rights. DeGeneres felt let down by ABC which, she charged, simply stopped advertising the show, and thereby effectively boycotting it.

DeGeneres received more media attention shortly after her coming out when she started a relationship with actress **Anne Heche**. The couple was often on the covers of tabloids and publicly claimed to be suffering from discrimination within the showbiz industry since they made their relationship public. After *Ellen* was cancelled, DeGeneres appeared regularly on the 1998 season of *Mad About You* and was one of the stars of Ron Howard's *EdTV* (1999). She also starred in the third episode of the HBO film *If These Walls Could Talk 2* (2000), where she plays opposite Sharon Stone as part of a lesbian couple trying to have a baby. In addition, HBO produced a special on her new 2000 stand-up tour. In 2001, DeGeneres returned to sitcoms with *The Ellen Show* on CBS. Her character was again a lesbian, but the show did not focus as strongly as the last season of *Ellen* on the character's sexuality. *The Ellen Show* was quickly cancelled as it failed to attract a considerable audience. However, the 2001 season saw her successful hosting of the Emmy Awards TV show, where she managed to find the right tone for such an event after the September 11 tragedy.

DeGeneres made a major comeback in 2003 when she lent her voice to a character in the highly successful Disney/Pixar animated film *Finding Nemo* and started a daytime television talk show, *The Ellen DeGeneres Show*. Its mixture of celebrity interviews, comic monologues by the host, and audience-participation games won good ratings and positive reviews. The show won two consecutive Emmys for Best Talk Show and Best Host. After Heche broke up with DeGeneres to marry cameraman Coley Laffoon, Ellen has been in relationships with photographer Alexandra Hedison and, currently, with actress **Portia De Rossi**.

In 2006, DeGeneres was chosen to host the 79th Academy Award Ceremony. Although her coming out was followed by a period of relative failures, DeGeneres seems to have fully returned to the public limelight and to personal success. Her coming out does not seem to have harmed her career, although it certainly made her a more political figure. Her public persona has helped to give visibility on television to gay and lesbian themes, particularly the crucial one of coming out.

Further Reading

DeGeneres, Betty. *Love, Ellen: A Mother/Daughter Journey*. New York: Rob Weisbach Books, 1999; Flint, Joe. "As Gay As It Gets? Prime-time Crusader Ellen DeGeneres Led TV into a New Era. But at What Cost to Her Show—And to Her?" *Entertainment Weekly* No. 430 (May 8, 1998): 26–32; Stockwell, Anne. "A Day in the Year of Ellen." Photos by Alexandra Hedison. *The Advocate* (January 18, 2005): 44–60; Tracy, Kathleen. *Ellen: The Real Story of Ellen DeGeneres*. Secaucus, NJ: Carol Publishing Group, 1999; Wieder, Judy. "Ellen: Born Again." *The Advocate* No. 807 (March 14, 2000): 28–33. http://www.highbeam.com/doc/1G1-60021910.html (accessed on April 7, 2007).

DE ROSSI, PORTIA (1973–)

Australian actress Portia De Rossi appeared in the critically acclaimed television series *Ally McBeal* and *Arrested Development*. Although she explicitly commented on her lesbianism only in a 2005 interview with the ***Advocate,*** De Rossi never denied her attraction for women. Even before the *Advocate* interview, she was on tabloid covers embracing her former partner, the singer Francesca Gregorini. As with many showbiz personalities, her lesbianism was an open secret. When De Rossi broke up with Gregorini in 2004 and got together with TV star Ellen DeGeneres, the media sensation that surrounded the new relationship made her one of the most visible lesbians within American popular culture.

De Rossi was born Amanda (Mandy) Lee Rogers on January 31, 1973, in Geelong in Victoria, Australia. Her father died of a heart attack when she was only eight years old and her mother had to take care of the family. At the age of 11, Mandy began her modeling career and, after a few years in the profession, changed her name to Portia De Rossi. She was soon aware of her attraction to other women, although she was not entirely comfortable with it. De Rossi partly ascribes the decision of changing her name to her being gay: "In retrospect, I think it was largely due to my struggle about being gay. Everything just didn't fit, and I was trying to find things I could identify myself with, and it started with my name" (Kort *Advocate* online, 2005) She also changed it to sound more European and, thus, more exotic on the Australian model scene. De Rossi started to have sexual intercourse with other women in high school: "They were straight women who I convinced to jump in the sack with me. I did a lot of fast talking as a youth; I was pretty good at it too....I just thought, This is so great and so interesting, and if only you knew how interesting this is and how great it feels! But these weren't real relationships with women who were gay—these were with women who were drunk!" (Kort *Advocate* online, 2005). After an unrequited crush on a fellow student, De Rossi graduated from high school and enrolled in law school at the University of Melbourne.

Yet, after only one year of academic studies, De Rossi was offered a role in the Australian film *Sirens* (1994), starring Hugh Grant and Sam Neil. Her performance earned the actress more TV and film parts. Soon De Rossi moved to Los Angeles to pursue her career. It was then that she became convinced that she must firmly remain in the closet to be a successful star. Although she identified as a bisexual, De Rossi admits that, for a long period of time, she would not even drive down Santa Monica Boulevard in the gay part of West Hollywood, in fear that someone would look in the car window and conclude that she was gay. In 1997, she was selected for the cast of Wes Craven's *Scream 2* and the following year she landed the role of Nelle Porter in *Ally McBeal*, Fox's popular comic series about an eccentric law firm. De Rossi stayed with the cast for the complete run of the show which ended in 2002. Although the series launched her career, De Rossi has mixed feelings about it. She felt the pressure that being a TV star put on her private life. Going to a lesbian coffeehouse the day before *Ally's* first episode was broadcast she remembers thinking that that was the last time she could be who she actually was. She also strongly disliked the exploitation of the lesbian theme in the episode where Calista Flockhart and Lucy Liu kiss: "I couldn't believe it, that whole episode—I hated it so much. It was just so upsetting to me as a gay woman" (Kort *Advocate* online, 2005). The huge pressure she felt because of the show caused her to have to struggle with anorexia for some time. After *Ally* was cancelled, De Rossi portrayed the vain heiress Lindsay Funke in another Fox series, *Arrested Development*, about a dysfunctional family. As for *Ally*, De Rossi remained in the cast until the end of the series in 2006.

De Rossi was briefly married to documentary filmmaker Mel Metcalfe, and she describes their relationship as deeply caring. Yet, her need to live her life as a lesbian was obviously in conflict with heterosexual marriage. De Rossi's relationship with singer Francesca Gregorini lasted for four years, until 2004, the year she met Ellen DeGeneres at a photo shoot. While De Rossi cared for Gregorini very much, she could not ignore her feelings for DeGeneres, who also split up with her long-time lover, the photographer Alexandra Hedison. Being together with DeGeneres obviously threw De Rossi's personal life into the spotlight. The actress finally relinquished her policy not to talk about her sexual orientation and started to give honest interviews about her lesbianism.

Further Reading

Anderson-Minshall, Diane. "Whatever Happened to Her?" *Curve* 12.4 (2001): http://www.curvemag.com/Detailed/447.html (accessed on February 7, 2007); Bennett, Sarah. "The Portia de Rossi Guide to Public Relations." *Afterellen*. http://www.afterellen.com/People/portia.html (accessed on February 7, 2007); Griffin, Nancy. "Flights of Fancy." *In Style* 9.4 (April 1, 2002): 410–13; Kort, Michele. "Portia Heart and Soul." *The Advocate* (September 13, 2005): 40–47. http://www.advocate.com/issue_story_ektid20037.asp (accessed on February 7, 2007); Lee, Luaine. "Portia de Rossi Definitely Is Not a Case of 'Arrested Development.'" *Knight Ridder/Tribune News Service* (November 3, 2003); Shaw, Jessica. "Portia Control." *Entertainment Weekly* 793 (November 19, 2004) 34–35.

DIVINE (1945–1988)

American drag artist Divine first attained success in the late 1960s and early 1970s with his appearances in **John Waters**'s early films such as *Pink Flamingos* (1972). He then went on to become an icon of gay and lesbian popular culture with his portrayal of outrageous women in camp shows. The 300-pound actor soon developed an international cult following for his ability to overturn bourgeois sexual and social morality thanks to his uncontrollable and anarchic energy. Although success made Divine an acceptable figure within mainstream culture too, the drag entertainer never forgot his gay fans: "They are the ones who gave me my start in show business. They're the one who supported me from the beginning. No matter what happens I will always play to them. That's just plain and simple" (Judell 1994, 37).

Born Harris Glenn Milstead on October 19, 1945, in Towson, Maryland, Divine grew up in Baltimore suburbs, where he first met future director John Waters. Two queers who could not fit in the sanitized world of American suburbia, the two became instant friends. "We were all kids trying to get away from suburbia," Waters recalls. "We all met downtown. It was gay people, it was straight people. Black and white. Left-wing political people and drag queens.... That was very important in our development of 'cinema rebellion.'... When Divine was young, he was preppy-ish. He was not at all flamboyant. Underneath all that was an anger. With Divine's

Divine as Babs Johnson, "the filthiest person alive," in John Waters's *Pink Flamingos.* Courtesy of Fine Line Features/ Photofest.

partnership, I came up with this character that was very very different from Glenn Milstead" (Rothaus 2001, *Knight Ridder* online).

Waters gave Divine his stage name. As the drag artist later explained, Waters always thought that inside him there was a divine person. Divine became part of Waters's Dreamlanders, the cast and crew of regulars that the director has used in his films. He appeared in Waters's films since his early 8mm *Roman Candles* (1966) and subsequently in his first 16mm feature *Eat Your Makeup* (1968). Divine also took part in *Mondo Trasho* (1969), which almost caused the arrest of the entire troupe for illegally shooting a scene involving a nude hitchhiker on the campus of Johns Hopkins University. However, the film that made Divine an underground star was Waters's *Pink Flamingos,* where the drag queen plays Babs Johnson, "the filthiest person alive," whose family successfully counters the vicious attacks of a rival criminal family, the Marbles. Called by the director himself "an exercise in poor taste," *Pink Flamingos* made Divine the protagonist of some shocking scenes. Her character performs oral sex on her son, urinates in public, steals meat by putting it in between her legs, and, most infamously, eats dog's feces. Divine continued his collaboration with Waters starring in his next film, *Female Trouble* (1974), where he plays Dawn Davenport, a criminal and a professional beauty. In the film, Divine also plays the role of an old maniac who sexually assaults Dawn. Just as *Pink Flamingos, Female Trouble* contains shocking scenes that center on the Divine character. Dawn, for example, kills her own daughter and is, in turn, executed on the electric chair.

In 1972, the same year *Pink Flamingos* was shot, Divine left his parents' house and was not reconciled with them until years later. At the time, Divine's mother Frances and his father were living in Fort Lauderdale, Florida, and a colleague of Frances's invited Frances to a show of the famous female impersonator named Divine. According to Frances, that was the first time she had known about her son's drag acts, although she had long worked out the fact that he was gay. The unexpected meeting brought about a family reconciliation.

Make-up artist and costume designer Van Smith was responsible for the creation of the Divine look in Waters's films. Such a look set new standards for drag impersonators that lasted long after Divine's sudden death. At the time when Divine started to make movies with Waters, drag queens reacted badly to a character so completely different from their own quieter images. Contrary to most drag queens of the period, Divine displayed make-up and clothes considered in bad taste. The Divine look was composed of three distinctive features: the hair was shaved back to the crown to leave more room for eye makeup; the makeup itself was extremely heavy with tons of eye shadow, arch eyebrows, long lashes, and a huge scarlet mouth; and the outrageous clothes, such as the red fishtail dress in *Pink Flamingos*, were the third characteristic element. Shimmering and skintight dresses gave Divine a larger-then-life, and aggressive female sensuality. Divine was instrumental in creating the image of camp, glittery decay that pervades John Waters's films.

Thanks to the success of *Pink Flamingos* and *Female Trouble*, Divine became a gay celebrity and also began singing in discos, first in San Francisco and then worldwide. In 1985 he released two hit singles, "Walk Like a Man" and "I'm So Beautiful." In the 1980s Divine also became a regular guest on TV shows. Yet, he also started to feel anxious for his artistic career, hoping for wider recognition both as a drag and character actor. Director Alan Rudolph offered him a role out of drag as a gangster in his *Trouble in Mind* (1985), which, however, failed at the box office. According to his agent and biographer Bernard Jay, Divine also grew increasingly tired of his life on the road and demanded more luxuries during his tours. The more expensive lifestyle meant a decrease in its net receipts while his private expenditures were growing at an alarming rate. The artist soon found himself embroiled in financial difficulties and also became worried about his weight. Jay reports a conversation where Divine confessed to him that he felt depressed both about his professional and private life: "I work and work and work dragging this ugly body around the world. And at the end of it all there's no money and no lover to go back home to" (Jay 1993, 213). Divine seemed worried about being forever trapped in the drag that had made him famous and not to be accepted by showbiz as a well-rounded artist: "They will never accept me....I hate what I am doing now. There's no fun left in these shows. It's the same old thing night after night....I am going to spend the rest of my life putting on the fucking dress and jumping up and down to stupid songs, making a fool of myself" (Jay 1993, 213).

Paradoxically, Divine's death came just when he was being accepted by mainstream film and television industry. After years of depression and worries in the mid-1980s, the actor made a major comeback in 1988 with another John Waters's film, *Hairspray*. As in *Female Trouble*, Divine plays a double role, one male and one female. The movie, and Divine's performance in particular, received rave reviews. *Hairspray* was a hit, bringing Divine to a mass audience and critics defined him as a star: "If the true test of a star," wrote one (Jay 1993, 239), "is that when he is on screen it is impossible to look at anyone else, then Divine is truly a star." The critical acclaim and the commercial success that surrounded the movie opened up new possibilities in Divine's career. Among other things, he was also offered a double role in Fox's long-running sitcom *Married...With Children*. Yet, just as the actor was preparing to begin his acting in the sitcom, he died in his sleep at 42 years of age in Los Angeles on March 7, 1988. Divine's talent, however, has continued to appeal to successive audiences, who have been able to discover his performances thanks to video and DVD releases. The artist has finally managed to reach beyond the queer communities. Best remembered for his extreme performances and his quest for stardom, Divine was actually a mixture of excess and more serious over-tones. In the obituary written for the **Advocate**, Brandon Judell (1994, 37) wrote that Divine's fans never realized what a "subdued soul" the actor really had: "Often wearing caftans that flowed about his ample frame, the quiet actor was the anti-thesis of his on-screen persona of sex-mad, evil-loving, big-bosomed sex goddess. He revealed this side of himself when I asked if he'd pose for a photograph mugging in character. 'That's just not me, honey,' he laughed. 'That's just a character I do. I'd look like a big fruit. I am actually a serious person. I'm shy.'"

Further Reading

Bernard, Jay. *Not Simply Divine: Beneath the Make-Up, Above the Heels and Behind the Scenes with a Cult Superstar*. New York: Simon & Schuster, 1993; Judell, Brandon. "Parting Words from a Divine Legend." *Long Road to Freedom: The Advocate History of the Gay and Lesbian Movement*. Thompson, Mark, ed. New York: St. Martin's Press, 1994. 337; Milstead, Frances, Kevin Heffernan, and Steve Yeager. *My Son Divine*. Los Angeles: Alyson Books, 2001; Rothaus, Steve. "Divine's Mom Looks Back on His Life, Career." *Knight Ridder Tribune* on-line. December 17, 2001. http://www.highbeam.com/doc/1G1-80874314.html (accessed on April 7, 2007); Waters, John. *Shock Value*. New York: Thunder's Mouth, 1981.

E

ETHERIDGE, MELISSA (1961–)

Academy and Grammy Award-winning singer and songwriter Melissa Etheridge has successfully combined her iconic status as a queer activist for gay and lesbian rights with a more mainstream position as a popular performer. Etheridge came out as a lesbian during President Clinton's first inauguration in January 1993 and, since then, has served as a model of activism for the queer community.

Etheridge was born in Leavenworth, Kansas, on May 29, 1961, from John Etheridge, a math teacher at the local high school, and Elizabeth Williamson Etheridge, a computer analyst for the U.S. Army at Fort Leavenworth. As a child she was fascinated by music and her parents encouraged Melissa's passion, buying her a guitar and sending her to music lessons. She was indeed a precocious musician giving her first public performance at a talent show when she was 11 and starting to sing with country and western adult groups by the age of 12. After graduating from high school, Etheridge enrolled at the Berklee College of Music in Boston. At Berklee she had the opportunity to explore her sexuality as she shared her room with a lesbian who introduced her to Boston's lesbian scene. However, Etheridge soon found that Boston was not well suited for her rock and roll ambitions and decided to go back to Leavenworth to earn enough money to go to Los Angeles, a city which she felt was a better choice to launch her music career. Back in her hometown, the singer worked as music assistant at the Army chapel and began dating other lesbians to the dismay of her mother who reacted particularly badly. She advised her daughter to seek treatment for her "psychological illness" and forbade her to bring women home if she wanted to carry on living with her parents. Her father was more supportive and Melissa came out to him when she finally left for Los Angeles, just before her twenty-first birthday.

In Los Angeles Etheridge stayed with an aunt, but she also got in touch with two paternal uncles who turned out to be gay and introduced her to the city's gay scene. Her musical talents soon earned her jobs in bars in the Los Angeles area where Etheridge developed a loyal following. One of her fans, Karla Leopold, persuaded

Melissa Etheridge at the 79th Annual Academy Awards. Courtesy of AMPAS/Photofest. Photograph by Matt Petit.

her husband Bill, a music manager, to represent Etheridge. It was difficult for Etheridge to find a label willing to offer a record contract and the singer had to wait until 1986 when Island Records founder, Chris Blackwell, decided to sign her for his label. Still, *Melissa Etheridge*, her first album, was hard to produce. Blackwell disliked the first version and tried to force more pop elements in it. Etheridge re-recorded the material and this second version eventually met with Blackwell's approval. The debut album came out in 1988 and met with good reviews which favorably compared Etheridge to Janis Joplin, a clear influence on the artist's music. Bruce Springsteen was also influential for the development of Etheridge's style. Her first album also brought Etheridge her first important romantic relationship. While shooting the video for the song "Bring Me Some Water," Etheridge met Julie Cypher, who was the project's associate director. There was an immediate attraction between the two women, although Cypher was then still married to actor Lou Diamond Phillips. Cypher eventually separated from Phillips and moved in with Etheridge. The singer's professional life flourished too: "Bring Me Some Water" was nominated for a Grammy Award, and both *Melissa Etheridge* and *Brave and Crazy* (1989), her second album, went platinum, selling a million copies.

Etheridge actively campaigned for Bill Clinton during his first Presidential race and, in January 1993, she was invited along with Cypher to the inauguration. While attending the Triangle Ball, the first inaugural event for gays and lesbians, Etheridge addressed the crowd by publicly stating that she was proud to say she was a lesbian. Her coming out did not damage the artist's career. During the same year, she won her first Grammy for "Ain't It Heavy" from her third album *Never Enough* (1992). Etheridge's fourth album, *Yes, I Am* (1993) was her most commercially profitable feature to date selling over 6 million copies and earning her another Grammy for the song "Come to My Window." With her increasing acceptance by the mainstream, Etheridge did not forsake her queer community. On the contrary, she used her success to campaign for GLBTQ rights such as same-sex unions and gay parenting. The ***Advocate*** appointed her Person of the Year for 1995 and the following year she appeared on a *Newsweek* cover for an issue devoted to gay families. Cypher and Etheridge contacted sperm donor David Crosby, and Cypher gave birth to the couple's two children in February 1997 and in November 1998.

In 2000, at the height of the singer's success and visibility as a lesbian icon, Etheridge and Cypher separated amicably and bought houses next to each other so that the children could still see both of them whenever they wished. Etheridge's 2001 album *Skin* reflects the sorrow for the break-up. In 2002, however, Etheridge met her new partner, actress Tammy Lynn Michaels, and the two artists exchanged wedding vows the following year in a ceremony presided by a non-denominational Agape Church minister. With Michaels at her side, Etheridge successfully battled against breast cancer for which she was diagnosed in 2004. She made a triumphant comeback on the music scene at the 2005 Grammy Awards Ceremony, going on stage bald from chemotherapy and performing "Piece of My Heart" with Joss Stone. Etheridge used her experience as a breast cancer survivor for the moving song "I Run for Life," which portrays a woman's successful battle against breast cancer. After the tragedy of cancer, Etheridge received more prestigious awards and experienced more personal joys. In April 2006 she was honored with the Stephen F. Kolzak Award at the annual GLAAD Media Awards. The prize is given to an openly gay member of the media and entertainment community for his or her work in defeating homophobia. In the same month, Etheridge and Michaels announced that Michaels was expecting twins conceived through artificial insemination. A daughter and a son were born in October 2006. In 2007, Etheridge's "I Need to Wake Up," her contribution to the soundtrack of the environmentalist Al Gore-moderated documentary *An Inconvenient Truth* (2006), earned her an Academy Award for Best Song.

In spite of being a champion of gay rights, Etheridge has always been careful to keep her music apart from her political campaigns. She has never written an explicitly lesbian love song, opting for a general and genderless "you" to address the beloved. The singer departed from this choice of keeping queer politics out of her music in 1998 when the murder of Matthew Shepard prompted her to write "Scarecrow," which condemned the homophobia that had led to the youth's death. The aim of Etheridge's music remains to be able to communicate emotions to people, regardless of their sexual orientation.

Further Reading

Etheridge, Melissa, and Laura Morton. *The Truth Is…My Life in Love and Music.* New York: Villard, 2001; Nickson, Chris. *Melissa Etheridge.* New York: St. Martin's Griffin, 1997; Wieder, Judy. "Melissa Etheridge: *The Advocate*'s Person of the Year on 1995's Battles, Triumphs, and Controversies." *The Advocate* 698/699 (January 23, 1996): 64–65.

EVERETT, RUPERT (1959–)

British film star Rupert Everett has been openly out as gay since 1989. He has helped to challenge popular stereotypes about homosexuality and has fought against Hollywood's suspicion of gay male actors. While the first part of Everett's career predominantly developed in Europe, the international success of *My Best Friend's Wedding* (1997) made him a well-known popular culture icon in the United States. Thanks to that box office hit, American media started to hunt for details of Everett's private life and frequently published accounts of Everett's life in Hollywood with his best friends Julia Roberts, Madonna, and other stars. Since then, Everett has come across as a confident and fulfilled gay star, although he has also repeatedly stated that Hollywood homophobia has cost him several roles. In spite of his uneven career, characterized by incredible successes and embarrassing flops, Everett has shown a remarkable versatility as an actor being comfortable in comic and dramatic roles both in European and American productions.

Everett was born into an upper-class British family on May 29, 1959, in Norfolk. He received his education at the Catholic college of Ampleforth in York from the age of seven. Everett's family was extremely right wing and traditional. Such background clashed with the boy's consciousness from the age of 1 to 10 to be "a seasoned cross-dresser." "I used to be taken out on these very macho things like hunting," the actor recalls (Glitz 2004, *Advocate* online), "and I would just be

Rupert Everett (right) and Madonna (left) in John Schlesinger's *The Next Best Thing*. Courtesy of Paramount Pictures/Photofest.

dreaming of being home and trying on my mother's nightdress." Everett was interested in theater from his adolescence and, at age 15, he left Ampleforth to attend the Central School for Speech and Drama in London, where he funded his acting education partly working as a male escort. The Central School dismissed him on grounds of insubordinate behavior and Everett completed his drama education in Scotland at the Glasgow Citizens' Company. The actor always took as role models controversial and troubled stars such as Marlon Brando, James Dean, and Montgomery Clift: "You felt they had experienced everything.... Their eyes were shocked and dead and alive and glowing like coals at the same time. And I think that was through experience, using your life as a tool. That's the way I wanted to conduct myself."

His breakthrough role was that of the British gay spy Guy Bennett (loosely based on Guy Burgess) in Julian Mitchell's play *Another Country* (1982), where Everett played opposite Kenneth Branagh. Everett also starred as Bennett in the film adaptation of the play directed by Marek Kanievska in 1984. He received more critical praise for the role of David Blakely in Mike Newell's biopic of Ruth Ellis, the last British woman to be executed in the United Kingdom. Orson Welles was so impressed by Everett's performances that he wanted the actor to star as himself in the movie adaptation of *The Cradle Will Rock*, which, however, collapsed just three weeks before filming. Everett then starred in a series of art-house releases such as Andrei Konchalovski's *Duet for One* (1986), Francesco Rosi's *Chronicle of a Death Foretold* (1987), based on a novel by Nobel Prize winner Gabriel Garcia Marquez, and Giuliano Montaldo's *The Gold Rimmed Spectacles* (1987). Thanks to these appearances, Everett became a well-known European actor and he also inspired Italian comic book author Tiziano Sclavi to create the horror investigator Dylan Dog. These films, however, failed to make Everett a Hollywood star. The actor thought his chance had come with Richard Marquand's *Hearts of Fire* (1987), a film conceived as a vehicle for singer Bob Dylan. However, the movie was a disastrous flop, suffering from an extremely limited theater run and from continuous rewritings of the script. Rumors of Everett's arrogance and unreliability on sets began to surface.

The box office failure of *Hearts of Fire* prompted Everett to return to the stage, where he played in drag the role of Flora Goforth, a dying woman remembering her life, in **Tennessee Williams**'s play *The Milk Train Doesn't Stop Here Anymore*. Everett also began a career as a novelist, publishing his first book, *Hello, Darling, Are You Working*, while living in Paris. Everett's decision to come out in 1989 was criticized by some as damaging for his chances of finding new film roles. Yet, it was shortly after that announcement that Everett's acting career was revitalized. In 1991, Everett obtained one of the leading roles in Paul Schrader's *The Comfort of Strangers*, based on the novel of Ian McEwan. Everett's return to success, however, was triggered by his participation as a character actor rather than as a lead in the critically acclaimed films *Prêt-à-Porter* (1994) by Robert Altman and *The Madness of King George* (1994) by Nicholas Hytner.

It was thanks to a more commercial film that Everett finally attained the role of Hollywood star. J.P. Hogan's *My Best Friend's Wedding* (1997) made Everett an overnight sensation. Playing the gay best friend of the Julia Roberts character, Everett became the main attraction for audiences. After initial previews of the movie, the positive response to the gay best friend embodied by the British actor was so unanimous that the producer and the director decided to shoot almost

20 more minutes with Everett. His character was not yet again another Hollywood gay sidekick. On the contrary, it challenged the flat comic representations of gayness, showing subtleness and appeal. After such a spectacular hit, Everett returned to elegant costume dramas such as the Academy Award–winning *Shakespeare in Love* (1998), where he played Marlowe, *An Ideal Husband* (1999), based on Oscar Wilde's play, and in the Shakespearean adaptation *Midsummer Night's Dream* (1999).

At the summit of his Hollywood fame, Everett embarked on a more personal and risky project which eventually resulted in the disappointing *The Next Best Thing* (2001). The film, directed by veteran gay director **John Schlesinger** and co-starring gay icon Madonna, centers on alternative families. Everett plays Robert, a gay man who fathers a child after a drunk one-night stand with his best friend Abbie (Madonna). The two begin to raise the child together, but, as another man enters Abbie's life, Robert decides to fight for custody. Everett put all his enthusiasm in the project, firmly believing that his own sexuality could give the character of Robert greater depth than that afforded by other celluloid gays. Yet, he was the first to be disappointed by the result. As Everett has recounted in interviews, *The Next Best Thing* did not start under the best of auspices. Everett did not like the original screenplay where Robert was an "overweight gay...whose answer to everything was to squirt cream in your mouth—a token acceptable Hollywood fag" (Hoggard 2004, *Independent* online), who, obviously, had no sex life whatsoever. Everett then started to rewrite the screenplay, although he had to compromise with the production. Robert, for example, still does not have much of a sex life in the film even after the rewrite. In addition, as the actor has admitted, the choice of Schlesinger for director was a wrong one. In the end, the movie was a "serious disaster," increasingly turning into a miniseries rather than the ambitious film of social critique that Everett had set out to make. Everett also went to arbitration for writing credits but lost. Since the failure of *The Next Best Thing*, Everett has continued to appear in important films, often in heterosexual roles as both lead and character actor. These include *The Importance of Being Earnest* (2002), *To Kill a King* (2003), the TV series *Les Liaisons Dangereuses* (2003), as well as the arthouse releases *Quiet Flows the Don* (2004) and *Stage Beauty* (2004), where Everett has a fantastic drag scene. He has also played Sherlock Holmes in the TV movie *Sherlock Holmes and the Case of the Silk Stocking* (2004) and has contributed his voice to the second and third chapters of *Shrek* and to *The Chronicles of Narnia* (2005).

Because Everett is a highly visible and openly out gay actor, he has stimulated debates in the media on how believable gay actors can be in heterosexual roles. Although Everett has successfully played gay roles, he does not want to be confined in those parts as he refuses to be cast solely as an upper-middle class Englishman (a belief that probably led him to turn down the Daniel Day Lewis's role in James Ivory's *A Room with a View*). Everett does not regret his coming out. Yet, both in his memoir *Red Carpets and Other Banana Skins* (2007) and in interviews, he has pointed out that his sexuality has caused him to lose important film parts, especially the lead in *About a Boy* (2002) which eventually went to his fellow countryman Hugh Grant. In a 2004 interview to the ***Advocate***, Everett took a particularly critical stance against Hollywood homophobia, saying that, although he is happy to have come out, he would not recommend other people in showbiz to do so: "Not in a trophy business like Hollywood. I don't think it's ideal. I think it's very lucky for me to have been

English and to have the opportunities to work in all the various different places that I could so I could keep going. French cinema, Italian cinema, theater, English movies, and getting a Hollywood one if I can" (Glitz 2004, *Advocate* online). As he turns middle age, Everett is becoming more critical of the glitz that surrounds the film industry and its stars. He is devoting an increasingly large part of his time to important political causes against **AIDS**, tuberculosis, and malaria.

Further Reading

"Bonbons with a Bitter Center. Rupert Everett's Memoirs Give an Edge to Hollywood Anecdotes." *Quad-City Times*. Sunday, October 1, 2006. http://www.qctimes.com/articles/2006/10/01/features/arts_leisure/doc451f40662d979310398663.txt (accessed on December 2, 2006); Everett, Rupert. *Red Carpets and Other Banana Skins: The Autobiography*. New York: Warner Books, 2007; Glitz, Michael. "Rupert's Return." *The Advocate*. November 9, 2004. http://www.advocate.com/issue_story_ektid02399.asp (accessed on December 2, 2006); Hoggard, Liz. "Prince Charming." *The Independent*. August 21, 2004. http://arts.independent.co.uk/film/features/article52377.ece (accessed on December 2, 2006).

F

Fierstein, Harvey Forbes (1954–)

Harvey Fierstein occupies a prominent position in gay and lesbian popular culture thanks to his award-winning performances of drag queens and homosexual characters as well as for his critically acclaimed plays. His work as an actor and playwright is closely linked to his outspoken support of gay rights. Fierstein has used both his acting and writing skills to depict people outside the boundaries of dominant society and their struggles to come to terms with mainstream culture. Fierstein himself seems to have made the transition from the New York avant-garde theaters of his debut to the mainstream productions of his maturity.

Fierstein was born on June 6, 1954, in Brooklyn, New York, from Jewish-American parents, Irving, a handkerchief manufacturer, and Jacqueline, a school librarian. Harvey was aware of his homosexuality at a very early age and came out to his supportive family at the age of 13. When he was still an adolescent, Harvey started a career as a drag queen in Manhattan gay clubs. His ease with the stage allowed him to land a role in Andy Warhol's *Pork* at La Mama Experimental Theatre in 1971. Two years later Fierstein earned a BFA in painting from the Pratt Institute.

Fierstein launched his career as a playwright in the early 1970s when his first plays, *In Search of the Cobra Jewels* and *Flatbush Tosca*, were performed in small venues. It was during the 1970s that Fierstein started to work on material that would finally become *Torch Song Trilogy* (1981). La Mama produced the early versions of the plays in 1978 and 1979. The three pieces were performed together off Broadway in 1981 and the production soon moved to Broadway, earning the playwright his first two Tony Awards (best performance and best play) and catapulting him to fame. *Torch Song Trilogy*, which also won an Obie Award and several other prestigious prizes, ran for almost three consecutive years at New York's Little Theatre (now the Helen Hayes Theatre) and was adapted into a film directed by Paul Bogart starring Fierstein himself, Matthew Broderick, and Anne Bancroft. *Torch Song Trilogy* is composed of three sections: "The International Stud," "Fugue in a Nursery," and "Widows and Children First!" They all tell different parts in the life of a Jewish drag performer, Arnold Beckhoff, who particularly specializes in torch songs, sentimental tunes where the singer laments an unrequited or lost love. In "The International Stud," Arnold falls in love with Ed, a bisexual who first returns his feelings, but then leaves him for a woman. "Fugue in a Nursery" chronicles the love story between Arnold and Alan, a model. They settle down together and decide to adopt a son, but Alan is killed in an homophobic attack. The third part, "Widows and Children First!," focuses on the relationship between Arnold and his mother, who criticizes him for his decision to adopt a son and to bury Alan in the family tomb. However, the act ends on a note of reconciliation.

Arnold is clearly identified as both gay and Jewish, although his sexual orientation, rather than his ethnicity, is the focus of the play. When Arnold's mother makes her appearance in the third act, the play does center on Jewishness more distinctly. Yet, as critics have pointed out, Mrs Beckhoff is not so much a well-rounded character as an amusing stereotype, a summary of all the neuroses usually associated with Jewish mothers in popular culture. The play also establishes a connection between queer-bashing and the persecution of Jews at the hands of the Nazis in the 1930s and 1940s. In spite of the unanimous praise heaped on both the play and the film, some queer critics find Fierstein's work disturbing. They take issue, for example, with the representation Fierstein gives of gay relationships, which seem to them to be too closely modeled after heterosexuals patterns. The gay characters in *Torch Song Trilogy* and in other Fierstein's plays want monogamous same-sex relations. Although Fierstein's characters lie outside the mainstream, they long for assimilation in it and eventually do so.

After the success of *Torch Song Trilogy*, Fierstein scored another hit: he wrote the libretto for the musical **La Cage Aux Folles** (1983). This earned him his third Tony Award. He also continued writing plays such as *Spookehouse* (1984), *Safe Sex* (1987), which reprises the same structures of three one-acts as *Torch Song Trilogy*, and *Forget Him* (1988), a one-act where a gay Jew finally finds a boyfriend in a synagogue. Fierstein's plays have continued to blend comfortably both a realistic and an experimental mode of writing. In 1988, Fierstein was hired to revise the libretto for a new musical about the gangster *Legs Diamond* (1988), which, like *La Cage Aux Folles*, was produced by Marvin Krauss. *Legs Diamond*, however, did not repeat the success of the latter show and was also embroiled in a lawsuit when choreographer Michael Shawn claimed he had been dismissed by Krauss because he had **AIDS**.

In the 1980s and 1990s, Fierstein started to appear in films such as Sidney Lumet's *Garbo Talks* (1984), Chris Columbus's *Mrs. Doubtfire* (1993), Woody Allen's *Bullets Over Broadway* (1994), and the blockbuster *Independence Day* (1996). He guest starred in episodes of the successful TV series *Miami Vice, Ellen, Cheers*, and *Murder She Wrote*. He also lent his voice for characters in *The Simpsons* and the animated Disney feature *Mulan* (1998). In 2000 he contributed to the Showtime movie *Common Ground*, a film focusing on the lives of gays and lesbians in a small Connecticut town in the 1950s, 1970s, and in 2000. Fierstein wrote and acted in "Amos and Andy," the last chapter of the movie, where a father has to come to terms with the intention of his son Amos to marry another man. The segment ends on a father-son reconciliation. Fierstein returned to Broadway in 2002 where he starred in the musical *Hairspray* based on the **John Waters** film of the same name. On stage, he had the role of Edna Turnblad that was played on the screen by the legendary drag queen **Divine**. This drag performance won Fierstein his fourth Tony Award and unanimous acclaim for his ability to portray drag queens outside the usual stereotypes of the wretched victim or the excessive diva.

In his plays, acting roles and public speeches, Harvey Fierstein has always made clear that difference, including sexual difference, should be valorized and not hidden. Although he has been accused of pandering to heterosexual models of relationships and of preaching assimilation, it should also be pointed out that his characters are not segregated from mainstream society. They eventually take an active part in it without renouncing their sexual identities.

Further Reading

Clum, John M. *Acting Gay: Male Homosexuality in Modern Drama*. New York: Columbia University Press, 1992; Cohen, Jodi R. "Intersecting and Competing Discourses in Harvey Fierstein's *Tidy Endings*." *Quarterly Journal of Speech* 77 (May 1991): 196–207; de Jongh, Nicholas. *Not in Front of the Audience: Homosexuality on Stage*. London: Routledge, 1992; Gross, Gregory D. "Coming Up for Air: Three AIDS Plays." *Journal of American Culture* 15 (Summer 1992): 63–67; Lawson, D. S. "Rage and Remembrance: The AIDS Plays." *AIDS: The Literary Response*. Nelson, Emmanuel S., ed. New York: Twayne Publishers, 1992. 140–54; Powers, Kim. "Fragments of a Trilogy: Harvey Fierstein's *Torch Song*." *Theater* 14.2 (Spring 1983): 63–67; Rich, Frank. "A Gentle Warning." *New York Times*. April 6, 1987: C13; Scott, Jay. "Dignity in Drag." *Film Comment* 25 (January–February 1989): 9–12.

G

GARLAND, JUDY (1922–1969)

Judy Garland is considered one of the greatest stars of Hollywood's Golden Age musicals. Her mixture of toughness and vulnerability has made her a revered gay icon and a popular cultural institution within the gay and lesbian movement. Garland was associated with several gay and bisexual men during her lifetime, including her two husbands Vincente Minelli and Mark Herron and her own father. According to her biographer David Shipman, Garland herself was bisexual and had several same-sex relationships. Shipman identified Garland's partners as, among others, her secretary Betty Asher, the songwriter and vocal arranger Kay Thompson, and the actress Katherine Hepburn. However, her popularity within the homosexual community was not merely based on acceptance of gays and her alleged same-sex relationships, which have been seriously questioned by other scholars. Her contradictions, both in her real existence and in her artistic persona, made her a symbol with whom many closeted gay men could identify. Like many of them, she lived a double life. She suffered from stage fright, yet repeatedly declared that her utmost happiness came from performing. Her repertoire included both songs depicting loneliness and passionate love. The tragic events in her life, five broken marriages, drug and alcohol addiction, debts, and premature death, made many gay men identify with her pain.

Although Garland may not be as well known among young gays in the new millennium, in more closeted times, when homosexuality was legally persecuted in the United States, gay men referred to each other as "friends of Dorothy" at social gatherings. This was a coded way to allude to one's sexual orientation without letting other people know what was the topic of the discussion. The expression was a homage to Judy Garland's role in *The Wizard of Oz* (1939), whose song "Somewhere Over the Rainbow" became a sort of gay national anthem. Garland has also been credited as the root of the Stonewall riots, which started the gay liberation movement in America. Although academic historians of the homosexual movement such as John Loughery and Martin Duberman have rejected this

Judy Garland as Dorothy Gale in the queer cult classic *The Wizard of Oz*. Courtesy of MGM/Photofest.

argument, many claim that it was anger and sorrow over Garland's death in 1969 that caused gays to respond against a police raid at the Stonewall Inn five days later.

Garland was born Frances Ethel Gumm in 1922 in Grand Rapids, Minnesota, the youngest daughter of Frank Avent Gumm, a vaudeville manager, and Ethel Marian Milne Gumm. Garland was only two years old when she debuted on her father's stage in a singing act with her two other sisters, under the name of Gumm Sisters. When her father was charged with having had an affair with a minor, the family was forced to move to southern California in 1926. While Frank Gumm managed the Valley Theater in Lancaster, his wife took care of her daughters' careers. Ethel's efforts won a part for the Gumm Sisters at the Ebell Theater in the show *Stars of Tomorrow* in 1931. The young Garland's voice and her stage confidence impressed the comedian George Jessel, who introduced the sisters act at Chicago's Oriental Theater in 1934, this time under the name of the Garland Sisters. Garland's first name was chosen from a popular Hoagy Carmichael song.

Success arrived quickly. Metro-Goldwyn-Mayer signed the sisters to appear in the short film *La Fiesta de Santa Barbara* (1935). In September the same year, Louis B. Mayer contracted Garland for seven years at a starting salary of $100 a week. The satisfaction for these early achievements was embittered by the sudden death of the entertainer's beloved father. In 1936, Garland appeared in a supporting role in her first feature film, *Pigskin Parade*. Yet, it was a short part in MGM's *Broadway Melody of 1938* (1937) that brought her to the attention of Decca Records and led to a recording contract. In the film Garland sang "You Made Me Love You," which became one of her most famous songs. In 1937 she graduated from Bancroft Junior High School and enrolled in University High School in Los Angeles. Her career languished in the next two years as MGM found it difficult to cast her because of her plump and plain look. Studio doctors, encouraged by her mother, began to prescribe Garland drugs to lose weight. These made her sleepless, forcing her to take sleeping pills and putting her in a vicious circle that would eventually kill her.

Garland made the most of the chance to revive her career when Fox refused to release the child star Shirley Temple for the leading role of Dorothy in MGM's *The Wizard of Oz* (1939). Garland got the part and the movie propelled her into stardom. The film also earned her the only prize she was to win from the Academy Award, a special miniature Oscar. The character of Dorothy, a misunderstood child from the black and white heartland who suddenly finds herself in a Technicolor world, mirrored gays' aspirations to better lives. Film scholar Alexander Doty (2000) defines the film as a popular culture touchstone that allowed him to understand his changing attitudes towards gender and sexuality. His reactions to the movie stand for those of entire generations of gays: "I was in love with and wanted to be Dorothy, thinking that the stark Kansas farmland she was trying to escape from was nothing compared to the West Texas desert our house was built upon. The Tin Man might stand in for my girlfriend's older brother (and subsequent crushes on older boys): an emotionally and physically stolid male who needed to find a heart so he could romantically express himself to me" (Doty 2000, 27). As Doty grew older and acquired an increased awareness of his homosexuality, he saw the Garland character as an image of the caring heterosexual woman who befriends gay men for her friendship with the camp Cowardly Lion. While the film has always been considered a popular culture institution for gay men, Doty also points out that it can be read as a teenaged girl's fantasy on the road to dykedom. His reading of the film, stressing the position of Dorothy as in between two models of lesbianism, the good femme (Aunt Em/Glinda the Good Witch) and the bad butch (Almira Gulch/the Wicked Witch of the West), gives new relevance to Garland's artistic persona for gay women as well as for gay men.

Garland's increasing star status did not make her more secure about her acting and singing ability nor did it solve her problems with drugs and depression. The Andy Hardy film series, where she teamed with Mickey Rooney, were all box office hits. They provided her with songs that would become classics in her repertoire, including George Gershwin's "I Got Rhythm" and "Embraceable You." Yet, her private life continued to be a source of sorrow and instability. In 1941 she married the composer David Rose, from whom, however, she soon divorced. The actress went on to star in *For Me and My Gal* (1942), together with Gene Kelly, and in the classic *Meet Me in St. Louis* (1944) by Vincente Minnelli, who became Garland's second husband in 1945. A year later, the couple had a daughter, Liza, who also became a popular actress and singer. In her early films, Garland portrayed innocent, girl-next-door characters whose complex and unrestrained emotions made them more than just stereotypes. *Meet Me in St. Louis* (1944) ended the actress's juvenile phase and advanced the American musical tradition with its use of songs to further the plot and to define characters' psychology. In the film, Garland sang "Have Yourself a Merry Little Christmas," which echoed feelings of loss and resilience shared by its wartime audiences.

Garland's other famous films of the decade included *The Harvey Girls* (1946), *Easter Parade* (1948), as well as her first non-singing role in *The Clock* (1945). Because of their commercial success, MGM put up with Garland's unpredictable and unreliable behavior on sets. Her contract was, however, eventually suspended in 1950 over disagreements during the shooting of *Annie Get Your Gun* and *Royal Wedding*. Only two days after her suspension from *Royal Wedding*, in June 1950, Garland was reported to have slit her throat with the shattered edge of a water glass. The studio account, which received coverage in the press, portrayed Garland as having inflicted the wounds in a "moment of vexation" during an "impulsive and hysterical act." Garland divorced Minnelli in 1951, blaming him for her depression. According to her testimony in court, his prolonged and unexplained absences made her ill and hysteric. Yet, this moment of despair was followed by a major comeback, following a pattern that became recurrent in the star's career. The same year Garland gave triumphant concerts at the London's Palladium and New York's Palace Theater, which led to a series of successful concert tours. These events were organized by her business manager Sid Luft, whom Garland married in 1952. The couple had two children, Lorna and Joey.

George Cukor's *A Star Is Born* (1954) marked her return to the big screen with a contract for Warner Brothers. The film went well over the planned budget, but was soon acclaimed as the greatest Hollywood musical ever made. It is also considered Garland's best performance: in the character of rising star Esther Blodgett, the actress infused many of her real-life upheavals. Critically acclaimed, *A Star Is Born* was, however, a disappointment at the box office, leading the studio to cut it after its initial release to reduce what they considered its overlong length of three hours. Although Garland was favorite in the Oscar race, she lost to Grace Kelly in what Groucho Marx defined as the greatest robbery in history. This led to another period of depression and self-doubt from which she re-emerged at the beginning of the 1960s. Overcoming the problems that had led to her disappearance from public scenes for half a decade, Garland gave memorable performances at the Palladium in London in 1960 and Carnegie Hall in New York the following year. The double album which recorded the concert, *Judy at Carnegie Hall*, sold two million copies, ranking number one for 13 weeks in the charts, and earned her five Grammy Awards. Garland was also back on the screen with a dramatic role in Stanley Kramer's historical recreation of the Nuremberg trials, *Judgment at Nuremberg* (1961). Her intense performance won her another Oscar nomination, this time as best supporting actress. In 1963 she starred in her last two films, *A Child Is Waiting* and *I Could Go On Singing*. In the same year, the TV network CBS broadcast 26 episodes of *The Judy Garland Show*, which was nominated for ten Emmy Awards, but failed to be renewed for a second season. The show suffered from direct competition with NBC hit western *Bonanza*, which was placed in the same time slot.

The failure to have her show renewed brought to an end Garland's hopes that the television series would finally give her financial security. In spite of her huge earnings during 30 years of career, Garland found herself in debt due to her business managers' negligence. For the rest of her life, the artist alternated artistic successes, such as the 1964 Palladium concert with her daughter Liza or the 1965 Forest Hills Tennis Stadium concert in New York, with health problems, cancelled engagements, and private unhappiness. In 1965 Garland divorced from Luft with protracted and embittered proceedings. The same year she was married to Mark Herron, but the couple split two years later. She was fired from the set of *Valley of the Dolls* (1967) when she did not report to the set. In June 1969, Garland died in her London flat due to an accidental overdose of sleeping pills, just a few months after her fifth marriage, to discotheque manager Mickey Deans. Her legacy for gays and lesbians is not simply a legacy of sorrow and despair. Although Garland started acting at a time when big studios had an overwhelming power over their contracted stars and manipulated their careers, she was willing to fight back to affirm her own true artistic identity.

Further Reading

Clarke, Gerald. *Get Happy: The Life of Judy Garland.* New York: Random House, 2000; DiOrio, Al, Jr. *Little Girl Lost: The Life and Hard Times of Judy Garland.* Greenwich, CT: Kearny Publishing, 1975; Doty, Alexander. *Flaming Classics: Queering the Film Canon.* New York: Routledge, 2000; Gross, Michael Joseph. "The Queen Is Dead." *Atlantic Monthly* 286.2 (August 2000): 62–70; Guly, Christopher. "The Judy Connection." *The Advocate* No. 658 (June 28, 1994): 48–56; Loughery, John. *The Other Side of Silence: Men's Lives and Gay Identities: A Twentieth-Century History.* New York: Henry Holt & Company, 1998; Shipman, David. *Judy Garland: The Secret Life of an American Legend.* New York: Hyperion Books, 1993; Vare, Eehlie A. *Rainbow: A Star Studded Tribute to Judy Garland.* New York: Boulevard Books, 1998.

GRANT, CARY (1904–1986)

English actor Cary Grant went on to become one of the greatest Hollywood stars of all times. In 1999 the American Film Institute named Grant the second Greatest Male Movie Star of All Times, preceded only by Humphrey Bogart. Grant embodied elegance and sophistication, personifying the quintessentially American debonair in spite of his British birth. The actor also signified sexual ambiguity as rumors about his attraction for men surfaced repeatedly throughout his career and after his death. However, Grant never identified himself as gay or bisexual. He stated he had nothing against homosexuals and had many gay friends, but when actor Chevy Chase joked about him being "such a gal" Grant sued him for slander. Beneath the idealized screen image celebrated by directors and film studios, the actor struggled to keep his off-screen persona private.

Cary Grant was born Archibald Leach on January 18, 1904, near Bristol in England. His childhood was an unhappy one, characterized by the separation of his parents when he was still a young boy. Since Grant's father was unable to pay for a divorce case, he decided to take a job in a Southampton military uniform factory. This gave him the opportunity of being far enough from his wife to start a new family also fathering a son out of wedlock. As the actor himself has recalled, Grant felt guilty about his father's departure as he was secretly pleased to have his mother all to himself. However, when he was 10 years old, the child returned home, where two of his older cousins lived, only to find that his mother had gone to a seaside resort for a while, as his relatives put it. The sudden disappearance of his mother further deepened the child's sense of insecurity and abandonment, a feeling that conditioned him for the rest of his life: "I [made] the mistake of thinking that each of my wives was my mother, that there would never be a replacement once she left. I found myself being attracted to [women] who looked like my mother—she had olive skin, for instance. Of course, at the same time, I [often chose] a person with her emotional makeup, too, and I didn't need that" (Eliot 2004, 43). Grant was later told that his mother had died, while, in fact, she had been committed to a mental institution because of a nervous breakdown. The actor did not learn the truth until the 1930s.

His insecurity led Archibald to seek praise and applause and thus drew him to an acting career. After being expelled from school just after his fourteenth birthday, the young adolescent joined Bob Pender's vaudeville troupe. In 1920 the troupe was invited to perform on Broadway by New York impresario Charles Dillingham. After the group finished their Broadway performances, it embarked on a nation-wide tour of the United States. When Pender returned to England in 1922, Grant decided to remain in the United States to continue his acting career. Completely alone in New York at the age of 18, Grant moved in with openly gay artist and future successful set designer Orry-Kelly, who offered the struggling actor to share his flat in the Greenwich Village. Throughout the 1920s, it was difficult for Grant to get roles in Broadway shows, which generally received mixed reviews and had limited runs. *Nikki*, opening in 1931 and closing after only 39 performances, was probably the most important of these shows in spite of its box office failure. Archibald was described by the *New York Daily News* reviewer as "a young lad from England" with a great future in movies.

When Orry-Kelly was invited by Jack Warner to work in Hollywood, Archibald followed him, quickly securing a five-year exclusive-services contract with Paramount

Randolph Scott (left) and Cary Grant (right) when they were carrying the buddy business too far. Courtesy of Photofest.

and changing his name to Cary Grant. In his early movies such as *This Is the Night* (1932), *Sinners in the Sun* (1932), *Merrily We Go to Hell* (1932), and *Devil and the Deep* (1932), Grant was generally cast in secondary roles. However, the good reviews that he received for his performances persuaded the studio to cast him as one of the male leads opposite Dietrich in *Blonde Venus* (1932), the fifth Von Stenberg/Dietrich collaboration. The film confirmed Grant as one of the most promising young Hollywood actors. In 1932 Grant also met fellow actor Randolph Scott on the set of *Hot Saturday* (1932). The two would become close friends, and, according to Grant's biographer Marc Eliot (2004, 99), the two began "one of the longest, deepest and most unusual love relationships in the history of Hollywood." Soon after their first meeting, Scott and Grant began to share a rented house which they called "Bachelor Hall." They continued to do so on and off for 12 years.

Grant's Hollywood career reached a decisive point when the actor was selected to play opposite Mae West in *She Done Him Wrong* (1933), an adaptation of West's hit Broadway play *Diamond Lil* (1928). The film was one of the highest-grossing ever produced in Hollywood and saved Paramount from bankruptcy. It also made Grant a star, although it was clearly West who was the film's primary focus. According to Eliot, the film also taught Grant an important lesson that would define his star image in years to come. In his future roles, Grant decided that he did not want to be the pursuer but the pursued. Working with West had shown him that as long as he was the pursuer the audience's attention would be on the object of his pursuit. Grant wanted to become that object himself as he wanted the audience to focus on him.

Grant appeared in a total of 72 films in a career that spanned three decades, from the early 1930s to the mid-1960s. The roles for which Grant is best remembered are those in the screwball comedies of the late 1930s and 1940s and his collaborations with Alfred Hitchcock of the 1940s and 1950s. Grant brought sophistication to the screwball comedy, perfecting his screen persona as an irresistible, if not completely reliable, man. Significantly, film critic Pauline Kael once described Grant as "the man from the dream city" (Eliot 2004, 2), a person equally capable of charming men as well as women. Following *She Done Him Wrong*, the actor starred in films such as *Sylvia Scarlett* (1935), *The Awful Truth* (1937), *Bringing Up Baby* (1938), and *The Philadelphia Story* (1940). These movies defined the conventions of the screwball comedy, a genre characterized by the farcical tensions generated by the romantic affair between two people who were opposites but, at the same time, destined to be together. Fast-talking and reversing the usual balance of gender power, making women the pursuers of men, these comedies also played on sexual ambiguity. For example, in *Sylvia Scarlett*, Katharine Hepburn masquerades as a male for most of the film and Grant remarks that he gets a "queer feeling" every time he looks at her/him. In addition, Grant invites Hepburn's young man to keep him warm in bed, in a situation which directly plays with the rumors of homosexuality surrounding the star. In *Bringing Up Baby*, when asked why he is wearing Katherine Hepburn's nightgown, Grant ad-libbed the famous line: "I've just gone gay, all of a sudden!" This was the first time the word was used in a context to indicate homosexuality.

Grant worked with Hitchcock on four films: *Suspicion* (1941), *Notorious* (1946), *To Catch a Thief* (1955), and *North by Northwest* (1959), which, according to many, represented the artistic and commercial peak of the actor's career. In these films Hitchcock emphasized Grant's darker side, turning the actor's screen image into a more complex and brooding persona. The characters Grant embodied for Hitchcock were men who were not what everyone perceived them to be, a definition that suited well the actor's on-going struggle to define his image and identity. Grant became Hitchcock's favorite actor. As he was one of the first stars to form his own independent production company in the mid-1950s, Grantley Productions, Grant was never awarded an Oscar during his active career, although he was nominated twice. Big studios never forgave him his quest for independence. Grant retired from films in the 1960s and finally received an Academy Award for Lifetime Achievement in 1970. He spent his last years touring the country with "A Conversation with Cary Grant," in which he showed clips from his films and answered questions from the audience. Before one of these meetings in Davenport, Iowa, Grant suffered a stroke and died on November 29, 1986.

Throughout his career, Grant was surrounded by rumors about his homosexuality, although he married five times and had well-publicized relationships with women. There is no conclusive evidence about his attraction for other men. Yet, some biographers, including Marc Eliot, have clearly defined his relationship with fellow actor Randolph Scott as a sentimental one. Eliot points out that the couple, who lived together before and in between their respective marriages, were well known in Hollywood for their carelessness in showing their mutual affection. This prompted Paramount executives to explicitly ask the stars to show up at parties and premieres accompanied by women. Hollywood gossip columnists began to wonder whether Scott and Grant were "carrying the buddy business too far," and their magazines ran stories with pictures depicting the two bachelors in their cozy domesticity, wearing aprons, having a meal together, or bathing in their swimming pool. Although both actors married, their friendship remained the focus of media attention. Yet, in spite of these rumors, Grant's career continued to flourish and the actor became the ultimate image of a movie star, synonymous with male sophistication and ambiguity.

Further Reading

Eliot, Marc. *Cary Grant: A Biography.* New York: Random House, 2004; Higham, Charles, and Ray Moseley. *Cary Grant: The Lonely Heart.* New York: Harcourt Brace, 1989; Loughery, John. *The Other Side of Silence: Men's Lives and Gay Identities: A Twentieth-Century History.* New York: Henry Holt & Company, 1998; McCann, Graham. *Cary Grant: A Class Apart.* New York: Columbia University Press, 1996; Wansell, Geoffrey. *Cary Grant: Dark Angel.* New York: Arcade Publishing, 1996.

H

HAINES, WILLIAM (1900–1973)

Hailed as Hollywood's first openly gay star, American actor William Haines was the top box office draw of the late 1920s and early 1930s. He lived his homosexuality openly and, when he refused a lavender marriage to silence rumors about his gayness, his studio, MGM, fired him. After his acting career ended, Haines became a successful interior designer and antique dealer, establishing one of the nation's most thriving firms together with his life partner Jimmy Shields.

Haines was born in Staunton, Virginia, on January 1, 1900, the third son of a cigar maker, George Adam Haines, and his wife, Laura Virginia Matthews, both descendants of ancient Virginian families. Because of his date of birth, Haines often described himself as "a true child of the twentieth century." From his early teens, Haines was aware of his homosexuality and showed impatience for his parents' way of life. He was particularly unhappy at the prospect of following his father's footsteps and taking over his cigar factory. When he was 14, he ran away from home for the first time, escaping with a boyfriend. After a brief return to Virginia, Haines settled down in New York in 1916 where he held a variety of odd jobs to support himself. He eventually moved into Greenwich Village. As George Chauncey documents in his *Gay New York* (1994), the Village was quickly acquiring a reputation for a center of unconventional behaviors, including sexual ones. The Village soon became of central significance for gays and lesbians throughout the American heartlands. They joined New Yorkers in their quest for a more tolerant milieu than what they found in their small towns. For Haines, who had been challenging conventions from a very early age, the Village represented a validation of his way of life and of his choice to live his homosexuality freely. According to his biographer William J. Mann (1998), Haines's sense of himself was shaped by the two years he spent in the Village, where a homosexual who lived his or her sexuality openly was not simply tolerated but often respected. During these years, Haines became friends with Mitchell Foster and designer Orry-Kelly, who would play an important part in Haines's second career as an interior designer.

The turning point in Haines's path to film stardom was his participation to the New Faces contest sponsored by the Samuel Goldwyn Studios at the end of 1921. Haines was the male winner of this talent search and, after a successful screen test, he was hired by the studio with a regular contract in 1922. However, it was not until 1924 that the studio began using Haines for leading roles. During his first two years in Hollywood, the actor had to content himself with bit parts, often uncredited. His first important role came with *Midnight Express* (1924), a film that would also define his screen persona of unreliable charming man who reforms following a tragic event that changes his life. Critics praised his performance. "I had one of those actor-proof roles," Haines (Mann 1998, 70) recalled later. "I was popular. Naturally, I was happy." With *Brown of Harvard* (1926), *Mike* (1926), and *Show People* (1928), Haines became a veritable star and, from 1928 to 1932, he was one of the top five box office stars of Hollywood. Contrary to many actors who started their career in the silent era, Haines was able to make a successful transition to sound films, starring in hits such as *Alias Jimmy Valentine* (1929) and *Navy Blues* (1929). Most of his films of the early 1930s are nowadays forgotten. Yet, they were incredibly popular at the time, making Haines the receiver of the greatest volume of fan mail among Hollywood stars.

Haines's homosexuality, however, cut short his promising career. The actor had chosen to live his homosexuality openly, and, since 1926, he had been together with former stand-in Jimmy Shields. Studios were wary of being associated with stars whose behavior could involve them in sex scandals. They were also worried that public exposure of homosexuality would fatally diminish the appeal of their stars. The social climate of the late 1920s and early 1930s was growing increasingly hostile towards homosexuality. As George Chauncey (1994, 353) writes, "the revulsion against gay life in the 1930s was part of the perceived 'excesses' of the Prohibition years and the blurring of the boundaries between acceptable and unacceptable public sociability." The Production Code made its explicit mission to expunge any reference to homosexuality in movies. Thus, MGM executives, including Louis B. Mayer himself, repeatedly tried to persuade Haines to marry. The actor, however, continued to refuse giving up his life with Shields. The termination of Haines's contract with MGM in 1932 after 11 years of successes has acquired the status of a Hollywood legend. It is not clear whether it was Haines's supposed arrest for having sex with a sailor or his refusal to give up his romantic commitment to Shields that finally prompted MGM to fire the star. No record of arrest has been found, although Haines and several friends have alluded to a similar episode in later interviews. Fact blends into fiction and melodrama, as with all Hollywood legends. Anita Loos significantly wrote (Mann 1998, 228) that "without even a hesitation, Bill opted for love and told L. B. [Mayer] to tear up his contract."

After his contract was terminated, Haines decided to devote his life to his other great passion: interior design. He used a business in antiques that he had established years earlier as a springboard into a successful career as interior decorator. Most of his clients included former colleagues such as Joan Crawford, Gloria Swanson, Carole Lombard, and **George Cukor**. Haines quickly acquired a national reputation for his projects and was invited to take part to the 1939 San Francisco World Fair. In the late 1940s, his neoclassical approach shifted towards a more modernist one and Haines is credited to have given a definite contribution to the definition of the Hollywood Regency style. Haines never returned to acting and spent the rest of his life with his partner Jimmy Shields. He died of lung cancer in Santa Monica, California, on December 26, 1973.

Further Reading

Chauncey, George. *Gay New York: Gender, Urban Culture, and the Makings of the Gay Male World, 1890–1940*. New York: Basic Books, 1994; Hadleigh, Boze. *Hollywood Gays*. New York: Barricade Books, 1996; Mann, William J. *Wisecracker: The Life and Times of William Haines, Hollywood's First Openly Gay Star*. New York: Viking Penguin, 1998; Official William Haines Web site http://www.williamhaines.com; Wentink, A. M. "Haines, (Charles) William ('Billy')." *Who's Who in Gay and Lesbian History from Antiquity to World War II*. Robert Aldrich and Garry Wotherspoon, eds. London and New York: Routledge, 2001. 197–198.

HARLEM RENAISSANCE

Several important gay and lesbian writers were prominent animators of the Harlem Renaissance, a moment of artistic and literary flowering in African American culture that took place in the 1920s and 1930s. Critics, artists, and poets central to the movement such as Alain Locke, Countee Cullen, Langston Hughes, Claude McKay, Wallace Thurman, Richard Bruce Nugent, Nella Larsen, Angelina Grimké, and Alice Dunbar-Nelson were all homosexuals or bisexuals. The most influential of the white patrons of the renaissance, Carl Van Vechten, was also gay. Studies that foreground the sexuality of these authors and the ways in which it shaped their writings were, however, slow to come. It was only during the early 1990s that critics began to mention homosexuality as an artistic influence. There are still many resistances to overcome before the cultural impact of gayness on the Harlem Renaissance can be fully acknowledged. The Harlem Renaissance contributed to the establishment of a gay tradition within African American literary culture and also to the development of unorthodox and queer events, such as drag balls, that were the marks of Harlem's rebel sexuality. How far homosexuality was really welcomed in Harlem, however, remains debatable.

The thrust for the movement came from the massive influx of African Americans from the rural South to the urban North and the resulting social and cultural changes. *The New Negro* (1925), the collection of essays, poetry, fiction, and visual art edited by Alain Locke, is generally taken as the manifesto of the movement, summing up its ideals and creative principles. Locke was a philosopher educated at Harvard and a professor at Howard University. Together with other important African-American intellectuals such as W.E.B. DuBois and James Weldon Johnson, Locke theorized that an elite of talented writers and artists might launch a vast campaign for reform and the social uplift of African Americans. The Harlem Renaissance can be seen as the response to James Weldon Johnson's appeal (2006, 13) to achieve greatness in literary and artistic expression to prove the greatness of African American people: "The world does not know that a people is great until that people produces great

Langston Hughes, one of the prominent animators of the Harlem Renaissance. Courtesy of Photofest.

literature and art. No people that has produced great literature and art has ever been looked upon by the world as distinctly inferior." As central as Locke was in the launch of the renaissance, his figure remains problematic within gay and lesbian culture. He favored the careers of many gay male artists and thus contributed to the development of a gay tradition within African American literary history. Yet, he was also a misogynist who hindered the careers of women artists (with the notable exception of Zora Neale Hurston) and contributed to the neglect to which Angelina Grimké and Alice Dunbar-Nelson were relegated until their rediscovery in the 1990s.

The renaissance was fuelled by gatherings of writers and artists at the salons of wealthy white patrons as well as by the literary forums and contests published in magazines such as *Survey, Crisis, Opportunity*, and the more avant-garde *Fire!* The African American A'Leila Walker, the daughter of an inventor of products to straighten African American women's hair, also provided important social occasions, which were characterized by the massive presence of homosexual artists. Walker's lavish parties and her own club, the Dark Tower, made her, in Langston Hughes's words (1993, 245), "the joy-goddess of Harlem's 1920s." Help to further the renaissance also came from white publishers who were largely of Jewish descent and based in New York such as Albert and Charles Boni, Alfred Knopf, and Horace Liveright. White patronage remains a controversial issue within the critical understanding of the Harlem literati's careers. It provided them with the chance of making their voices heard. Yet, some critics charge that the movement's eventual failure to provide general uplift for the race can be attributed to the necessity black artists felt to pander to the tastes of their white patrons. These, the argument continues, were more interested in superficial primitivism than in an actual understanding of African American culture.

Homosexuality occupied an ambivalent position within Harlem. On the one hand, Harlem was, as John Loughery (1998, 45) has described it, "a slummer's paradise," offering thrills to people of all classes and tastes. Homosexuals felt they could be freer to live their sexual identities in the African American cultural capital.

The existence of gay bars and speakeasies where white and black men could dance together and drag queens were regulars is well documented. The only openly gay writer of the renaissance, Richard Bruce Nugent, recalls (Loughery 1998, 50) that "You did just what you wanted to do. Nobody was in the closet. There wasn't any closet." On the other hand, the uneasiness of the African American protagonists of the renaissance about their homosexuality is equally well documented, alerting us that, perhaps, homosexuals were more an exotic commodity to lure even more white tourists to the already glamorous setting of the so-called Negro Mecca. When Nugent himself published his homoerotic story "Smoke, Lilies and Jades" in *Fire!*, now hailed as the first gay African-American short story, he only signed it with his first and middle name to avoid the identification of his family with the piece. W.E.B. Du Bois did not have any qualms in firing the business manager of *The Crisis* when his homosexuality was brought out by a police raid in a subway toilet. Claude McKay, Wallace Thurman, and Countee Cullen all felt the pressure to marry, although their marriages were short-lived. They only addressed homosexual themes and characters in their novels and poems through a coded language that, according to Christa Schwarz (2003), they borrowed from the Greek tradition and Walt Whitman. The closet can be seen to be both oppressive and inspiring for the Harlemites as it hindered an explicit revelation of their homosexuality in their art; yet, it also helped them to develop an artistic discourse about homosexuality that protected them from discrimination and gave them access to mainstream publishers.

Contrary to his contemporaries, Langston Hughes, now unanimously considered as the central figure in the renaissance, never married. Yet, he also never openly spoke about his private life or sexual orientation, and critics have been only too willing to ignore or, at best, downplay the possibility of his homosexuality. Many of his poems, including "Young Sailor," "Waterfront Streets," "Joy," can be read as coded references to homoeroticism. "Cafe: 3 a.m." openly describes an early morning scene in a gay club: "Detectives from the vice squad/with weary sadistic eyes/spotting fairies" (Vendler 2003, 45). Homosexual characters appear in the background of Hughes's memoir *The Big Sea* (1940), mostly as pathetic aging queens. Hughes did not include homosexuals as protagonists of his fiction until the early 1960s with the publication of "Blessed Assurance," a short story about a father's inability to accept the effeminacy of his talented son. Black gay culture has been eager to include Hughes in its canon. In the documentary *Looking for Langston* (1998), the filmmaker Isaac Julien explored the impact of homosexuality on Hughes's production. Hughes's estate did not allow his poetry to be used in the film, a confirmation of the cultural resistance to a full assessment of the role of homosexuality within the Harlem Renaissance.

Gays and lesbians "in the life" (as African Americans referred to homosexuality) found many nightspots that catered to their tastes in Harlem during the 1920s and 1930s. Yet, as Lillian Faderman (1991, 69) points out, this apparent acceptance was instrumental in presenting white tourists with "one more exotic drawing card" and lure them in the queer capital of the New Negro. In turn, racist assumptions of superiority reassured white homosexuals that they could behave as they pleased in Harlem. Homosexuality and bisexuality were flaunted in many clubs and both white gay males and lesbians openly displayed their sexuality in a way that they would not even dare to think of doing in their white society. They conceptualized Harlem as a world of fantasy where they could experiment with unconventional behavior because common standards did not apply in that free zone and because their whiteness sheltered them from insult. Black entertainers, on the other hand, banked on their provocative image. Gladys Bentley, for example, was a famous male impersonator who wore men's clothes also when she was not performing. Audiences were so fascinated with her ambiguous image. Although bisexual, Bentley chose to publicize her lesbian side more than her heterosexual one by marrying a woman in a New Jersey civil ceremony. Wedding ceremonies among lesbians in Harlem were quite common at the time. More often than not real licenses were obtained, Faderman (1991, 73) reminds us, "by masculinizing a first name or having a gay male surrogate apply for a license for the lesbian couple." The butch/femme pattern also became highly visible in Harlem's lesbian communities and such visibility helped to give it an important position within queer culture.

Bisexuality and lesbianism were common among African American jazz singers. Bessie Smith was a married woman; yet, her attraction for other women was well-known. Smith's mentor, Ma Rainey, was even arrested in 1925 for hosting an orgy at her home with other women from her chorus. Her arrest, however, did not hurt her reputation. On the contrary, Rainey's launch of her song "Prove It on Me Blues," where a woman sings her love for other women, was supported by advertising posters portraying a plump woman, looking not unlike Rainey, talking to two women with a policeman observing the scene from the background. Alberta Hunter, Ethel Waters, and her lover Ethel Williams were other women involved in the show business who did not hide their love for women. Contrary to Waters and Williams, however, Smith, Rainey, and Hunter were all married and thus also promoted a heterosexual image. At the same time, the lyrics of their blues reproduced this ambivalence towards lesbianism, speaking of unconventional female sexuality, but also ridiculing "bulldikers" for their mannish behavior. Lesbian sex is defined, at once, as both "dirty" but extremely "good" (Faderman 1991, 78).

The same combination of fascination and uneasiness towards lesbianism is reflected by the lesbian characters in the fiction of the gay/bisexual males of the renaissance. Claude McKay's *Home to Harlem* (1928), for example, features a dialogue between Raymond, an intellectual black waiter, and Jake, a kitchen porter, where the two discuss lesbianism. Raymond starts from a liberated standpoint, celebrating Sappho's poetry and declaring lesbian "a beautiful word." Jake is not so liberated and objects that all lesbians are "ugly women." Raymond tries to persuade Jake that not all lesbians are ugly; however, he concedes, "Harlem is too savage about some things" (Faderman 1991, 69). In Wallace Thurman's novel *The Blacker the Berry* (1929) the heroine Emma Lou encounters several lesbian and bisexual women. Although they can live through the streets of Harlem undisturbed, it is clear that they are not so much accepted as merely tolerated. Lesbianism was seldom mentioned in the fiction of gay and bisexual women. In her two novels *Quicksand* (1928) and *Passing* (1929), Nella Larsen denounces traditional gender roles as constricting for women and describes the sphere of domesticity as a trap for women through the metaphor of the quicksand. *Passing* focuses on the relationship between two women without explicitly defining it as lesbian. However, the novel is charged with lesbian overtones and suggests that a whole subtext of repressed impulses is at work in the narrative. The characters fear the acknowledgement of their own homosexual desire, a fear that may well lead to the death of one of the women and the suspicion that the other is implicated in the murder. Angelina Weld Grimké focused on the pervasiveness of racism in her play *Rachel*, published in 1920 and representing one of the first works of the renaissance, where a woman refuses to marry and become a mother rather than seeing her children subject to lynching and racial hatred. Grimké's poetry, which was largely unpublished during her lifetime, addresses instead the writer's attraction for other women. Alice Dunbar-Nelson, who was married to the poet Paul Laurence Dunbar, also had lesbian relationships throughout her life and Gloria Hull (1987) has suggested that her unpublished novel *This Lofty Oak* documents the life of her lover Edwina Kruse. Her diaries, more than her published poetry, document Dunbar-Nelson's other lesbian affairs as well as her involvement in the lesbian circles of the Renaissance. The fact that all these three women faded into obscurity after the 1940s and were not rediscovered well into the 1980s by feminist and black scholars suggests that the so-called new negroes were not as liberated about lesbianism as the glamorous appeal of bisexual entertainers and clubs would first lead us to believe.

The glitter of Harlem's clubs and salons was cut short by the Depression. The renaissance did not succeed in generating that general uplift for African Americans that Locke wanted to pursue. Yet, it decisively contributed in injecting a distinctive gay and lesbian tradition into African American literary heritage and popular culture.

Further Reading

Anderson, Jervis. *This Was Harlem: A Cultural Portrait, 1900–1950*. New York: Farrar, Straus, & Giroux, 1981; Avi-Ram, Amitai F. "The Unreadable Black Body: 'Conventional' Poetic Form in the Harlem Renaissance." *Genders* 7 (1990): 32–45; Baker, Houston A. *Afro-American Poetics: Revisions of Harlem and the Black Aesthetic*. Madison: University of Wisconsin Press, 1988; Baker, Houston A. *Modernism and the Harlem Renaissance*. Chicago: University of Chicago Press, 1987; Chauncey, George. *Gay New York*. Basic Books, 1994; Cooper, Wayne F. *Claude McKay: Rebel Sojourner in the Harlem Renaissance, A Biography*. Baton Rouge: Louisiana State University Press, 1987; Fabre, Michel. *From Harlem to Paris: Black American Writers in France, 1840–1980*. Urbana: University of Illinois Press, 1991; Faderman, Lillian. *Odd Girls and Twilight Lovers: A History of Lesbian Life in Twentieth-Century America*. New York: Columbia University Press, 1991; Garber, Eric. "A Spectacle in Color: The Lesbian and Gay Subculture of Jazz Age Harlem." *Hidden from History: Reclaiming the Gay and Lesbian Past*. Martin Duberman, Martha Vicinus, and George Chauncey, Jr., eds. New York: New American Library, 1989. 318–331; Hughes, Langston. *The Big Sea: An Autobiography*. New York: Hill and Wang, 1993; Hull, Gloria T. *Color, Sex, and Poetry: Three Women Writers of the Harlem Renaissance*. Bloomington: Indiana University Press, 1987; Johnson, James Weldon. *The Book of American Negro Poetry*. New York: BiblioBazaar, 2006; Loughery, John. *The Other Side of Silence. Men's Lives and Gay Identities: A Twentieth-Century History*. New York: Owl

Book, 1998; Maxwell, William J. *New Negro, Old Left: African American Writing and Communism between the Wars*. New York: Columbia University Press, 1999; Nugent, Richard Bruce. *Gay Rebel of the Harlem Renaissance: Selections from the Work of Richard Bruce Nugent*. Edited by Thomas H. Wirth with a foreword by Henry Louis Gates. Durham: Duke University Press, 2002; Rampersad, Arnold. *The Life of Langston Hughes, Volume I: 1902–1941, I Too, Sing America*. New York: Oxford University Press, 1986; Rampersad, Arnold. *The Life of Langston Hughes, Volume II: 1941–1967, I Dream a World*. New York: Oxford University Press, 1988; Reimonenq, Alden. "Countee Cullen's Uranian 'Soul Windows.'" *The Journal of Homosexuality* 26:2–3 (Fall 1993): 143–165; Schwarz, Christa A. B. *Gay Voices of the Harlem Renaissance*. Bloomington: Indiana University Press, 2003; Vendler, Helen. *The Anthology of Contemporary American Poetry*. New York: I. B. Tauris&Co, 2003.

HARRIS, E. LYNN (1955–)

Openly gay African American novelist E. Lynn Harris combines in his bestselling semi-autobiographical novels entertaining plots and a gossipy style with complex themes. These include sexual and racial identity, **AIDS**, bisexuality, and closeted homosexuality within the African American community.

Harris was born on June 20, 1955, in Flint, Michigan, but grew up in Little Rock, Arkansas. After graduating in journalism from the University of Arkansas at Fayetteville, Harris worked as a successful computer sale executive for more than a decade. Yet, in 1990, he left his profitable job due to depression and alcoholism caused by his struggle to accept his homosexuality. Moving to Atlanta, Harris resorted to therapy and writing to overcome his problems. As he confessed in his memoir *What Becomes of the Brokenhearted* (2003, 255), "Writing saved my life." Encouraged by author Maya Angelou and urged by a friend who was dying of AIDS to write about their friendship, Harris set down to write what would eventually become his first novel, *Invisible Life* (1992), whose title pays homage to Ralph Ellison's *Invisible Man* (1952).

The novel introduces Raymond Tyler, a recurring character in Harris's subsequent fiction, a young lawyer struggling to come to terms with his homosexuality and to reconcile his love for Kelvin with his relationship with Sela. Wishing to put these relationships behind, Tyler moves to New York, where, however, he starts again to lead a double life dating Nicole, an actress, and Quinn, a married stockbroker with children, at the same time. Tyler longs for a form of relationship approved by society, yet he increasingly finds sexual intercourse with men more satisfying. The outbreak of AIDS in Tyler's sphere of friends leads the lawyer to reject those men like Quinn who describe themselves as heterosexual but have sex with other men. These characters who live "on the down low" (in the closet) constitute a particular focus of Harris's fiction.

Written within a few months, *Invisible Life* was initially rejected by all the 12 publishers to whom it had been submitted. Harris then resorted to his skills as sales executive, self-printing 5,000 copies of the novel and selling them door to door. Thanks to word of mouth, the novel sold all its copies within nine months and

Doubleday accepted it for publication in July 1992. Its success led to the sequel *Just As I Am* two years later. In the sequel, Raymond Tyler is a sports lawyer in Atlanta, still struggling with his sexual identity, while Nicole is trying to get a career in Broadway. Basil Henderson, a closeted football player first introduced in *Invisible Life*, re-enters Raymond's life, further complicating his doubts about his sexual identity. However, as in Harris's previous novel, a veritable epiphany for Tyler occurs when his friend Kyle is struck down by AIDS, and Raymond goes to New York to be close to Kyle during his last months. Kyle's death leads both Raymond and Nicole to be honest with each other and find true happiness with other partners. *Abide with Me* (1998) portrays Raymond and Nicole in their new satisfying relationships and focuses again on Basil Henderson who also returns in *Not a Day Goes By* (2000) and in *A Love of My Own* (2002). The latter novel takes place after Raymond's long-term relationship has ended and the lawyer is once again on his quest for emotional balance.

The easy and accessible writing style, the most praised feature of Harris's books, is also the most frequent source of criticism directed at the writer. Harris's fiction has been criticized by some as superficial and over-relying on easy melodrama. Yet, his books have helped to popularize homosexual themes and characters within the black community, which has traditionally resisted them. In his novels, Harris firmly places homosexuality within the black middle class. In spite of his honest portrayals of African American homosexuals or, perhaps, because of his liberating appeal, Harris has become a popular culture icon within the black community. He was featured in the 2000 *Essence* Win a Dinner with E. Lynn Harris contest and was nominated for an NAACP Image Award for *Abide with Me*. Through his fiction, Harris has contributed to give visibility to homosexuality within African American literature and culture.

Further Reading

Boykin, Keith. "Just As He Is: An Interview with Lynn Harris." *Lambda Book Report* 6.5 (1997): 1, 6–7; Harris, E. Lynn. *What Becomes of the Brokenhearted*. New York: Doubleday, 2003; Labbé, Theola S. "E. Lynn Harris: Black Male, Out and on Top." *Publishers Weekly*. 248.31 (July 30, 2001): 53–54.

HAWTHORNE, NIGEL (1929–2001)

Sir Nigel Hawthorne was one of Britain's most accomplished actors. He was the first openly gay actor to be nominated for an Oscar for his performance in *The Madness of King George* (1994). In addition to this Oscar-nominated role, Hawthorne's popular fame rests also on the character of Sir Humphrey Appleby for the British hit television series *Yes, Minister*. The media, however, devoted closest attention not so much to Hawthorne's acting skills as to his sexual orientation. While promoting *The Madness of King George* in the United States, the actor had spoken openly to the ***Advocate*** about his long-time partner Trevor Bentham. Hawthorne had never been exactly closeted, living together with Bentham, but he never spoke publicly about their relationship and his homosexuality. The article in the *Advocate* represented such first instance, and caused a tabloid furor in Britain with headlines like "The Madness of Queen Nigel." These reactions shocked the actor who resented all this publicity about his private life. He further claimed that the American gay and lesbian magazine had not respected his request for privacy. A reserved man, Hawthorne did not want to be identified as a spokesperson for the gay and lesbian movement.

Nigel Hawthorne was born on April 5, 1929, in Coventry, England, but grew up in South Africa where his family emigrated when he was two. Hawthorne attended strict Catholic schools and had a difficult relationship with his father. These two features of Hawthorne's childhood made him insecure and lonely. The actor started to appear in plays in South African theaters in 1951. His father tried to prevent his son from becoming an actor as he wanted him to join the diplomatic corps. In spite of his father's plans, the year following his South African debut, Hawthorne went back to England to pursue an acting career. His beginning as an actor was far from promising as Hawthorne only got roles as understudy and, after 19 months, returned to South Africa where he continued to act.

In the early 1960s Hawthorne decided to try again his luck on the British stage. Although popular fame did not arrive until the late 1970s, the actor was more successful in this second effort and his acting career took off. Hawthorne appeared in a number of stage productions, both comic and dramatic, thus demonstrating his versatility and acquiring a solid reputation as a character actor. The turning point in Hawthorne's career was the series *Yes, Minister*, for which he was selected in 1977. His portrayal of a scheming politician earned him four BAFTA awards and made him a well-known television star in Britain. The series ran for five seasons and was later broadcast by PBS in the United States, making Hawthorne a familiar face on American television too. In 1989 Hawthorne became even more visible for American audiences when he took the role of writer C. S. Lewis in *Shadowlands*, which enjoyed a two-year run on Broadway. His performance earned him a Tony Award, but Anthony Hopkins was chosen to star in the film adaptation because he was thought to have wider international appeal than Hawthorne.

For *The Madness of King George*, however, Hawthorne was chosen for both the play and its film adaptation, as playwright Alan Bennett particularly insisted for him to be cast. Nominated for an Academy Award for Best Actor, Hawthorne found himself at the center of media attention on both sides of the Atlantic. After the *Advocate* published an interview with the actor where he candidly spoke of his private life for the first time, British tabloids concentrated on his 20-year relationship with his manager Trevor Bentham. In the interview, Hawthorne (Clarkin 1995, *Advocate* online) had conceded that he was not "somebody who sets himself up as an icon of sexual orientation," but, he added, "my private life has never been a secret. I've never been a closet queen." The media attention for an Academy Award nominee clearly caught Hawthorne off-guard and he found the unexpected interest in his private life difficult to bear. "The headlines were absolutely awful and hurtful, dreadful stuff," Hawthorne later admitted in an interview with the British paper the *Observer* (Barber 1999, *Observer* online). "We were held up to ridicule. I just thought it was so trashy. We've got over it now, and, in a way, things are better, but I was very angry at the time." In the same interview, he explicitly distanced himself from other British actors "like Simon Callow and **Ian McKellen**, who seem to use [being gay] as a platform." Contrary to them, Hawthorne stated that he had never wanted to do that: "I've always wanted a private life; that's what I was after. And I thought just by living as we did and going everywhere together, it would be assumed, without my ever having to make a public statement about it." Significantly, commenting on his relationships with other gay actors after his coming out, Ian McKellen quotes Hawthorne as someone frightened by queer visibility: "And I think some other gay actors are frightened of me, because they think, 'Oh if I do come out, I'll have to do what Ian McKellen does, and be a spokesperson.' That's what Nigel Hawthorne felt. He said, 'I don't want to be a spokesperson—leave me alone'" (Garfield 2006, *Observer* online).

This partial coming out did not ruin Hawthorne's career. On the contrary, probably also for the resulting fame of the Academy Award nomination, Hawthorne's last years were his most successful ones and the actor was knighted by Queen Elizabeth II in 1999. He gave critically acclaimed screen performances in Nicholas Hytner's *The Object of My Affection* (1998), where he portrays a gay character, and David Mamet's *The Winslow Boy* (1999). Hawthorne died on December 26, 2001, after an 18-month struggle against cancer.

Further Reading

Barber, Lynn. "The King and I." *The Observer Magazine*. September 5, 1999. 14–18. http://observer.guardian.co.uk/life/story/0,267151,00.html (accessed on November 15, 2006); Clarkin, Michelle. "Acting Out." *The Advocate*. April 4, 1995. 45–47. http://www.advocate.com/html/stories/854_5/854_5_hawthorne_678.asp (accessed on November 15, 2006); Garfield, Simon. "The X Factor." *The Observer*. April 30, 2006. http://film.guardian.co.uk/interview/interviewpages/0,1765778,00.html (accessed on November 15, 2006); Hawthorne, Nigel. *Straight Face*. London: Hodder & Stoughton Ltd, 2002; Koenig, Rhoda. "Mad about the Boy." *The Independent: The Weekend Review*. October 16, 1999. 5.

HAY, HARRY (1912–2002)

Harry Hay has been unanimously credited as one of the most important founders of the organized modern gay movement in the United States. His life, political choices, and cultural stances were entirely devoted to the improvement of civil rights for gays and lesbians. He was the co-founder of the first semi-public organizations for homosexuals such as the Mattachine Society and the Radical Fairies. Hay contributed to promote social and cultural awareness of gay people as an oppressed minority within the United States and devised a program for cultural and political liberation. Hay's diverse experiences were all informed by the rejection of homosexual assimilation to the rest of society. Hay always insisted on celebrating the cultural diversity of gay people from heterosexuals.

Harry Hay Jr. was born in Worthington, Sussex, England in 1912, the son of Harry Hay Sr. and Margaret Neall Hay. Both of Harry's parents were Americans living in South Africa, where his father was a manager for Cecil Rhodes's mining company. A few months before Harry was born, his mother moved to England where she remained with Harry for the first two years of his life. When World War I broke out, the family reunited in Chile where Harry's father had secured another mining job. In 1916, after Harry senior had had a serious mining accident, the family moved back to the United States, first to southern California and then to Los Angeles. The relationship between father and son was often tense and Harry later declared that his determination to live a life completely different from his father's stemmed from his sheer hatred of the man. Thus, while his father urged him to pursue scientific studies that would ensure him a profitable career, Harry excelled in artistic and literary subjects and was particularly attracted to drama and music. He graduated from Los Angeles High School in 1929 and enrolled at Stanford University the following year.

During the early 1930s, Hay suffered from a serious sinus infection that forced him to leave university. When he was unable to re-enroll for financial reasons, Hay started his singing and acting career, eventually working in 1933 with Will Geer and becoming his lover. The couple attended Communist Party meetings and both Hay and Geer became members. Hay was an active in the Communist Party from the 1930s to the early 1950s. Caught by what he described as "the siren song of Revolution" (Stryker 1996, 26), Hay, like many of his generation, conceived Communist membership and militancy as an important step towards changing the world for the better. Yet, for him, his political involvement also marked the beginning of an enduring alienation: the party prohibited homosexuals from becoming members and treated homosexuality as a disease of bourgeois decadence. Hay, like Geer, was eager to comply with party directives and, in 1938, married Anita Platky, who, when their marriage ended, perceptively said that Harry had not married her but the Communist Party. Being married certainly made things easier for Hay within the party. Yet, marriage and political activism could not erase his homosexuality, and, during his married years, Hay continued to have same sex relationships and to think about ways in which to organize homosexuals. In 1950 Hay met Rudi Gernreich and the two became partners. This encounter caused Hay to rethink his life entirely and led to the founding of the Mattachine Society, the first semi-public gay organization in the United States. The Mattachines were masked folk dancers who performed satiric and parody shows during the Middle Ages in Italy and in France. These performers challenged the Catholic ban on social satire. Hay chose the name hoping that, just like the masked performers of the Middle Ages who fought for the oppressed, the Mattachines would be a society of homosexual men living in disguise in American society but fighting, at the same time, for the rights of their oppressed minority. Hay's meeting with Gernreich was also the catalyst for the end of his marriage and his consequent break with the Communist Party.

In April 1951, Hay came out to his wife and informed her about the Mattachine. By September, the couple had divorced. The same year also marked Hay's resignation from the party. Because of the aggressive anti-Communist propaganda of Cold War America, the CPUSA was holding one of its re-registration campaigns. These were held to make sure that members were not politically vulnerable to the blackmails of McCarthyism and to protect the party from the increasing number of FBI informers. Hay used this opportunity to discuss his situation as a gay man openly. In a report he outlined both his services to the party and his involvement with the Mattachine. The party line was that, while Hay was recognized as an original thinker and an important asset, he and other homosexuals were "security threats." Thus, because allegiance to the party was superior to any others, Hay was asked to name the names of other homosexual members. Since Hay was the first militant to discuss so openly and candidly his homosexuality within the Communist orthodoxy, the party had difficulty handling the case and it took a year and a half to reach a decision. Hay, as he himself had recommended, was expelled by the party, although due to his years of service as a Marxist teacher he was credited as "a lifelong friend of the people." Stuart Timmons (1990) documents that the rank-and-file reactions to Hay's coming out were at times even worse than the party's official line on the issue, and Hay was repeatedly insulted by fellow comrades. The party's desertion of Hay became clear in May 1955 when he was summoned to testify before the House Un-American Activities Committee for his Marxist teaching in Southern California. His coming out had isolated him from the rest of the party and, while party members could count on a group of few but determined and sympathetic lawyers and fundraising parties, Harry Hay could not. His case was, however, quickly dismissed.

During the early 1950s, the Mattachine Society increased its membership. The society came to the public attention when one of its founding members, Dale Jennings, was arrested and charged with soliciting a police officer. The Mattachine formed a committee to defend Jennings whose lawyer successfully demonstrated that the police officer had lied. In spite of the fierce opposition of one juror, the judge dismissed the case. This is considered one of the first victories for gay rights in America. Membership of the society soared and the Mattachine started to produce the monthly periodical *ONE*, which was also at the center of a controversial court case after the Los Angeles postmaster refused to distribute it. However, this long court battle proved another success for the American gay and lesbian movement when, in 1958, the Supreme Court declared that talking about homosexuality could not constitute obscenity. In the "Society Missions and Purposes" (Hay and Roscoe 1996, 132), the Mattachines argued that their organization "serves as an example for homosexuals to follow, and provides a dignified standard upon which the rest of society can base a more intelligent and accurate picture of the nature of homosexuality than currently obtains in the public mind." The public attention devoted to the society, however, also caused allegations of subversion and Hay, in particular, was branded as a Marxist teacher by the press. These charges were dangerous ones in the Cold War climate and the new members of the society successfully called for a change in the society leadership. Without Hay's charisma, however, the society declined.

For most of the 1950s and until the mid-1960s, Hay was isolated from the movement for gay and lesbian rights that he had helped to found. Yet, his meeting and subsequent relationship with John Burnside rekindled in him the urge to activism. The two founded a gay and lesbian collective, the Circle of Loving Companions, and were active in demonstrations and picket lines both before and after Stonewall. In the 1970s the couple moved to New Mexico, where Hay had the chance of studying the Native Americans and their culture which had fascinated him for years. These were also the years when the Radical Fairies movement started, turning the derogative definition of homosexuals into a proud affirmation of cultural difference and an identification with so-called sexual others. The Fairies conceived homosexuals as a separate tribe and borrowed their spiritual elements from Native American and New

Age culture. Holding their meetings in rural areas far away from the growing gay mainstream culture of urban centers, the Radical Fairies experimented with communal lifestyle in sanctuaries throughout North and Central America emphasizing the importance of personal self-development.

Hay's status within the gay and lesbian movement was again obscured during the 1980s, to be rediscovered at the end of the twentieth century. A formal recognition of Hay's pioneering work in gay and lesbian culture and rights came in 1999, three years before his death for lung cancer, when he was publicly elected as grand marshal for San Francisco Gay, Lesbian, Bisexual, and Transgender Pride Parade.

Further Reading

D'Emilio, John. *Sexual Politics, Sexual Communities.* Chicago: University of Chicago Press, 1983; D'Emilio, John. "The Homosexual Menace: The Politics of Sexuality in Cold War America." *Making Trouble.* New York: Routledge, 1992; Edge, Simon. *With Friends Like These: Marxism and Gay Politics.* London: Cassell, 1995; Faderman, Lillian. *Odd Girls and Twilight Lovers: A History of Lesbian Life in Twentieth-Century America.* New York and London: Penguin Books, 1992; Hay, Harry, and Will Roscoe, eds. *Radically Gay: Gay Liberation in the Words of Its Founder.* Boston: Beacon Press, 1996; Lorde, Audre. *Zami: A New Spelling of My Name.* London: HarperCollins, 1982. Loughery, John. *The Other Side of Silence: Men's Lives and Gay Identities: A Twentieth-Century History.* New York: Henry Holt & Company, 1998; Stryker, Susan, Jim Van Buskirk and Armistead Maupin, eds. *Gay by the Bay: A History of Queer Culture in San Francisco Bay Area.* San Francisco: Chronicle Books, 1996; Timmons, Stuart. *The Trouble with Harry Hay: Founder of the Modern Gay Movement.* Boston: Alyson Publications, 1990.

HAYNES, TODD (1961–)

American film director Todd Haynes has moved from the underground fringes of independent cinema and the New Queer Cinema to the mainstream of the American film industry. His movie *Far from Heaven* (2002), an homage to, and a rewriting of, Douglas Sirk's melodramas of the 1950s, was unanimously hailed as a masterpiece, sweeping a host of prestigious international awards and obtaining four Oscar nominations. Like the careers of **Gus Van Sant**, David Lynch, and the Cohen brothers, Todd Haynes's professional biography represents the dynamics that turn maverick directors into Hollywood's hottest cultural properties, thus increasingly blurring the boundaries between independent and industry cinema. Haynes's films, however, remain distinctively queer, not only for the homosexual themes that they directly or indirectly treat, but also for their subversion of conventional narrative structures and their complex cultural references.

Haynes was born on January 2, 1961, in Los Angeles. He was passionate about cinema from a very early age, a passion that he sustained by watching movies from different genres and historical periods. Once an art and semiotics student at Brown University, Haynes developed a particular interest in avant-garde cinema. After

Jonathan Rhys Meyers as a David Bowie look-alike in Todd Haynes's homage to glam rock, *The Velvet Goldmine*. Courtesy of Miramax/Photofest.

graduating in 1985, he decided to actively promote independent films by launching Apparatus Production, an organization which supports underground movies. He also became involved in **AIDS** activism through ACT-UP, a move which the filmmaker has credited as inspiring his earlier queer films. Central to all of Haynes's shorts and full-length features is the director's investigation of how identities are constructed, shattered, and repressed. Whether concerned with the death from anorexia of the Carpenters' female singer Karen or with an adaptation of Jean Genet's stories, Haynes's films warn about the dangers of letting others define one's own personal identity.

The short on Karen Carpenter, *Superstar* (1987), focuses on how social norms manipulate female bodies, suggesting a dangerous identification of identity with the physical body. What begins as a parody with Ken and Barbie dolls cast in the leading roles soon turns into a bitter reflection on the social and cultural constructions of illness and identity. The three episodes of *Poison* (1991) and, in particular, "Homo," the most directly indebted to Jean Genet's stories, show the dangers of repressing one's innermost sexual desires. A recipient of funds from the National Endowment for the Arts and the winner of the Grand Jury Prize at the Sundance Film Festival, *Poison* soon became the defining work of New Queer Cinema. Set in a prison, the scenes of explicit homosexual sex in the "Homo" episode caused the film to be targeted by the American Family Association. Yet, the National Endowment for the Arts proudly defended its choice to partly fund the film lending artistic credentials to the New Queer Cinema. According to Keith Ulhich (*Senses of Cinema* online), *Poison* is really about reconstructing "the interior psychology of a single homosexual male—represented at different ages and in different time periods by the main characters in each segment—and how he ultimately succumbs to or transcends how society views him." The movie moves backwards from the present-day suburbia of "Hero," to the 1950s Cold War paranoia of "Horror" and the years when homosexuality was still a crime of "Homo."

Although *Safe* (1995) does not have an explicit homosexual content, it is a powerful reflection on the social and cultural significance of diseases, including, obviously, AIDS. It focuses on an upper-middle-class woman, played by Julianne Moore, who discovers that she is infected with a mysterious and invasive disease for which there is no treatment. The film criticizes the public processes that confer people a distinctive identity because of their diseases. At the same time, *Poison* targets also the supposedly miraculous treatments for such diseases. Through these different aspects of his critique, Haynes challenges the ways in which AIDS is conceptualized in contemporary society. However, Murray Pomerance, a contributor to James Morrison's 2006 volume on Haynes points out how the director may eventually end up sharing some of the complacency he seems to satirize.

Velvet Goldmine (1998) looks at the queer world of glam rock of the 1970s and early 1980s. Following the efforts of British journalist Arthur Stuart (Christian Bale) to trace rock star Brian Slade (Jonathan Rhys-Meyers), the film depicts how glam artists used music and excessive spectacle to challenge social rules and gender distinctions. Awarded the Grand Jury Prize for Artistic Contribution at Cannes, *Velvet Goldmine* rejects the so-called biopic conventions and does not set out to reconstruct the lives of the artists, such as David Bowie and Iggy Pop, that acted as a source of inspiration. "I wanted it to be," Haynes stated (Dickinson 2005, *Biography* online), "about the relationship between the fan and his idol." The film is built on the conviction that all history writing is partial and the director takes full advantage of his artistic freedom to recreate history. The director traces the origins of glam to Oscar Wilde and has him appear at the beginning of the movie. "I don't know if Oscar Wilde was as apparent to Ferry and Eno as he seems in the movie," he concedes, "but all the roads lead back to him. Wilde is the most articulate spokesperson for this moment—the last really mainstream explosion of these kinds of ideas that run very counter to the traditional notions of art and truth and direct emotional communication by the artists. Instead it elevates art as camp and irony and wit, evokes questions about sexual identity. Oscar Wilde was a very popular bourgeois hit in his time, and so was glam rock" (Dickinson 2005, *Biography* online).

Far from Heaven was Haynes's most successful film to date, starring Julianne Moore as Cathy, an upper-class housewife in 1950s America who discovers that her husband Frank (played by Dennis Quaid in one of his best performances) is sexually attracted to other men. A film about homophobia, sexual repression, and racism, *Far from Heaven* takes the 1950s melodramas of Douglas Sirk as its privileged point of reference, mimicking and reinterpreting the iconography of *Magnificent Obsession* (1954), *All That Heaven Allows* (1955), and *Imitation of Life* (1959). This last one, in particular, shares with *Far from Heaven* a critique of racism, a critique, however, that is stronger in Haynes's film. *Magnificent Obsession* and *All That Heaven Allows*, both starring Rock Hudson, are reinterpreted by Haynes as films with a strong gay subtext dealing with closeted homosexual desire due to their star's real sexual orientation. In his progressive interpretation of themes derived by Sirk's melodramas, Haynes skillfully links the oppression of women, gays, and African-Americans. The film shows Frank attaining a certain degree of happiness in a gay relationship, which, however, has to remain well hidden. Cathy, on the contrary, cannot experience a fulfilling relationship with her black gardener when their affair comes out in the open.

Although *Velvet Goldmine* and *Far from Heaven* garnered important official recognitions and the latter, in particular, received rave reviews in mainstream media, the cinema of Todd Haynes continues to challenge conventional Hollywood narratives both in terms of form and content. The director's films question stereotypical and totalizing conceptions of identity, and, tellingly, his forthcoming project on Bob Dylan (*I'm Not There: Supposition on a Film Concerning Dylan*) will have the singer played by many actors and actress. James Morrison (2006, 6) reads this choice as an enduring "critique of humanist notions of coherent selfhood, offering hope to those who expect that Haynes will continue his work in the cinema of transgression."

Further Reading

Aaron, Michele. *New Queer Cinema: A Critical Reader*. New Brunswick, NJ: Rutgers State University Press, 2004; Dickinson, Peter. "Oscar Wilde: Reading the Life after the Life." *Biography*. Volume 28, Number 3, Summer 2005. 414–432. http://www.highbeam.com/doc/ 1G1-137269360.html (accessed on March 12, 2007); MacDowell, James. "Beneath the Surface of Things: Interpretation and *Far from Heaven*." *Offscreen*. Volume 10, Issue 5 (May 31, 2006). http://www.off-screen.com/biblio/phile/essays/beneath_surface/ (accessed on March 12, 2007); Morrison, James ed. *The Cinema of Todd Haynes: All That Heaven Allows*. London: Wallflower Press, 2006; Stephens, Chuck. "Gentlemen Prefer Haynes." *Film Comment* 31.4 (1995): 76–81; Ulhich, Keith. "Todd Haynes." *Senses of Cinema*. http://www.sensesofcinema.com/contents/directors/02/haynes.html (accessed on March 12, 2007).

HECHE, ANNE (1969–)

American actress, screenwriter, and director Anne Heche holds a controversial place in gay and lesbian popular culture. On the one hand, she has contributed to making lesbianism the object of media hype thanks to her much-publicized relationship with **Ellen DeGeneres** in the late 1990s. Heche and DeGeneres became the most talked about couple in Hollywood, titillating the interest of popular tabloids. They attended White House receptions as partners and announced their relationship on *Oprah!* On the other hand, however, Heche has been taken to task for the development of her persona after her relationship with DeGeneres ended in 2000. Her marriage to cameraman Coley Laffoon has led critics to speculate that many of the lesbians who achieve visibility in the Hollywood mainstream do so only because they can quickly switch back to heterosexuality. In addition, Heche's autobiography *Call Me Crazy* (2001) may be problematic to gay and lesbian audiences for its connections between insanity and lesbianism.

Heche was born on May 25, 1969, in Aurora, Ohio, but grew up in New Jersey, where her family moved when she was five. Her father Donald Heche was a Baptist minister and, according to Heche's autobiography *Call Me Crazy*, he abused her during her childhood. In the 1980s the family discovered that Donald was gay and that he was dying of **AIDS**. Heche's childhood was also marked by the death of her older brother Nate in a car accident. Heche reacted against the strict Baptist upbringing from an early age. Her acting career started at the age of 18 when she was offered the double roles of the twins Vicky Hudson and Marley Love Hudson in the soap opera *Another World* (1987–1991). For her performance as these good and bad twins, she won a Daytime Emmy Award.

Heche continued her career starring in important films such as *Donnie Brasco* (1997), the action drama *Volcano* (1997), and the political satire *Wag the Dog* (1997). Heche and DeGeneres announced their relationship shortly after Heche was cast for the female lead in the romantic comedy *Six Days, Seven Nights* (1998) opposite Harrison Ford. Heche thus became the first openly lesbian actress to act in a romantic comedy. Since the movie was mainly targeted to a heterosexual audience, her decision to come out was challenged by film critics as well as by the movie's director Ivan Reitman. In 1998 she also starred in **Gus Van Sant**'s shot-for-shot remake of Alfred Hitchcock's *Psycho* in the role of Marion Crane, played by Janet Leigh. While they were a couple, Heche and DeGeneres worked together on a number of projects. Heche directed the documentary *Ellen DeGeneres: American Summer Documentary* (2001) and the third segment of the lesbian-themed TV movie *If These Walls Could Talk 2* (2000). The couple often complained to be the victim of Hollywood discrimination against homosexuals as they claimed their contracts diminished after their coming out.

After her split with DeGeneres, Heche was again in the national headlines for her memoir *Call Me Crazy*. In the book, she claimed that she had suffered from mental insanity for more than 30 years, she talked about her father's sexual abuses against her, and argued she had an alter ego called Celestia who was the daughter of God and half-sibling of Jesus. Heche married Coley Laffoon in September 2001, which gave her Christian-fundamentalist mother the excuse to say that her prayers to God had cured her daughter of her homosexuality. Heche, however, denied that there had been a change in her sexual orientation and that she preferred not to label herself as either lesbian or straight. Heche's career has continued with appearances in less successful films such as *John Q.* (2002) and *Birth* (2004). While she has not appeared in leading roles on the big screen, she has starred opposite Treat Williams in the third season of the TV series *Everwood*. In 2006, she played relationship coach Marin Frist, the protagonist of the ABC series *Men in Trees*. The series centers upon Frist's misadventures when she relocates from her native New York to Alaska after discovering that her fiancé has been cheating on her. To Marin, the move will mean starting her life anew. The series was created by one of the head writers and executive producers of *Sex and the City*.

With her statements and actions when she was the partner of Ellen DeGeneres, Heche has contributed to take lesbianism into the mainstream of American popular culture. However, because of further developments in Heche's life, many see the actress's place within the gay and lesbian community as problematic. In her article "Making Her (In)Visible: Cultural Representations of Lesbianism and the Lesbian Body in the 1990s," Ann M. Ciasullo (2001) has explicitly taken Heche as the example of the lesbian that can be soon turned into a heterosexual with a comforting effect for heterosexual viewers. Wondering how the lesbian has been allowed to enter the mainstream, Ciasullo examines a number of magazine articles as well as recent television and film representations of lesbians. The critic concludes that these representations create a paradox: the lesbian becomes invisible as the result of her hypervisibility. Contemporary mainstream cultural representations of lesbianism are always predicated on the possibility that "she who is lesbian (e.g., Anne Heche) can 'unbecome' lesbian (e.g., Anne Heche)." These lesbian bodies are thus "comfortable and comforting" (Ciasullo 2001, *Feminist Studies* online). They are not butch bodies which challenge conventional representations of gender roles. The interest of tabloids for Heche is indicative of the fact that the butch body remains invisible and marginal within contemporary culture. It does not conform to the heterosexual notion of desirable woman. Thus, it remains a matter for debate how far Heche's success as an actress and her frequent appearances on tabloid covers in the late 1990s have really modified mainstream representations of the lesbian or have lent support to them.

Further Reading

Ciasullo, Ann M. "Making Her (In)Visible: Cultural Representations of Lesbianism and the Lesbian Body in the 1990s." *Feminist Studies.* Fall 2001. 27:3. 577–608. http://www.highbeam.com/doc/1G1-81889004.html (accessed on May 20, 2007); Heche, Anne. *Call Me Crazy.* New York: Washington Square Press, 2001; Weisel, Al. "Anne Heche." *US Magazine.* February 1998. 61–62, 89.

HUDSON, ROCK (1925–1985)

Throughout his career, American movie star Rock Hudson hid his homosexuality and became an icon of Hollywood heterosexuality. His good looks, the 1950s melodramas directed by Douglas Sirk, and the 1960s romantic comedies opposite Doris Day made Hudson one of the top moneymaking Hollywood stars. His homosexuality, however, abruptly emerged in the early 1980s when the media announced that Hudson was suffering from **AIDS**. As the first Hollywood celebrity to die of AIDS, Hudson drew attention to the disease, although it took two more years before American President Regan, a long-time friend of the actor, decided to publicly mention AIDS and to reconsider the allocations of funds for prevention and treatment. Yet, Hudson's pivotal importance in people's awareness about AIDS cannot be underestimated. As gay journalist Randy Shilts wrote at the beginning of his history of AIDS, *And the Band Played On:* "By October 2, 1985, the morning Rock Hudson died, the word [AIDS] was familiar to almost every household in the Western world."

Hudson was born Roy Harold Scherer, Jr., in Winnetka, Illinois. He was the only child of Roy Harold Scherer, Sr., a mechanic, and Katherine Wood, a

Rock Hudson and Phyllis Gates shortly after their studio-arranged marriage in 1955. Courtesy of Universal Pictures/Photofest.

telephone operator. When Hudson was four years old, his parents divorced and, in 1932, his mother married Wallace Fitzgerald, who legally adopted Hudson. This second marriage also ended in divorce. Hudson graduated from New Trier High School in 1943 and then served in the navy until 1946. Once discharged, he moved to Los Angeles where he embarked on his acting career. He was rejected by the University of Southern California's dramatics program because of his poor grades. Before the agent Henry Willson, who was also gay, changed his name and introduced him to director Raul Walsh, Hudson worked at different odd jobs. The beginnings of the actor's career were not auspicious. His screen test for Twentieth Century-Fox was so terrible that it was shown to beginners' classes as a classic example of poor acting. Walsh signed the actor for his first film role in *Fighter Squadron* (1948). However, legend has it that Hudson needed 38 takes to utter his one line in the film. The following year Hudson's contract was sold to Universal, where the actor remained until 1965.

After a string of B movies, mainly Westerns, émigré director Douglas Sirk provided Hudson with the role that would launch his career as a star. In Sirk's melodrama *Magnificent Obsession* (1954). Hudson played a ruthless man who repents and devotes his life to a woman (played by Jane Wyman) he has blinded. Melodrama suited Hudson who went on to star in the majority of Sirk's so-called women's films of the 1950s: *All That Heaven Allows* (1955), again opposite Jane Wyman, *Written on the Wind* (1956), and *The Tarnished Angels* (1957). These big hits consolidated Hudson's status as a star as did his performance as a traditional Southern cattle owner in *Giant* (1956), which won Hudson his only Academy Award nomination. The actor's new star status required silencing the rumors about Hudson's homosexuality. Thus, a marriage between Hudson and his agent's secretary Phyllis Gates was arranged in 1955, although it only lasted for three years. Many have come to suspect that Gates herself was homosexual and that, after the divorce, she tried to blackmail her former husband.

Pillow Talk (1959) was a turning point in the actor's screen persona. After a series of melodramatic roles, it was Hudson's first comedy. In it he plays a handsome womanizer who falls for an interior decorator (Doris Day) with whom he shares a telephone line. The mix of sexual innuendo, witty script, and fast-paced developments made *Pillow Talk* successful with audiences and critics alike. The film received several Oscar nominations, although Hudson did not, and obtained enthusiastic reviews. Hudson had proved to the box office that his appeal extended beyond melodramas and adventure films. *Pillow Talk* codified the conventions for the so-called sex comedies that made Hudson's popularity rocket in the 1960s. He was cast again opposite Day in *Lover Come Back* (1961) and *Send Me No Flowers* (1964). His other female partners included Gina Lollobrigida in *Come September* (1961) and *Strange Bedfellows* (1965), Paula Prentiss in Howard Hawks's *Man's Favourite Sport?* (1964), and Leslie Caron in *A Very Special Favor* (1965). All these comedy vehicles made Hudson one of the most profitable actors in Hollywood and the winner of several popularity polls and theater owners' awards. Between 1957 and 1964, the actor was on the top 10 list of box office stars drawn by cinema owners every single year. His international reputation was certainly not confined to the United States as he also won five German Bambi Awards in the category of the most popular male actor.

Paradoxically, Hudson never felt too comfortable in the roles that crowned him as the "king of sex comedies." Throughout the 1960s, he tried to complement his comic roles with more dramatic ones, including a lone sheriff in *The Last Sunset* (1961) and an atheist converted to faith in *The Spiral Road* (1964). However, these characters were less appreciated by both critics and audiences. Although thousands of letters poured every month in his fan club, when Hudson became a free agent in 1965, he decided to relinquish comedy roles altogether. He formed his own production company, Gibraltar Productions, and purposefully hunted for roles that could prove his dramatic abilities. John Frankenheimer's *Seconds* (1966) was certainly the most critically acclaimed of these efforts. It follows the story of disillusioned banker Arthur Hamilton (John Randolph) who contacts a secret organization to assume the identity and the body of the younger Tony Wilson (Hudson). As Wilson is murdered, Hamilton takes on his life and his body (Hudson plays the transformed banker at this point). He becomes an artist and starts a relationship with a woman, but is plagued by the guilt of having caused the death of a person and of having betrayed his previous family. Hudson considered *Seconds* one of his best films, but, unfortunately, it flopped at the box office. Undaunted by the commercial disappointment, the actor continued his pursuit of dramatic roles, starring in *Ice Station Zebra* (1968), a Cold War spy-thriller, and in *The Undefeated* (1969), a Civil War drama where Hudson plays a Confederate colonel who finds himself forced into cooperation with a Yankee colonel (John Wayne).

The shift from romantic comedy to drama proved damaging for Hudson's film career, which, by the 1970s, started to decline. His films of the decade were largely undistinguished such as the western *Showdown* (1973), the sci-fi *Embryo* (1976), and the catastrophic *Avalanche* (1978), in which he acts opposite Mia Farrow. Rather than going back to his comedy roles, he turned to television where he played the lead in the popular mystery series *McMillan and Wife* (1971–1977). He also starred in several TV movies and miniseries, such as the adaptation of Ray Bradbury's *The Martian Chronicles* (1980), an ambitious project, which, however, suffered from negative publicity from Bradbury himself, and *The Devlin Connection* (1982). He briefly returned to cinema to join the all-star cast of the rather bland Agatha Christie's mystery *The Mirror Crack'd* (1980). His appearances on the TV series *Dynasty* brought his career full-circle as he returned to the world of melodrama from where he had started.

By the time he joined the *Dynasty* cast, Hudson was already seeking treatment for AIDS. On the set he suffered from memory losses and had to use cue cards. His worn-out look attracted wide media coverage and people started to speculate on the actor's health, given that Hudson's homosexuality had always been rumored and that, in the early 1980s, AIDS was still considered a gay plague. When asked by friends and by his partner Marc Christian, Hudson tried at first to deny he had AIDS, explaining that his emaciated appearance was due to liver cancer and anorexia. In July 1985, Hudson joined Doris Day for the TV launch of her show "Doris Day's Best Friends." In the show he appeared even slimmer than in the *Dynasty* episodes and his speech was increasingly incoherent. The show revived media and public attention towards the actor's health. It was veteran gossip columnist Army Archerd who wrote in *Variety* that Hudson was seeking experimental treatment for AIDS in Paris. Hudson's publicist Dale Olson initially denied the story, but on July 25 he issued a press statement in which Hudson admitted that he was gay and that he had full-blown AIDS. Before his death Hudson stated (Official Rock Hudson website), "I am not happy that I am sick. I am not happy that I have AIDS. But if that is helping others, I can at least know that my own misfortune has had some positive worth." It remains debatable whether Hudson would have revealed his condition without Army Archerd's column. He died at his home in Beverly Hills, California, on October 2, 1985.

Hudson's revelations on his homosexuality and his death from AIDS caused a press furor. Many speculated whether Hudson could have infected *Dynasty* actress Linda Evans whom he had kissed in the TV series. His sexual life, which he had successfully kept secret for many years, suddenly received unprecedented attention. Hudson's partner Marc Christian, who had not been informed of his positive status, successfully sued the actor's estate. It also emerged that Hudson's agent Henry Willson had to constantly persuade celebrity gossip magazines not to run stories on Hudson's homosexuality. In particular, Willson was willing to sell *Confidential* stories about the homosexuality of his less successful clients, including Rory Calhoun and Tab Hunter, to preserve Hudson's heterosexual mask.

Hudson's predicament threw AIDS in the limelight and started to change the attitude of politicians and journalists towards the disease. Hudson was entirely different from the portrayals of people with AIDS made by the press in those days. Media described AIDS as an illness of those groups who were on the margins of society. Yet, here was Rock Hudson, a Hollywood legend who was white, enormously rich, an international icon of rugged heterosexuality, and a staunch Republican supporter. The actor gave a face to the virus, as actress Morgan Fairchild summarized. AIDS activists were able to exploit the new media interest in the virus to expose the growing number of positive diagnoses in the United States and the lack of resources to fight the epidemic. As Stuart Byron remarked in the **Advocate** four years after Hudson's death, the actor's "illness and death marked the turning point in opening up funding for and public sympathy to the AIDS epidemic." Byron then went on asking bitterly, "How many lives might have been saved had there been...uncloseted stars and athletes testifying before Congressional committees and leading AIDS marches?"

Rock Hudson was a product of Hollywood's celluloid closet. His career and the careful construction of his public heterosexual persona testify to the burden of the closet for gay and lesbian actors. As Michelangelo Signorile has pointed out, Rock Hudson's death exposed the Hollywood mechanism to impose heterosexuality on actors and to marginalize homosexuals. However unwittingly, Hudson's greatest achievement as a gay star might have been precisely to begin to smash that celluloid closet.

Further Reading

Davidson, Sara, and Rock Hudson. *Rock Hudson: His Story.* New York: Bantam, 1986; Hofler, Robert. "Outing Mrs. Rock Hudson." *The Advocate.* 28 February 2006; Official Rock Hudson Website. http://www.cmgworldwide.com/stars/hudson/about/quotes.htm (accessed on June 17, 2007); Klinger, Barbara. *Melodrama and Meaning: History, Culture, and the Films of Douglas Sirk.* Bloomington: Indiana University Press, 1994; Royce, Brenda Scott. *Rock Hudson: A Bio-Bibliography.* Westport, CT: Greenwood Press, 1995; Signorile, Michelangelo. *Queer in America: Sex, the Media and the Closets of Power.* New York: Random House, 1993; Thompson, Mark, ed. *Long Road to Freedom: The Advocate History of the Gay and Lesbian Movement.* New York: St. Martin's Press, 1994.

I

ISHERWOOD, CHRISTOPHER (1904–1986)

Anglo-American novelist Christopher Isherwood is a major figure in gay and lesbian popular culture. Although the author only explicitly revealed his homosexuality in the autobiography of his parents, *Kathleen and Frank*, in 1971, he has written about homosexuality and gay characters in all his novels. His early works of the 1930s do not always treat gayness in an explicit way, but, even in their covert allusions, they differ from contemporary literary pieces on homosexuality where same-sex desire is portrayed as a symptom of psychological malaise or decadence. Isherwood's later novels of the 1960s and 1970s focus on homosexual characters more explicitly. Together with the author's participation in the early phases of the gay liberation movements, novels such as *A Single Man* and autobiographical works such as *Kathleen and Frank* and *Christopher and His Kind* (1976) made Isherwood a popular icon of gay culture. Isherwood's centrality in gay culture was also established thanks to his overseeing the publication of E. M. Forster's gay novel *Maurice*, a task entrusted to him by Forster's himself. **Edmund White** has hailed Isherwood's novel *A Single Man* (1964) as the founding text of modern gay fiction. Both Isherwood's early and later novels are characterized by a strong autobiographical element. Many gay authors have adopted Isherwood's semi-autobiographical narrative technique to create the genre of the so-called coming out novel and Isherwood's works have influenced gay writers such as **Gore Vidal, Tennessee Williams, Armistead Maupin**, and Paul Monette.

Christopher William Bradshaw Isherwood was born into a distinguished Cheshire family at Wyberslegh Hall, near the villages of Disley and High Lane, England, on August 26, 1904. He was brought up in England and Ireland and his childhood was marked by the violent death of his father, Frank Isherwood, who was killed in 1915 during World War I and whose body was never found. Isherwood's mother never recovered from her husband's death and spent most of her remaining life mourning. Christopher was educated at St. Edmund's School, Hindhead, Surrey, where he first met the future poet and fellow homosexual W. H. Auden, and then at Repton School, Derby. In 1924, Isherwood won a history scholarship at Corpus Christi College, Cambridge. In his two years in Cambridge, Isherwood met Auden again and also made friends with Stephen Spender. The friendship with Auden was to shape many of Isherwood's future decisions, including his settling down in Berlin and in the United States. The three friends formed the core of the Auden Group, which, in the 1930s, would recruit talented left-wing writers. The group became a predominant literary force on the British scene. When Isherwood left Cambridge without a degree in 1925, he earned his living in London as a private tutor and as secretary to the French violinist André Mangeot and his Music Society String Quartet. In 1928 he enrolled at university again, this time at King's College, London, to study medicine, but he soon gave up medical studies to follow his friend Auden to Berlin, where he lived from 1930 to 1933. In Weimar Berlin, where homosexuality was a visible feature of everyday life, Isherwood found a way to liberate himself from the world of stifling social conventions that had characterized his family life in Britain. These conventions form the main targets of the author's early novels, *All the Conspirators* (1928) and *The Memorial* (1932).

Isherwood's first two novels do not explicitly define the gayness of their main characters. Yet, both in the case of *All the Conspirators* and, more clearly, of *The Memorial*, the main characters are usually interpreted as prototypes for the more explicitly homosexual figures of Isherwood's later fiction. Both novels are auto-biographical in their rejections of English class society and family life. They are written in the modernist style typical of the previous generation of British novelists. From writers such as Virginia Woolf and D. H. Lawrence, Isherwood borrows the techniques that had deeply innovated the genre of the novel in the 1910s and early 1920s, including the stream-of-consciousness narration and the non-chronological arrangement of events. In addition to the homosexuality of the characters, one can see Isherwood's own homosexuality finding its way into the author's works. The fascination for anti-heroes and for alienated characters who live on the margins of society, the revolt against middle-class respectability, the search for a father figure, and the ironic observations that pervade Isherwood's early works can be related to the author's sexuality. Both *All the Conspirators* and *The Memorial* are characterized by a central ambivalence: the author's desire to express the anxieties of a generation clashes against his refusal to define clearly his personal investment in them.

The same ambivalence shapes Isherwood's most famous writings of the 1930s, his Berlin novels *Mr. Norris Changes Trains* (1935) and *Goodbye to Berlin* (1939). These have had a lasting impact on popular culture as they formed the source material for the hit musical and film *Cabaret*. Both novels translate Isherwood's experiences in pre-Hitler Berlin into fictional sketches, using both social realism and what Isherwood himself described as a detached "camera" perspective. The combination of social realism and modernist detachment is an apparent influence of Bertolt Brecht's epic theater, one of the distinctive cultural features of Weimar Berlin. Both novels were started in Berlin, but were completed after Isherwood had moved back to London to collaborate with German film director Berthold Viertel for the screen adaptation of Margaret Kennedy's novel *Little Friend*. This experience helped Isherwood perfect two techniques that became the typical aspects of his fiction: the revelation of characters' psychology through surface observation and telling details, and the "camera-eye" perspective adopted by the narrator. Both

Mr. Norris and *Goodbye to Berlin* describe Berlin society and its colorful expatriate community and create two alter egos for Isherwood, William Bradshaw, Isherwood's middle names, and Christopher Isherwood. The creation of these fictional figures obviously blurs the boundaries between autobiography and fiction in Isherwood's narratives. The William Bradshaw and Christopher Isherwood devices reveal the author's longstanding dissatisfaction with the two conventional forms of narration. Isherwood disliked first-person narration as it limited the narrative to the eyes of an egotistic storyteller. He was equally dissatisfied with third-person narration as it assigned the narrator too much authority. William Bradshaw and Christopher Isherwood served the purpose of striving towards a more objective observation, however impossible this ultimate goal is in literature. Isherwood conceived his narrator as a participant-observer of the events, but not the main part of the action that he was describing. The beginning of *Goodbye to Berlin* literally compares the narrator to a "ventriloquist dummy" and later to a camera with the shutter open to record the surrounding reality. What the camera records will have to be fixed and developed at a later stage.

What remains mostly hidden from view in the Berlin stories is the narrator himself and, particularly in the case of William Bradshaw, his homosexuality. Yet, as Claude J. Summers (1980) points out, this is part of Isherwood's technique not to sensationalize homosexual culture, but rather to present same-sex desire without the melodramatic attitude that characterizes its treatment in writings of the period. In his Berlin stories, Isherwood displays considerable insight in his depiction of homosexual relationships. *Mr. Norris Changes Trains* and *Goodbye to Berlin* do not depict gay characters as unhappy because of their homosexuality, but because they are part of that interwar Europe threatened by the menace of contrasting totalitarianisms. The gay and straight characters of Isherwood's Berlin novels ultimately share a common fate as citizens of a European continent on the brink of the cultural and social tragedy of fascism. Both the gay characters and the straight ones, such as Sally Bowles and Mr. Norris, are forced to live on the margins of society.

During the 1930s Isherwood also collaborated with Auden on three stage plays for London's Group Theater: *The Dog beneath the Skin* (1935), *The Ascent of F6* (1936), and *On the Frontier* (1938). These experimental plays are clearly influenced by the theater of Brecht and contain a critique of British and European governments. These avant-garde works confirmed both Isherwood's and Auden's left-wing sympathies, from which, however, both writers would start to distance themselves at the end of the decade. The two intellectuals also collaborated on the reportage of the Sino-Japanese War, *Journey to a War* (1939). At the beginning of 1939, both writers emigrated to the United States, where they spent the rest of their lives. While Auden settled down in New York, Isherwood went to live in Los Angeles, where he worked as a screenwriter in Hollywood for Metro-Goldwyn-Mayer. When Isherwood decided to emigrate he was considered one of the major English writers by British critics. Somerset Maugham famously stated that Isherwood had the future of the English novel in his hands. Yet, moving to the United States irreversibly damaged Isherwood's British reception and critics in the United Kingdom never paid much attention to the writer's American works. Isherwood's posthumously published diaries are a helpful source to reconstruct his early years in America. They show the writer engaged in the study of the Vedanta philosophy, a branch of

Hindu religion. In the early 1940s Isherwood was a resident student at the Vedanta Society of Southern California and, together with his guru Swami Prabhavananda, served as editor for the magazine *Vedanta and the West*. He also translated into English the *Bhagavad-Gita*, one of the sacred books of the Hindu religion. Isherwood's encounter with Hinduism and his work as a screenwriter in Hollywood form the basis for his next novel *Prater Violet* (1945), a transitional work between the author's Berlin stories and his later American books. Set in Austria between 1933 and 1934 at the time of the Socialist uprising and its following suppression, the novel fictionalizes Isherwood's work with Viertel on the adaptation of *Little Friend*. The narrator, named Christopher Isherwood, is the same of the Berlin stories, but he is more generous in giving personal details. The title of the novel is the same of the trivial comedy on which the character Isherwood is working and the situations of the film are contrasted with the tragic events that constitute the novel's historical background.

Isherwood became an American citizen in 1946, and in 1953 he met his life partner, the artist Don Bachardy, then a young art student, with whom he settled down in Santa Monica, near Los Angeles. Isherwood's American production is more explicit about homosexual themes and focuses more insistently on the specific difficulties that gay people encounter within mainstream society. In his novel *The World in the Evening* (1954), set in the 1940s, Isherwood gave one of the very first sympathetic representations of a gay activist in American literature. Bob Wood, the main character of the novel, faces both personal and institutional obstacles to his development as an activist. His Jewish boyfriend cannot stand Bob's militancy and, at the end of the novel, Wood joins the Navy not so much out of patriotic fervor, but because he wants to fight against the military ban on homosexuals. Worried that readers might find the gay content of *The World in the Evening* offensive, the publisher tried to persuade Isherwood to tone down the homosexual parts of the book, but the author refused. *Down There on a Visit* (1962) returns to the episodic structure of the Berlin novels and to the same subgenre of so-called fictional autobiography. The book is also similar to the Berlin tales in its emphasis on loneliness and alienation. For example, Ambrose, one of the characters, attempts to establish a community of homosexuals on a Greek island where heterosexuality is illegal, but can be tolerated if practiced in private. The ironic reversal of everyday reality is obviously symptomatic of the alienation and exclusion that many homosexuals feel from larger society.

At the end of the 1950s, Isherwood began to combine his activity as a writer with university teaching. He was guest professor of modern English literature at Los Angeles State College from 1959 to 1962. He was then Regents Professor at the University of California at Los Angeles and later at Riverside. As an academic, he was one of the first to address the topic of gayness in literature and, in 1974, he was invited to the Modern Language Association conference with a talk on "Homosexuality in Literature." By then, Isherwood's academic reputation was firmly established and his American life became increasingly characterized by political activism on behalf of queer causes. *A Single Man* (1964) is unanimously considered the writer's best American novel and has been hailed as the founding text of modern gay literature. Following the typical structure of modernist novels such as Joyce's *Ulysses* (1922) and Woolf's *Mrs. Dalloway* (1925), *A Single Man* (1964) focuses on a day in the life of George, a middle-aged gay literature professor, whose surname remains unknown. The character shares important traits with his creator, although there are also crucial differences. The novel, seen entirely through the eyes of its main character, challenges the notion of a unified self as George almost becomes a different person according to the roles he takes in the various events of the narrative. The underlying theme of the novel is the grievance for the loss of George's lover, an ordeal never experienced by Isherwood. Thus *A Single Man* celebrates male homosexual love. George's sexuality is presented matter-of-factly without problems of self-hatred or of neurosis to be treated. In addition, with the advent of the AIDS epidemic, George's narrative has acquired an oddly prophetic status for entire generations of gay men as it shows a gay male grieving alone for the loss of his partner.

A Meeting by the River (1967) was Isherwood's last work of fiction, focusing on the controversial relationship between two brothers, a film producer, and a younger novice in a Hindu monastery who is about to take his vows as a swami. Isherwood's following two books represented a return to the autobiographical genre that is so central to the author's entire production. *Kathleen and Frank* (1971) is a biographical account of Isherwood's parents, where the writer starts to talk frankly about his own homosexuality. This aspect of his biography is further reconstructed in his last volume, *Christopher and His Kind* (1976). Isherwood died on January 4, 1986, in Santa Monica, California. Several critics have faulted Isherwood for a certain degree of self-absorption as he repeatedly examined his own life through the lenses of autobiography and fiction. Yet, his centrality in gay and lesbian popular culture is indisputable. With his books, Isherwood contributed to an increased visibility of homosexuality with American fiction and autobiography. He was also one of the first well-known American personalities and intellectuals to stand up for homosexual rights, an inspiring example to many of subsequent generations.

Further Reading

Berg, James and Chris Freeman, eds. *The Isherwood Century: Essays on the Life and Work of Christopher Isherwood*. Madison: University of Wisconsin Press, 2000; Cunningham, Valentine. *British Writers of the Thirties*. Oxford: Oxford University Press, 1988; Philips, Adam. "Knitting." *London Review of Books* (November 16, 2000): 6–7; Schwerdt, Lisa M. *Isherwood's Fiction: The Self and Technique*. London: Macmillan, 1989; Summers, Claude J. *Christopher Isherwood*. New York: Ungar, 1980; Summers, Claude J. *Gay Fictions: Wilde to Stonewall*. New York: Continuum, 1990; Wade, Stephen. *Christopher Isherwood*. London: Macmillan, 1991.

J

JETT, JOAN (1960–)

Although 1980s rock icon Joan Jett has never issued a public discussion of her sexual orientation, she has developed a devoted lesbian following. She has also appeared at many events in support of queer rights throughout the United States. The singer has stimulated rumors about her sexuality, performing with the sticker "Dykes Rule" on her guitar and claiming that she does not care how people label her sexuality. Some of her songs, such as "A.C.D.C.," "Androgynous," and "Everyone Knows," have an unmistakably queer content. Jett's passion for rock music dates back to her early teens, when she founded the first all-girl teen rock band, the Runaways. Her aggressive leather look, her characteristic rough voice, and her punk-influenced music made the singer the forerunner of the so-called riot grrrl genre and challenged the gender barriers of the world of rock. At the time of Jett's debut, most women performed as mellow pop or folk singers; Jett's spellbinding success, made of nine Top 40 hit singles and eight Platinum and Gold LPs, demonstrated that rock was not only for men.

Born Joan Larkin in Philadelphia on September 22, 1960, Jett grew up in Baltimore and moved with her family to Los Angeles in 1972. She became interested in rock music at an early age, especially in British glam artists, but has often complained that there were no role models for women at the time: "There just weren't any females role models. Suzi Quatro made records and I liked some of them. And I thought if she can do it, I can do it. Then I saw her a few times and that's where I got the idea for the Runaways" (Harrington 1987, *Washington Post* online). Jett was intrigued by starting an all-girl rock band: "Sure, it was great with one girl up there, but what if you had four or five girls doing sweaty rock 'n' roll? Nobody'd seen that before, and I thought, 'Wow, what a great idea.' I thought we would be the next Rolling Stones" (Harrington 1987, *Washington Post* online). Yet, as Jett herself later admitted, "it was a 15-year-old's pipe dream" and the band had difficulties to be taken seriously, especially in the United States. Also due to their manager's promotion strategy, the group would perform before almost all-male

Lesbian rock icon Joan Jett. Courtesy of Columbia TriStar/ Photofest.

audiences expecting "some sort of a sex show.... I don't know why girls wouldn't come to see us as a rock 'n' roll band" (Harrington 1987, *Washington Post* online). Although the Runaways were successful in Europe and Japan, the fact that they could not make a breakthrough on the American market led to their dissolution in 1979, only three years after their founding.

Regardless of what were the gender roles prescribed for women singers, Jett decided to pursue her solo career in the world of punk and rock. She produced an album with the punk band the Germs and performed with several former members of the Sex Pistols. However, it was with her newly established band, the Blackhearts, that Jett became a rock star. After difficult beginnings which forced the band to self-produce their first album, the Blackhearts topped the charts in 1982 with the title track of their second album *I Love Rock 'n' Roll*, which was number one for eight consecutive weeks. The song was covered in 2001 by Britney Spears, who, however, infamously identified it as a Pat Benatar song at a press conference. During the 1980s, Jett had a string of Top 40 singles and toured with world-famous bands such as The Police, Queen, and Aerosmith. While she could not replicate the success of *I Love Rock 'n' Roll*, her albums *Up Your Alley* (1988), *The Hit List* (1990), and *Notorious* (1991) sold well and contributed to make Jett a feminist and queer icon. *Fit to Be Tied* (1997) collected her greatest hits. Jett continued to produce albums into the late 1990s and in the new millennium. These include *Fetish* (1999), *Unfinished Business* (2001), *USA: Joan Jett and the Blackhearts* (2002), *Naked* (2004), and *Sinner* (2006). The latter celebrates the 25th anniversary of the singer's recording label, Blackheart Records.

In 1987 the singer also started her acting career when she appeared in Paul Schrader's *Light of Day* with Michael J. Fox and Gena Rowlands. Jett performed the title song of the movie, specially written by Bruce Springsteen for her. Since then, she has appeared in several indie movies and, in 2001, she was part of the Broadway cast for *The Rocky Horror Picture Show*. With the years, the lyrics of her songs have become more overtly political and several of her songs have also taken up explicitly queer themes. "A.C.D.C.," from *Sinner*, is an ode to bisexuality, with an impressive video featuring Jett together with glamour model and actress Carmen Electra, who confessed to having had a long-standing crush on Jett. "A.C.D.C."

is a cover of an old Sweet song and brings Jett back to her adolescence: "That's what I grew up on in the '70s, when the Runaways were forming. There was this teenage nightclub I would go to, and the deejay would play Bowie, Slade, Sweet and these other great British bands American kids were never exposed to" (Joan Jett Official Website). "Everyone Knows" has also a clear homosexual content and is a hymn to sexual nonconformity. The song finished with an affirmation of difference and devotion among partners who are considered "freaks" by mainstream society. Her shift towards a more militant and political attitude is signaled by the title of the radio show she hosts for Sirius Satellite radio, *The Radio Revolution with Joan Jett*.

With her albums in the 1980s and early 1990s, Jett has contributed to modifying the image of the rock artist as a quintessentially male figure. Her signature look and her hardcore punk music made her an important influence of the queercore movement. With her more militant and politically committed lyrics of the albums of the new century, Jett also demonstrated how music can respond to, and advance, controversial social debates.

Further Reading

Harrington, Richard. "Joan Jett, Rocking to Runaway Success." *The Washington Post*. January 9, 1987. http://www.highbeam.com/doc/1P2-1299907.html (accessed on February 4, 2007); Joan Jett and the Blackhearts Official Web site: http://www.joanjett.com (accessed on February 4, 2007); Juno, Andrea. "Joan Jett." *Angry Women in Rock Volume One*. Andrea Juno, ed. New York: Juno Books, 1996. 69–81.

JOHN, SIR ELTON (1947–)

In a career spanning over four decades, British singer and composer Elton John has become a prominent icon of rock and popular music. He has won five Grammy Awards and one Academy Award. Because of his remarkable commercial success, Elton John has had a profound impact on popular music, often setting the standards of the industry and perfectly adapting to the new tastes of international audiences thanks to his renowned versatility. His charisma, his flamboyant and glitzy outfits, his distinguished voice, and his unique melodies have fascinated successive generations of admirers as much as his famous diva-like tantrums. Although he has experienced temporary crises of creativity, John was the bestselling pop star of the 1970s and he continues to attract adulation from a large fan base and respect from music critics. Since his coming out after the collapse of his marriage to Renate Blauel, John has also been a vocal supporter of gay and lesbian causes. He has contributed to the struggle for **AIDS** awareness and, in 1992, established the Elton John AIDS Foundation, which fights for HIV/AIDS prevention and for the elimination of prejudice and discrimination against individuals affected by the virus. On December 21, 2005, the first day the British law allowed same-sex unions, he entered into a civil partnership with his longtime companion David Furnish. In addition to the sentimental meaning, John gave a political nuance to his partnership, using it as an opportunity to comment on discrimination and homophobia.

John was born Reginald Kenneth Dwight in Pinner, Middlesex, on March 25, 1947. His parents Stanley Dwight, a Royal Air Force officer, and Sheila Harris, who was educated at the Royal Academy of Music, were keen record buyers and exposed Reginald to music from a very early age. The child learned to play the piano at four, and at Pinner Country Grammar School, Reginald showed a natural inclination for musical composition. At 11, he won a scholarship to the Royal Academy of Music in London. However, John was impatient to go into the music business and in 1961 he joined his first band, Bluesology, who were backing touring American soul and R&B musicians. John split from Bluesology only five years later due to artistic differences with the bandleader, Long John Baldry. In the mid-1960s, he answered an advertisement for songwriter placed by Liberty Records. At the audition, he was given lyrics written by Bernie Taupin, who had also answered the ad and who would become his regular professional partner. The two artists began corresponding and Reginald, who had changed his name to Elton John borrowing the first names of two Bluesology members, started to write music for Taupin's lyrics. The cooperation proved rewarding for both artists, who wrote easy-listening tunes for other singers.

In 1969 John had its first hit album, *Elton John*, whose single "Your Song" catapulted the singer to fame both in Britain and the United States. After the second album, *Tumbleweed Connection*, also proved a success, John and Taupin began to produce records at a frenetic pace. Between 1972 and 1976, the pair John/Taupin scored 16 Top 20 hits in a row. In 1973 John founded his own label, *Rocket*, which was distributed by MCA, to record young promising artists but did not become a Rocket recording artist himself, preferring to stay with MCA for a record-breaking $8 million contract in 1974. Songs written during these years, such as "Daniel," "Don't Let the Sun Go Down on Me," "Rocket Man," "Goodbye Yellow Brick Road," and "Candle in the Wind," have proved continuously popular with audiences. During the 1970s, John also developed his defining performing style in

Elton John with a pair of his distinctively bizarre glasses at the height of his success as an unlikely rock icon in the 1970s. Courtesy of Photofest.

sold-out concerts. His shyness was concealed by an increasingly camp performance style. His bizarre outfits, ranging from feather boas and the Statue of Liberty to astronaut suits and Mozart impersonations, all topped by a never-ending collection of glasses, became a distinguishing feature of John's persona. His excessive performances made up for his short stature, chubby build, and balding head, characteristics that do not usually help a career as a rock idol. Yet, John successfully overcame these physical inadequacies and became the hottest rocker of the 1970s. During that decade, John also collaborated with two legendary artists: John Lennon and Pete Townshend. He covered The Beatles' "Lucy in the Sky with Diamonds" and Lennon's "One Day at a Time" and was featured with his band on Lennon's comeback single "Whatever Gets You Thru the Night." Lennon and John performed live at Madison Square Garden on Thanksgiving Day 1974 in what turned out to be Lennon's last live performance. In 1975 Pete Townshend of the Who offered John to play the character of Pinball Wizard in their rock-opera *Tommy.*

Such a frenzied schedule, together with drug and alcohol addiction, soon took its toll on John, who, in 1977, announced he was retiring from performing. Stress and personal insecurities also momentarily ended the professional relationship with Taupin, who began writing for other singers. The albums released at the end of the 1970s attracted little commercial and critical notice, and John's artistic persona relinquished the flamboyance that had catapulted him into music stardom in favor of a more reserved and secluded personality. The 1980s, however, witnessed the reunion of John and Taupin and the albums *21 at 33* and *The Fox* restored the singer to the success of British and American charts. Yet, John's personal life remained plagued by insecurities due to his sexual orientation and his physical appearance. His alcohol and cocaine addictions only worsened. John had candidly announced in a 1976 interview with *Rolling Stone* that he was bisexual and that he thought everyone was bisexual to a degree. Such an interview might have seem daring at the time, yet it was already a compromise as John subsequently admitted that he already very well knew that he was gay. In spite of being aware of his queerness, in 1984 John took the media and his fans by surprise when he married German recording engineer Renate Blauel. The couple divorced only four years later.

The reunion of John and Taupin proved commercially rewarding, although the pair could never match their 1970s hits. John's albums of the 1980s such as *Jump Up!* and *Too Low for Zero* went gold and generated several Top 10 singles both in the United Kingdom and the United States. These included "I Guess That's Why They Call It the Blues" featuring Stevie Wonder, "Little Jeannie," "Nikita" (which also featured a video directed by Ken Russell), and "I Don't Wanna Go On with You Like That." In 1985 he reached number one with the single "That's What Friends Are For," a collaboration with Dionne Warwick, Gladys Knight, and Stevie Wonder that raised funds for AIDS research. HIV became a prominent concern of the singer, who, during the mid-1980s, developed a close friendship with Ryan White, a teenage hemophiliac who contracted the virus through a blood transfusion. White was at the center of a bitter controversy when he was expelled from his middle school in Kokomo, Indiana, due to his positive status. John supported Ryan and his family and sang "Candle in the Wind" at his funeral in April 1990.

He also helped Ryan's mother to start the Ryan White Foundation for the prevention of AIDS.

During the 1980s, John had to confront his alcohol and drug addictions as well as his personal insecurities, which made him an easy target for the tabloid press. When *The Sun* alleged that John was having underage sex, the singer reacted by filing a libel suit which he won in 1987. After successful appearances at Wham's farewell concert and at the Live Aid concert in 1985, John collapsed on stage while performing in Australia the following year. He underwent throat surgery and in 1988, after five sold-out concerts at Madison Square Garden, he symbolically auctioned his costumes together with pieces of memorabilia and his record collection at Sotheby's. The auction represented John's eagerness to start a new life, free from drugs and alcohol. Over the next two years he was successfully treated for drug addiction and bulimia. A sobered up Elton John made a major comeback in 1992 with the album *The One*, which peaked at number eight on the U.S. charts and went double platinum. In the same year, John established his own AIDS Foundation, which has contributed million of dollars to HIV causes worldwide. John announced that he would donate all royalties from his single to AIDS research. The year 1992 also saw John's participation to the *Freddie Mercury Tribute Concert*, an AIDS charity event held at Wembley Stadium, London, in honor of Queen's late lead **Freddie Mercury**.

The One, his highest charting release since *Blue Moves* (1976), sparked a veritable renaissance in the artist's career and, together with Taupin, John signed a record contract with Warner/Chappell Music for an estimated $39 million. In 1994 he collaborated with lyricist Tim Rice on the songs for Disney's animated feature *The Lion King*. "Can You Feel the Love Tonight," from the movie's soundtrack, won the Academy Award for Best Original Song. At the ceremony, John acknowledged his partner David Furnish. Rice and John reunited in 1998 for a Broadway adaptation of Verdi's opera *Aida*. The 1990s ended with tragedy and success for John, who lost two of his closest friends, fashion designer Gianni Versace and Princess of Wales Diana. Deeply affected by Diana's death, John produced a special version of "Candle in the Wind," which he also performed at the Princess's funeral in Westminster Abbey. The single became the fastest selling record of all times, eventually grossing £55 million for the Princess of Wales Memorial Fund.

The New Millennium has reserved more personal successes for Elton and more fruitful collaborations with other artists. His duet with Eminem for the rapper's song "Stan" at the 2002 Grammy Awards Ceremony proved particularly controversial given Eminem's homophobic reputation. John also features in Blue's "Sorry Seems to be the Hardest Word" (2003) and Tupac's posthumous "Ghetto Gospel" (2005), both reaching number one in the United Kingdom. In 2005 John teamed up with playwright Lee Hall for the West End production of *Billy Elliot—The Musical*. In 2006 he authored another musical, *Lestat*, with Bernie Taupin, based on Anne Rice's vampire novels. Unfortunately, the project was both a commercial and a critical disappointment.

During the twenty-first century, John has become increasingly political. He was one of the performers at the Live 8 concert at Hyde Park in London in 2005. In December the same year he entered into civil partnership with David Furnish and used the event to campaign against President Bush's proposed amendment outlawing gay marriage. In an article written for the British Sunday newspaper the *Observer*, John (2005, online edition) condemned homophobia and encouraged gays and lesbians to fight against it: "I have long been a supporter of Amnesty International which estimates that around 80 countries still have laws that criminalize adult same-sex relations, from the Caribbean and Latin America, to Africa, the Middle East and even Europe....I strongly believe we can make a difference if we show solidarity with those who are bullied and ill-treated for their sexuality by bombarding the authorities with letters, faxes and emails making it clear that we know about these abuses and calling for them to end." John's artistic and personal achievements constitute an inspirational example for queer artists and citizens.

Further Reading

Cochrane, Robert. "The Fall and Rise of Reginald Dwight." *Gay Times.* June 2000, issue 261; Decker, Ed. "Elton John." *Contemporary Musicians: Profiles of the People in Music.* Stacy A. McConnell, ed. Detroit: Gale Research, 1997. 20: 107–111; Heatley, Michael. *Elton John: The Life and Music of a Legendary Performer.* London: CLB International, 1998; John, Elton. "We'll Celebrate Our Love, but Others Live in Constant Fear." *The Observer.* December 18, 2005. 8–9. http://arts.guardian.co.uk/news/story/0,1670098,00.html (accessed on January 23, 2007); Norman, Philip. *Sir Elton: The Definitive Biography.* New York: Carroll & Graff, 2001; Official Web site: http://www.eltonjohn.com.

JOHNSON, HOLLY (1960–)

British singer and artist Holly Johnson rose to international fame as the lead singer of the controversial and meteoric band Frankie Goes To Hollywood who helped define the British New Wave music movement, a mixture of funk, rock and reggae sound. He later launched a solo career, whose success was clouded by a protracted legal battle with the group's record company ZTT Records. The case was settled in Johnson's favor in 1989 in what was considered a landmark ruling for the music business. Since the mid-1990s, he has also embarked on a critically-acclaimed career as a painter.

Holly Johnson was born in Wavertree, Liverpool, on February 9, 1960. He attended Liverpool Collegiate Grammar School for boys where his strong personality and his queer appearance made him an easy target of homophobic attacks. The singer was attracted to music and queer culture since his school days. He listened to David Bowie and The Velvet Underground and read the French novelist and playwright Jean Genet and also William Burroughs, one of the chief animators of the **Beat Generation**. In the field of the visual arts, he was especially keen on Derek Jarman and **Andy Warhol**. When he was thirteen, Johnson got his first acoustic guitar through cigarette coupons which he had traded for his collection of Bowie ephemera. In 1976 he dropped out of school and the following year became a member of the New Wave group Big In Japan. After being ousted by the other band members, Johnson formed Frankie Goes To Hollywood with Paul Rutherford, Nasher Nash, Mark O'Toole and Peter "Ped" Gill, but the group had to wait two more years before they could get a recording contract with Trevor Horn's ZTT Records.

"Relax," the first piece the band recorded in 1983, catapulted them to international fame and controversy. A superb dance track with a clear sexual innuendo, "Relax" was banned from BBC radio and television when it had already entered the charts. Yet, the ban only stimulated more public curiosity around the song, which peaked at number one in the United Kingdom for five weeks from January 1984, selling almost two million copies. The promotion behind Frankie Goes To Hollywood banked on such curiosity, combining laddish appearance with the bold homosexuality of Johnson and Rutherford. The promotion campaign for the group also included the production of best-selling T-shirts with the message "Frankie Say Relax Don't Do It." "Relax" shot to number one in many other countries and a version of the video was used in Brian DePalma's 1984 thriller *Body Double* as a scene taken from a pornographic movie.

The single was the first in a string of impressive hits which were all released in 1984, the band's golden year. Released in May, "Two Tribes (We Don't Want To Die)" entered the British charts at number one and maintained that position for nine consecutive weeks. The success of "Two Tribes" also rekindled attention for "Relax" which reentered the charts at number two, a total domination only experienced before by The Beatles. The song confronted the threat of an atomic holocaust and of global destruction. To add to the song's authenticity and capture the spirit of the Cold War, the band included in the piece the voice of British actor Patrick Allen who had narrated a series of instructive governmental videos on how to survive in case of a nuclear explosion. The video showed caricatures of President Ronald Reagan and Soviet leader Chernenko wrestling and was acclaimed as one of the best products of the period. The double debut album *Welcome to the Pleasuredome* responded to the pressure of producing a record for the Christmas market. It included several interesting covers and went to number one selling more than 3 million copies. The year finished triumphantly with the single "The Power of Love," Johnson's signature song, reaching number one again.

During the band's first world tour which also included the United States, Johnson met art collector Wolfgang Kuhle who became his new manager and partner. Back from the tour, Frankie Goes To Hollywood began working on their second album, *Liverpool*, which came out in 1986. The single "Rage Hard" reached number four in the United Kingdom, but Johnson grew progressively dissatisfied with the band and left in 1987. Launching a solo career proved difficult, as the artist was involved in a bitter legal battle with ZTT Records which wanted to prevent him from releasing solo material with his new label MCA Records. The court case was finally settled in favor of Johnson who was awarded artistic freedom and substantial damages in a ruling that was to have vast resonance in the British music industry. In 1989 the singer could finally release his first solo album, *Blast*, which reached number one in the United Kingdom and went platinum. It included the hit singles

"Love Trains," "Americanos," "Atomic City," and "Heaven's Here." Yet, disagreements between Johnson and MCA over the marketing of his second solo album, *Dreams That Money Can't Buy* (1991), prompted the artist to leave the label.

In November 1991, Johnson discovered that he was HIV-positive, a fact that he would make public two years later in the British newspaper *The Times*. His positive status led the artist to withdraw temporarily from the spotlight of the music scene and the showbiz world. Yet, this period of self-scrutiny proved rewarding when his 1994 biography *A Bone in My Flute* was published by Century, Random House, and received good reviews, becoming a bestseller. The cover of the book featured a portrait of the author by French queer artists Pierre et Gilles. Since the 1990s, Johnson has been mainly active as a painter whose works have been exhibited at prestigious venues such as London's Tate Modern and The Royal Academy of Arts. In 1999, however, the artist returned to music, recording the album *Soulstream* with his own label Pleasuredome.

Further reading

Catacunzino, Maria. "I was expecting that call from Liz Taylor." *The Independent.* March 17, 1994. http://findarticles.com/p/articles/mi_qn4158/is_19940317/ai_ n14859968 (accessed October 23, 2006); Johnson, Holly. *A Bone in My Flute.* London: Century, 1994.

Joplin, Janis (1943–1970)

American singer Janis Joplin is one of the icons of the 1960s. Her lifestyle, made of rock and roll, flamboyant clothes, liberated sexuality, drug taking, and heavy drinking, summarizes the excesses of the youth counterculture of the decade. Her powerful voice allowed Joplin to experiment with a wide musical repertoire and her persona created a completely new image for women in the musical industry at a time when it was still dominated by men.

Janis was born into a middle-class family on January 19, 1943, in Port Arthur, Texas. Her father Seth was an engineer and her mother Dorothy was the registrar of a business college. Port Arthur is known for its oil refineries and shipbuilding facilities and was a hostile milieu for Janis's artistic ambitions. From an early age, Joplin took an interest in black singers such as Billie Holiday and Bessie Smith, an unconventional curiosity for a Southern white girl of the 1950s. In high school, Joplin also developed a passion for Beat Poetry as well as for the writings of F. Scott Fitzgerald and his wife Zelda. Her ambition as a teenager, however, was to become a visual artist. After her graduation from high school in 1960, she took arts classes at Lamar State College of Technology and then at the University of Texas at Austin, but she never succeeded in getting a degree. According to her own reconstructions, her childhood was an unhappy one and she always felt a misfit both at home and at school. Although some biographers have pointed out that Joplin exaggerated her plight, her shy character and weird interests certainly made her a likely outcast in the society she grew up.

Countercultural icon Janis Joplin. Courtesy of Photofest.

Joplin's first professional performance dates back to 1961 at the Halfway House in Beaumont. Shortly afterwards, she first visited California, a state which will have a central importance in her personal and professional biography. For the summer months, Joplin stayed with an aunt in Los Angeles and worked as a keypunch operator for the Los Angeles Telephone Company. At Venice Beach Joplin first came into contact with the beatniks communities that would constitute a point of reference for her future artistic career. Returning to Texas from Los Angeles, Joplin started to perform in the country and western clubs of Houston.

In 1962 Joplin moved to Austin where she enrolled in a course of fine arts. She decided not to live in the campus dormitory, but settled in a rundown block called "the ghetto," which was the center of Austin's rising countercultural movement. She performed at various bars while in Austin. Her confidence, however, was easily undermined and, when her classmates voted her "the ugliest man on campus" in 1963, she dropped out. With her friend Chet Helms, who was to become her manager, Joplin went to San Francisco where she became increasingly dependent on amphetamines. She was concerned by this growing addiction and, in an attempt to reform, she went back to Lamar State College to study sociology. Yet, Helm, who, by then had become a successful rock manager in San Francisco, offered her the role of lead singer in the hard-rock band Big Brother and the Holding Company. Joplin accepted and returned to San Francisco, where the band made its debut at the Avalon Ballroom in June 1966. Joplin's characteristic voice, with its combination of harsh and gentle tones, created a considerable local following for the band, which made its first national appearance at the Monterey International Pop Festival in June 1967. Monterey was the first of the big outdoor festivals of the decade and a major event in the Summer of Love. Joplin's performance was acknowledged as one of the best at the festival.

The success in Monterey allowed Joplin and Big Brother to get a contract with a small company, Mainstream, for their debut album *Big Brother and the Holding Company, featuring Janis Joplin* (1967). Success arrived a year later with the second album, *Cheap Thrills*. Produced by the major label Columbia, the album went to number one and included the famous single "Piece of My Heart." Once reviled as "the ugliest man on campus," Joplin went on to become an aggressive sex symbol of hard-rock music. In those years, which predated the women's liberation movement, it was not easy for a woman to get to the top of the still male-dominated world of rock. In addition, Joplin's frantic, sexually allusive style and her repertoire inclusive of African American music did not always comply with the expectations that general audiences might have had about a white female singer. Her persona crossed the racial, sexual, and gender boundaries that were so dear to many of her contemporaries, even within hippie circles. Joplin refused to define herself as a heterosexual, lesbian, or bisexual. She had many affairs with women, and even, as Peggy Caserta's contentious first-hand account *Going Down with Janis* (1973) shows, long-term relationships. She was engaged twice, but she never married. Joplin's unwillingness to conform took its toll on her, and she began using heroin and drinking more heavily.

After *Cheap Thrills*, Joplin left Big Brother and founded the Kozmic Blues Band. They reached number five in 1969 with *I Got Dem Ol' Kozmic Blues Again Mama!* and, the same year, they performed at Woodstock, the most famous of the 1960s countercultural events. At the apex of her career, Joplin left the Kozmic Blues Band and started the Full-Tilt Boogie Band to produce her new project, *Pearl*, which would be released only after her death. This posthumous album, whose title refers to Joplin's nickname, is often hailed as the artist's finest work, with the outstanding performance of "Me and Bobby McGee," written by Kris Kristofferson. Her heroin addiction became worse during the recording of the album. Joplin was found dead due to drug overdose in her room at the Landmark Motor Lodge in Hollywood on October 4, 1970.

Joplin's legacy for the world of rock and for queer popular culture consists in her explosive charisma and sexual charge as a performer who was able to show that female rockers could be just as electrifying and shocking as male performers. Joplin's style and attitude defeated decades of stereotypes about female singers, thus becoming a point of reference for an entire generation of women's artists.

Further reading

Amburn, Ellis. *Pearl: The Obsession and Passions of Janis Joplin*. New York: Warner Books, 1993; Dalton, David. *Piece of My Heart: A Portrait of Janis Joplin*. New York: Da Capo Press, 1991; Echols, Alice. *Scars of Sweet Paradise: The Life of Janis Joplin*. New York: Metropolitan Books, 1998; Friedman, Myra. *Buried Alive: The Biography of Janis Joplin*. New York: Harmony Books, 1992; Joplin, Laura. *Love, Janis*. New York: Villard Books, 1992.

K

KRAMER, LARRY (1935–)

The Jewish-American activist, essayist, novelist, and playwright Larry Kramer has contributed many provocative and challenging insights to the popular debate on the **AIDS** crisis. As a founder of the Gay Men's Health Crisis (GMHC) and the AIDS Coalition to Unleash Power (ACT UP) and the author of many literary responses to the epidemic, Kramer has proved an outspoken, and often controversial, voice. His efforts to raise general awareness of AIDS have caused him to come into conflict with his sexual and ethnic communities. Kramer's censure of homosexual promiscuity and of the slowness in adopting safe sex practices drew criticism from the gay community. In addition, his comparison of the crisis to the Holocaust, a trope Kramer also used as the title of his *Reports from the Holocaust* (1989), attracted the anger of Jewish groups. In Kramer's interpretation, homosexuals were behaving just like the Jews had done when faced with Hitler's project of extermination: they were doing nothing to save themselves.

Kramer was born in Bridgeport, Connecticut, in 1935. Although he was born at the time of the Great Depression, his family was a relatively wealthy one. His grandparents owned a grocery shop, while his father was an attorney. Because of his father's work, the Kramers moved twice during Larry's childhood and adolescence: first to Mount Rainier, Maryland, and later to Washington, DC. Kramer started to like the theater and the arts from a very young age, in spite of his father's encouragement to pursue more masculine interests such as sports. In 1953 Kramer unwillingly entered Yale University. He would have preferred other institutions, but it was a family tradition to attend Yale, so his father forced him to go there. These were difficult years for Kramer as he suffered from depression from the very first year and began seeing a psychiatrist for a cure. He started a relationship with one of his professors, which was, however, short-lived. Kramer confided in his brother, who told their parents about his homosexuality, putting a considerable strain on their relationship. Larry graduated from Yale in 1957 with a B.A. in English and served in the army for a year. In 1958 Kramer started working for Columbia Pictures, a job that he would keep throughout the 1960s. At the end of the decade, he was hired by United Artists, which gave him the opportunity of writing the screenplay for *Women in Love* (1969). The screenplay was nominated for an Academy Award; yet Kramer suffered a major setback with his script for the musical *Lost Horizon* (1971), one of the greatest flops of the 1970s.

Disappointed by the film industry, the writer turned to the theater. His first play was *Sissie's Scrapbook* (1973) and had a successful original run, but was later panned by the *New York Times* when it was produced in the Greenwich Village with the new title of *Four Friends.* The play centered around the lives of a gay man and three straight friends. The publication of Kramer's first novel *Faggots* in 1978 made the author the chief satirist of New York gay life before the advent of AIDS. The central character of the novel is Fred Lemish, a gay screenwriter who is about to turn 40. Through his sexual encounters, we come into contact with a world of detached and unemotional sex, peopled by promiscuous homosexuals. Because of its assumption that gays should chiefly blame themselves for their unhappiness, the novel obtained mixed reviews in the gay press. Kramer was accused of being a self-loathing homosexual for his condemnation of promiscuity. The impact of AIDS on the gay community and the changes in the lifestyle that the disease brought about made *Faggots* more acceptable when it was re-issued in 1987.

Although Kramer has been an activist for gay rights since the 1970s and an AIDS campaigner since the beginning of the crisis, he has had to contend with the accusation of being a homophobic homosexual for most of his life. Kramer started to collect funds for research almost as soon as the then-unidentified so-called gay cancer appeared. In 1981 he published his first article on the disease in the *New York Native* and founded the Gay Men's Health Crisis (GMHC). His piece in the *New York Native*, in which Kramer demanded funds for research into Kaposi's sarcoma, a rare form of skin cancer that was becoming particularly common in gay males, spurred negative reactions from many homosexuals. Kramer was accused of identifying a particular illness with homosexuality and of spreading unjustified alarm. In fact, the main aim of the GMHC was to educate gay men about the disease. The group started a telephone helpline and a newsletter. It also organized public meetings to give information about the virus and recruited volunteers for its initiatives. Yet, Kramer's iconoclasm was soon too much even for a group like the GMHC, which feared that Kramer would completely alienate government's officials from the cause. So his involvement with the organization progressively diminished. Kramer continued to contribute pieces on AIDS to the *New York Native*, including the famous "1, 112 and Counting" (1983), an attack against the neglect with which the government had responded to the crisis. As usual for Kramer, the piece also contained criticism against the gay community for its inability to adopt behaviors that could slow down the spread of the epidemic. When the GMHC distanced itself from the central theses in "1, 112 and Counting," Kramer resigned from the organization's board.

These critical stances against the responses to the AIDS crisis by both the political establishment and the gay community also inspired Kramer's theatrical work of the 1980s. The play *The Normal Heart* (1985) focused on the life of Ned Weeks, an AIDS activist and founder of an important HIV awareness group, recounting his problems both within the organization and with his brother who has difficulties to accept Ned's homosexuality. As all other works by Kramer, *The Normal Heart* proved controversial also within the gay community, but received several important awards and a nomination for an Olivier Award. The original run of the play at New York City's Public Theatre was successful, leading to a full year of performances. The role of Ned Weeks was played by bisexual actor Brad Davis who died of AIDS in 1991. It has subsequently been played by such accomplished actors as Richard Dreyfuss, Joel Grey, Martin Sheen, and Tom Hulce. In 1988 Kramer returned to the early days of the AIDS crisis with the farce *Just Say No* (1988), which targeted New York mayor Ed Koch and the Reagan administration for their lack of concern about the epidemic.

As Kramer increasingly separated from the GMHC, he decided to found a more radical organization to fight against AIDS: the AIDS Coalition to Unleash Power (ACT UP), which was originally conceived at a meeting in New York in 1987. ACT UP soon made it to the national headlines for its spectacular protests such as the stopping of traffic on Wall Street during the rush hour. The organization succeeded in mobilizing a large number of gay men and soon spread outside of American boundaries. Kramer himself tested HIV-positive in a test following a chronic hepatitis B diagnosis. He did not withdraw from public life as a result of his status. On the contrary, he continued to campaign with more strength than before. He also wrote a sequel to *The Normal Heart*, *The Destiny of Me* (1992), which obtained an Obie award and was short-listed for the Pulitzer. In this second chapter of Ned Weeks's life, the activist discovers he is HIV-positive and seeks experimental treatment. *The Destiny of Me* expands on Weeks's difficult relationship with his family, touching also on Kramer's problems with his father. Kramer has also collected most of his pieces on the AIDS crisis in the non-fiction book *Reports from the Holocaust*. Since the late 1970s, he has been working on a huge novel called *The American People*.

Larry Kramer has never feared to be, in Susan Sontag's definition of him, a troublemaker. When former President Ronald Reagan died, he was one of the few dissenting voices against the chorus of praise that followed. Kramer took the statesman to the test for his stance against AIDS. Characteristically, Kramer (2004) compared Reagan to Hitler stating that the former President hated gays as much as Hitler hated Jews. Although Kramer's style is aggressive and his positions have often targeted the gay community itself, he has played a pioneering role in the AIDS movement. He has forced gay people to rethink critically about their lifestyles and models. One can only agree with Susan Sontag's hope that Kramer will never lower his voice.

Further Reading

Bergman, David. *Gaiety Transfigured: Gay Self-Representation in American Literature*. Madison: University of Wisconsin Press, 1991; Kramer, Larry. "Adolf Reagan." *The Advocate*. July 6, 2004; Mass, Lawrence D. *We Must Love Each Other or Die: The Life and Legacies of Larry Kramer*. New York: St. Martin's Press, 1999.

KUSHNER, TONY (1956–)

Tony Kushner has made important contributions to queer culture both with his complex and metaphysical plays and with his activism for gay and lesbian rights. His fiction and non-fiction writings focus on political and philosophical issues such as the place of homosexuals and Jews in contemporary society, the impact of **AIDS** on the gay community, and the portrayal of common people at times of political crises. Kushner's style blurs the boundaries of history and magic, often linking different historical periods or the natural and the supernatural. Kushner's most famous cycle of two plays, *Angels in America* (1991), has earned him the Tony Award, the Pulitzer Prize, and international acclaim. Since *Angels*, Kushner has been identified as a spokesperson for gay rights and AIDS activism.

Tony Kushner was born in New York on July 16, 1956, into a Jewish-American family. His parents, both classical musicians, moved to Lake Charles, Louisiana, shortly after Tony's birth. As one of the few Jews in the south of Louisiana, Kushner felt an outsider from a very early age, a feeling that certainly informed his political and literary interest for people outside the American mainstream. Kushner's fascination with the theater dates back to his childhood: his mother was also an actress and Kushner enjoyed watching her perform. Kushner was aware of his homosexuality very early on in his life, but only started to practice a gay lifestyle when he returned to New York to study at Columbia University. In his literary career, Kushner has used the potentialities implicit in both his ethnicity and sexuality to provide him with an outsider's point of view on social phenomena. After his graduation in 1978, the playwright spent several years operating a switchboard at the United Nations. He soon decided, however, that he wanted a career in the theater and thus attended New York University's graduate program in directing, obtaining his MFA in 1984. Through Carl Weber, his mentor at NYU, Kushner deepened his knowledge of German Marxist playwright Bertolt Brecht, who became an important influence on his own works. With his emphasis on political art, Brecht has clearly informed Kushner's attention for how common people respond to times of crises. Weimer's social critic Walter Benjamin, instead, provided Kushner with an apocalyptic vision of history comprised of a succession of historical turning points. The playwright often takes such turning points from different eras and blends them together in a single work.

In 1985 Kushner started working as an assistant director at the St. Louis Repertoire Theatre. Two years later, he returned to New York where he worked for several arts organizations and gave university lectures. He also produced several plays, both adaptations (of, for example, Goethe's *Stella* and Pierre Corneille's *L'Illusion Comique*) and originals. *A Bright Room Called Day* is typical of Kushner's technique of blending together two different historical periods through moments of politically charged crises. The main plotline follows the lives of several radicals during the fall of the German Weimar Republic in the 1930s. Yet, this narrative is interspersed with the comments of a Jewish-American woman living during the Reagan Presidency, which links the decline of Weimar to contemporary issues. Through this device, the audience is led to equate Reagan and Hitler.

International fame arrived in the early 1990s with the performances of *Angels in America: A Gay Fantasia on National Themes*. Composed of two plays, *Millennium Approaches* (1991) and *Perestroika* (1992), *Angels in America* was performed both in the United States and Europe to critical and commercial acclaim. The play was eventually adapted by Kushner himself into an HBO miniseries, which was directed by Mike Nichols in 2003 with an all-star cast including Al Pacino, Meryl Streep,

Joe Mantello (left) and Stephen Spinella (right) in Tony Kushner's award-winning play *Angels in America*. Courtesy of Joan Marcus/Photofest.

and Emma Thompson. Like the play, the series was both a critical and a commercial success, winning the Golden Globe and the Emmy for Best Miniseries, and obtaining the best ratings for a made-for-cable movie in 2003. The play has also been adapted into an opera. *Angels in America* has a complex plot, which, as usual with Kushner's works, intertwines different lives and different historical periods. As Prior Walter is getting increasingly sick with AIDS he is deserted by his lover. While in the hospital, he is visited by an angel who tells him that he has been chosen as a prophet. Prior's African American friend Belize is the nurse assigned to the closeted right-wing lawyer Roy Cohn who is secretly dying of AIDS, haunted by the ghost of Ethel Rosenberg. Prior's former lover, in the meantime, has started an affair with Cohn's Mormon protégé who has constantly repressed his homosexuality and is married. The play mixes historical figures such as Roy Cohn and Ethel Rosenberg with fictional characters. It also combines the everyday realm with the supernatural one. For example, Prior meets a group of angels who want him to be their prophet. Yet, he rejects them as their teaching that humanity must stop growing, comes dangerously close to the projected outcome of AIDS, the disease he is dying of. The play is a political indictment of the Reagan administration and of right wingers for their failure to respond effectively to the AIDS crisis.

Angels in America was followed by *Slavs! Thinking about the Longstanding Problems of Virtue and Happiness* (1994), which obtained less enthusiastic reviews. The play is set in the last days of the Soviet Union, before and after the Chernobyl nuclear accident. The political decline of the USSR is paralleled by that of the relationship between two women. After several adaptations and the play on the slave *Henry "Box" Brown* (1998), Kushner returned to the attention of critics and the media with *Homebody/Kabul* (2001), which opened just four months after the September 11 attacks and the American bombing of Afghanistan. In its first part, the four-hour long play focuses on the thoughts of a British housewife, who decides to travel alone to Kabul in 1998. The second part is concerned with the efforts of her husband and daughter to discover what has happened to her after her disappearance during the Taliban regime. Kushner has been a strenuous opponent of Bush administration's war on terror: the first scene of *Only We Who Guard the Mystery Shall Be Unhappy* (2003) shows the First Lady reading bedtime stories to the ghosts of dead Iraqi children.

In 2003 Kushner teamed up with composer Jeanine Tesori for *Caroline, or Change*, an autobiographical musical which portrays the relationship between the African American maid Caroline and the son of her Jewish employers in the backdrop of the deep south during the Civil Rights Movement. In spite of its relatively short run on Broadway, the musical was nominated for several Tony Awards and won the category of best supporting actress. In 2006 Kushner was nominated for an Academy Award for the script of the Steven Spielberg's movie *Munich* (2005). He has also written a children's book and several collections of essays which document his activism for gay rights and the AIDS movement.

Although Kushner has been unable to match the success of *Angels in America*, he has continued to produce important works that are challenging and stimulating for American culture and society. His works conceptualize the categories of ethnicity and sexuality as fluid, rather than stable entities. In the best tradition of left-wing literary production, Kushner's writings are politically charged without being didactic, confronting audiences with the dilemmas of moral responsibility during socially repressive times.

Further Reading

Brask, Per, ed. *Essays on Kushner's Angels.* Winnipeg, MB: Blizzard Publishing, 1995; Fisher, James. *The Theater of Tony Kushner: Living Past Hope.* New York: Routledge, 2001; Freedman, Jonathan. "Angels, Monsters, and Jews: Intersections of Queer and Jewish Identity in Kushner's *Angels in America.*" *PMLA* 113:1 (1998): 90–102; Geis, Deborah R., and Steven F. Kruger. *Approaching the Millennium: Essays on* Angels in America. Ann Arbor: University of Michigan Press, 1997; Vorlicky, Robert, ed. *Tony Kushner in Conversation.* Ann Arbor: University of Michigan Press, 1998.

L

LANE, NATHAN (1956–)

When openly gay American actor Nathan Lane was summoned to London to save the musical *The Producers* from financial disaster in 2004, the *Observer* (Smith 2004, online edition) described him as Broadway's "hottest property." Much better known in North America than in the United Kingdom and Europe, Lane still obtained rave reviews when he was called to replace Richard Dreyfuss, who left the show a week before its first previews. American critics and fans have long hailed Lane as one of the most accomplished actors of his generation, capable of incredible versatility, switching easily from dramatic to comic roles. The actor has also embodied several gay characters in plays and films such as *Frankie and Johnny* (1991) and *The Birdcage* (1998). His stage persona has been described as "funny on top, bleeding underneath." An American reviewer (Dezell 2003, *Boston Globe* online) has aptly summed up Lane's impressive versatility: "Bombastic but fleet-footed, subtle yet outrageously funny, the kind of old-fashioned stage virtuoso who makes 'em laugh, breaks their hearts, belts it to the second balcony, and brings cheering crowds to their feet."

Born Joseph Lane on February 3, 1956, in Jersey City, New Jersey, the actor has described his childhood as something from a bad Eugene O'Neill play. He was the youngest of the three sons of Daniel Lane, a truck driver, and Nora Lane, a secretary. His father became unemployed shortly after Joseph's birth, when his eyesight deteriorated. Unable to find another job, he started drinking heavily, a habit that would eventually lead to his death when his son was 11. As her husband's health deteriorated, Nora Lane began suffering from manic depression and had to be hospitalized several times. Joseph studied at various Catholic schools in Jersey City, including St. Peter's Preparatory School, where his passion for acting was first appreciated as he appeared in several student productions. Because of these roles, he was awarded a partial scholarship to study drama at St. Joseph's University in Philadelphia, but his family could not meet the rest of the required tuition. Joseph thus started working as a stand-up comedian and as a performer in dinner theater and children's plays, while also supporting himself with odd jobs, including bail interviewer, telemarketer, and singing telegram singer. When Joseph registered with Actor's Equity, he discovered that there already existed a Joseph Lane. He then decided to change his first name, taking Nathan in homage to his favorite character, Nathan Detroit, in the musical *Guys and Dolls*.

The turning point in Lane's acting career was his successful audition for the TV series *One of the Boys*, starring Mickey Rooney. The situation comedy was not a big hit, running for only 13 episodes in 1982, but it brought Lane to the attention of a larger audience than his club acts. In the same year, the actor made his Broadway debut in Noel Coward's *Present Laughter*, alongside George C. Scott. His performance was critically acclaimed and helped Lane land more parts. He was selected for the cast of two musicals, Elmer Bernstein and Don Black's *Merlin* (1982–1983) and William Perry's *Wind in the Willows* (1985–1986), which, however, flopped at the box office. In 1987 Lane made his first screen appearance as a ghost in Hector Babenco's *Ironweed*, starring Jack Nicholson and Meryl Streep.

The playwright Terrence McNally, who once called Lane his muse, has provided him with some of the most interesting roles in his acting career. In 1989 Lane was Mendy in McNally's *Lisbon Traviata*, a role that earned the actor a Drama Desk

Nathan Lane (left) and Matthew Broderick (right) in the film version of *The Producers*. Courtesy of Universal Studios/Photofest.

Award. His collaboration with McNally included more plays such as *Bad Habits* (1990), *Lips Together, Teeth Apart* (1991). and *Love! Valor! Compassion!* (1994). His sensitive depiction of a man living with AIDS in this last play won Lane another Drama Desk Award. Commenting on Lane's career, McNally (Smith 2004, *Observer* online) has voiced his admiration: "I don't think he's gotten better. He was touched with genius in the theater from the very beginning. Nathan was born for the stage and most truly exists there."

In 1992 Lane had the chance to return to Broadway with the character after which he took his name: Nathan Detroit in *Guys and Dolls.* He was unanimously praised by critics and went on to win another Drama Desk Award. Since the 1990s, Lane's career has been constellated by many hits and the occasional flop. In 1996 he won his first Tony Award for Best Actor in the revival of **Stephen Sondheim**'s *A Funny Thing Happened on the Way to the Forum.* In the same year, he achieved increasing visibility thanks to the international success of Mike Nichols's film *The Birdcage.* Although *The Birdcage* was accused of stereotypically representing gay people like the original French film that it remakes, *La Cage Aux Folles*, Lane showed incredible energy in the portrayal of drag queen Albert Goldman. Film scholar Lucy Mazdon (2000) has also toned down the negative judgments on the film's representation of queerness, stating that *The Birdcage* ironically interrogates notions of gender, family, morality, although it is unable to fully embrace a liberal agenda. Lane won his second Tony Award for Mel Brooks's musical *The Producers* (2001), one of the biggest Broadway hits at the turn of the millennium.

The actor has never been particularly secretive about his homosexuality, coming out to his family when in his early twenties. Some gay activists, however, have criticized him for failing to discuss publicly his sexual orientation until after the assassination of college student Matthew Shepard. In an interview with the *New York Times* magazine, Lane (Smith 2004, *Observer* online) explained his reserve. "We're talking about someone's life, not a to-do list. From the time I told my mother, I've been living openly. But really, I was born in 1956. I'm one of those old-fashioned homosexuals, not one of the newfangled ones who are born joining parades. My family referred to them as 'fags,' and that was it. And yes, careerwise, I didn't want to be branded as a big fruitcake and that's all I could do. On a personal level, I don't immediately open up to anybody, even about what colors I like, much less something like this. I am my mother, OK? Just without the housedress and slippers."

Further Reading

Dezell, Maureen. "Nathan Lane Goes beyond Broadway." *Boston Globe*, October 19, 2003. Online edition. http://www.boston.com/news/globe/living/articles/2003/10/19/nathan_lane_goes_beyond_broadway/ (accessed on September 12, 2007); "Lane, Nathan." *Contemporary Theater, Film and Television.* Michael J. Tyrkus, ed. Detroit: Gale Group, 2000. 201–203; Mazdon, Lucy. *Encore Hollywood: Remaking French Cinema.* London: BFI Publishing, 2000; Smith, David. "Bring On the Clown." *The Observer.* November 7, 2004. http://arts.guardian.co.uk/features/story/0,11710,1345473,00.html (accessed on

September 12, 2007); Vilanch, Bruce. "Citizen Lane." *The Advocate* (February 2, 1999): 30.

LANG, K. D. (1961–)

Grammy Award-winning Canadian singer and songwriter k. d. lang had already become an icon for the gay and lesbian community well before her coming out in a 1992 interview with the ***Advocate***. Queer audiences have always been attracted to lang for her gender-bending appearance and for her intense singing performances. After her coming out, her position within queer communities became even more relevant. She was pointed out as an example of courage to follow. In "Queer Manifesto," the closing chapter of his seminal book *Queer in America*, Signorile (1993, 365) cited lang, alongside Barney Frank, **Martina Navratilova**, and David Geffen as a hero of gays and lesbians that could encourage queers to come out: "Deep down you know why you must now come out and why it is wrong for you not to....Just think: You'll be one of the people who have decided to be honest and make a world a better place for all queers. You'll be another. You'll be a hero." Throughout her career, lang has given particular importance to the connection with her audience. She has described herself as an artist "who craves the communal experience of sharing new ideas and sounds. The ideal scenario is to have an interactive give-and-take with your audience; to build and nurture a bond with them" (Official website).

Lang was born Kathryn Dawn Lang in the small Canadian farming town of Consort in Alberta on November 2, 1961. While attending college, she became fascinated with country music and was particularly drawn to the figure of Patsy Cline. Together with guitarist Ben Mink, in 1983 she founded the Reclines, a band which was intended as a tribute to Cline. In the same year, the Reclines recorded their debut album, *Friday Dance Promenade*, and in the following year, they rose to national attention in Canada with their second feature, *A Truly Western Experience*, which attracted positive reviews. Although lang's gender-bending outfits took the country music establishment by surprise, she was awarded a Canadian Juno Award for Most Promising Female Vocalist in 1985. Lang received more critical acclaim for her 1987 album *Angel with a Lariat*. The turning point in the singer's career came during that same year when rock-and-roll pioneer Roy Orbison chose her to record a duet for his classic song, "Crying." The collaboration earned lang a Grammy Award for Best Country Collaboration with Vocals.

In 1988 lang launched her solo career with *Shadowland* and she performed at the closing ceremonies of the fifteenth Winter Olympics in Calgary, Alberta. Her following album *Absolute Torch and Twang* (1989) won her another Grammy Award and the single "Full Moon of Love" reached number one in the Canadian Country chart. With her 1992 single "Constant Craving," from the album *Ingénue*, lang achieved her most popular song, which brought her international sales and critical acclaim as well as a third Grammy for Best Female Pop Vocal Performance. *Ingénue* also represented a shift from the world of country music to that of sophisticated pop. The move proved to be commercially successful as the album went double platinum. Lang recorded another original album in 1995, *All You Can Eat*, and, two years later, she put together *Drag*, a compilation of old songs that shared the common theme of smoking. For three years, lang stopped recording and devoted herself to her personal life, moving from Vancouver to Los Angeles and falling in love with actress and musician Leisha Hailey. "Over the last three years I really slowed down," she stated in an interview with the *Advocate* (Kort 2000, online edition). "It's been more than rejuvenating—it's almost as if I'm born again. I took time off to change my batteries: buy a house, cook, get a dog, drive home and see my mom in Canada. Do things I never had a chance to do in the last 15 years, when I was always on a plane, backstage, onstage, on a bus to a hotel, recording" (Kort 2000, *Advocate* online). When she returned to recording, she obtained rave reviews for *Invincible Summer* (2000), an album of love songs whose success also generated an accompanying tour. *Invincible Summer* took its inspiration from lang's three-year break: "The album's really about taking the time to find that core sunshine that burns inside of me." Following *Live by Request* (2002) and *Wonderful World* (2003), in which she duets with Tony Bennett in songs inspired by Armstrong, lang returned to her Canadian heritage with *Hymns of the 49th Parallel* (2004). In this album, lang performs several works by her favorite Canadian songwriters such as Leonard Cohen, Joni Mitchell, and Neil Young. "These songs," she maintains (Marti 2004, online), "are part of my cultural fabric, my Canadian soundtrack. They have nurtured my musical DNA." *Hymns* is, therefore, an homage to the songs that have inspired lang throughout her career.

Lang is hard to categorize as her music falls into different musical genres. In addition to her career as a singer, she has also appeared in films and sitcoms. She starred in Percy Adlon's art-house release *Salmonberries* (1991), in which she played Kotzebue, a woman who passes as a man to work in an Alaska mine. In 1999 lang joined Ewan MacGregor and Ashley Judd in the thriller *Eye of the Beholder*. In 2006 her iconic lesbian status was emphasized by Brian De Palma's film *The Black Dahlia*, in which lang makes a cameo appearance as a singer in a lesbian nightclub. Lang has also made guest appearances in popular sitcoms such as *Ellen* and *Dharma and Greg* and has contributed to the soundtracks of popular films such as *Midnight in the Garden of Good and Evil* (1997), *Tomorrow Never Dies* (1997), *Home on the Range* (2004), and *Happy Feet* (2006). She wrote almost the whole soundtrack for **Gus Van Sant**'s ill-fated project *Even Cowgirls Get the Blues* (1993). Lang's versatility has made the artist popular with a diverse and multi-generational following. Some queer critics were angered by lang's statements (Kort 2000, *Advocate* online) that she would "rather connect with a person one-to-one, not connect as a lesbian to a straight person" and that her sexuality is "an aside." Yet lang has been active in promoting a number of gay and lesbian causes and has contributed to AIDS-fundraising events. She takes pride in the distinctiveness of gay and lesbian culture. Her comments on the impracticality of gay marriage should be read precisely as an act of pride rather than shame and self loathing. Asked by the *Advocate* (Kort 2000, online edition) to comment on gay marriage, lang argued that marriage "is a tradition and an institution to a certain majority of people. Why go there? Create a new language, create a new tradition, then approach the government about tax rights and rights in hospital. Instead of fitting into something that's not ours, we have to build our own culture." Lang has undoubtedly contributed to the building of such culture and will continue to do so for many years to come.

Further Reading

Allen, Louise. *The Lesbian Idol: Martina, k. d., and the Consumption of Lesbian Masculinity*. London: Cassell, 1999; Kort, Michele. "k. d.: A Woman in Love." *The Advocate*. 814 (June 20, 2000): 50–54. http://www.highbeam.com/doc/1G1-62741790.html (accessed on April 13, 2007); Marti, Kris Scott. "Review of k. d. lang's *Hymns of the 49th Parallel*." July 2004. http://www.afterellen.com/archive/ellen/Music/72004/hymns.html (accessed on April 13, 2007); Martinac, Paula. *k. d. lang*. New York: Chelsea House Publishing, 1997; Official Web site: http://www.wbr.com/kdlang/index.html (accessed on April 13, 2007); Robertson, William. *k d. lang: Carrying the Torch*. Toronto and East Haven, CT: ECW Press, 1993; Signorile, Michelangelo. *Queer in America*. New York: Abacus Books, 1993; Starr, Victoria. *k. d. lang: All You Get is Me*. New York: St. Martin's Press, 1994.

LEAVITT, DAVID (1961–)

The Jewish-American writer David Leavitt is one of the most influential figures of the gay literary movement and of American literature in general. In his multiple roles as fiction writer, essayist, reviewer, and editor, Leavitt has sought to capture the gay experience challenging the stereotypes usually associated with it in popular fiction. The lives of both his homosexual and heterosexual characters are effectively observed. Leavitt describes human relationships without idealizing them, taking into account their emotional and intellectual complexities. Since his first short story, "Territory," was published in the *New Yorker* when the writer was only 21, Leavitt has received numerous literary prizes, including an O. Henry Award, a National Endowment for the Arts grant, and a Guggenheim fellowship. He has also held teaching posts of creative writing at various academic institutions such as the Institute of Catalan Letters in Barcelona and the University of Florida. Ever since "Territory," Leavitt has encountered controversies for its frank depiction of homosexuality, including a highly publicized legal battle with British novelist Stephen Spender in 1995.

Born on June 23, 1961, in Pittsburgh, Leavitt is the son of Harold Leavitt, a university professor, and Gloria Rosenthal, a liberal activist. David grew up in Palo Alto, California, and graduated from Yale University in 1983 with a B. A. in English. Leavitt was still a student at Yale when "Territory" was published in *The New Yorker* and the magazine soon accepted a second story of his, "Out Here." *Family Dancing* (1984), which contained the two previously published pieces along with seven new ones, was Leavitt's first published collection of short stories and provided its author with critical acclaim and popular success. It was nominated for the National Book Critics Circle Award and for the PEN-Faulkner Award. In the nine stories of the book, Leavitt introduces gay themes within middle-class America, carefully dissecting its sexual repression and its material desires. The characters in *Family Dancing* set the type for many of the figures that people Leavitt's fiction: they are mainly secular Jews who cannot closely and completely identify with their ethnic and religious rituals. Some of the stories' plotlines will also be developed in the author's later works such as the troubled relationship of a gay son with his mother in "Territory," coming to terms with broken marriages in "The Lost Cottage" and "Family Dancing," a mother struggling against cancer in "Radiation," homosexuality in supposedly heterosexual people in "Danny in Transit," and the love of a heterosexual woman for a gay man in "Dedicated."

Coming two years after *Family Dancing*, *The Lost Language of the Cranes* (1986) was Leavitt's first novel. It centered on the relationship between Philip Benjamin, who has just come out as gay, and his parents, his father Owen, who is also gay but has chosen to hide and repress his sexual orientation, and his mother Rose who struggles to accept her son's homosexuality and her husband's lack of attention for her. Leavitt's narrative, which takes place under the shadow of the threat of the **AIDS** epidemic, draws sympathy for each of the characters and skillfully plays with the readers' expectations from a coming out story. These are successfully subverted when the coming-out story of the book turns out to be not the son's, but the father's, unveiling as it does years of deceits and lies in the lives of two professional, middle-class heterosexuals. The novel was later adapted into a stunning BBC movie.

Contrary to its title taken from a poem by W. H. Auden, *Equal Affections* (1989) focuses on a series of unequal relationships described through a broken chronological order. The novel centers around the Coopers, a Jewish family. The character of Louise Cooper, the mother, is the person who keeps the different narrative threads together through her 20-year battle against cancer. The book follows Louise's doubts about her religious faith and her attraction for Catholicism, her husband's extramarital affair, her gay son's suburban and monogamous life and her lesbian daughter's feminist rejection of family conventions, including her artificial insemination with the sperm of a gay man.

With *A Place I've Never Been* (1990), Leavitt returned to the short story form with pieces initially composed in 1984. Several stories return to themes and situations already explored in *Family Dancing*. "My Marriage to Vengeance" and "Houses," for example, both feature two married heterosexuals struggling to come to terms with their homosexual tendencies, which, in the end, they choose to ignore or repress. Clelia, the woman at the center of *Family Dancing*'s "Dedicated," and her gay love Nathan both return in "When You Grow to Adultery." Some stories, such as "Ayor" (an acronym which stands for "At Your Own Risk"), also present promiscuous behavior and explicit sex scenes within the aftermath of AIDS. With this collection, Leavitt expanded his focus from the world of gay American urban life to portray the existence of American expatriates in Europe, thereby inviting comparisons to the fiction of Henry James. As James, Leavitt too has divided his life between his native America and Europe, where he and his partner have bought a house in Tuscany, Italy.

After the promising beginnings and the critical acclaim of the 1980s, Leavitt increasingly found himself embroiled in scandals and controversies during the 1990s. *While England Sleeps* (1993) chronicles the love story between Brian Botsford and Edward Phelan on the backdrop of the Spanish Civil War and the split in the left-wing republican front. David Streitfeld, the reviewer for the *Washington Post*, noticed that the story bore resemblances with Stephen Spender's 1950 autobiography *World within World*. The British writer was offended by what he considered thinly disguised references to himself and lengthy pornographic love scenes. Spender's accusations led to a prolonged legal case which was, however, settled out of court. Parallel to the legal battle, Leavitt and Spender exchanged mutual accusations on the pages of literary magazines. Leavitt charged that Spender's reaction was caused by homophobia, an interpretation rejected by the British author who claimed that his life belonged to himself only. In his article "Did I Plagiarize His Life?," Leavitt (1994, *New York Times Magazine* online) wrote that he was not trying to pass off Spender's writing as his own. On the contrary, Spender's autobiography merely served as the inspiration for his historical novel. "Homophobia is global," argued Leavitt, "what is unique about English homophobia is that it is part and parcel of a national fervor about gay sex in comparison to which the national fervor to accuse writers of plagiarism seems tame." Leavitt also pondered on "what greater homage could be paid to a writer than to see his own life serve as the occasion for fiction." A settlement was finally reached causing the novel to be withdrawn and revised in several parts, although the love scenes were left as in the original edition. *While England Sleeps* was reissued by Houghton Mifflin with an interview to the author. Leavitt's subsequent work, the novella "The Term Paper Artist" proved equally controversial. Originally written for publication in *Esquire*, the story was rejected by the magazine's editor for its explicit language which, they feared, might offend their readers. The piece focuses on the link between authors' lives and their works. Its main character is David Leavitt, a novelist and the author of a book called *While England Sleeps*, who writes term papers for UCLA undergraduate students in exchange for sex. The story was included in the collection *Arkansas* (1997), which also features "Saturn Street," where a writer works as a volunteer to deliver lunches to AIDS patients forced into their homes by the illness, and "The Wooden Anniversary," where Clelia and Nathan's story further develops.

Leavitt was skillful enough to exploit the controversies of the early 1990s for his own artistic and literary inspiration. "The Term Paper Artist" already dramatized the tensions between its protagonist's early successes and his fears not to be able to live up to these expectations. Its character acknowledged that "[c]ompetitiveness, not to mention a terror to lose the stature I had gained in my early youth, played a much more singular role in my life than I have heretofore admitted" (Leavitt 1997, 5). Leavitt's novel *The Page Turner* (1998) further explored the fears and expectations of an aspiring artist, the 18-year-old piano prodigy Paul Porterfield, who falls in love with the famous pianist Richard Kennington. A mutual fascination leads the two to start an affair while they are in Rome. Paul admires Kennington for the fame he has achieved. Yet, Kennington too is fascinated by Paul and his ambition to make it in the world of classical music. In the younger pianist he sees a reflection of himself as he was before his success, a success that has not brought him any happiness. On the contrary, Kennington feels that his life has become an arid series of musical tours. His success generates in the artist a sense of failure. As usual in Leavitt's fiction, *The Page Turner* also focuses on the life of a middle-class, middle-aged woman, Pamela, Porterfield's mother who finds herself confronted both with her husband's infidelity and her son's gayness. Catalonian director Ventura Pons adapted the novel into the film *Food of Love* (2002).

Told in a confessional first-person narration, *Martin Bauman: Or a Sure Thing* (2000) continues Leavitt's play with the blurring of boundaries between the author's life and fiction. Martin Bauman is yet another ambitious young writer who moves within New York literary circles, aspiring to achieve literary fame with a great novel and romantic fulfillment with a lasting gay relationship. In his quest for recognition, Martin also has to struggle to gain independence from his former mentor Stanley Flint whose approval, however, he constantly seeks. *Martin Bauman* ironically portrays the personalities and the institutions behind New York's literary circles which serve as the milieu to the protagonist's bildungsroman.

The Marble Quilt (2001) interestingly alternates short stories set in the nineteenth and twentieth centuries, shifting between Europe and the United States. "The Infection Scene" actually moves between the two centuries within its narrative as it progresses from the story of Lord Douglas, Oscar Wilde's cruel lover, to that of Christopher, a gay man living in contemporary San Francisco and seeking to become infected with HIV. Common to both characters is their self-loathing. After *The Body of Jonah Boyd* (2004), focusing again on the relationship between an older and a younger writer, Leavitt turned to biography with *The Man Who Knew Too Much: Alan Turing and the Invention of the Computer* (2006), on the life of the gay British mathematician who committed suicide in 1954. Together with his partner Mark Mitchell, Leavitt has also written a travel book, *Italian Pleasures* (1996), and edited three gay literary anthologies. In spite of the mixed reviews that his books have received since the publication of *While England Sleeps*, Leavitt has continued to write and has successfully developed a faithful readership both within and outside of the gay and lesbian community.

Further Reading

Guscio, Lelia. *"We Trust Ourselves and Not Money. Period.": Relationships, Death and Homosexuality in David Leavitt's Fiction*. New York: Peter Lang, 1995; Kekki, Lasse. *From Gay to Queer: Gay Male Identity in Selected Fiction by David Leavitt and in Tony Kushner's Play Angels in America I-II*. New York: Peter Lang, 2003; Lawson, D. S. "David Leavitt." *Contemporary Gay American Novelists: A Bio-Biographical Critical Sourcebook*. Emmanuel S. Nelson, ed. Westport, CT: Greenwood Press, 1993. 248–253; Leavitt, David. "Did I Plagiarize His Life?" *New York Times Magazine*. April 3, 1994. 36–37. http://www.nytimes.com/books/97/03/30/reviews/leavitt-plagiarize.html (accessed on July 8, 2007); Leavitt, David. *Arkansas: Three Novellas*. New York: Houghton Mifflin Company, 1997; Lilly, Mark. *Gay Men's Literature in the Twentieth Century*. New York: New York University Press, 1993; Spender, Stephen. "My Life Is Mine; It Is Not David Leavitt's." *New York Times Book Review*. September 4, 1994. 10–12.

LIBERACE (1919–1987)

With his lavish and elaborate music shows, the charismatic American entertainer and pianist Liberace became the personification of **camp** and flamboyance.

Although critics panned his skills as a performer, Liberace was incredibly popular with American audiences and, throughout the 1950s, was the highest grossing entertainer in the country, drawing to his shows audiences which were comparable in size to those of Frank Sinatra and Elvis Presley. Yet, in spite of the pervading glitter of his unlikely costumes, Liberace repeatedly issued contemptuous denials against the rumors that he was gay. His career was punctuated with legal battles about his sexuality. The artist's struggle with his own queerness points to his own double persona. On stage, he was completely in control and his shows were perfect creations where Liberace successfully interacted with his audience, mostly made of adoring middle-aged women. Off stage, however, Liberace was not as flamboyant and was ill at ease with his homosexuality.

Wladziu Valentino Liberace was born on May 16, 1919, in West Allis, Wisconsin, in a family of Polish and Italian descent. He learned to play the piano at a very young age. Since his early career, Liberace discovered that his renditions of popular songs and tunes were more appreciated by his audiences than his classical repertoire. Therefore, despite his classical training and his debut with the Chicago Symphony in 1940, the performer soon changed the nature of his act, which he defined as "pop with a bit of classics" or "classical music with the boring parts left out." In the mid-1940s, his career reached a turning point as he started to perform in Las Vegas, a desert town that was booming thanks to legal gambling. Liberace's shows had a positive impact on the casinos where he was playing. His boyish good looks were perfect for business, attracting sizable audiences. It was while playing in Las Vegas that Liberace was first noticed by the man who then became his manager, Seymour Heller.

Heller decided to try the artist, who, by the 1950s, started to bill himself only as Liberace, on television. At the time, TV was still an exciting and experimental industry, although it would soon change the nature of entertainment in America. TV producers wanted someone who could charm audiences in their homes and Liberace proved to be the right solution. As the medium was still in its infancy, there were no conventions set and Liberace created his own by talking directly to the camera as if it was a person. His flirting and beaming at the camera while playing, along with his distinctive and ever-present silver candelabrum on top of his piano, bewitched American audiences, who were accustomed to much more formal performers. Beginning in 1952, *The Liberace Show* was a tremendous hit, becoming the most watched TV program in the country. The show was also one of the first to manage to attract advertisers, who, at the time, were still skeptical about the usefulness of the TV medium, still considering it a gimmick. Liberace quickly realized that his show would stand or fall by his ability to attract commercial sponsors and he managed to secure the Citizens National Bank of Los Angeles. On his show, Liberace performed with the top stars of the day and turned into a universally appealing product of the early TV days. *The Liberace Show* was aired until 1956 and provided the performer with a huge fan base. Liberace's trademarks, such as his candelabrum, his flashy and glittery costumes and his huge rings, would reverberate through popular culture for years to come.

Because of Liberace's status as a TV star, audiences flocked to see his live shows as well. Such popularity obviously led to intense media scrutiny about the performer's private life. Liberace's family was ever present in his shows, his brother George leading the backing band. Liberace constructed an image of his family as living in opulent bliss, the perfect American family that had produced the perfect American boy. In public, the artist was always surrounded by adoring women. He also told a raunchy story of how he had lost his virginity to a female blues singer when he was barely 16. In 1953 Liberace caused the dismay of his thousands of women fans when he came up with a fiancée: dancer and aspiring actress Joanne Rio. The story was in every paper, but the couple eventually called off their engagement, a split orchestrated by Liberace's manager as the performer could not go on with a fake wedding. Far from media attention, however, Liberace was unmistakably gay. Young handsome boys sunbathed around his piano-shaped pool. His brother privately complained about "too many fags" hanging around the house and this led to a growing rift between the two brothers.

Liberace and his trademark, the ever-present silver candelabrum. Courtesy of Photofest.

In 1956 Liberace embarked on a European tour that made him a transatlantic star, but also sentenced the entertainer to life-silence about his sexuality. When Liberace arrived in England, he was greeted by thousands of adoring fans, but also by critics who reacted with disgust to his show. In his Cassandra column in the tabloid *Daily Mirror*, William Connor described Liberace as "the summit of sex—the pinnacle of Masculine, Feminine and Neuter. Everything that He, She and It can ever want." The journalist went on with an impressive strings of adjectives which termed the performer as a "deadly, winking, sniggering, snuggling, chromium-plated, scent-impregnated, luminous, quivering, giggling, fruit-flavored, mincing, ice-covered heap of mother love." To Connor, Liberace was "the biggest sentimental vomit of all time." The performer sued for libel claiming that the article had damaged his career because it implied that he was a homosexual. At a time when being gay was still considered a custodial offence in Britain, homosexuality received an unprecedented press coverage. When cross-examined, Liberace was directly asked the question, "Are you a homosexual?" He vehemently denied, stating that he was against homosexuality as "it offends conventions and it offends society." Liberace won the case and was awarded £8,000 in damages. It was, however, a Pyrrhic victory: he had denied his own sexuality under oath and could now never admit to being gay. Since the Cassandra article, Liberace's career would be punctuated with legal skirmishes about his sex life. The entertainer's $25 million libel suit against *Confidential*, which had run a cover story with the title "Why Liberace's theme song should be, 'Mad About the Boy!,'" contributed to the magazine's shutdown.

In spite of these legal battles, Liberace continued to perform to adoring audiences of middle-aged women who found his high camp style irresistible. His lowbrow cocktail of pop tunes, flashy costumes, and elaborate sets made Liberace the highest paid entertainer in America, reaching a salary of $50,000 a week during the 1950s. His shows, which grew more outrageous with the years, became a regular feature of the Las Vegas scene. Although critics detested Liberace as the man who had stripped the classic out of classical music, the artist's salary remained phenomenally high throughout his career. In the 1970s, however, Liberace grew increasingly worried about his legacy and about how he would be remembered by future generations. The Liberace Museum opened in Las Vegas in 1979, quickly becoming the third most popular attraction in Nevada. Yet, in spite of Liberace's attempts to institutionalize his own closeted life, the 1980s witnessed renewed public attention for the entertainer's sexuality. After an acrimonious split, Scott Thorson, who had been Liberace's partner for five years, filed a palimony suit against the artist. Liberace continued to deny his homosexuality. He dismissed his former lover, whom he had sent to his own plastic surgeon to have him remade in his own image, as an employee who had been fired because of his alcohol and a drug abuse. The case was settled out of court and, once again, Liberace was able to exploit the publicity to his own ends. He made a triumphant, record-breaking appearance at Radio City Music Hall in New York City, scoring a victory in the very milieu where all his critics were based.

As his shows grew increasingly campy, Liberace also found himself becoming a hip gay icon. This was somewhat paradoxical as the entertainer fought against the very notion that he was gay until his death. As Liberace appeared slimmer and was plagued by health problems, the media again speculated about his sexuality. After Rock Hudson's death of **AIDS** in 1985, journalists were in search of the next celebrity victim. Liberace died in his Palm Springs house on February 4, 1987. His death finally smashed the closet that had been so carefully constructed throughout the entertainer's career. Liberace was horrified by Hudson's public admission of his homosexuality and HIV-positive status, telling a friend that he did not want to be remembered as an old queen who died of AIDS. Although Liberace's death was quickly attributed to emphysema, the Palm Springs coroner surprisingly ordered an autopsy to determine the true cause of Liberace's death. The public persona of Liberace died with the artist in a city morgue, the first time, perhaps, that both his private and public existences coincided. Ironically, due to the entertainer's life-long battle with his own sexual difference, Liberace's influence on popular culture was, as biographer Ray Mungo (1995) argues, to make it acceptable to be a screaming queen on stage. Liberace paved the way for camp and glitter to be adopted by a whole generation of pop stars.

Further Reading

http://www.bobsliberace.com/decades/1950s/1950s.11.html. Excerpt from the William Connor's column in the *Daily Mirror* (accessed on June 18, 2007); Faris,

Jocelyn. *Liberace: A Bio-Bibliography*. Westport, CT: Greenwood Publishing Group, 1995; Liberace. *An Autobiography*. New York: G. P. Putnam's Sons, 1973; Liberace. *Liberace Cooks*. New York: Barricade Books, 1970; Liberace. *The Things I Love*. New York: Grosset and Dunlap, 1976; Liberace. *The Wonderful Private World of Liberace*. Tony Palmer, ed. New York: Harper & Row, 1986; Miller, Harriet H. *I'll Be Seeing You: The Young Liberace*. Las Vegas: Leesson Publisher, 1992; Mungo, Ray. *Liberace*. Lives of Notable Gay Men and Lesbians. New York: Chelsea House Publishing, 1995; Pyron, Darden Asbury. *Liberace: An American Boy*. Chicago: University of Chicago Press, 2000; Thomas, Bob. *Liberace: The True Story*. New York: St. Martins Press, 1988; Thorson, Scott, with Alex Thorleifson. *Behind the Candelabra: My Life with Liberace*. New York: Dutton, 1988.

LOUGANIS, GREG (1960–)

Olympic diving champion Greg Louganis publicly came out as a gay man in 1994 at the Gay Games in New York. He subsequently talked candidly about his sexual orientation and positive HIV-status in a much-publicized "20/20" interview with Barbara Walters and in his bestselling autobiography *Breaking the Surface* (1995), which was also adapted as a TV movie. Although officially closeted during his athletic career, Louganis has actively supported queer causes and has appeared as an actor in gay-themed plays since his coming out. With his example, Louganis has contributed to give visibility to homosexuality within the world of sports, which still remains pervaded by homophobic attitudes. Although progress was made in the last decades of the twentieth century, the organization of most sports along same-sex lines and the connection between athletic achievement and masculinity have proved a fertile ground for heterosexism. Louganis's support of the Gay Games, as well as several of his speaking events, go precisely in the direction of instilling self esteem in the gay community through sport.

Gregory Louganis was born on November 29, 1960, in San Diego to unmarried teen parents of Samoan and Northern European descent. He was adopted by a Greek-American family when he was less than a year old and grew up in the suburbs of San Diego. Louganis was attracted by athletic disciplines from a very early age, starting as a gymnast first and then switching to diving. The athlete went through a difficult time during his childhood and adolescence as he was the target of homophobic scorn by his peers who called him a nigger for his dark skin, a sissy, and a retard (due to his dyslexia). His relationship with his alcoholic adoptive father was characterized by abuse and violence. Louganis was prey to several bouts of depression, lack of self-confidence, and suicide attempts, all problems that he has frankly written about in his autobiography. Sport was an important emotional outlet for the athlete, who, barely 16, took part in the 1976 Summer Olympics in Montreal. In the 10m platform, Louganis won the silver medal, second only to the Italian Klaus Dibiasi. Two years later, he won his first world title in the same event.

In the meantime, Louganis had been offered a diving scholarship at the University of Miami where the athlete also started to explore his sexuality, an element of his identity that he had repressed until then. Eager to take part in the Moscow Olympics (1980), where he was confident he could have won the gold medal, Louganis was prevented from competing because of the American boycott of the games in retaliation against the Soviet invasion of Afghanistan. He then started to train for the next Olympics, transferring from the University of Miami to the University of California, Irvine, where he was coached by Ron O' Brien. The 1980s were years of incredible athletic achievements for Louganis, who swept the 1982 springboard and platform titles at the World Championships and won gold medals at the 1984 Olympic Games in both springboard and platform. Louganis was the first athlete to win both competitions since 1928.

At the Seoul Olympics in 1988 he repeated his double triumph in both springboard and platform. Yet, this event was the center of a heated controversy after Louganis

Diver Greg Louganis interviewed by Mike Adamle in 1979. Courtesy of NBC/Photofest.

came out and revealed he had **AIDS**. While taking a two-and-a-half pike from the springboard, the diver hit his head and came out of the pool bleeding. At the time, Louganis already knew he was HIV-positive, but he had not informed anyone except for his coach about his status. Although the 1980s had been a decade of professional feats for the athlete, his private life had been marked by short and abusive relationships with men, one of whom had confessed to Louganis he had AIDS just while the diver was training for the games. Louganis tested positive in March 1988 but decided not to inform the Olympic Committee of his status thinking that diving was not a contact sport. After he injured his head, the diver still neglected to inform the doctors that he was HIV-positive. The risk of infecting someone following the injury to his head was very low. Yet, Louganis was in sheer panic, as he recounts in the opening chapter of *Breaking the Surface*. In spite of this, he did not withdraw and went on to perform some of the best dives in his career. After the diver's coming out, the chairman of the Seoul Olympic organizing committee, Park Seh Jik, said it had not been "morally right" for Louganis to compete in the final round of the Olympics and not disclose his condition. Yet, the International Olympic Committee maintained that Louganis was not required to disclose his positive status.

Louganis stated that his coming out on *20/20*, which coincided with the launch of his autobiography, aimed to "motivate those people who are HIV-positive to be responsible and also to understand that life isn't over yet, that HIV and AIDS is not a death sentence." Some people, even from within the gay community, blamed Louganis for being, in the words of David Kirp (1995) in the *Nation*, "out for dollars." Kirp charged that Louganis's coming-out interview with Walters was not "an act of moral self-examination" but "the titillating tidbit meant to coax people into buying his new book." Yet, generally, queers regard Louganis's coming out as a defining moment in their history, and one which can contribute to fight homophobia in the world of sport. The ***Advocate*** included the diver's coming out in the events that shaped the consciousness and awareness of the younger generation of gays and lesbians over the last 30 years of the twentieth century.

Further Reading

Anderson, Eric. "Openly Gay Athletes: Contesting Hegemonic Masculinity in a Homophobic Environment." *Gender and Society* 16, no. 6 (December 2002): 860–877; Kirp, David. "Out for Dollars." *The Nation.* March 20, 1995. http://findarticles. com/p/articles/mi_hb1367/is_199503/ai_n5597558 (accessed on November 17, 2006); Louganis, Greg. http://www.louganis.com (accessed on November 17, 2006); Louganis, Greg, and Eric Marcus. *Breaking the Surface.* New York: Random House, 1995; Lutes, Michael A. "Greg Louganis." *Gay and Lesbian Biography.* Michael J. Tyrkus, ed. Detroit: St. James Press, 1997. 297–299.

M

Mapplethorpe, Robert (1946–1989)

The works of American photographer Robert Mapplethorpe caused heated debates both within critical circles and the larger American society because of their frank depiction of male nudity, homosexuality, and extreme S-M practices. Different critics disagreed over the question whether to consider Mapplethorpe's sexually explicit photographs art or obscenity, a debate that contributed, in the end, to treat the two terms not as mutually exclusive but as compatible features of a creative work. More progressive critics also challenged the photographer's depiction of black men as perpetrating racial stereotypes reducing them to their sexual attributes. Frantz Fanon's famous statement in *Black Skin, White Masks* on "the eclipse of the Negro" and his turning into a penis has been applied to Mapplethorpe's photographs of black men by queer critics such as Essex Hemphill and Vivien Ng (1997, 225–228). In addition, the sexual nature of a significant part of Mapplethorpe's artistic production sparked a more general controversy about the National Endowment for the Arts and its funding policies, a crucial phase in what has been described as the "culture wars of the arts" in the early 1990s. Because of these controversies, the name of the artist has become inextricably tied with censorship and homosexuality although his production is not limited to sexually explicit images but also includes still lifes and portraits of celebrities. Mapplethorpe's application of rigorous formal composition to extreme subject matter made the photographer one of the most successful American photographers of the post-World War II era. Mapplethorpe's photographs, which he managed to market as luxury objects, became increasingly expensive in the 1980s and their prices skyrocketed after the artist's death from **AIDS**-related complications at the end of the decade. The photographer's print of **Andy Warhol**, purchased in 2006 for over $600,000, was one of the most expensive photographs ever sold.

Mapplethorpe was born into a Catholic family in Queens, New York, on November 4, 1946. He enrolled at the Pratt Institute, Brooklyn, in 1963 not, however, to study photography but painting and sculpture. As a student, Mapplethorpe came into contact with New York's bohemian world and, during these years, he met singer and poet Patti Smith who became one of his favorite models. The two began to share an apartment in Brooklyn and then moved to the Chelsea Hotel in Manhattan, a gathering place for artists, writers, and musicians in the early 1970s. Mapplethorpe's first creations were not photographs, but collages and mixed-media objects that incorporated pornographic images of men. The artist's decision to create his own images for these works stimulated his interest in photography and Mapplethorpe soon started to work as a photographer for Andy Warhol's *Interview* magazine. Because his collages were rejected by the many galleries that the artist approached in the early 1970s, he increasingly chose photography as his privileged form of art. Mapplethorpe's decision to take up photography full time was also encouraged by the artist's encounters with John McKendry, Curator of Prints and Photography at the Metropolitan Museum of Art, New York, and Sam Wagstaff, a curator and collector who became the artist's manager and lifetime partner. Mapplethorpe's first photographs were black-and-white Polaroids and mainly included self portraits. These early pictures already show the artist's interest in sexuality as Mapplethorpe portrays himself in various acts of masturbation. The Polaroids anticipate the major themes of the photographer's later and more controversial Portfolios. These self portraits constituted the material of Mapplethorpe's first solo exhibition which took place at the Light Gallery, New York, in 1973.

The artist's fame progressively increased throughout the 1970s. In 1975, when Patti Smith signed a contract with Arista Records, Mapplethorpe took the photograph that constituted the cover of Smith's first album, *Horses*. The picture of Smith in an androgynous outfit is widely regarded as the peak of Mapplethorpe's early career. The photographer's subsequent creations broadly fall in three categories: male nudes, still lifes, and portraits of celebrities and socialites. In the late 1970s, Mapplethorpe increasingly focused on the depiction of S-M practices. These photographs constitute the main part of his *X Portfolio* and were exhibited in 1977 at the Kitchen in New York. That same year, Mapplethorpe had another important show in New York at the Holly Solomon Gallery, centering on the photographs of flowers of the *Y Portfolio*. Thanks to these two portfolios, the photographer acquired an international reputation and solo exhibitions rapidly spread throughout the United States and Europe. After these two first collections of works, Mapplethorpe published a third volume, the *Z Portfolio*, in 1981. This new series reflects the artist's interest in black male bodies and, together with the more widely distributed *The Black Book* (1986), prompted controversies on Mapplethorpe's sexual objectification of black bodies. What unites the three main strands in the photographer's production is Mapplethorpe's detached attitude towards his subject matters, even the most extreme ones, and his attention for formal elegance and composition. Whether photographing flowers or well-endowed black men, Mapplethorpe emphasized structural symmetry, complex color gradations, and attention for visual details. He presented most of his pictures as luxury objects, printing them on linen or surrounding them with elegant fabrics such as silk and velvet. His portfolios were initially published in limited editions. To Mapplethorpe, aesthetic qualities were not intrinsic in subject matters: "I don't think there's much difference," he controversially stated, "between a photograph of [a] fist up someone's ass and a photograph of carnations in a bowl" (Dubin 1992, 172). He summed up his artistic goal as reaching "the perfection in form. I do that with portraits. I do it with cocks. I do it with flowers."

In the mid-1980s, when the artist was at the peak of his celebrity, his private life was devastated by the advent of AIDS. The photographer was diagnosed with the illness in 1986 and the following year his partner Sam Wagstaff died of AIDS-related complications. In 1988 Mapplethorpe established the Robert Mapplethorpe Foundation, a charity that funds AIDS research and photography exhibitions. He also had four major exhibitions devoted to his work at prestigious venues: the Stedelijk Museum, Amsterdam; the Whitney Museum of American Art, New York; the Institute of Contemporary Art, Philadelphia; and the National Portrait Gallery, London. Mapplethorpe died on March 9, 1989, in Boston.

The controversies generated by his photographs, however, did not stop with Mapplethorpe's death. The Institute of Contemporary Art in Philadelphia decided to take its retrospective exhibition, "The Perfect Moment," partially funded by the National Endowment for the Arts (NEA), on tour. The show enjoyed record attendance in both Philadelphia and Chicago, the second stop on the tour. However, as the Corcoran Art Gallery in Washington, DC, prepared to house the exhibition, Republican Senator Jesse Helms began a campaign against NEA in reaction to its funding of controversial photographer Andres Serrano and his photograph "Piss Christ." The Corcoran director, anxious that the images of the *X Portfolio* might provide further ammunition for Helms against NEA, cancelled the Mapplethorpe show. Yet, her decision only served to escalate the controversy. Reacting against the cancellation of the exhibition, protesters gathered outside the Corcoran and projected the Mapplethorpe images on the wall of the Gallery. The press coverage of the protest brought Mapplethorpe to the attention of Helms and other right-wing groups such as the American Family Association and the Christian Coalition. The work of Mapplethorpe was taken as an example of the degrading of American art encouraged by NEA's careless funding. The Washington Project for the Arts eventually took on the exhibition, but Helms's campaign and histrionics (he destroyed an exhibition catalog on the floor of the U.S. Senate) caused a backlash against NEA that significantly restricted public funding for the arts. The controversy helped "The Perfect Moment" to reach record-breaking attendance in Washington too. When the exhibition moved to Cincinnati's Contemporary Art Center (CAC) in 1990, police forces stopped admittance on the opening day to review the works. At the end of the inspection, seven photographs out of the 150 that made up the show were classified as "obscene," and this led to the arrest and trial of CAC's director Dennis Barrie on charges of obscenity and child pornography. Barrie was later acquitted as the jury did find the photographs obscene, but could not determine that they did not have artistic merit. The verdict sanctioned, at least partially, that an object could be both artistic and obscene, an argument which Mapplethorpe himself would have espoused.

Criticism of Mapplethorpe's works has not come only from conservative and homophobic quarters. Progressive and even gay critics have challenged the photographer's fascination with black men as perpetrating the worst racist stereotypes and as reducing black males to walking phalluses. These critics target in particular Mapplethorpe's *Z Portfolio* and *The Black Book*. According to them, pictures such as "Man in a Polyester Suit" (1980) show a fetishization of the black male body. The photograph portrays a black man in a three piece suit, but it is cut at the chest and above the knees. What features most prominently in it is the black man's large and semi-hard penis, a representation of black identity that many find reductive at best and at worst, complicit with other demeaning racist depictions of black males. Yet, others, Kobena Mercer (1991, 188) among them, have interpreted photographs like "Man in a Polyester Suit" as problematizing racist beliefs. In Mercer's view, Mapplethorpe's works on black subjects is not "a repetition of racist fantasies but…a deconstructive strategy that lays bare psychic and social relations of ambivalence in the representation of race and sexuality."

Mapplethorpe made a vital contribution to the transformation of sexual culture thanks to his creations of elegant visual records of marginalized and despised practices. He revolutionized the world of photography by applying the formal rigor of classical sculptures to S-M acts, thus lending them that artistic dignity that they were previously denied. "I wanted people to see that even those extremes could be made into art," the photographer (Rushton *Independent*, online) said shortly before his death. "Take those pornographic images and make them somehow transcend the image." Mapplethorpe's photographs blurred the boundaries separating the realms of art and obscenity. His works also gave clear visibility to homosexual desire, stimulating debates that eventually helped to lift, though partially, the veil of censorship against the representation of homosexuality in artistic creations.

Further Reading

Bolton, Richard, ed. *Culture Wars: Documents from the Recent Controversies in the Arts*. New York: New Press, 1992; Danto, Arthur C. *Playing with the Edge: The Photographic Achievement of Robert Mapplethorpe*. Berkeley: University of California Press, 1996; Dubin, S. C. *Arresting Images, Impolitic Art and Uncivil Actions*. New York: Routledge, 1992; Kardon, Janet. *Robert Mapplethorpe: The Perfect Moment*. Philadelphia: Institute of Contemporary Art, 1988; Marshall, Richard, Richard Howard, and Ingrid Sischy. *Robert Mapplethorpe*. New York: Whitney Museum of American Art, 1988; Mercer, Kobena. "Skin Head Sex Thing: Racial Difference and the Homoerotic Imaginary." Bad Object Choices, *How Do I Look? Queer Film and Video*. Seattle: Bay Press, 1991. 169–210; Meyer, Richard. "Robert Mapplethorpe and the Discipline of Photography." *The Lesbian and Gay Studies Reader*. Henry Abelove, Michele A. Barale, and David Helperin, eds. New York: Routledge, 1993. 360–380; Meyer, Richard. "The Jesse Helms Theory of Art." *October* 104 (Spring 2003): 131–148; Ng, Vivien. "Race Matters." *Lesbian and Gay Studies*. Andy Medhurst and Sally R. Munt, eds. London: Cassell, 1997. 215–231; Rushton, Susie. "Body of Evidence." *The Independent*. September 11, 2004. http://findarticles.com/p/articles/mi_qn4158/is_20040911/ai_n12798306 (accessed on December 7, 2006).

MCKELLEN, IAN (1939–)

Openly gay English actor Sir Ian McKellen has earned many prestigious awards and honors for his fine performances as both stage and screen actor. He has acted in many Shakespearian productions and, since the mid-1990s, he became a well-known actor in North America too with his appearances on TV in series such as *Tales of the City* (1993) and in films such as *And the Band Played On* (1993). With his participation to the *X-Men* and the *Lord of the Rings* cinematic sagas, Ian McKellen has achieved the status of a popular culture icon. In spite of his star status and his knighthood, McKellen has never been timid about campaigning for queer rights. He publicly came out in the late 1980s to fight against Section 28 of the Local Government Act, which prohibited the promotion of homosexuality and the teaching of homosexuality as a "pretended family relationship." McKellen was also one of the co-founders of Britain's first gay lobbying group *Stonewall*. In a profile, the British Sunday newspaper *The Observer* (Garfield 2006, online edition) has described McKellen as "a national treasure."

Ian Murray McKellen was born on May 25, 1939, in Burnley, Lancashire. He grew up in a family of non-orthodox Christian background. The actor's parents both died when he was still young. McKellen's mother died when Ian was only 12 years old, while his father, a civil engineer and a lay preacher, died when he was 24. McKellen attended Bolton School Boys Division where he appeared in several school plays. His passion for the theater was supported by his family and his parents often took him to see shows at local theaters. McKellen won a scholarship to study at St. Catherine's College, University of Cambridge, from where he graduated in 1961. During his university years, the actor appeared in 21 student productions. Since there was no drama school at Cambridge, these plays represented his training for the stage. The same year of his graduation, McKellen made his professional debut at the Belgrade Theater in Coventry. After three years of touring regional theaters, the actor obtained his first part in a London production, James Saunders's *A Scent of Flowers*, for which he was awarded the Clarence Derwent Award for best supporting actor. From the mid-1960s, McKellen began to appear regularly at the National Theater and he also made his first appearance as a screen actor, although the theater still remained the major focus of his career.

In the 1970s, McKellen acquired a reputation as a spokesperson for British actors when he founded the Actors' Company, an organization democratically run by its members. He also started directing London productions and made his debut for the Royal Shakespeare Company, playing leading roles in *Romeo and Juliet*, *Macbeth*, and *The Alchemist*. In 1979 the actor took the gay role of Max in Martin Sherman's play *Bent*, which, for the first time, drew public attention to the Nazi persecution of homosexuals. The following year McKellen made his first appearance on the Broadway stage as Salieri in Peter Shaffer's *Amadeus*, a role that earned him a Tony Award for Best Actor. Appearing on Broadway was, McKellen recalls, the crowning of his lifelong ambition.

In the 1980s, the actor began working more regularly in films, where he soon landed leading roles. In particular, after his coming out in 1988, he enthusiastically took up the part of disgraced Conservative politician John Profumo in Michael Caton-Jones's *Scandal* (1989). Profumo was a famed womanizer. He became the center of a Cold War sex scandal when his affair with call girl Christine Keeler, who was also sleeping with Yevgeny Ivanov, the senior naval attaché at the Soviet Embassy, emerged as a possible threat to national security. To McKellen, this role would prove that he was still believable in heterosexual roles after his coming out. The actor's coming out did not have a negative impact on his career. On the contrary, this continued to flourish even after his announcement that he was gay during a BBC radio broadcast. McKellen's decision to come out was primarily motivated by the decision of the Conservative government led by Margaret Thatcher to introduce Section 28 in the Local Government Act. The proposed legislation ambiguously prohibited the "intentional promotion of homosexuality" by local governments. The section effectively banned council funding of books, plays, leaflets, films, or any other material depicting homosexual relationships as normal and positive. In spite of widespread opposition, Section 28 was enforced from 1988 to 2003. An important part of McKellen's campaigns for gay and lesbian rights, including the foundation of Stonewall, was geared to the repeal of the clause.

The decision to confer a knighthood to the actor in 1991 put McKellen at the center of a national controversy, which was surprisingly orchestrated not by right-wing homophobes, but by prominent members of the queer community. Commenting on McKellen's acceptance of the honor, gay director Derek Jarman publicly accused the actor of being complicit with Margaret Thatcher's homophobic government. A group of famous British gay and lesbian artists, including actor Simon Callow and director **John Schlesinger**, published an open letter in the national newspaper the *Guardian* supporting McKellen's decision to accept the knighthood. It is a proved fact that, since his coming out, McKellen has used his prominence as an actor to campaign for gay rights. In addition, in his professional career, he has accepted many roles in important gay-themed films such as *And the Band Played On*, where he portrays gay activist Bill Kraus dying of AIDS, and *Gods and Monsters* (1998). For his performance as gay director James Whale in the latter film, McKellen was nominated for an Academy Award for Best Actor.

It was thanks to the roles of Magneto in *The X-Men* series and Gandalf in *The Lord of the Rings* saga that McKellen reached international stardom, becoming a popular culture institution. Although not explicitly identifiable as gay-themed, *The X-Men* films have a clear gay subtext which hinges on McKellen's Magneto. In spite of his participation to these blockbusters and other mainstream Hollywood films such as *The Da Vinci Code* (2006), McKellen has remained a vocal critic of the homophobia embedded in the American film industry. Talking about the failure of *Brokeback Mountain* to win the Oscar for Best Picture, the actor (Garfield 2006, *Observer* online) commented: "It's called homophobia. Nobody has ever looked to Hollywood for social advance. Hollywood is a dream factory. I love the way that conservatives think that Hollywood is a bed of radicalism—it couldn't be more staid and old-ladyship if it tried." In 2002 McKellen served as Grand Master for the Gay Pride Parade in San Francisco. McKellen is a self-confessed left-winger. Yet, he has openly criticized British Prime Minister Tony Blair and his Labor government for failing to grant gay people the possibility of calling their civil partnerships a marriage: "I suppose I'm a bit mean-spirited, but I really can't see why the government couldn't just say gay people can get married—that would have been true equality and so much simpler. But that hasn't been done because they couldn't face the furore. So they've passed a law that is not available to straight people—straight people cannot have a civil partnership, they have to get married—extraordinary" (Garfield 2006, *Observer* online). Because of his acting achievements and his commitment for social change, we can expect that Ian McKellen will continue to be a defining personality in setting the cultural and political agenda for the queer community for many years to come.

Further Reading

Bronski, Michael, Christa Brelin, and Michael J. Tyrkus, eds. *Outstanding Lives: Profiles of Lesbians and Gay Men*. Detroit: Visible Ink, 1997; Garfield, Simon. "The X-factor." *The Observer Magazine*. April 30, 2006. http://observer.guard ian.co.uk/magazine/story/0,1762453,00.html; Gibson, Joy Leslie. *Ian McKellen*. London: Weidenfeld and Nicolson, 1986; Official Web site. http://www. mckellen.com; Russell, Paul Elliott. *The Gay 100: A Ranking of the Most Influential Gay Men and Lesbians, Past and Present*. New York: Birch Lane Press, 1994.

MERCURY, FREDDIE (1945–1991)

Freddie Mercury was one of the most innovative rock icons of the twentieth century. As the front man of Queen, one of the world's most popular rock groups, he was responsible for the creation of rock anthems whose fame still endures today. He also created lavish stage performances and a gender-bending androgynous persona whose reign as international rock star seemed destined to last forever, until he became rock's first **AIDS** casualty. Mercury was able to keep his status as a rock icon in spite of constant media hostility and scrutiny into his sexuality. His death due to AIDS-related complications helped to raise worldwide awareness of the disease although Mercury only revealed his positive status 24 hours before his death. In spite of the rock star's silence, the emotion that followed his death contributed to make people around the world more sensitive to AIDS causes.

Mercury was born Farrok Bulsara on September 5, 1946, on the island of Zanzibar in the Indian Ocean, then a British colony. The island's ethnically diverse population included Africans, Indians, and Arabs. A small community of Parsees also lived on the island. They followed the Zoroastrian faith and had fled from Persia in the seventh and eighth centuries to avoid persecution from Muslims. Mercury's family was of Parsee background and his parents, Bomi and Jer Bulsara, raised him in the Zoroastrian faith. Bomi, Mercury's father, worked for the British government and the family was well-off. When he was eight, Farouk was sent to St. Peter's boarding school, near Bombay in India. It was here that Mercury was first called Freddie by his schoolmates. He proved to be a good student, a promising athlete, and a fine artist. He was awarded trophies for his school achievements. He also took piano lessons and sang in the school choir. Freddie clearly had a natural penchant for performing. He soon started his own band, which played at school functions.

When Zanzibar became independent from Britain in 1963, ethnic tension exploded and the African population staged a revolution. British and Indian citizens fled and Freddie's family emigrated to England where they stayed with relatives in Middlesex, near London. In the fall of 1966, Freddie enrolled to study graphic design at the Ealing School of Art where many of his fellow students shared his interest in pop music. During these years, Freddie was particularly impressed by the new rock star Jimmy Hendrix. In the summer of 1969, he joined Ibex, a struggling band from Liverpool, whose repertoire mainly included Rod Stewart's and Beatles's covers. Freddie's increasing flamboyant style of performing made his bandmates

Freddie Mercury (second from left) and the other Queen band members in the mid-1970s. Courtesy of Elektra Records/Photofest.

uneasy. After leaving Ibex, Freddie started his own band, Wreckage, receiving, however, little attention from audiences and critics. His big opportunity arrived with Smile, a band which included future Queen guitarist Brian May and drummer Roger Taylor. Freddie liked the music of Smile, although he advised them to take more care in their stage performances. In May 1970, Taylor and Mercury formed a new band, which Mercury insisted on calling Queen, as he wanted a name that would be punchy and campy at the same time. The name obviously had a gay connotation, but Freddie did not come out as gay or bisexual. On stage, though, Freddie played with stereotypes associated with sexual ambiguity: as a performer he was allowed to have secret and multiple identities. Thus, it was only logical for him to drop his old Parsee name and adopt a new identity as Freddie Mercury, taking his new surname after the messenger of the gods.

The music of Queen was not yet profitable enough to live on, so Mercury and Taylor began selling clothes at a Kensington Market stall. On the fashion scene Freddie met Mary Austin, the manager of an elegant London boutique. To general surprise, the two fell in love and soon moved in together. In the meantime, John Deacon was selected to become the fourth member of Queen. All four artists remember the beginning of Queen as full of hopes and ideas. Yet, almost every major label turned down the band's first demo. Mercury, May, Taylor, and Deacon were not discouraged, and in 1973 they signed a deal with EMI for Europe and with Electrorecords in America. The label's manager enthusiastically wrote to his staff that he had seen the future of pop music: "It is a band called Queen." In July 1973, Queen released their debut album. Although the music failed to enthuse critics and audiences, what was noted was the band's campy and flamboyant way of performing. To some critics, this was a far from positive trait: was there, they asked, any musical substance behind the nail varnish and the shiny designer's outfits? Critics also reacted with hostility to the implied queerness in both the name of the group and in Mercury's effeminate look.

Mercury was not discouraged by the lack of interest reserved for Queen's first album and secured a place for the band in the tour of Mott The Hoople, then at the height of their commercial success. Mercury retained his campy style and also designed the band's logo, a phoenix and a crown, putting together the four artists' zodiac signs. Mercury's aim was to communicate with his audiences and make them connect with his songs emotionally. In February 1974 Queen made their first appearance on BBC's *Top of the Pops* TV show and the following month they started their first British tour. Their live performances proved extremely popular and helped their second album, *Queen II*, to climb the British charts and get to number five. The same year Queen also went on their first American tour, once again supporting Mott the Hoople, although the tour was suddenly stopped when May contracted hepatitis. *Sheer Heart Attack*, their third album, brought Queen their first U.S. Top 20 hit single, "Killer Queen," in 1975. In February Queen launched their first American tour as a solo group, but Mercury's persistent throat problems forced the band to cancel several dates. Queen were, however, finally reaching to international stardom: their Japanese tour caused a national hysteria, an anticipation of what the group would soon experience worldwide. In October 1975 Queen submitted to EMI Records an ambitious single provisionally entitled "Bohemian Rhapsody," which Mercury described as a "mock opera." The single was over six minutes long and, when the label refused to release it without cuts, Queen slipped a copy to London's Capital Radio, which broadcast it 14 times. Popular demand forced EMI to release the single without shortening it. "Bohemian Rhapsody" remained at number one in the U.K. for two months and entered the U.S. Top 10. Queen's new album *A Night at the Opera* made it to the Top 10 around the world. Fame opened the way for a world tour, which featured more elaborate and pyrotechnic performances. "We Are the Champions" and "We Will Rock You" from the album *News of the World* (1977) closed the 1970s with more commercial success and became standard anthems at sports events. Their popularity has endured well into the twenty-first century.

As he himself stated, excess seemed to come naturally to Mercury, and he enjoyed all the excesses that stardom could give him. By 1976 Austin and Mercury separated, although they remained close friends and Mary often accompanied Freddie to official events. Mercury became increasingly more open about his bisexuality. In 1978 Queen decided to move away from Britain to avoid the high British income tax and the group relocated to Munich. Far from the scrutiny of the British tabloids, Mercury could explore Munich gay scene. In the early 1980s, Mercury also underwent a major change of image. He relinquished his characteristic long hair, flashy clothes, and nail varnish in favor of a more macho persona dressed in leather and eventually even grew a moustache. In spite of this radical transformation, Queen's hits continued. The Elvis Presley-inspired single "Crazy Little Thing Called Love," from the album *The Game*, topped U.S. and U.K. charts. "Another One Bites the Dust" represented another change of direction as it was influenced by the funky and disco music. Written by John Deacon, it became the band's bestselling single to date, topping the U.S. disco, soul, and rock charts. After such a spectacular result, however, the fame of the band started to decline in the United States, but Queen continued to score impressive strings of number one hits around the world, although their initial revolutionary potential had somehow diminished with the years.

Hot Space, featuring the single "Under Pressure" in collaboration with **David Bowie**, obtained a mixed reception. Queen fans demanded that the band turned back to the synthesizer-less pure rock of their beginnings. Disappointed by this cold reception and exhausted by their long tours, Queen took off the entire 1983, and this even led to rumors that they were breaking up. Mercury, in particular, felt increasingly isolated in spite of the masses of adoring fans that adulated him. He loved performing as a way of trying on different identities. Success had brought him money, but he still did not have what he desired the most: a loving relationship. In interviews, Mercury never even hinted at the fact that he could have male partners. The only relationship he kept referring to was that with Mary Austin, the one-time girlfriend who had turned into a loyal friend. In the second half of the 1980s, Mercury started to pursue several solo projects. His 1987 remake of the Platters' classic "The Great Pretender" continued to generate debate on who the real Freddie Mercury really was. The song, as a part of the ongoing speculation about the true nature of his identity, proved to be successful. Mercury also scored a big hit in his collaboration with Spanish opera diva Montserrat Caballé for "Barcelona" (1987).

Despite the tensions that had characterized the early 1980s, Queen remained together, but they found themselves embroiled in the biggest controversy of their career when they accepted to perform at the Sun City resort in South Africa in 1984. At the time, South Africa was still enforcing the regime of segregation and persecutions of African citizens known as *apartheid.* Queen issued press statements emphasizing that they were not a political group and that they by no means supported *apartheid.* Yet, their concerts at Sun City cost them a lot of respect from the international community. The following year, however, the group, and Mercury in particular, stole the show at the Live Aid Concert for Africa in London. After the Live Aid Concert, Queen's popularity soared once again and all the members of the band, reunited and reinvigorated by the success, collaborated on the hit single "One Vision." Renewed popularity, however, brought back Mercury's personal life into the tabloid spotlight. Rumors began to circulate in the second half of the 1980s that Mercury was HIV-positive. In 1987 Mercury responded to these rumors stating that AIDS had changed his life. He described himself as having been extremely promiscuous but as having adopted a radically different lifestyle after the onslaught of the epidemic. He concluded his statement by encouraging those who had a promiscuous behavior to get tested and by reaffirming that he was "fine and clear." Mercury knew, in fact, that he was positive, but kept the illness to himself. He only told the other members of Queen about his positive status when it became impossible to conceal it and swore them to secrecy. The disease and the awareness that time was running out drew the band members closer to each other. Despite Mercury's frail health, the band produced the album *Innuendo* for which they also recorded music videos.

As the disease progressed, Mercury sought refuge from the tabloid press in the privacy of his Kensington estate where he lived virtually as a prisoner. On November 23, 1991, Mercury finally acknowledged that he had AIDS in a statement to the press. The following day he died, leaving a large following of fans shocked by the revelation. Mercury had never made a definitive statement about his private life or sexuality during his lifetime. His long-term relationship with his gardener Jim Hutton, who stayed with Mercury until the artist's death, was never acknowledged in public.

Further Reading

Bret, David. *The Freddie Mercury Story: Living on the Edge*. London: Robson Books, 1999; Evans, David, and David Minns. *Freddie Mercury: The Real Life, the Truth behind the Legend*. London: Antaeus, 1997; Freestone, Peter. *Freddie Mercury: An Intimate Memoir by the Man Who Knew Him Best*. New York: Music Sales, 2000; Hutton, Jim, with Tim Wapshott. *Mercury and Me*. New York: Boulevard Books, 1994; Jones, Lesley-Ann. *Freddie Mercury. The Definitive Biography*. London: Hodder & Stoughton, 1997.

MICHAEL, GEORGE (1963–)

British singer and songwriter George Michael has enjoyed global success since the mid-1980s, first as part of the duo WHAM! and later in his solo career. He has sold more than 80 million records worldwide, including 6 U.S. No. 1 singles, 11 British No. 1 singles, and 6 No. 1 albums. He has also displayed a remarkable social and political awareness, taking part in important concerts such as Live Aid, the Nelson Mandela Freedom Concert, and the **Freddie Mercury** Tribute. He has also spoken out against the Bush Administration. Yet, scandals and failures have been part of Michael's artistic record too. His sexuality was the subject of much speculation in the popular press throughout the first part of his career. Michael's arrest in October 1998 in a park restroom in Beverly Hills for "lewd behavior" definitely outed the singer. Since then, the artist has become more open about his homosexuality, discussing it in interviews and publicly acknowledging his relationships with male partners.

George Michael was born Georgios Kyriakos Panayiotou in North London on June 25, 1963, the son of a Greek-Cypriot restaurant owner. As a young boy, Michael was shy and overweight. He was also desperate for fame. At the local comprehensive school, the singer met his future artistic partner, Andrew Ridgeley. In 1981 they formed their first band, The Executives, but soon changed to the duo that would propel them to international fame, WHAM! The following year WHAM! were signed up by Innervision Records and released their first two albums, *Fantastic* (1982) and *Make It Big* (1984). "Wham Rap" was their debut single, but it was with their second single "Young Guns (Go for It!)" that the duo scored the first in a string of Top 10 hits, including the irresistible "Wake Me Up before You Go-Go," "Club Tropicana," "Last Christmas," and "Freedom." From a teenage ugly duckling, Michael soon transformed into an international sex symbol. WHAM! became known worldwide for their so-called bubblegum pop, featuring catchy melodies and lightweight lyrics. They also projected a homoerotic image, although Michael later maintained that they were not conscious of it at the time: "Andrew [Ridgeley] and I didn't realize how homoerotic our image was. We had leather jackets; we had these cuffed jeans. We just thought it was cool. Andrew was the stylist—ironic that it was the straight one that was doing the styling!" (Wieder 1991, *Advocate* online). WHAM! were soon an international hit. Yet, the duo found it difficult to be taken seriously by critics who were largely dismissive of WHAM!'s artistic worth. In the mid-1980s, Michael also started to release solo singles such

George Michael (right) with Andrew Ridgeley (left) as WHAM! Courtesy of Photofest.

as the hit ballad "Careless Whispers," which became one of the signatures of the 1980s. The song represented a shift from the pop sound of WHAM! toward a more soul-influenced composition.

At the peak of their success, WHAM! dissolved amicably, bidding their fans farewell with a sold-out concert at Wembley. Michael now faced the excitement but also the challenge of a solo career, where the influence of soul music would eventually become increasingly prominent. In 1987 he was the first white artist to duet with soul artist Aretha Franklin in "I Knew You Were Waiting," which became an immediate worldwide hit. In the same year, Michael recorded and released his first solo album *Faith*, which went to No. 1 in both Europe and North America. *Faith* was better received by critics than Michael's previous WHAM! songs and sold more than 10 million copies. The album spawned four U.S. No. 1 singles, with the title track, "Father Figure," "One More Try," and "Monkey" all reaching the top. Inspired by the Motown sound, *Faith*, along with the duet with Franklin and the songs "Careless Whispers" and "A Different Corner," established Michael as a serious songwriter. The album collected a series of prestigious prizes, including a Grammy for Album of the Year and the American Music Awards for Best Pop Male Vocalist, Best Soul/Rhythm and Blues Vocalist, and Best Soul/Rhythm and Blues Album. With *Faith* Michael was also the first white artist to top the Black Album Chart. The album also caused some controversy as one of its singles, "I Want Your Sex," was widely interpreted as encouraging casual sex in the age of **AIDS**. The singer countered that the song was really about monogamous sex. In the video of the song, Michael actually wrote "Explore monogamy" on a woman's back.

AIDS has had an important impact in both Michael's career and in his private life. The artist has given a considerable amount of his huge earnings to AIDS charities and has taken part in awareness events such as the Tribute to Queen singer Freddie Mercury. He was also involved in the production of albums and singles, such as the duet with **Elton John**, "Don't Let the Sun Go Down on Me" (1991), whose proceedings went entirely to organizations fighting against the virus. HIV also entered the singer's private life when his partner, Brazilian designer Anselmo Feleppa, died because of AIDS-related complications in 1993. His death prompted Michael to come out to his parents, who were supportive and more concerned about their son's loss than about his sexuality. In his coming-out interview to the *Advocate* (Wieder 1991, *Advocate* online), Michael stated that AIDS helped him on his journey to self-discovery: "The occasional times that I'd invite a man home, I was very careful. There was no way I was having sex without a condom, and there were only certain things I would do. Then it got to the stage where AIDS became common enough that I thought I could no longer, with good conscience—condom or not—have sex with a woman if she didn't know that I was bisexual."

The second album in the artist's solo career, *Listen without Prejudice Vol. 1* (1990), continued the singer's ongoing search for a more personal style, but also provoked the first tensions with Michael's label Sony which eventually led to a lengthy and bitter court case. Songs such as "Praying For Time" confirmed the singer's exploration of the legacy of black music and jazz. Stardom was probably taking its toll on Michael, who decided not to appear at promotional events of the album. Sony claimed this decision damaged the sales, while the singer maintained that the label did not do enough to support the new direction he was taking with his music. In October 1993 Michael took Sony to court to get free from his contract. He described Sony as "a giant electronics corporation which appears to see artists as little more than software." The case went on for almost three years and came close to ending the singer's career. The first ruling was in favor of Sony, concluding that the singer fully expected his new style to damage his sales and that he thus could not blame his label for this. Only in 1995, faced with Michael's refusal to record anything for Sony, did the company agree to release the singer from his contract. Freedom came at the harsh conditions dictated by Sony: the rights to a greatest hits package, a share in the profits from future albums, and a £25 million ($40 million) lump sum from his new labels, Virgin in the United Kingdom and the Spielberg-Geffen's SGK Music in the United States. Michael later stated that much of the anger he directed against Sony was a projection of his rage for the declining health of his partner.

Michael's first album for Virgin was *Older* (1996), which included the moving and incredibly successful "Jesus to a Child." The song mourns the death of a beloved partner and was inspired by the feeling of loss experienced after Feleppa's death. *Older* also included livelier songs such as "Fastlove" and the success of the album and its singles demonstrated that Michael was still a box office certainty even after three years of silence. *Older* was followed by the double CD *Ladies and Gentlemen—The Best of George Michael* in 1998. *Ladies and Gentlemen* came out with Michael's former label as part of the singer's settlement contract with Sony. It was number 1 for eight weeks and sold over two million copies. In the same year Michael was arrested while cruising in a public toilet in Los Angeles. The singer's image, however, was not damaged by the arrest. On the contrary, Michael used the potentially embarrassing situation to come out with humor, talking to the *Advocate* about his homosexuality shortly after the arrest and using the event for his music video *Outside*. The video is a challenging parody of the singer's arrest and the ensuing media furor. In the interviews after the arrest, Michael also explained why he had not come out earlier. Initially, this was due to insecurity about his own sexuality. Later in his life, however, Michael came to dislike the press and journalists so much that he would not give them what they wanted from him. In the *Advocate* interview with Judy Wieder (1991, online edition), Michael defined the press as trying to make him answer to them and to the public all the time. "So, I had this thing of, 'Fuck you! I'm not going to give you my private life! I'm just trying to work it out myself, thank you very much!' And by then it was like two dogs with a bone. I kept trying to see how I could be clever and retain my dignity, not denying my sexuality but not giving them the three words they wanted." Michael also claimed that while not officially out, he was out to everyone since his meeting with Feleppa. The gay community welcomed Michael's coming out. One dissenting voice was that of **Boy George**, who told the *Advocate* (Galvin 1998, online edition) that the only way Michael could face his sexuality was by actually being caught doing something embarrassing. The British DJ and Culture Club icon further claimed that George Michael's arrest offered a sad image of gays as people who "go to toilets and wank, and they don't have relationships, and they don't love each other."

Michael's fourth solo album was *Songs From the Last Century* (1999), a collection of famous covers originally performed by such artists as Sting and Frank Sinatra. Michael's two following singles, "FREEEK!" (2003) and, particularly, "Shoot the Dog" (2004), were more controversial. In the latter song and video, the singer explicitly took issue with the war on terrorism of the Bush administration and of Tony Blair's British government. His overtly political stance was criticized by right-wing media. By doing so, they dramatically revealed their homophobic bias. Tabloids urged him to focus on the topics he knew best, public toilets. Fellow singers also attacked Michael. Noel Gallagher (Hattenstone 2005, *Guardian* online), for example, commented on "Shoot the Dog" dismissing Michael's credibility in the political arena because of his closeted past: "This is the guy who hid who he actually was from the public for 20 years, and now all of a sudden he's got something to say about the way of the world. I find it fucking laughable!" When accused of being anti-American, Michael replied that, having been in love with a Texan, Kenny Goss, for over six years, the definition was most unfair.

In 2004 Michael reunited with Sony Music, releasing his fifth album *Patience*, which reached number one in the United Kingdom within its first week. In the development of his career, George Michael has reconciled himself with his sexuality and has found the strength of putting it in words in the songs included in *Patience*. In "Please send me someone to love (Anselmo's song)", for example, Michael urges his dead lover to send him someone to love "now that you're gone." In "American Angel," the singer compares his partner Kenny Goss, a "horny cowboy," to an angel who takes the fear away from him and that has dried his tears. George Michael's career dramatizes the conflicts that besiege many queer icons of popular culture and how these can be successfully resolved.

Further Reading

Galvin, Peter. "Boy Will Be Boy." *The Advocate*. June 23, 1998. http://findarticles.com/p/articles/mi_m1589/is_n762/ai_20856094/pg_3 (accessed on March 9, 2007); Hattenstone, Simon. "There Was So Much Death." *The Guardian*. December 9,

2005. http://arts.guardian.co.uk/filmandmusic/story/0,1662016,00.html (accessed on March 9, 2007); Larkin, Colin, ed. *The Encyclopedia of Popular Music.* 3rd ed. New York: Muze, 1998. 5:3652–3653; The Official George Michael Web site. http//www.georgemichael.com (accessed on March 9, 2007); Rampson, Nancy. "Michael, George." *Contemporary Musicians: Profiles of the People in Music.* Julia M. Rubiner, ed. Detroit: Gale Research, 1993. 9:169–172; Wieder, Judy. "All the Way Out George Michael." *The Advocate* 799 (January 19, 1999). http://www.georgemichael-tribute.com/TheAdvocate1999.html (accessed on March 9, 2007).

MOOREHEAD, AGNES (1900–1974)

Although she married twice and never explicitly identified as a lesbian, American actress Agnes Moorehead has become a central icon of gay and lesbian popular culture, particularly for the campy role of Endora in the successful TV series *Bewitched* (1964–1972). The cult following that her participation to *Bewitched* earned her has, however, partially obscured a long previous career through which Moorehead consistently played supporting characters that could be defined as lesbians. Rumors about Moorehead's own homosexuality have been frequent since the actress's death. Although dismissed by her biographer Charles Tranberg, such rumors were confirmed by *Bewitched*'s gay co-star Paul Lynde (White 1995, 92): "Well, the whole world knows Agnes Moorehead is a lesbian—I mean classy as hell, but one of the all-time Hollywood dykes."

Agnes Robertson Moorehead was born on December 6, 1900, in Clinton, Massachusetts, the daughter of a Presbyterian minister. In the characteristic fashion of many Hollywood actresses of the time, she later took off six years from her age, claiming that she was born in 1906. Because of her father's pastoral assignments, Moorehead moved with her family to Hamilton, Ohio, and later to St. Louis. Although interested in an acting career since her high school years, Moorehead also continued her academic education. She earned a bachelor's degree from the Presbyterian Musking College in New Concord, Ohio, and then obtained a master's degree in English and public speaking at the University of Wisconsin in Madison. In 1926 Moorehead went to New York to pursue post-graduate studies at the American Academy of Dramatic Arts, from where she graduated three years later.

In 1930 Moorehead married actor John Griffith Lee, from whom she divorced in 1952. The following year she married another actor, Robert Gist, but their union was short-lived and they divorced in 1958. Meanwhile, the actress had launched a successful career, first on the stage with Orson Welles and his Mercury Theatre Group, and then, because of the adverse effects of the economic depression on the theater, for the radio. During the 1940s and 1950s, Moorehead was one of the most demanded actresses for radio programs. One of her most celebrated performances was for Lucille Fletcher's suspense radio thriller *Sorry, Wrong Number* in 1943. The actress would revive this role several times in her career. Moorehead plays a neurotic woman who overhears a murder plotted on the phone and soon

Agnes Moorehead (center) as Endora between her co-stars from *Bewitched*. Courtesy of Photofest.

realizes that she is the intended victim. The actress also took part in many important films of the 1940s and 1950s such as Orson Welles's *Citizen Kane* (1941) and *The Magnificent Amberson* (1942), Delmer Daves's Bogart-Bacall noir vehicle *Dark Passage* (1947), Jean Negulesco's *Johnny Belinda* (1948), Douglas Sirk's *Magnificent Obsession* (1954) and *All That Heaven Allows* (1955). These roles made Moorehead one of the most praised and in demand character actresses in Hollywood. She took part to over 60 films in total. She was nominated for four Academy Awards for Best Supporting Actress and won two Golden Globes for her performances in Tay Garnett's *Mrs. Parkington* (1945) and Robert Aldrich's *Hush . . . Hush, Sweet Charlotte* (1964). Patricia White (1995, 100) defines Agnes Moorehead's long career before *Bewitched* as encompassing "a gallery of types connoting female difference." Generally playing stern, unmarried women, Moorehead often embodied "nurses, secretaries, career women, nuns, companions, and housekeepers," all characters that "connote, not lesbian identity, but a deviation from heterosexualized femininity" (White 1995, 94–95).

In spite of her long career, Agnes Moorehead is best remembered for her role as Endora, the bossy mother of the beautiful witch Samantha and herself a witch, in ABC's TV comedy series *Bewitched.* For her performance, the actress received six Emmy nominations, although the only Emmy she eventually won was for her appearance in *The Wild Wild West* (1967). As White (1995, 108) has pointed out, Endora represents the culmination of a defining trait of Moorehead's star persona: her meddlesomeness. Her character, constantly disapproving of her daughter's husband, "literally casts a dark shadow over heterosexual relations." Endora has a central relevance to the series: with her spells, she upsets her daughter's married suburban life and it is her who generates the plots of the episodes. Endora clearly appeals to gay and lesbian audiences for her **camp** status: her image, built on exaggerated costumes, eccentric hairstyles, and overbearing personality, suggests artifice and theatricality. After *Bewitched*, Moorehead continued acting, most notably in a revival of George Bernard Shaw's *Don Juan in Hell*, a play that she had also successfully directed in the 1950s, and in the Broadway musical *Gigi*. She remained active until a few months before her death due to lung cancer. She died in Rochester, Minnesota, on April 30, 1974.

The queer career of Agnes Moorehead has made her an enduring icon of gay and lesbian popular culture. The actress was extremely reserved about her private life and rumors about her lesbianism have found confirmations, but also documented confutations. Yet, as Patricia White (1995, 92–93) writes, "Moorehead is a prime candidate for gay hagiography. Her best known incarnation, Endora, is a camp icon; she passes even the cinephile test, having been featured in films by auteurs such as Welles, Sirk, Ray and Aldrich." More importantly still, "her ubiquity and longevity as a character actress are such that she can be identified with the very media in which she triumphed, with the regime of popular entertainment itself, and with the continuities and ruptures in gender and sexual ideology that can be read off from it."

Further Reading

Kear, Lynn. *Agnes Moorehead: A Bio-Bibliography*. Westport, CT: Greenwood Press, 1992; Madsen, Axel. *The Sewing Circle: Hollywood's Greatest Secret: Female Stars Who Loved Other Women*. New York: Carol Publishing Group, 1995; Tranberg, Charles. *I Love the Illusion: The Life and Career of Agnes Moorehead*. Albany, GA: BearManor Media, 2005; White, Patricia. "Supporting Character: The Queer Career of Agnes Moorehead." *Out in Culture: Gay, Lesbian and Queer Essays on Popular Culture*. Corey K. Creekmur and Alexander Doty, eds. Durham, NC: Duke University Press, 1995. 91–114.

MUSCLE MAGAZINES

Magazines such as *Physique Pictorial, Vim, Trim, Grecian Guild Pictorial, Adonis, Body Beautiful*, and *Tomorrow's Man* became increasingly popular in the 1950s and 1960s, catering to the erotic fantasies of gay men. They offered pictures and illustrations that emphasized masculinity, presenting images of tough and muscled male bodies. Models were almost always young and white, with little body hair, defined pectorals and a bulging so-called basket. Muscle or beefcake magazines, as they were also called, forged an entire new field in popular art, that of the nude male. While pictures of naked women had always enjoyed wide popularity, figures of nude males had not had comparable circulation. Of course, these magazines could not explicitly define themselves as gay, although they had clear homosexual nuances and even had ads for pen pals from time to time. Their official mission was to provide tips on body building to improve male muscles. Yet, they were almost the only source of images of naked males in the early post-war years and thus encountered the favors of gay men.

The man behind this erotic revolution that challenged the bigoted notions of taste of the McCarthy era was Bob Mizer, a California aircraft factory worker and amateur photographer, who founded the Athletic Model Guild in 1945. Mizer pretentiously defined the guild as a modeling agency, although some of his so-called models had just come out of prison and had no experience whatsoever in the profession. He initially set up a studio in the family garage and took pictures of men who were either naked or partially dressed as gladiators and farmers. He sold the pictures for a nickel each and soon found himself sending them to an ever-growing mailing list of 5,000 people. Mizer got his clients with advertisements published in the back of men's magazines, especially weightlifter periodicals, which announced catalogs of photos of invaluable importance for artists and for body builders. Under pressures from the Postmaster General, however, these magazines stopped publishing Mizer's ads. He thus decided to gather other artists and photographers in the physique field and form his own magazine, *Physique Pictorial. Physique* started to be published in the late 1950s and was mailed to readers. The first issue consisted of 16 pages entirely filled with images of male bodies, without any articles or editorials. Several artists who would become the most popular in the field, including George Quaintance, Al Urban, and Bob Delmonteque, were involved in the project from its early years. Illustrators such as **Tom of Finland** and Etienne joined from the second half of the 1950s and their work has since developed a cult following. Pictures of movie stars such as Tony Curtis, Marlon Brando, and television-Tarzan Gordon Scott were also included in physique magazines in the mid-1950s.

The success of Mizer's publication was immediate and the print run grew with each new number. By the end of 1952, *Physique Pictorial* was available nationwide and was also sold in Europe. Mizer's achievement was to photograph nude males not to inspire ideals of health as was common in body building magazines, but to please the (male) viewer. Although Mizer did not openly transgress the legal boundaries of the times and never pictured full frontal nudity, censors repeatedly attacked physique art. Mizer himself had to stand trial on charges of running a prostitution ring. Yet, very few of these cases went to trial and censors hardly ever won. The success of *Physique Pictorial* led to the birth of many other competing magazines. Joe Wieder, for example, modified the outlook of some of his body building/health magazines to exploit the boom of the physique field. His *Body Beautiful* and *Adonis* were the first ones to include color photos and adopt the a larger format that would become the standard. In the repressive atmosphere of the McCarthy years, which succeeded to make homosexuals a comparable target to communists, beefcake magazines not only stimulated the erotic fantasies of gay men, but also, and perhaps more importantly, told them that they were not alone. Without being explicitly labeled as gay, these publications were clearly assembled by and for gay men. By the mid-1950s, the sales of *Physique Pictorial* and *Tomorrow's Man* skyrocketed to 40,000 copies each.

The 1960s witnessed the progressive collapse of those censorship rules that had constantly endangered the existence of the muscle magazines. The more liberal climate finally led newer magazines such as *Butch* and *Drum Magazine* to publish frontal male nudes in 1965, while *Physique Pictorial* published its first frontal male nude in 1969. Yet, as more graphic erotic pictures and illustrations became legally acceptable, physique magazines found themselves out of date and could not survive the important changes in the industry. Mizer's Athletic Model Guild was the last of the physique studios to close in 1993, while Joe Wieder once again reconverted his publications to the body building/health sector. In spite of their eventual demise, muscle magazines played a fundamental part in the development of a gay male erotic imagination in America.

Further Reading

Hooven, F. Valentine. *Beefcake: The Muscle Magazines of America, 1950–1970.* Cologne: Benedikt Taschen Verlag, 1996; Loughery, John. *The Other Side of Silence. Men's Lives and Gay Identities: A Twentieth-Century History.* New York: Henry Holt & Company, 1998.

N

NAVRATILOVA, MARTINA (1956–)

Czech-born American player Martina Navratilova is considered one of the greatest tennis champions of all times. Throughout her career, she smashed several tennis records and won Wimbledon singles titles nine times, a target she went after with particular determination. Since her early career as an American player, it became apparent that Navratilova would challenge the standards of femininity considered acceptable in sports. Her muscular outlook and her powerful style of play revolutionized women's image in tennis. Her training techniques, initially criticized, became standard for many women athletes. In addition, her openness about her sexuality made her a central icon in gay and lesbian popular culture. Since she was outed in 1991 following a palimony suit, Navratilova has championed queer causes with the same passion and determination that marked her successful career as tennis player. Because of her activism, she was quoted by Michelangelo Signorile as an example for all closeted queers to follow. In "Queer Manifesto," the closing chapter of his seminal book *Queer in America*, Signorile (1993, 365) wrote: "Deep down you know why you must now come out and why it is wrong for you not to....Just think: You'll be one of the people who have decided to be honest and make a world a better place for all queers. You'll be another Barney Frank, another Martina Navratilova, another k. d. lang, another David Geffen. You'll be a hero."

Navratilova was born on October 18, 1956, in Prague, then part of Czechoslovakia. Her parents divorced soon after Martina's birth and her mother remarried Mirek Navratil, a ski instructor, when the child was six years old. Her stepfather proved an affectionate parent and became her first tennis coach. Navratilova immediately excelled at tennis and entered her first tournament when she was only eight. By 16, she was number one in her mother country and started to compete internationally. Navratilova soon realized that her full professional development would be forever thwarted in Communist Czechoslovakia. In 1975, after losing the semifinals of the U.S. Open to Chris Evert, she defected to the United States. In later interviews, Navratilova recalled that she was never comfortable with the

Tennis player Martina Navratilova winning her ninth women's single championship at Wimbledon, England, 1990. Courtesy of Photofest.

Czech totalitarian regime as she did not like to be told what to do and how to do it. The decision to defect was a difficult one for the 18-year-old Navratilova because it meant that she would probably not be able to visit her family for many years to come. It was this decision, however, that made her an international tennis champion. Six years later, in July 1981, Navratilova became an American citizen.

Navratilova soon acquired the fame of an aggressive serve-and-volley player. Left-handed, she exhibited a forceful muscular body that stretched the boundaries of social acceptability for women in tennis. She was also one of the first players to adopt graphite racket technology. In 1978 Navratilova reached the World No. 1 ranking for the first time. She established a double record of 156 consecutive weeks and 331 total weeks as the World No. 1 singles player. German player Steffi Graff eventually broke those records, although she failed to surpass Navratilova's 168 singles titles, a record both for female and male players in the Open Era. Navratilova's other startling records include 9 Wimbledon singles titles, 20 total Wimbledon championships (including doubles matches) tying Billie Jean King's record of 20 Wimbledon titles, 74 consecutive victories in 1984, and 20 Grand Slam (the U.S., Australian, and French Open events and Wimbledon) doubles titles. Navratilova's professional tennis career earnings surpassed $20 million. In the 1980s, she was named the Female Athlete of the Decade by the *National Sports Review* and was inducted into the International Tennis Hall of Fame in 2000. Although she officially retired in the mid-1990s, Navratilova returned to play doubles, and, more rarely, singles from 2000 to 2006. In 2004 she was the oldest player to win a singles match in the Open Era. In 2006 she played in what she said would be her last Wimbledon matches, losing both in the women's and mixed doubles. Yet, in the same year, she won the mixed doubles title at the U.S. Open with Bob Bryan. Navratilova's best-known rival was the all-American Chris Evert. Nancy Spencer (2003) has pointed out that the rivalry was constructed in its press coverage to re-create impressions of Evert as quintessentially American and straight while positioning Navratilova as quintessentially "other," a foreigner and a lesbian.

When Navratilova applied for asylum in the United States, she described herself as bisexual, confirming her reputation of being frank and honest. Her honesty has won her the respect of many fans and her opponents on the tennis court. When a former lover sued her in a bitter palimony case in 1991, Navratilova was outed as a lesbian by the press which scrutinized her private life. Since her outing, the athlete has taken seriously her role as one of the very first public lesbian figures in the world of sport. She has supported gay and lesbian causes and has spoken vocally in favor of queers' rights. Her decision to be open about her lesbianism cost her many commercial endorsements, which had never come in large numbers even before she became active in the gay and lesbian campaigns. In interviews, Navratilova (Palmieri, online interview) recalled her initial difficulty of being perceived as a lesbian: "When I came out publicly it was difficult for me because that became the first thing people thought about when they would see me...It wasn't what I looked like or what I had accomplished or how many animals I had rescued. It was lesbian. That was the first thing. And that is a personal thing. If I were a heterosexual I wouldn't have to trumpet it to the world. So that was a little difficult. I resented the fact that it had to be an issue. But it was an issue and still is an issue and will always be an issue until we have equal rights across the board." Navratilova described the lack of financial endorsements as the price she had to pay for keeping her integrity. In 2000, however, Subaru signed her to appear in advertisements for their Forester model.

Navratilova did not shy away from controversies. On many occasions, she displayed her characteristic self-assurance that has been interpreted by many as arrogance. She took issue with the media portrayal of Magic Johnson as a hero when he told the press he had contracted HIV through countless heterosexual intercourse. Surely a woman admitting to the same sexual conduct, Navratilova argued, would be disparagingly branded as immoral. Whenever members of the tennis community made homophobic comments, Navratilova was quick to respond. The player also fought a high profile battle against Colorado's Amendment 2 which barred antidiscrimination laws protecting gays and lesbians. When voters approved the amendment in 1992, Navratilova supported the suit filed by the American Civil Liberties Union (ACLU). Navratilova and the ACLU scored a big victory when the Supreme Court deemed the amendment as unconstitutional. In 1993 she took part to her first major gay and lesbian event as a keynote speaker at the March on Washington. In her speech, the athlete stressed the importance of being open about one's sexual orientation. It was also at this event that she felt the inspiration for the launch of the Rainbow Card, a VISA card to raise money for queer non-profit groups. The project was extremely successful, raising $50,000 in its first year and accumulating over

$1.5 million by 2002. The project was designed to harness the economic power of the LGBT community. In 2005, Navratilova also launched an endorsement deal for the lesbian travel company Olivia. She has also authored several novels and autobiographies, as well as fitness books.

In addition to her activism for gay and lesbian rights, Navratilova is a fundraiser for women's groups, the Susan G. Komen Breast Cancer Foundation, and female political candidates. She also supports environmental causes and People for the Ethical Treatment of Animals (PETA). With her example, Navratilova has set an inspirational blueprint for activists both inside and outside the gay and lesbian community.

Further Reading

Allen, Louise. *The Lesbian Idol: Martina, kd, and the Consumption of Lesbian Masculinity*. Washington, DC: Cassell, 1997; Blue, Adrianne. *Martina: The Lives and Times of Martina Navratilova*. Secaucus, NJ: Carol Publishing Group, 1995; Kort, Michele. "Martina Navratilova and Amelie Mauresmo." *The Advocate* No. 817–818 (August 15, 2000): 26–28; Official Web site http://www.martinanavratilova.com; Palmieri, Jimmy. "Time Out for Martina Navratilova." http://www.gaysports.com/page.cfm?typeofsite=storydetail&Sectionid=1&ID=754&storyset=yes (accessed on March 9, 2007); Silvas, Sharon. "Martina! Serving On and Off the Court." *Colorado Woman News* 2, no. 18 (June 30, 1992): 17; Spencer, Nancy E. "'America's Sweetheart' and 'Czech-mate.' A Discursive Analysis of the Evert-Navratilova Rivalry." *Journal of Sport & Social Issues* 27 (2003): 18–37.

O'DONNELL, ROSIE (1962–)

Rosie O'Donnell is an American stand-up comedian, actress, and a popular talk-show host who has openly supported gay and lesbian causes since her coming out in 2002. O'Donnell has never feared controversy and, throughout her career, has tackled several contentious issues. She is a staunch advocate of gay parenting and a harsh critic of American policies on gun ownership which she considers too lax. She has also criticized the polices against terrorism of the Bush Administration after the 9/11 attacks and has explicitly likened Christian and Islamic fundamentalisms.

The third of five children, O'Donnell was born in Queens, New York, on March 21, 1962, into a family of Irish Catholic origins. She grew up on Long Island and her unhappy childhood, marked by the death of her mother and the emotional detachment of her father, rendered her particularly sensitive to children's rights. O'Donnell attended Dickinson College and Boston University, without, however, completing a degree. She started her career touring the East Coast as a stand-up comedian and, later in the 1980s, hosting VH1 stand-up series. In 1992 she was cast in the leading role in Fox's *Stand by Your Man*, an American adaptation of the popular BBC sitcom *Birds of a Feather*. Contrary to the British show, the American series only ran for a few months before being cancelled due to poor ratings. In the early 1990s O'Donnell launched her movie career, acting in several comedy films, including *A League of Their Own* (1992), *Sleepless in Seattle* (1993), and *Another Stakeout* (1993). After these initial hits, she appeared in less successful films but her career revived in the mid-1990s when she began hosting *The Rosie O'Donnell Show*. A daytime talk show, it earned her five consecutive Daytime Emmy Awards for Best Talk Show and six for Best Talk Show Host. *The Rosie O'Donnell Show* ran from 1996 to 2002 and crowned O'Donnell as the Queen of Nice for her style and her support of several charitable causes. Although O'Donnell did not completely like the title, her show, which also featured numbers from Broadway musicals, restored a certain degree of civility to the talk show genre which had become synonymous with trash, sensational stories, and insults.

Outspoken TV host Rosie O'Donnell with the Muppet Elmo. Courtesy of Warner Bros. Television/ Photofest.

The Queen of Nice is actually quite vocal about her support for liberal causes and has often brought them to the attention of her viewers. In 1999, while interviewing Tom Selleck, she criticized him for his stance on guns and his involvement in the National Rifle Association. One of the causes that she feels particularly strongly about, the adoptive rights of gay parents, prompted her to come out. O'Donnell was long rumored to be a lesbian, and her orientation was well-known in the gay and lesbian community. Before her coming out, she had starred as a lesbian in a guest role in the gay series *Will and Grace.* In March 2002, shortly before leaving *The Rosie O'Donnell Show,* she confirmed that rumor in a interview with Diane Sawyer on *Primetime Thursday.* Talking about the refusal of adoption agencies to grant adoptive rights to gay parents, she stated: "I don't think America knows what a gay parent looks like: I am a gay parent." O'Donnell challenged the policy of limiting the choice of adoptive parents, doubting that it was beneficial to the rights of foster children. As she affirmed in her coming-out interview, O'Donnell is a gay parent: she adopted her first son, Parker Jaren, in 1995, her daughter Chelsea Bell in 1997, and a second son, Blake Christopher, in 1999. O'Donnell and her partner Kelli Carpenter have been together since 1998 and, in November 2002, Carpenter gave birth to the couple's fourth child, Vivienne Rose. The couple married in San Francisco in February 2004, although the marriage license was later voided by the California Supreme Court.

O'Donnell's coming out was one of the many sources of controversy in the artist's life. Her critics pointed out that her decision to come out coincided with the end of *The Rosie O'Donnell Show*, scheduled for May 2002. It also corresponded with the promotion of her memoir *Find Me* (2002), where she described her involvement with a woman suffering from personality disorders. O'Donnell was also involved in a lengthy legal battle against publisher Gunner & Jahr. In 2000, O'Donnell had launched her own magazine *Rosie*, planning to make it a forum for honest discussion of topics such as breast cancer, depression, and foster care. The failure of the publication caused the court battle between O'Donnell and her publishers. The case received wide media attention, but was eventually dismissed by the judge who ruled that neither of the parties deserved damages. O'Donnell was also criticized as a hypocrite when she allowed an armed bodyguard to accompany her son to school. Other parents pointed out that this was at odds with her highly publicized stance against guns and in support of gun control.

In 2003 O'Donnell took **Boy George**'s musical *Taboo* to Broadway, where it got cold reviews and ran for only a hundred performances. O'Donnell's career, however, does not seem to have suffered from her artistic failures nor from several damaging comments made about her allegedly bullying personality during the *Rosie* court case. On the contrary, over the years, the TV star has consolidated her reputation as a lesbian pop culture icon. O'Donnell has appeared in important Broadway and television productions. In 2005 she was cast in the Broadway revival of *Fiddler on the Roof*, opposite **Harvey Fierstein**. She also produced CBS's *Riding the Bus with My Sister* and starred in it as the mentally retarded protagonist. In 2006 O'Donnell starred in an episode of the series *Nip/Tuck* and returned to TV hosting, replacing Meredith Vieira as the moderator of ABC talk show *The View*. Together with her partner, O'Donnell owns R. Family Vacations, a travel agency catering to gay and lesbian families.

Further Reading

Goodman, Gloria. *The Life and Humor of Rosie O'Donnell: A Biography*. New York: William Morrow, 1998; Hunter, Carson. "Rosie by Any Other Name." *Girlfriends* (June 2001): 18–19, 42–43; Nordlinger, Jay. "Rosie O'Donnell, Political Activist." *National Review* (June 19, 2000): 33–36; O'Donnell, Rosie. *Find Me*. New York: Warner Books, 2002.

P

Pet Shop Boys

The Pet Shop Boys are central to the developments of popular music in the 1980s and 1990s. Formed by Neil Francis Tennant (1954–) and Christopher Sean Lowe (1959–), the band has achieved worldwide success, particularly in Europe and Britain, where they have had 39 top thirty singles including 4 number ones: "West End Girls" (also a U.S. number one), "It's a Sin," "Always on My Mind," and "Heart." The Pet Shop Boys were also very successful in the United States in the mid-1980s, although their popularity there started to decline after 1988 when they had their last Top 40 single with "Domino Dancing." The Pet Shop Boys's longevity and enduring success are due to many diverse factors: the striking combination of Tennant's refined vocals and Lowe's creative use of synthesizers; their melodic songs; their ability to defy expectations; and their remarkable performing style pairing opera and theater staging with avant-garde tailored fashion. Alongside more traditional love songs, several of the Pet Shop Boys's songs deal with social and political issues. In their music, Tennant and Lowe have also embraced queer causes such as the battle against **AIDS** and prejudice and the repeal of the infamous British Section 28 which prohibited the promotion of homosexuality by government agencies. Their disco-influenced albums also pay homage to disco's importance as a popular musical genre in gay popular culture. The group's famous versatility makes it possible for them to be equally at ease both covering **The Village People's** "Go West" and writing a modern score for Eisenstein's classic 1925 silent film *Battleship Potemkin*.

Neil Tennant was born on July 10, 1954, in North Shields, Northumberland, while Chris Lowe was born five years later on October 4 in Blackpool, Lancashire. Both artists played in local groups and went to university during the 1970s: Neil was a member of Dust, based in Newcastle, and Lowe played the trombone in a band called One Under the Eight. In the mid-1970s Tennant moved to London where he studied history at the Polytechnic of North London and later worked for publishing houses. In 1978 Chris enrolled at Liverpool University to study architecture and, three years later, he too moved to London to work in a London architectural practice. The Pet Shop Boys were born out of a chance meeting between Tennant and Lowe that took place on August 19, 1981, in an electronics shop at King's Cross. They immediately realized they shared the same interest in dance music and began working together first calling themselves West End and then adopting the name of Pet Shop Boys. This name derived from some friends working in a pet shop in the London suburb of Ealing. In March 1985 Tennant and Lowe signed a recording contract with the EMI-label Parlophone Records and, in October, "West End Girls" was released. The following January the single reached number one in the United Kingdom and proved a worldwide hit, selling 1.5 million copies.

"West End Girls" received a number of important awards and paved the way for international recognition, which reached an impressive peak in October 2003 when former Soviet President Mikhail Gorbachev presented the Pet Shop Boys with the World Arts Award. The award was given to Tennant and Lowe "for their extraordinary dedication to art, their social engagement and their unique contribution to popular music as well as their overall patronage of the arts." During more than 20 years of career, the Pet Shop Boys have often collaborated with other artists who are considered gay icons such as Dusty Springfield, Patsy Kensit, Liza Minnelli, Kylie Minogue, and Madonna. They have also worked together with other queer artists, greatly contributing to heightening the visibility of gays and lesbians in music and in the visual arts. Particularly worth mentioning are the collaborations with British queer director Derek Jarman for the video of their smashing hit "It's a Sin" (1987), a song exposing the Catholic Church's sexual prohibitions and its policing of desire, and with photographer **Bruce Weber** for "Being Boring" (1991). Tennant and Lowe have also produced **Boy George**'s cover of Dave Berry's "The Crying Game," which featured in Neil Jordan's homonymous film about transgenderism. In 2001 they teamed up with playwright Jonathan Harvey, the author of the modern gay classic *Beautiful Thing*, to work on a musical. The result was *Closer to Heaven* which played for five months in London's West End to considerable critical

Chris Lowe (left) and Neil Tennant (right) as the British duo Pet Shop Boys. Courtesy of EMI/Photofest.

acclaim and the approval of gay icon **Elton John**, who said that the Pet Shop Boys had blown apart "the comfortable world of the West End musical" (Pet Shop Boys Official Website).

The Pet Shop Boys have never been coy in confronting issues relating to homosexuality in their songs. In a 1994 interview with the British gay lifestyle magazine *Attitude*, Tennant states that he has always written songs from a gay point of view. Recurrent motifs in their works which are relevant for gay and lesbian popular culture include **AIDS** ("Go West," "Being Boring," "Dreaming of the Queen") and coming out ("Metamorphosis").

Further Reading

Burston, P. "Honestly." *Attitude* 1.4 (August 1994): 62–69; Frith, S. *Performing Rites*. Cambridge: Harvard University Press, 1996; Gill, John. *Queer Noises: Male and Female Homosexuality in Twentieth-Century Music*. Minneapolis: University of Minnesota Press, 1995; Pet Shop Boys official Web site: http://www.petshop boys.co.uk (accessed on March 15, 2007); Robertson, Textor A. "Review Essay: A Close Listening of the Pet Shop Boys' 'Go West.'" *Popular Music and Society* 18.4 (Winter 1994): 91–96.

PHILADELPHIA

Following the TV movie *And the Band Played On* (1993), Jonathan Demme's *Philadelphia* (1993) was the second big-budget Hollywood film to address the issue of **AIDS**. Similarly to *And the Band Played On*, it had an all-star cast that included Tom Hanks and Denzel Washington as the two leads as well as Joan Woodward, Jason Robards, and Antonio Banderas in supporting roles. *Philadelphia* won two Academy Awards for Best Actor in a Leading Role (Hanks) and for Best Music, Song (Bruce Springsteen's "Streets of Philadelphia"). The film contributed to the shift in the film representation of gay men that took place in the 1990s towards a more realistic depiction. However, gay audiences were not entirely pleased with the movie, and many argued that a fundamental flaw of the movie was the lack of intimacy between the two gay lovers, which suggests a de-sexualization of gay relationships.

Philadelphia was partly inspired by the Geoffrey Bowers case. A New York attorney, Bowers filed one of the first AIDS discrimination lawsuits to go to a public hearing. In 1986 he sued his law firm Baker and McKenzie after being fired following the appearance of lesions on his face. The case was finally resolved in favor of Bowers, who, however, died before the final sentence was reached. In Demme's movie, Hanks plays the up-and-coming Andrew Beckett, a successful lawyer employed in the largest law firm of Philadelphia. Andy is gay, but he keeps his sexuality and his relationship with Miguel (Banderas) secret from colleagues. However, when he develops lesions typical of Kaposi's sarcoma on his face, he cannot hide the truth any longer. Not only is he gay, but he is also ill with AIDS. Following his admission, Andrew is immediately fired by the homophobic head of the firm

Philadelphia's narrative allows HIV-positive Andrew Beckett (Tom Hanks, right) to hold a baby, but not to kiss his partner Miguel Alvarez (Antonio Banderas, left). Courtesy of TriStar Pictures/Photofest. Photograph by Ken Regan.

(Robards). When he tries to find a lawyer who can help him to sue his firm for damages, Andrew discovers that none is willing to take his case except for Joe Miller (Washington). In spite of his own homophobia, Miller takes Andrew's case and, little by little, he modifies his views on gay people. The relationship which Miller and Andrew develop is based on mutual respect and trust. In the end, Miller successfully shows that Andrew was fired because of his illness.

Demme's film certainly had many merits. In the early 1990s, homosexuality, let alone AIDS, was still a taboo at the movies. The success of the film, which grossed over $40 million in its first two months, helped to bring the disease to the American heartland. Demme repeatedly stressed that he wanted to make a movie not so much for the people living with AIDS, but to reach those who did not know people with AIDS or those who looked down on people with AIDS. Yet, to reach to the malls, the director had to make his own compromises. The script started out as more politicized, but was subsequently toned down. Demme stated that rather than responding angrily to the homophobia and the discrimination against people with AIDS, he and his gay screenwriter Ron Nyswaner decided to focus on Andrew's determination to stay alive. Activists and critics like **Larry Kramer** were outraged that the film did not show any kissing or any signs of affection between the two lovers. Demme responded that audiences were still not ready to see two men kissing or two men in bed together. *Philadelphia* did not want to bank on shock value. "It's a real concern. When we see two men kissing, we're the products of our brainwashing—it knocks us back twenty feet. And with *Philadelphia*—I'm sorry, Larry Kramer—I didn't want to risk knocking our audience back twenty feet with images they're not prepared to see. It's just shocking imagery, and I didn't want to shoehorn it in" (DeCurtis 1994, *Rolling Stone* online).

Activists also took issue with the representation of Andrew Beckett's family, who is incredibly supportive not only of Andy's homosexuality but also of his AIDS status. Andrew even gets to rock his baby nephew in his arms. Many critics of the film pointed out that this rosy family portrayal did not do justice to the harsh treatment that most people with AIDS received in their very families. While Demme claims that the film is gay-oriented, most of the viewers will identify not so much with Andy as with Joe Miller. Andrew's African American lawyer accepts his client's homosexuality and his relationship with Miguel. Yet, this acceptance does not lead him to embrace fully the cause of the gay community. As the *Cineaste* review of the film points out (1993, online edition), Miller functions as a safety valve for most of the audience: "*Philadelphia* . . . succeeds in severing a legal agenda from its moral foundation. The film makes a case for legal equality for both homosexuals and PWAs (although in the film the distinction between the two is not always clear), yet it refuses to follow suit by morally condemning homophobia." *Philadelphia* is a landmark film because it takes what was at the time such a taboo subject at the core, and makes it into a big-budget, all-star narrative. Its representation of this taboo, however, in spite of its self-proclaimed liberal agenda, is unable to radically challenge the homophobia of middle America, eventually overwhelming ideology with emotion. As the film closes, the news that justice has prevailed in the court case strengthens the viewers' faith in that very system which causes discrimination against gays and lesbians in the first place.

Further Reading

DeCurtis, Anthony. "Rolling Stone Interview: Jonathan Demme." *Rolling Stone.* March 24, 1994. http://www.storefrontdemme.com/rollingstone.html (accessed on January 17, 2007); Grundmann, Roy, and Peter Sacks. "Review of *Philadelphia.*" *Cineaste.* 20: 3 (Summer, 1993). http://www.lib.berkeley.edu/MRC/Philadelphia.html (accessed on January 17, 2007).

PINK NARCISSUS

Released in 1971 though probably shot during the previous seven years, *Pink Narcissus* represents a turning point in gay underground films. Credited to an anonymous director, but now rightfully ascribed to photographer Jim Bidgood, the film synthesizes all the major features of gay underground movies of the 1960s, opening, at the same time, new directions for the genre. Although it did not capture the attention of audiences and reviewers when it first hit the theaters, *Pink Narcissus* has since gained a central position in gay popular culture.

The film focuses on the sordid life and the sexual fantasies of a handsome male prostitute (played by Bobby Kendall). Like the mythological figure of Narcissus, he is in love with himself. Obsessed by his beauty and perfection, he is the center of his own sexual fantasies. In them, the hustler is both a Roman emperor and the slave the emperor can dispose of at his wish, a bullfighter with tight clothes attacked by a bullman, and a sultan in a male harem. Narcissus's fantasies are interwoven with grim scenes from his life in an unnamed contemporary metropolis. The film follows him while he cruises public toilets and rundown neighborhoods. Yet, the boundaries between reality and fantasy become increasingly blurred as the narrative unfolds. Lofty fantasy scenes soon turn into sexually degrading events by the eruption of the real world into them. In a sudden revelation at the end of the movie, it becomes clear that the young hustler himself has turned, with age, into a client of handsome male prostitutes.

Bidgood was already working within gay underground culture before *Pink Narcissus*. He was an amateur photographer whose portrayals of naked men were published in mail-order circuit magazines such as *The Young Physique*, *Muscleboy*, and *Big*. He began working on *Pink Narcissus* while taking pictures of his favorite model Bobby Kendall. The long shooting, which, for the most part, was done in Bidgood's New York's apartment, eventually annoyed the independent production company Sherpix. In 1971 the company took the existing footage away from Bidgood and gave it to Martin Jay Sadoff who proceeded to edit it. *Pink Narcissus* was thus released without Bidgood's consent, who, in protest, withdrew his name as the director. When the film came out, it attracted few spectators, but soon acquired cult status within gay and lesbian popular culture. The VHS edition in the 1990s contributed to a wider circulation of the film, as did the DVD release which also contains commentary by Bidgood. Shot in 8 mm later blown up to 35 mm and with characteristic fluorescent lighting, *Pink Narcissus* had a crucial impact on the erotic imagination of gay males and has influenced international gay directors such as R. W. Fassbinder and Pedro Almodovar.

As film scholar Richard Dyer (1990, 165) has pointed out, "the film has imagery from most phases of the underground." It clearly owes to the photographs of Pierre & Gilles and the underground cinema of **Andy Warhol**, Kenneth Anger (who, for some time, was rumored to be the actual director), and George Markopoulos. Like the movies of Warhol and Anger, *Pink Narcissus* features a melancholy hero and is strongly visionary in nature with its use of glittering colors. The film is also peopled by a crowd of hustlers and sailors, while exuding eroticism and unashamedly showing the seediest of details: all characteristics which it shares with underground movies. At the same time, *Pink Narcissus* takes all these elements to such extremes as to innovate its sources. Its images purposefully border into kitsch aesthetics filtered through a constant use of the pink color, one of the symbols of gayness. With its overt sexuality, the film also edges on the boundary of pornography, although the director is careful to hint and suggest rather than to show explicit sexual acts (except for a money shot with sperm splashing directly on the camera). Richard Dyer's description of the film as "underground, kitsch, [and] softporn" (1990, 164) captures the film's complexity and its longing for a gay utopia, which will never materialize. The film's sense of sadness and nostalgia is also heightened by the fate of its hero, who, in spite his good looks, will always be confined into a claustrophobic world of his own creation.

Further Reading

Benderson, Bruce. *James Bidgood*. Berlin: Benedikt Taschen Verlag, 1999; Dyer, Richard. *Now You See It: Studies on Lesbian and Gay Film*. London and New York: Routledge, 1990.

QUEER AS FOLK

The American/Canadian series *Queer as Folk* was based on the British series created by Russell T. Davies and lasted for five seasons, drawing strong ratings both in the United States and Canada. Initially targeted primarily at gay men, the series, broadcast by Showtime and Showcase, appealed also to a large number of straight women. As its British counterpart, the American *Queer as Folk* stretched the representational boundaries of gay sexuality on television, venturing on grounds that were not always considered acceptable and inciting both favorable and negative reactions within the gay community.

Queer as Folk takes its title from the colloquial expression from the northern part of Britain, "there's nought so queer as folk," which means "there's nothing as weird as people." The series follows the lives of a group of gay men (Brian, Justin, Michael, Emmett, Ted), a lesbian couple (Lindsay and Melanie), and their friends and families in Pittsburgh (although most of *Queer as Folk* was shot in Canada due to tax incentives). Since the first episode, the series presented a graphic and honest depiction of gay sex, showing mutual masturbation, anal sex, and rimming for the first time on American television. *Queer as Folk* also featured a frank portrayal of drug use and casual sex. The producers were careful to emphasize that the series did not represent all of gay society, but was simply a celebration of the lives and passions of a group of gay friends. A disclaimer in that sense appeared before every episode of the American series. Showtime was also wary to stress that the series did not champion any particular cause in spite of addressing particularly controversial issues such as gay parenting, artificial insemination, same-sex marriages, child prostitution, and bug-chasers (HIV-negative people actively seeking to be infected with the virus).

The main thread of the narrative is Michael's seemingly unrequited love for his childhood mate Brian, an up-and-coming advertising executive, who has agreed to become a father by artificially inseminating his college friend Lindsay. The earlier episodes introduce the different characters and their relationships, while subsequent chapters tackle political themes more explicitly. Much of the last season, for

The complete cast of Showtime's steamy *Queer as Folk* series, season 1. Courtesy of Showtime/Photofest.

example, takes its inspiration from the several legislative initiatives that have sought to restrict the rights of gays and lesbians in the United States. The main characters of the series find the family balances that they have struggled so much to gain endangered by "Proposition 14," a political campaign aimed at outlawing same-sex marriages and other family rights. The protagonists of *Queer as Folk* actively fight against the proposition and the show increasingly focuses on the discrimination and hatred that they encounter. Homophobia explodes towards the end of the last season when an event at a gay bar to support opposition to the proposition is disrupted by a bomb. This horrible event leads Brian to declare his love for Michael so that the two friends finally become partners, although they decide against marrying.

Queer as Folk quickly became Showtime's most successful program and still enjoyed such status after its last season. The network apparently did not broadcast a sixth series for fears of being considered too gay-oriented. In spite of its success, the series did not win unanimous praise within the gay community. On the contrary, like its British counterpart, *Queer as Folk* drew criticism from gay viewers for some aspects that were considered particularly problematic. In spite of the initial disclaimer about the representation of a simple segment of gay life, the show was still charged of representing queer lifestyle with little realism. This was due to an almost exclusive focus on white people and to the excessive portrayal of sex in public places such as bars. The focus on sexuality also risked associating infidelity with gay people, thus lending arguments to those who are opposed to same-sex unions. Those who came to the defense of the program stated that, in spite of its graphic depiction of sex, *Queer as Folk* also showed its main characters engaged in various meaningful relationships, including the first one in a TV series between an HIV-negative man and his HIV-positive partner. They praised the show for the heightened media exposure that it gave to gay and lesbian themes and characters.

Life partners Ron Cowen and Daniel Lipman, who served as the program's executive producers, emphasized that *Queer as Folk* "is the story of boys becoming men" (Rowe 2003, *Advocate* online). Responding to the charges of misrepresenting the gay community, the producers argued that their primary responsibility was to the story they were telling and that they hoped that the community could find some truth in that particular story. As Lipman pointed out, "When we say we're 'politically incorrect,' we don't mean that we're out to offend anyone; we're out to tell the truth. Sometimes the truth is not pretty—sometimes people behave in flawed ways. But it's human, and we have to go with 'human' over political correctness" (Rowe 2003, *Advocate* online). Cowen went as far as challenging the very notion of a gay community: "I'm starting to feel more and more that there is less and less of 'a community,' in the sense that all gay people are not the same, like all straight people aren't. There are gay people who want to assimilate and move into the straight world, and there are others who want to stay within the gay community. Those people all have different attitudes and expectations of the show, and it's hard to satisfy everyone" (Rowe 2003, *Advocate* online). In addition to challenging the boundaries of sexual representations on television, *Queer as Folk* has thus also stimulated debates on the reception of gay-themed fiction within their primary community target and even on the very existence of that community.

Further Reading

Rowe, Michael. "The Men behind *Queer as Folk.*" *The Advocate*. April 15, 2003. http://www.highbeam.com/doc/1G1-99850364.html (accessed on April 13, 2007); Skeggs, Beverly, Leslie Moran, Paul Tyrer, and Jon Binnie. "*Queer as Folk:* Producing the Real of Urban Space." *Urban Studies* 41.9 (2004): 1839–1856.

QUEER EYE FOR THE STRAIGHT GUY

The Emmy Award-winning television series *Queer Eye for the Straight Guy* premiered on the Bravo television network in 2003, immediately becoming a surprising hit and one of the most debated TV programs of the season. It has also generated spinoff series throughout the world, although none of these has been as successful as the American series, often leading to their cancellation after a few episodes. At the beginning of its third season, the show shortened its name to simply *Queer Eye* to reflect its broader focus, which was no longer limited to making over straight people, but also women and gay people themselves. Although some gay critics pointed out that the show perpetrated the usual stereotypes associated with gay men, *Queer Eye for the Straight Guy* emphasizes that gay and straight men can easily bond and that they do not pose threats to their respective sexualities.

The show intersects with the genres of reality TV and the so-called makeover programs. It features the Fab Five, five openly gay men who take care of a helpless straight man. Each member of the gay team is an expert in a particular field and helps the straight man to make progress in it. The protagonist of each episode is assisted by Kyan Douglas for his hair and grooming, Thom Filicia for interior designing, Jai Rodriguez to improve his culture, Ted Allen for advice on food and wine, and Carson Kressley for the latest fashion. Throughout the episode, the man willingly experiences a total transformation and he is usually so pleased with it that, in the end, he does not really want the Fab Five to leave. The team of gay experts has not focused only on making over straight men: some episodes have focused on gay people, one on a female-to-male transgender, and one on the entire Red Sox baseball team.

As Kylo-Patrick Hart (2004) has argued, *Queer Eye for the Straight Guy* challenges the stereotype, which has been reinforced by many televised representations of queers, that gay men are obviously inferior to heterosexuals because of their sexual

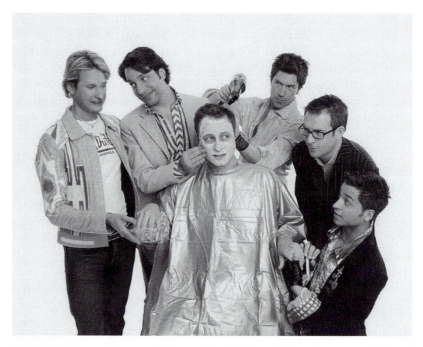

The Fab Five working on their straight fashion victim. Courtesy of Bravo/ Photofest.

orientation. Other critics have been less enthusiastic about the show, arguing that it is predicated upon the tired stereotype of gay men having a natural penchant for style, fashion, and art that straight, masculine men lack. Gay men are ultimately feminized as fairies in the program, and yet Hart finds precisely in this detail the subversive potential of *Queer Eye*. The show's representation of gay men as feminized does not imply that they are inferior to the straight man that they have to make over. On the contrary, they are superior to him in every respect. The show thus presents homosexuals as non-threatening to heterosexuals, yet, at the same time, affirms their superiority over the latter. In addition, although *Queer Eye* apparently feminizes its gay team, it establishes a different power dynamic than those usually associated with gay/straight relationships. The straight man is completely cast in the passive role as he surrenders himself to the gay team for his make over. Gay culture becomes the dominant one in the show, and gays mould the new identity of the straight man.

Queer Eye for the Straight Guy makes extensive use of humor to subvert common stereotypes about gay men and to make fun of the straight protagonist. In this way, the show challenges the power dynamics between gays and straights showing how easy it is for gay men to make fun of heterosexuals. In televised representations, gays are usually made fun of. *Queer Eye* focuses instead on how to make fun of straight men. The humor directed at the straight guy, however, is benevolent and, by the end of each episode, the Fab Five establish a significant bond with the straight man. As Kylo-Patrick Hart has remarked (2004), the Fab Five are represented as a team of gay superheroes who come to the rescue of the straight guy with their superpowers in their different areas of expertise.

Through its good-natured approach, *Queer Eye for the Straight Guy* communicates to a vast audience positive images of gay people and shows how they can lead a straight man to better himself. As David Collins, the show's executive producer, has argued (Hart 2004, *Journal of Men's Studies* online), the Fab Five make the straight guy discover a whole new set of possibilities for his life: "gay guys [and] straight guys may do things a little different in the bedroom, but in the end, they're just men.... Guys are guys, and all we want [is] to feel good about ourselves."

Further Reading

Hart, Kylo-Patrick R. "We're Here, We're Queer—and We're Better Than You: The Representational Superiority of Gay Men to Heterosexuals on 'Queer Eye for the Straight Guy.'" *The Journal of Men's Studies* 12.3 (Spring 2004): 241–253. http://www.highbeam.com/doc/1G1-117988723.html (accessed on October 4, 2006).

R

Real World, The

MTV's longest-running program, *The Real World* was one of the first reality shows to gain a vast audience at a national level and to include gay and lesbian characters in its cast. It thus helped to give increasing visibility to homosexuals on television. Since 1992, its formula has proved immensely successful and has become the canvas for many other reality television programs. In its 1994 season, filmed in San Francisco, *The Real World* was also the first show to include an openly gay cast member, Cuban-American Pedro Zamora, who was struggling with **AIDS**.

The Real World focuses on the lives of seven twenty-something strangers who have to live in a house together for several months while cameras record their relationships and interactions. Cameras follow the participants' lives not only in the house but also when they are out in public and at work (or looking for employment). Although interaction with the public was minimal in the first seasons, the group is now given a common task at the beginning of the series. The program moves to a different city with each new season. As the opening message says, the seven strangers will "find out what happens, when people stop being polite, and start getting real." The characters' taped lives are then broadcast in a series of 13 half-hour episodes. During its first season in New York, *The Real World* included a gay man in the cast of seven strangers, Norman Korpi. Korpi was the first homosexual whose life was portrayed in a television series after Lance Loud came out in the 1970s during PBS's docudrama *An American Family*. While the nation was shocked in the seventies by Loud's coming out, Korpi's participation in *The Real World* was greeted by positive responses as he came across as the most sensible and politically aware of the seven strangers. This has become a recurring characteristic of the gay and lesbian participants of the show and one which sets *The Real World* in contrast to other reality shows, such as CBS's *Survivor* and ABC's *The Mole*, where homosexuals are also part of the cast. These programs tend to reinforce damaging stereotypes about queers as untrustworthy and egocentric. Thus, when homosexual contenders such as *Survivor*'s first-season Richard Hatch eventually emerge as the winners, their success may be read negatively as evidence of gay people's scheming skills.

While *The Real World* itself is not immune from stereotypes, it is far more nuanced and socially conscious in its presentation of gays and lesbians with whom even heterosexual viewers can identify. It portrays gays as involved in their community's quest for equal rights with heterosexuals. In the New York season, for example, Korpi encouraged his housemates to attend a march in Washington to grant gays reproductive rights. Other seasons have stimulated discussions on gay marriages and the presence of gays in the military. In the Los Angeles series, lesbian Beth Anthony vocally supported gay marriages and, at the end of the show, got married to her partner Becky. In the San Francisco season, Pedro Zamora exchanged wedding wows with his boyfriend. It was Danny Roberts of the New Orleans cast who helped to engineer a discussion of the "Don't Ask, Don't Tell" policy about gays in the U.S. military. Roberts's boyfriend was in the military at the time of the show and, to protect his identity, his face was blurred every time he appeared on camera.

The San Francisco season of *The Real World* is commonly referred to as the most poignant and socially challenging for its depiction of Pedro Zamora's life with AIDS. Zamora used his appearance on the show to educate viewers about the virus. His own initial response to his positive status was one of denial. During his school years, Zamora had received very little sex education and his promiscuous behavior, partly the result of his mother's death when he was only 13 years of age, had exposed him to the infection. Even when he tested positive in 1989, Zamora did not start to seek help immediately. However, after a severe case of shingles, he decided not only to start treatment but also to educate himself and others about his disease. Zamora thus gave up academic education to devote himself fully to his career as AIDS educator. His activities attracted media attention before Zamora was cast on *The Real World.* He was interviewed on several talk shows, including Oprah's, and even testified before Congress arguing for more comprehensive and comprehensible AIDS programs specifically targeted to reach young men.

Being selected for *The Real World* allowed Zamora to be shown on national television lecturing in schools about the virus. His discussion on HIV with his fellow participants obviously reached a wider audience than his usual listeners at conferences. His health was already deteriorating while Zamora was recording *The Real World* and Pedro died the day after the broadcast of the last episode in the series. Zamora's participation to *The Real World* brought AIDS to American homes and families. After the San Francisco series of the show, very few Americans could still say that they did not know anyone with AIDS. Zamora was praised because of his fight against AIDS by President Clinton, who also arranged for all the members of the Zamora'a family who were still in Cuba to join Pedro in the United States shortly before his death. Fellow Real Worlder Judd Winick created mainstream comic books inspired by his friendship with Zamora.

Throughout its numerous seasons, *The Real World* has brought gay and lesbian themes and people to American television. Its portrayal of gay men and lesbians is more affirmative and less stereotypical than that found in other reality shows. *The Real World* emphasizes that queers are men and women with a distinct personality and character. It praises their strength and their commitment to the social and political goals of their community and, at the same time, it is careful not to define their identity solely in terms of their sexuality. As one gay participant to *The Real World* makes clear, "I love men. But that's just part of me. That's not all of me."

Further Reading

Brenton, Sam, and Reuben Cohen. *Shooting People: Adventures in Reality TV*. London: Verso, 2003; Johnson, Hillary, and Nancy Rommelmann. *MTV's The Real Real World*. New York: MTV Books, 1995; Pollet, Alison. *MTV's The Real World New Orleans Unmasked*. New York: MTV Books, 2000; Winick, Judd. *Pedro and Me: Friendship, Loss and What I Learned*. New York: Henry Holt & Co, 2000.

REUBENS, PAUL (1952–)

American actor, comedian, and writer Paul Reubens is best remembered in gay and lesbian popular culture for the creation of the character of Pee-wee Herman, informed by an apparent homosexual sensibility. Refused at the auditions for the 1980–1981 season of *Saturday Night Live*, Reubens made Pee-wee the main character in a stage show that proved so popular that it soon transferred from clubs and theaters to children's television. As Bruce La Bruce (1995) has noticed, the sexual ambivalence of the character was particularly baffling for critics and reviewers. This was due to their "reluctance to deal with the implications of an implicitly gay icon who is adored by children, and whose appeal cuts across a surprisingly wide range of youth subcultures" (La Bruce 1995, 382–389). Reubens's unwillingness to discuss his private life has been the subject of much speculation, which was further stimulated by the two sex scandals in which the actor found himself embroiled.

Reubens was born Paul Rubenfeld on August 27, 1952, in Peekskill, New York, from Jewish-American parents, but grew up in Sarasota, Florida, where his family owned a lamp store. Rubenfeld was interested in acting since he was 11. At that age, he joined the local theater group in Sarasota and appeared in a number of plays throughout his high school years. After his graduation, he enrolled at Boston University and studied there for a year before deciding to change his surname into Reubens and pursue an acting career in Hollywood. He first attended the California Institute for the Arts as an acting major and, in the 1970s, he joined The Groundlings, an improvisational theater group based in Los Angeles. During the years he spent with The Groundlings, Reubens started to develop the Pee-wee Herman character. Pee-wee is an eccentric man who acts as a child, always clothed with his characteristic grey suit that is too small for him. La Bruce (1995, 383) also points out that Pee-wee has an androgynous nature, wearing "pancake makeup, rouge, and a hint of lipstick" and talking in a weird falsetto. The name apparently came from the brand of a miniature harmonica and, to Reubens, it was the kind of name that parents would give to a child they did not care about.

Reubens debuted with the *Pee-wee Herman Show* at the Groundlings Theatre in 1980 and later moved to the Roxy where the cable network HBO recorded one of the performances and broadcast it in 1981. Reubens gained more fans with his guest

Paul Reubens (right) as Pee-wee Herman with Laurence Fishburne as Cowboy Curtis on CBS's series *Pee-wee's Playhouse*. Courtesy of CBS/Photofest. Photograph by John Duke Kisch.

appearances as Pee-wee on *Late Night with David Letterman*. In 1984 he performed to a sold-out Carnegie Hall in New York. The following year, the then-newcomer Tim Burton directed Reubens in his first film, *Pee-wee's Big Adventure*, which proved surprisingly popular at the box office. The success of the character earned him a place on CBS's Saturday morning children's programs. *Pee-wee's Playhouse* first aired in 1986 and went on for the next five years. Because the program was mostly watched by children, the sexual innuendo of the shows was toned down. Yet, the show proved successful with adults too and contributed to stretch the boundaries of what was considered acceptable on children's TV. *Playhouse* won 22 Emmys during its run, heaping up critical praise for its queer challenges against racism and heterosexism. Most of Pee-wee's closest friends on the show are black and their sexualities are over-exaggerated, making them parodies. Alexander Doty (1993), who has analyzed the figure of Pee-wee at length, argues that the show challenges and satirizes popular notions of gender and sexuality. In addition, the character of Pee-wee functions as an affirmation of the figure of the effeminate gay man. "I'm just trying to illustrate," Reubens stated in an interview (Marcor *St. James's Encyclopedia* online), "that it's okay to be different—not that it's good, not that it's bad, but that it's all right. I'm trying to tell kids to have a good time and to encourage them to be creative and to question things."

Although Reubens had already decided not to sign on for a sixth season, his arrest for masturbating in a pornographic movie theater in Los Angeles on July 26, 1991, caused CBS to stop broadcasting the reruns of the series. Reubens was given a clear record in return for a fine and a few public service announcements. Doty (1993) claims that the disproportionate media reaction to Reubens's arrest was generated by the connection of Pee-wee's queerness with that of his creator. The actor's arrest created a link between Pee-wee's difference and Reubens's sexual body. This flaunting of difference was too much for a children's program. Reubens was subject to a second arrest in 2002 in connection with child pornography, although this charge was later dropped after Reubens pleaded guilty to a separate misdemeanor obscenity charge.

Since 1991, Reubens has not been able to revive his Pee-wee character although he and director Tim Burton are said to be working on a movie based on *Pee-wee's Playhouse*. His career, however, has continued even after the actor's two arrests. He has earned particularly good reviews for his recurring role in the hit TV series *Murphy Brown* (1988–1998, for which he obtained his only Emmy nomination for a non–Pee-wee character) and for his portrayal of a gay drug dealer in the film *Blow* (2001). With Pee-wee Herman, however, Reubens created a career-defining character, one which is informed by **camp** subversion. As La Bruce concludes (1995, 384), behind Pee-wee's "naivety and ingeniousness always lurks a naughty understanding of his own seditious behavior."

Further Reading

Doty, Alexander. *Making Things Perfectly Queer.* Minneapolis: University of Minnesota Press, 1993; La Bruce, Bruce. "Pee Wee Herman: The Homosexual Subtext." *Out in Culture: Gay, Lesbian and Queer Essays on Popular Culture.* Corey K. Creekmur and Alexander Doty, eds. Durham, NC: Duke University Press, 1995. 382–388; Macor, Alison. "Pee-wee's Playhouse." *St. James Encyclopedia of Pop Culture.* http://findarticles.com/p/articles/mi_g1epc/is_tov/ai_2419100938 (accessed on May 7, 2007); Nericcio, William Anthony. "Watching Critics, Watching Journalists, Watching Sheriffs, Watching Pee-wee Herman Watch: The Extraordinary Case of the Saturday Morning Children's Show Celebrity Who Masturbated." *Iowa Journal of Cultural Studies* 4 (Spring 2004): 43–70; Russo, Vito. *The Celluloid Closet: Homosexuality and the Movies.* New York: Harper and Row, 1981.

ROSEANNE

The American sitcom *Roseanne* aired on ABC from 1988 to 1997. Starring outspoken stand-up comedian Roseanne Barr and John Goodman, it became one the most successful and unusual sitcoms in TV history, getting in the top five places of Nielsen Ratings for its first six seasons. The show occupies a special place within gay and lesbian popular culture as it gave a fundamental contribution to the access of gay, lesbian, and bisexual themes within mainstream television. Setting itself in sharp contrast to the sitcoms of the time, *Roseanne* focused on a working-class family living in a fictional Illinois town and honestly depicted controversial issues, including homosexuality.

Initially conceived as a stand-up act, *Roseanne* evolved into a series with a strong female matriarch at its center. Roseanne's husband is often in the dark about family matters. "I figure by the time my husband comes home at night, if those kids are still alive, I've done my job": this is Roseanne's way of dealing with the problems of the Conner family. In its matriarchal and working-class focus, *Roseanne* stood in sharp contrast to the other popular sitcom of the 1990s, *The Cosby Show*. While the latter focused on a well-to-do family with a strong father figure, *Roseanne* decidedly favored a more divided group centered upon a mother figure. In addition to Roseanne and her husband Dan, the Conners included their daughters Darlene and Becky, their son D. J. and Roseanne's sister Jackie. Over time, the household came to include Becky's husband Mark and Darlene's boyfriend David. The Conners periodically experience money problems and hold a variety of jobs, including managing their own diner, the Lanford Lunch Box.

Several recurrent characters in the series are gay, including Roseanne's sister, whose homosexuality, however, is not revealed until the surreal last episode of the final season. Roseanne's mother reveals lesbian yearnings in the last season too, although her lesbian orientation is revealed to be an invention of Roseanne in the

The cast of ABC's sitcom *Roseanne*. Courtesy of ABC/Photofest.

last episode. In spite of this, her character is the first almost lesbian grandmother in a TV series. Leon Carp, Roseanne's boss at the luncheonette inside Rodbell's Department Store, is gay and, after dating many men, he finds happiness with his partner Scott. The two also marry with a public ceremony. Nancy, played by Sandra Bernhard, is one of Roseanne's best friends and co-owner of the Lanford Lunch Box. She is a bisexual and often dates attractive women; her first girlfriend was played by Morgan Fairchild. Because of these gay and lesbian characters, as well as several other controversial issues, such as masturbation and birth control, the show often challenged the boundaries of what was acceptable by network standards.

Controversy surrounding the gay and lesbian themes in the sitcom openly exploded in March 1994 with the airing of the episode "Don't Ask, Don't Tell." The episode actually started to cause animated debates even before it was aired, as it became known that Roseanne would be kissed by another woman. Right-wing groups put pressure on ABC to either edit out the kiss or cancel the whole episode. In turn, Roseanne held her ground, threatening to switch networks if ABC gave in to the pressure. The episode was aired after countless debates and clips of the incriminated kiss had made it a highly publicized commodity. It centers on Roseanne's visit to a gay bar with Nancy and her latest girlfriend (Mariel Hemingway). Through its star's entrance into the queer community, the episode challenges many lesbian stereotypes and leads viewers to reflect on the persistence of homophobia within American culture. Although ABC finally agreed to air the entire episode, "Don't Ask, Don't Tell" had to be preceded by a warning on its mature content, thus advising parental discretion. The warning signaled that, although the primetime lesbian kiss was aired, gays and lesbians still remained marginalized subjects within American society, their visibility perceived as a threat. As Suzanna Walters (2003) has shown in her detailed reading of the episode, "Don't Ask, Don't Tell" was particularly effective as, rather than making gays the target for parody, it made fun of homophobia, forcing America's favorite working-class character to address the discomfort she experiences after being kissed by a woman.

Roseanne was not simply the first sitcom to feature a primetime lesbian kiss or a gay male wedding. In Walters's words (2003, 72), the show integrated gay and lesbian characters in its narrative not simply as "token signs of cultural hipness and diversity." It depicted them as part of both the dominant culture and a more marginalized one signified by their gayness.

Further Reading

Arnold, Roseanne. *My Lives.* New York: Ballantine, 1994; Dresner, Zita Z. "Roseanne Barr: Goddess or She-devil." *Journal of American Culture.* Vol. 16, Issue 2 (Summer 1993). 37–44; Dworkin, Susan. "Roseanne Barr: The Disgruntled Housewife as Stand-up Comedian." *Ms. Magazine* (New York), July–August 1987. 107–108, 205–206; Lee, Janet. "Subversive Sitcoms: Roseanne as Inspiration for Feminist Resistance." *Women's Studies: An Interdisciplinary Journal* 21. 1. 87–101; Rowe, Kathleen. *The Unruly Woman: Gender and Genres of Laughter.* Austin: University of Texas Press, 1995; Walters, Suzanna Danuta. *All the Rage: The Story of Gay Visibility in America.* Chicago: University of Chicago Press, 2003.

RUDNICK, PAUL (1957–)

Out playwright, novelist, and screenwriter Paul Rudnick has authored several comedies that prominently feature gay and lesbian themes and, as in the case of the successful *In and Out* (1997), challenge homophobic hypocrisies in society. Even when Rudnick has addressed dramatic social themes such as **AIDS**, he has done so with characteristic wit and dark humor. He is also the writer of long-running columns and humorist pieces in mainstream magazines such as *Premiere Magazine*, *Vanity Fair*, *Vogue*, *Esquire*, and *The New Yorker.*

Rudnick was born in 1957 in New Jersey. Both his father, a physicist, and his mother, an arts publisher, were extremely supportive when he told them he was gay. Rudnick grew up in the New York City suburb of Piscataway, which gave him insights on "what it's like to live in a town where everyone has to know everyone else's business" (*Spliced* online, 1997). These would be particularly useful for the writing of *In and Out*, although Rudnick was never in the position of the protagonist, who was played by Kevin Kline. Since his childhood and adolescence, Rudnick wanted to be a playwright, so he enrolled at Yale University for a B.A. in theater. After graduating, he supported himself with odd jobs while writing his first play *Poor Little Lambs* (1982). The mixed reception given to the play prompted Rudnick to change literary genre and write two novels: *Social Disease* (1986) and *I'll Take It* (1989), which earned him a reputation for satirizing American obsessions with nightlife and shopping respectively.

Rudnick's surreal second play *I Hate Hamlet* (1991) featured the ghost of legendary actor John Barrymore advising a television performer on how to act the role of Shakespeare's prince. The piece met with a cold reception from both audiences and critics to start with, but has since had successful reruns. Rudnick finally obtained critical and commercial recognition with his third play *Jeffrey* (1993), which observed the impact of AIDS on gay relationships with humor and with an affirmative attitude. As with Rudnick's subsequent script for *In and Out*, the focus in *Jeffrey* is not merely on gay sexuality but on gay romance, which the author sees as far more threatening to the audience's imagination. The play received an Obie Award, an Outer Critics Circle Award, and the John Gassner Award for Outstanding New American Play. Filtering AIDS through humor may seem controversial. Yet, Rudnick is neither interested nor bothered by political correctness. As he stated in an interview about his next play *The Naked Eye* (1996), no character or interest group is sacred in his works: "Political correctness is actually an enemy of comedy. I believe if there is a political platform that can be destroyed by humor, then it wasn't very strong to begin with. I'm interested in celebrating absurdity" (Graham, *The Naked Interview* online).

Jeffrey challenges the conservative notion that AIDS can be avoided through abstinence. Its main character initially decides to become celibate to avoid the virus, but then comes to the conclusion that abstaining from same-sex intercourse means giving up life. To Rudnick, humor is part and parcel of being gay and a tool for survival. *Jeffrey* is an homage to the way the gay community has dealt with AIDS, using what the playwright calls the natural gay resources of humor and style to get through an absolute nightmare. Far from trivializing the disease, the play shows how the humor and the style of the gay community were instrumental in getting through the crisis. The play eventually celebrates the strength of the gay community. Rudnick continued to challenge conservative and fundamentalist beliefs with the play *The Most Fabulous Story Ever Told* (1998), which recasts the story of the Book of Genesis through the same-sex couples formed by Adam and Steve and Jane and Mabel. *Valhalla* (2004) explores the link between homosexuality and beauty through the parallel stories of Ludwig II of Bavaria and James Avery, a small-town Texan homosexual who served in Germany during World War II.

In the meantime, Rudnick also started a successful career as a screenwriter. Thinking of Bette Midler as a protagonist, he wrote the first version of *Sister Act* (1992), but demanded to use a pseudonym in the film credits when the production made it a Whoopi Goldberg vehicle. Rudnick was also involved in the scripts of *The Addams Family* (1991), *Addams Family Values* (1993), and *The First Wives Club* (1996). In 1995 he adapted *Jeffrey* for the screen version that starred Steven Weber, Sigourney Weaver, Patrick Stewart, and **Nathan Lane**. The film was not as successful with mainstream audiences as the play, but attracted the attention of the gay community.

Rudnick's most successful film to date was the comedy *In and Out*, directed by Frank Oz and starring Kevin Kline, Tom Selleck, and Matt Dillon. Rudnick's script concerns the outing of a teacher (Kline) by a former student on national television. The situation is further complicated by the fact that the teacher is about to marry, lives in a small town, and has to weather an unexpected wave of media attention on his private life. The film contains a long kiss between Kline and Selleck which, to Rudnick (*Spliced* online, 1997), was the center of the whole narrative: "I think the length is completely the secret of that kiss. It's a way of saying, the movie says, 'We mean this. Get over it.'" The film refuses to treat outing and coming out as problems; on the contrary, it addresses them through the conventions of the screwball genre.

By turning gay stereotypes on their head and using surreal situations for humor, Rudnick's works address important social issues related to homosexuality. His plays are peopled by body builders, opera buffs, interior decorators, and waiters. However, instead of being simply employed as side characters for comic relief, they become the veritable heroes of the playwright's pieces, and the center of his narratives. With his writings, Rudnick thus cautions not to lose sight of the enormous potential of gay and lesbian popular culture for self-parody.

Further Reading

Graham, Shawn René. "The Naked Interview." American Repertory Theater Web site. www.amrep.org/people/rudnick.html; "Out With It." 1997; *SPLICEDwire*. http://www.splicedonline.com/features/rudnick2.html

RuPaul (1960–)

African American drag queen, singer, and actor RuPaul rose to international fame in the 1990s. Through his numerous appearances on TV programs and films, and at famous disco venues around the world, he has contributed to give drag a visible place in mainstream American popular culture.

RuPaul Andre Charles was born into a working-class family in San Diego on November 17, 1960. As a child, he loved the music of the Supremes and went through the trauma of his parents' separation and bitter divorce. Every time his parents started arguing, RuPaul recalls that, together with his sisters, they "would run into the bedroom and hold each other crouching down as though it were an air raid" (Official Web site). The divorce was "as ugly and nasty as it could have gotten" (Official Web site), something for which the child blamed himself. The traumatic separation caused RuPaul's mother to have a serious nervous breakdown. Because of her health, she was unable to hold a steady job for a long time. Once on welfare, the kids became the adults of the household, taking care of each other and of their mother too. They learned how to keep "secrets from social workers, daddy and anyone else who could threaten [their] family" (Official Web site). The artist was conscious of being effeminate at a young age. In his biographical notes, he recounts being called a sissy by neighborhood kids when he was 5 and being mistaken for a girl when he was 10. He was also well aware of his love for boys, a feeling that he had learned to keep hidden.

A different type of drag queen: RuPaul. Courtesy of Photofest.

When he was 12, RuPaul first got acquainted with acting, enrolling in San Diego Children's Theater. In September 1975 he started to attend Gompers Jr. High School, but was expelled only four months later for his poor attendance. The following year he moved in with his married sister Renetta and, after a few months, they moved together to Atlanta, a city that the performer has loved ever since. His school marks, however, did not improve and the only class he did not skip was drama. By 1978 RuPaul had dropped out of high school and started to work full time for his brother-in-law's used car business, a job that he kept until 1982. During these years, the artist began exploring his sexuality and had his first intercourse with men. In spite of his job as a car seller, RuPaul never abandoned his dream of entering showbiz. His brother-in-law was a formative influence, teaching him "how to go out into the world and get what [he] wanted": "He taught me how to listen and how to articulate my thoughts. I learned how to negotiate with people in business and above all, I learned that I had as much right to fulfill my dreams as any white person had" (Official Web site).

In the early 1980s RuPaul decided that time had come to fulfill his own dreams and he founded RuPaul and the U-hauls. The band performed at clubs in Atlanta and as an opening act for local rock and punk groups. The artist also started his career as an actor, appearing in drag in underground films. By the end of the decade, RuPaul had become a well-known figure in Atlanta, but he began to feel constrained there and wished for a larger recognition. He thus moved to New York, where, after a difficult beginning, he became a regular drag performer on the club scene. In 1989 he was voted "Queen of Manhattan" by club owners and DJs and selected by the B-52s for a cameo in the video of their hit "Love Shack." In 1993 RuPaul released his first dance album, *Supermodel*, which included the hit singles "Supermodel (You Better Work)" and "Back to My Roots." Topping the U.S. dance charts, RuPaul developed a new image for drag queens based on gentleness and warmth rather than on the bitchy remarks that had characterized the previous generations of performers. He was also the first drag queen to sign a modeling contract for a cosmetics firm, the Canadian MAC Cosmetics. Thanks to his position, he has helped to set up the MAC Aids Fund and has been one of its most effective fundraisers.

Since his music debut, RuPaul has released more successful albums and has recorded duets with internationally renowned artists such as **Elton John**. His acting career has flourished too, working with directors such as Spike Lee (*Crooklyn*, 1993), Wayne Wang (*Blue in the Face*, 1995), and Beeban Kidron (*To Wong Foo, Thanks for Everything, Julie Newmar*, 1996). He has also appeared out of drag in the film *But I'm a Cheerleader* (2000) as a former gay turned into a counselor for a rehabilitation camp to turn homosexuals into heterosexuals. From 1996 to 1998, the artist hosted his own television show, *The RuPaul Show*, on VH1, which ran six days a week. He interviewed a string of music celebrities and popular culture icons. He also devoted some episodes to controversial issues, such as pornography (interviewing porn personalities such as underground director Chi Chi LaRue).

One of RuPaul's most often-quoted sentences states that "we are born naked, all the rest is drag." It summarizes well the artist's conception of drag as something which affects all of us, and should therefore be given visibility into popular culture. Through a dramatic shift from the catty personae of his predecessors to his own more reassuring and less threatening image, RuPaul has vitally contributed to this visibility. Although the performer has reached a position within mainstream culture, he has consistently affirmed his identity as a gay man and has performed at queer events. He has also made clear that he wants to distance himself from the stereotypes that portray homosexual men as secretly wanting to be women. He has repeatedly stressed that he does not impersonate females, but simply drag queens, as his clothes would be too uncomfortable for women to wear.

Further Reading

Charles, RuPaul Andre. *Lettin' It All Hang Out*. New York: Hyperion, 1995; Charles, RuPaul Andre. http://rupaul.com/index.html. Official Web site (accessed on

July 10, 2007); Feinberg, Leslie. *Transgender Warriors: Making History from Joan of Arc to RuPaul*. Boston, Beacon Press, 1997; Trebay, Guy. "Cross-dresser Dreams: Female Impersonator RuPaul Andre Charles." *New Yorker* 69.5 (March 22, 1993): 49–56; Yarbrough, Jeff. "RuPaul: The Man behind the Mask." *The Advocate* 661–662 (August 23, 1994): 64–73.

S

SARGENT, DICK (1930–1994)

American actor Dick Sargent is best remembered for his role as the so-called second Darrin in ABC's comedy series *Bewitched*. As most of the gay actors who began their careers in the 1950s, Sargent kept his homosexuality secret, although he had a 20-year romantic relationship with another man. He came out in 1991, only three years before his death due to prostate cancer. For Sargent, coming out meant lifting a heavy burden. Working for 40 years in the business as a closeted homosexual was, according to the actor's own words (Signorile 1993, 323), "a terrible way to live." "It totally felt dirty and second-class and had all of those negative emotions. . . . Nobody should have to do it." After his coming out, Sargent became an outspoken supporter for gay and lesbian causes. He declared it was "a whole new mission in life" (Keehnen, online interview). Together with *Bewitched* co-star Elizabeth Montgomery he acted as Grand Marshal for the Los Angeles Pride Parade in 1992.

Born Richard Cox in Carmel, California, on April 19, 1930, Dick Sargent had a difficult relationship with his father, Elmer Cox, who had served as a Colonel in the Army during World War I. Elmer later became the business manager of Hollywood personalities such as actor Douglas Fairbanks and director Erich Von Stroheim. Sargent's mother, Ruth McNaughton Cox, was an actress in silent films. Because of his father's military background, Richard attended the San Rafael Military Academy, an institution that he detested, and Menlo School, both in California. He went on to Stanford University to study acting and he appeared in several student productions. While at Stanford, Cox also became increasingly aware of his homosexuality, a self-discovery that scared him. Intending to pursue an acting career, he held odd jobs to fund his ambition, until he landed a small role in *Prisoner of War* (1954) and changed his surname into Sargent. Slowly, the actor was able to get roles, albeit small ones, in more successful films such as *Operation Petticoat* (1959), *That Touch of Mink* (1962), and the Elvis Presley vehicle *Live a Little, Love a Little* (1968). He also had a leading role in the TV series *One Happy Family* (1961) and appeared in episodes of *Dr. Kildare* (1961), *Gunsmoke* (1962), and *Broadside* (1964). Sargent

(Signorile 1993, 323) has recalled the negative effects he feared that the revelation of his homosexuality might have on his career and decided not to talk about his orientation to anyone, not even with the other gays in showbiz. "My first agent was gay, and I didn't even talk to him about it." Sargent went as far as putting a fictitious ex-wife in his biographical notes for the studios.

Sargent joined the cast of *Bewitched* in 1969 for the last three seasons. He had originally been offered the role of Darrin when the series debuted in 1964, but could not take it up due to previous contractual obligations to Universal Studios. Yet, in 1969, Dick York, who had played Darrin in the first five seasons of the show, withdrew due to health reasons. Sargent then stepped in the role of the ordinary middle-class man married to the beautiful witch Samantha. **Agnes Moorehead** and Paul Lynde, themselves rumored to be gay, were part of the cast. Yet, although by the late 1960s the rumor of homosexuality would not necessarily destroy one's career, Sargent still did not talk to his co-stars about it. He became good friends with his co-star Liz Montgomery: "She and her husband and my lover and I socialized. We'd play tennis together, have Christmas parties, that kind of stuff, but [Liz and I] never discussed my being gay until years later. As long as you didn't say anything, nobody ever gave a damn in that [*Bewitched*] crowd" (Signorile 1992, 323). Guest star Paul Lynde was a case in point: "Paul Lynde was always around, always coming to parties and he was flamboyant and obvious and always trying to shock people. Everyone had to know, but it was never talked about" (Signorile 1993, 323). Although replacing a beloved actor as Dick York was not an easy task, Sargent ultimately won unanimous praise, including York's.

After *Bewitched* ended in 1972, Sargent continued to star in films and TV series including *The Streets of San Francisco, Taxi, Murder, She Wrote, L.A. Law,* and *Down to Earth.* He was badly affected by the death of his life-partner in 1980 and began to socialize with gays who were out of the closet. Although he did not publicly declared his homosexuality until 1991, he began to live more openly and less secretively. In April 1991 the tabloid *Star* outed him, an event which the actor described as "terrible" but that, at the same time, pushed him to realize that he needed to live his life more honestly. Another factor which motivated him to talk openly about his sexual orientation was the decision of then California governor Pete Wilson to sign a bill against the discrimination of gays and lesbians on the workplace. Choosing October 11, 1991, National Coming Out Day, to make his announcement, Sargent discussed his homosexuality on *Entertainment Tonight* and was excited about becoming an adult role model for those many gay teenagers that were coming to terms with their own sexual difference. Since his coming out, the actor became a gay rights activist. He compared the experience of coming out to feeling cleansed. "I'll probably never be allowed to play a father symbol again," he admitted. "I'm afraid for my career. I'm probably gonna lose a whole lot of work....I may even have to sell the house someday, but this is more important. I like myself, probably more than I have most of my life."

Unfortunately, this new happiness was short-lived as Sargent was diagnosed with prostate cancer in 1989, and, although the disease seemed curable, it progressed in spite of the radiation cycles the actor underwent. Sargent died on July 8, 1994. In his study of outing, *Queer in America,* Michelangelo Signorile has praised Sargent as someone who made history, becoming one of the very first television stars to come out.

Further Reading

Keehnen, Owen. "No More 'Straight Man'; Dick Sargent Is Out and Proud." http://www.harpiesbizarre.com/sargent_interview.htm; Signorile, Michelangelo. *Queer in America: Sex, the Media and the Closets of Power.* New York: Random House, 1993.

SCHLESINGER, JOHN (1926–2003)

Academy Award–winning director John Schlesinger contributed with many of his films to the visibility of homosexual characters in both British and American cinema. Most of his cinematic works are concerned with gender relations and, as his reputation became more established, Schlesinger grew more explicit in his treatment of homosexuality. Same-sex desire is the main theme in at least three of his films (*Midnight Cowboy* [1969], *Sunday Bloody Sunday* [1971], and *The Next Best Thing* [2001]) and in the highly praised television dramas *An Englishman Abroad* (1983) and *A Question of Attribution* (1991). Many of his other films include gay characters in minor roles and display a clear homosexual sensibility. Openly gay, Schlesinger lived with his partner Michael Childers from the 1960s until his death in 2003.

Schlesinger was born into a Jewish middle-class family in London on February 16, 1926, the eldest of five children. His mother Winifred was a musician and his father Bernard a pediatrician. Schlesinger's education contributed to his love of art, music, and literature. After serving in World War II, Schlesinger studied English literature at Oxford from where he graduated in 1950. In his Oxford years, he performed with the Oxford University Dramatic School and the Experimental Theater Club. His career as a filmmaker started with a series of documentaries he shot for the BBC in the late 1950s. One of these, *Terminus*, earned him a prize at the prestigious Venice Film Festival. His first films were part of the social unrest that permeated the 1960s and of the exciting British youth culture of those years. With *A Kind of Loving* (1962), which won the Golden Bear at the Berlin Film Festival, *Billy Liar* (1963), *Darling* (1965), and *Far from the Madding Crowd* (1967), Schlesinger inscribed himself in the group of social realist British directors such as Karel Reisz and Tony Richardson, who were preoccupied with a depiction of working-class life and aspirations. The films contributed to the launching of the careers of British stars such as Alan Bates and Julie Christie, who starred in all of them and won an Academy Award for her performance in *Darling*. Schlesinger too was nominated for Best Director.

For his first American film, Schlesinger chose the controversial *Midnight Cowboy*. The movie focuses on the relationship between Joe Buck (Jon Voight) and Ratso Rizzo (Dustin Hoffman). Joe is a male hustler who has just arrived in New York with the plan to be the kept man of rich women. Rizzo is an ailing con who first robs Joe, but then starts a partnership with him becoming his manager. The two live in Rizzo's rundown apartment whose block is about to be demolished. With time, it is actually Rizzo who becomes increasingly dependent on Joe because of his health problems. Their friendship becomes deeper and Joe, who often finds himself hustling for male clients, begins to make plans for them as a couple. He robs and beats one of his clients to get enough money to take Rizzo to the warmer climate of Florida where he also plans to find an honest work. Rizzo, however, dies just as they are approaching Miami. The movie received an X-rating, but won Academy Awards for Best Picture and Best Director and both its actors were nominated. A typical product of the New Hollywood, which targeted the hypocrisy of the big studios, *Midnight Cowboy* was praised for its lucid observation of American urban life and its gritty details. Worldwide success rewarded Schlesinger of his daring choice of material and allowed him to make an even more personal film.

Thanks to the triumph of *Midnight Cowboy*, Schlesinger returned to Britain to shoot the introspective *Sunday Bloody Sunday* (1971), in which a middle-aged Jewish gay man (Peter Finch) and a divorced woman (Glenda Jackson) both become attracted to a younger man (Murray Head). The film was released after only four years from the decriminalization of sexual acts between male adults in Britain and contained explicit scenes of lovemaking between men. The director considered this his most personal work and "a breakthrough film, where gay characters were not tortured, suicidal, mean, bitchy, dishonorable, or tragic—they were portrayed as normal, loving human beings with real lives, real careers, real feelings filled with compassion, and many of the compromises which life and relationships bring" (Vary 2003, *Advocate* online). With *Sunday Bloody Sunday*, Schlesinger received more Oscar nominations and more international awards, including the BAFTA for Best Direction.

Since the 1970s, Schlesinger divided his production between mainstream big-budget films such as the thrillers *The Marathon Man* (1976), *Pacific Heights* (1990), and *The Innocent* (1993), and more personal projects like the television dramas *An Englishman Abroad* and *A Question of Attribution*, which focus on Guy Burgess and Anthony Blunt respectively. Both Burgess and Blunt were homosexuals who were part of the Cambridge Spy Ring, which passed British secrets onto the Soviets during the Cold War. Schlesinger also directed several operas and served as associate director of the National Theater, London.

The Next Best Thing (2001) represents an inadequate ending for an otherwise brilliant career. Abbie (Madonna) and Robert (**Rupert Everett**) are best friends who, during a drunken one-night stand, conceive a son. They decide to raise him together, unmarried and without giving up their own sexual lives. In spite of gay icons Madonna and Rupert Everett, the film is badly scripted and, as a result, its characters are psychologically underdeveloped and stereotypical. Although *The Next Best Thing* asks important questions about the legal rights of queers to parenting and to constitute a nontraditional family, its solutions appeal more to the conservative logic of tolerance and respectability than to the potentialities within queer culture. Robert is bored with the excesses of the gay community and is shown to have no success at relationships. He is desexualized and alone. His representation comes as a disappointment from a director who, 30 years before, had powerfully deconstructed stereotypical representations of gay sexuality with *Midnight Cowboy* and *Sunday Bloody Sunday*. Schlesinger died on July 25, 2003, in Palm Springs, California.

Further Reading

Brooker, Nancy. *John Schlesinger: A Guide to References and Resources*. Boston: G. K. Hall, 1978; Garnett, Tay. "John Schlesinger." *Directing*. London: The Scarecrow Press, 1996. 228–233; McFarlane, Brian. "John Schlesinger." *An Autobiography of British Cinema*. London: Methuen, 1997. 509–514; Philips, Gene. *John Schlesinger*. Boston: Twayne, 1981; Porton, Richard, and Lee Ellickson. "Reflections of an Englishman Abroad." *Cineaste* 4 (1994): 38–41; Vary, Adam B. "Darling John: Maverick Director John Schlesinger Forever Changed the Face of Gay Cinema." *The Advocate*. September 2, 2003. http://findarticles.com/p/articles/mi_m1589/is_2003_Sept_2/ai_110737684 (accessed on April 3, 2007).

SONDHEIM, STEPHEN (1930–)

Award-winning musical composer and lyricist Stephen Sondheim deeply innovated American musical theater in the 1960s and 1970s. Although Sondheim's works do not include gay characters and he does not show particular pride for his homosexuality, his musicals and songs have enthused gay and lesbian audiences who have conferred to the author's compositions a cult status comparable to those reserved to illustrious predecessors such as Cole Porter and Noël Coward. In his works as well as in his life, Sondheim has eschewed open militancy in favor of queer rights. On the contrary, he has adopted an ambiguous and oblique critique of the traditional musical form, which includes as its targets the representation of idealized heterosexual romances and sexuality.

Sondheim is the only child of Herbert Sondheim, a dress manufacturer, and Etta Janet Fox Sondheim, a dress designer. He was born in New York and grew up in Manhattan in a wealthy, nonreligious Jewish family. When Stephen was 10, his parents separated and he went to live with his mother on a farm in Pennsylvania. Sondheim first studied in military school, then attended George School, a preparatory academy in Pennsylvania, and finally graduated in music from Williams College in Massachusetts in 1950. He also studied privately with composer Milton Babbitt. However, the main influence on Sondheim's education was exerted by his Pennsylvanian neighbor and musical lyricist Oscar Hammerstein II. Stephen, who had a tense relationship with his mother, identified Hammerstein as a father figure. As the composer would later state, he decided to write for the theater to emulate Hammerstein. Their close relation continued throughout Sondheim's career, until Hammerstein's death in 1960.

In the early 1950s, Sondheim worked as a scriptwriter for the television series *Topper* and composed the score for the musical *Saturday Night*. This was to be Sondheim's debut on Broadway, however, when its producer died, the musical was shelved and was not produced until 1997. Sondheim finally made his Broadway debut in 1957 with the lyrics for **Leonard Bernstein**'s *West Side Story*, a big hit which has since developed into a classic. Two years later, Sondheim wrote the lyrics for another Broadway hit, *Gypsy*, accompanying the music by Jule Styne. Both stories were tragic in tone and subverted the standard light spectacle which audiences would expect from musicals. Their unconventional nature attracted Sondheim to these projects. *West Side Story* is a modern adaptation of Shakespeare's *Romeo and Juliet*. The musical became central to queer popular culture of the 1960s. *Gypsy* focuses on the controversial relationship between Gypsy Rose Lee, the famous striptease performer, and her mother, Mama Rose, the first of a long series of manipulative mother figures in Sondheim's theater.

Sondheim was responsible for writing both the score and the lyrics of his next work, *A Funny Thing Happened on the Way to the Forum* (1962). The plot, adapted from different comedies by Plautus, the ancient Latin playwright, involves a humorous sex farce organized by Pseudolus, a slave who wants to conquer his freedom. *Forum* went on to become a big success and won a Tony Award for Best Musical. Originally played by Zero Mostel, the role of Pseudolus has been played by such diverse actors as **Nathan Lane** and Whoopi Goldberg. Although the score of *Forum* was initially coolly received and was not even nominated for a Tony Award, it represents a pioneering innovation on the traditional musical form. *Forum* departs from the integrated tradition in which the score furthers the plot. On the contrary, the songs in *Forum* break up the fast pace of the narrative.

After these successes, Sondheim went through a series of disappointments which lasted until the end of the 1960s. His next musical, *Anyone Can Whistle* (1964), introduced Angela Lansbury to Broadway, starting a long-lasting collaboration between the composer and the actress. Yet, the musical was ahead of its times and flopped badly, closing after only nine performances. Once again, the topic departed radically from the reassuring plots of traditional musicals, featuring corruption in municipal administrations and the subtle boundaries between sanity and insanity as its main themes. *The Time of the Cuckoo*, a more conventional collaboration with Hammerstein's professional partner Richard Rodgers, also proved a disappointment for Sondheim, who later declared he regretted agreeing to write the lyrics for the project. The relationship with Rodgers proved difficult and the musical was not well received. In 1966 Sondheim returned to a darker subject matter with his adaptation of John Collier's short story, "Evening Primrose," for television. Collier's fantasy about a community of people living in isolation from the rest of humanity in a department store did not succeed on the small screen.

Sondheim made a major comeback to Broadway with *Company* (1970), a so-called concept musical, which disrupted the genre's traditional chronological development in favor of a series of sketches in no linear order. *Company* centers on the relationships between a New York bachelor, who is about to turn 35, and several married couples whom he befriends. It further developed the composer's notion that music should comment on, rather than convey, action. Sondheim described *Company* as a musical about middle-class people with middle-class problems, highlighting the musical's unconventional concern with adult crisis. *Company* was a big hit with critics and audiences alike, winning the New York Drama Critics Circle Award and the Tony Award for Best Musical and reviving Sondheim's passion for experimentation with new techniques. It also started a productive collaboration between the composer and director Harold Prince which resulted in the creation of five more musicals between 1970 and 1981: *Follies* (1971), an homage to the vaudeville tradition; *A Little Night with Music* (1973), based on Ingmar Bergman's film; *Smiles of a Summer Night, Pacific Overtures* (1976), a complex piece on the westernization of Japan; *Sweeney Todd* (1979), bringing cannibalism on the Broadway stage; and *Merrily We Roll Along* (1981). After the success and the praise of the 1970s, *Merrily* opened the new decade with a bitter failure for Sondheim as it closed after less than 20 performances. It also marked the end of the Sondheim-Prince collaboration which was briefly resumed in 2003 for *Bounce*, which, however, was never staged on Broadway.

After the failure of *Merrily*, Sondheim considered retiring from musical writing. Yet, both the 1980s and the 1990s were decades of notable achievements in Sondheim's career, although his critical success was not always equaled by box office results. After breaking up his professional partnership with Harold Prince, Sondheim found a new, inspiring collaborator in James Lapine. The Pulitzer Prize winner *Sunday in the Park with George* (1985) was their first production. It is a meditation on art and the painful estrangement from communities that artists may feel. The musical takes as its point of departure the French artist Georges Seurat's obsession for painting. Sondheim and Lapine revisited the Brothers Grimm's fairy tale in the popular *Into the Woods* (1987) and the critically acclaimed, but commercially disappointing *Passion* (1994). Sondheim also won an Oscar for Best Song with "Sooner or Later (I Always Get My Man)," written for the film *Dick Tracy* (1990). This made him one of the few winners of an Academy Award, a Pulitzer Prize, and several Grammy and Tony Awards.

Throughout his career, Sondheim has eschewed categorization, drawing on constantly diverse sources of inspiration for his works. His musicals reject the reassuring image of America and the West that is characteristically inscribed in traditional Broadway fare. On the contrary, they portray Western capitalist society as predatory and alienating. "Life is all right in America / If you're all white in America," sing the Puerto Rican characters in *West Side Story*, pointing to the composer's lifelong concern with social exclusion. Although they never directly broach gay themes, Sondheim's productions have developed a cult following within queer popular audiences. His songs have often served as official scores for different generations of gays and have also played a central part in **AIDS** fundraising events.

Further Reading

Banfield, Stephen. *Sondheim's Broadway Musicals*. Ann Arbor: University of Michigan Press, 1993; Clum, John M. *Something for the Boys: Musical Theater and Gay Culture*. New York: St. Martin's Press, 1999; Goodhart, Sandor, ed. *Reading Stephen Sondheim: A Collection of Critical Essays*. New York: Garland, 2000; Gordon, Joanne. *Art Isn't Easy: The Theater of Stephen Sondheim*. Updated ed. New York: DaCapo Press, 1992; Gordon, Joanne, ed. *Stephen Sondheim: A Casebook*. New York: Garland, 1997; Miller, D. A. *Place for Us: Essay on the Broadway Musical*. Cambridge, MA: Harvard University Press, 1998; Secrest, Meryle. *Stephen Sondheim: A Life*. New York: Knopf, 1998; Zadan, Craig. *Sondheim & Co*. Second ed., updated. New York: DaCapo Press, 1994; The journal *The Sondheim Review* is fully devoted to the composer.

STANWYCK, BARBARA (1907–1990)

Although American award-winning actress Barbara Stanwyck never identified herself as lesbian and kept her private life as hidden as possible from public life, the strong female characters that she embodied on the screen made her a lesbian icon. Whether playing the murderous femme fatale Phyllis Dietrichson in Billy Wilder's seminal noir film *Double Indemnity* (1944) or the moral matriarch of the hit TV series *The Big Valley*, Stanwyck appealed to gay women for her intelligence and self-reliance. Although she only played one lesbian character throughout her career, the actress was an affirming image for women in love with other women. As her biographer Axel Madsen (1994, 84) points out, to the lesbians growing up in the conformist American society of the 1940s and 1950s, "the Barbara Stanwyck screen image defined her as 'one of us.'" The screen characters that she played "defined themselves in their own terms and were comparatively independent of men and of household expectations."

Born Ruby Stevens on July 16, 1907, in Brooklyn, New York, Stanwyck was the fifth, and last, child of Byron and Catherine McGee Stevens, working-class immigrants from Massachusetts. When Ruby was three years old, her mother died, knocked to the ground by a drunkard after stepping off a streetcar. A few weeks after his wife's death, Ruby's father enlisted to join a work crew digging the Panama Canal and abandoned his family. Ruby grew up with an elder sister and in foster homes with her brother Byron, an experience that the actress never commented upon at length in later life. She just pointed out (Madsen 1994, 9) that where she grew up "kids existed on the brink of domestic or financial disaster." She also put down her determination to succeed to the poverty she experienced as a child. The accomplishments of other people from her neighborhood inspired her; they were "the promise and proof that we weren't puppets. Hapless, maybe, but not helpless, not hopeless. We were free to work our way out of our surroundings, free to work our way up—as far as we could dream of" (Madsen 1994, 10). At 13 Ruby left school and started to work as a wrapper of packages for a Brooklyn department store, although her true ambition was to become a chorus girl.

Barbara Stanwyck often played defiant and independent women that made her a favorite with lesbian audiences. Courtesy of Photofest.

She fulfilled her plans two years later when she was hired by a Times Square nightclub. After a few months in the club, she obtained a small part in the 1922 edition of the *Ziegfeld Follies.*

Ruby's career took off when she starred under the stage name of Barbara Stanwyck in the play *The Noose*, which became a big hit in the 1926 season, running for nine months and 197 performances. Stanwyck received positive reviews for her role and this led to Hollywood interest in the actress, who was then able to translate successfully her stage career to the big screen. Her Hollywood career started with the silent film *Broadway Nights* (1927) and continued with sound films throughout the 1960s. In spite of the flops of *The Locked Door* (1928) and *Mexicali Rose* (1929), her second and third film, Stanwyck was selected by Frank Capra for *Ladies of Leisure* (1930), where she portrayed the first of the strong and somewhat immoral women who made her a star. Her first Oscar nomination arrived in 1937 for *Stella Dallas*, directed by King Vidor. Stanwyck was also nominated for her performances in Billy Wilder's *Balls of Fire* (1941) and *Double Indemnity* and in Anatole Litvak's *Sorry, Wrong Number* (1948). Although she never won an Academy Award, she received a Honorary Award from the Academy in 1982 for her "unique contribution to the art of screen acting" and the American Film Institute gave her a Lifetime Achievement Award in 1987. Stanwyck had a reputation of a true professional, and she was considered one of the easiest screen stars of her era to manage on sets. Yet, she was notoriously more difficult with younger female co-stars.

Stanwyck reached the peak of her career in the 1940s thanks to films such as *Lady Eve* (1941), *Meet John Doe* (1941), and *Double Indemnity.* The strings of hits that she collected in the early 1940s made Stanwyck the highest paid woman in the United States in 1944. Few of her films of the 1950s and 1960s were as successful. She craved acting as she herself admitted: "I would go mad if I retired. I'm ready to work anytime. I'll take every part that comes along. I don't care about the money or the size of the role. All I care about is working" (Madsen 1994, 336). This often led Stanwyck to appear in films that were only worth watching for her performance. As her career started to decline in the late 1950s, the actress began appearing on television, one of the first Hollywood stars to make such a move. Her *Barbara Stanwyck Show* ran from1960 to 1961 and, although its ratings were not exceptional, it earned the actress her first Emmy. From 1965 to 1969, Stanwyck played the matriarch in the western series *The Big Valley.* Broadcast by ABC, the series made her one of the most popular TV stars and was worth a second Emmy. Stanwyck's performance in the steamy TV melodrama *Thorn Birds* (1983) gave the actress her third Emmy. In 1985 she joined the cast of *The Colbys*, a spin off from the more popular soap *Dynasty.* This was a largely disappointing experience for Stanwyck, who walked out at the end of the first season. Plagued by ill health due to her heavy smoking, Stanwyck died on January 20, 1990, in Santa Monica, California.

Throughout her career, Stanwyck kept her private existence as hidden as possible from the media, refusing to author an autobiography or collaborate with writers on a biography. In the last years of her life, publishers became insistent for the Stanwyck story, but she always rejected their offers, saying that she was incapable of total honesty: "I had a scrapbook as a kid, but I never wrote down the bad things that happened" (Madsen 1994, 356). Stanwyck married twice: in 1928, with established stage actor Frank Fay, and in 1939, with fellow star Robert Taylor. Both marriages, however, ended in divorce. Stanwyck's union with Fay lasted seven years, while the actress and Taylor divorced in 1951. Stanwyck and Fay also adopted a son, Dion, although he later became estranged from his mother. Stanwyck and Fay's marriage suffered from the actors' professional competition. While Fay was never able to translate his successful stage career to the screen, Stanwyck became a Hollywood star. Fay's resentment was certainly a factor in their divorce. Significantly, many film critics believe that the film *A Star Is Born* was modeled after the Stanwyck-Fay union. Stanwyck's marriage to Robert Taylor was equally turbulent after its early years due to enduring rumors about Taylor's extramarital affairs. Some critics have suggested that both of Stanwyck's marriages were in fact covers for her, and her husbands', homosexuality.

Axel Madsen (1994, 83) has pointed out that "people would swear that [Stanwyck] was . . . Hollywood's most famous closeted lesbian, that 'everybody' knew." Yet, he concludes, "unearthing the truth about her sexuality would remain impossible," as none of the people who proclaimed themselves sure of Stanwyck's lesbianism could substantiate their claim with definite evidence. What remains indisputable is the actress's 30-year long friendship with her press agent and career counselor Helen Ferguson. Stanwyck never defined herself by her feelings for Ferguson and no one ever publicly questioned their friendship as something more than a working relationship. Yet, according to Madsen (1994, 82), "their affection for each other was lasting." Ferguson lived on and off at the different Stanwyck estates, and she was always present at critical moments in the actress's life. The press agent was responsible for Stanwyck's off-screen persona and managed to talk to the media about the star without seriously revealing her innermost feelings.

Stanwyck was uncomfortable about the gay liberation movements of the 1970s and 1980s. Madsen writes that when asked by a gay activist about her sexuality, the actress threw him out of her house. Yet lesbians could identify with Stanwyck's screen persona throughout the star's career. Although she only played a lesbian once (in the critical and commercial flop *A Walk on the Wild Side*, 1962), Stanwyck acquired the status of icon within lesbian communities. They did not care whether the star's characters were required to marry on the screen. To them, Stanwyck was a woman whose life was arranged in such a way as to shun public censure, yet whose screen persona challenged respectability because of the strong and independent women she embodied during the 1940s. Her characters were also often able to manipulate men, signaling a different way of relating to the opposite sex than other stars. As the lesbian movement became more visible in the 1960s, the younger lesbians who animated it still considered Stanwyck an important point of reference. According to Madsen (1994, 338), Victoria Barkley, Stanwyck's character in *The Big Valley*, appealed to them even more than the actress's earlier roles. To them, Victoria seemed genderless and radiated a sense of control: "Here she was a woman in full possession of her powers—no man needed."

Further Reading

Kaplan, E. Ann ed. *Women in Film Noir.* London: BFI Publishing, 1998; Madsen, Axel. *Stanwyck.* New York: HarperCollins, 1994; McLellan, Diana. *The Girls: Sappho Goes to Hollywood.* New York: St. Martin's Griffin, 2000.

STEIN, GERTRUDE (1874–1946)

Gertrude Stein and her life partner Alice B. Toklas have achieved iconic status within gay and lesbian popular culture as the first fully visible lesbian couple. Until recent recuperation from feminist and gay critics, therefore, Stein was primarily notable as a personality and as the inventor of such famous phrases and expressions as "a rose is a rose is a rose" and "the Lost Generation." She was one of the leading animators of the modernist movement and, during the 1920s, her Parisian household became a vital center of social and intellectual debates where French artists mingled with American expatriates and other international visitors. Stein's social celebrity overshadowed her literary achievements. Stein was an extremely eclectic author who produced poems, novels, autobiographies, opera librettos, essays, and literary and art criticism. During her lifetime, however, her works were often turned down by publishers and, with the exception of the bestseller *The Autobiography of Alice B. Toklas* (1933), they were not widely read. Stein's experimental style made her literary pieces difficult and challenging, and some critics have argued that her work should be considered a forerunner of postmodernism. Others have also pointed out that the coded references to lesbianism in her books can prove disorienting for mainstream readers.

Gertrude Stein was born in Allegheny, Pennsylvania, on February 3, 1874, the youngest of five children. She grew up in a wealthy Jewish family of German background and spent most of her childhood between Vienna and Paris until her family settled down in Oakland, California, after Gertrude's fifth birthday. Stein's childhood and adolescence were marked by the premature death of both her parents. Her mother died when Stein was 14 and her father died in 1891, leaving Michael, the eldest brother, in charge of the family investments, which, skillfully managed, provided good incomes for the children throughout their lives. Stein received her high school education in Oakland and San Francisco. When her closest brother Leo went to Harvard University in 1892, Stein followed him, enrolling in the Harvard Annex (later known as Radcliffe College). There she took courses in philosophy and psychology with the leading intellectuals of the day such as George Santayana and William James. From 1897 to 1901, Stein studied medicine at Johns Hopkins Medical School in Baltimore, but never completed her degree. During her years at Medical School, Stein grew increasingly aware of her lesbianism. This new awareness led her to rebel against the constraining maternal roles assigned to women and the predominant views of female bodies of the period. Her interest in sexuality, however, also distanced her from contemporary feminists such as Charlotte Perkins Gilman, who considered sexuality as an obstacle for women to gain independence from men. Stein's decision to leave Johns Hopkins was also probably due to the unrequited love for May Bookstaver, a fellow student who was already involved with another woman, Mabel Haynes. Stein described her exclusion from the love triangle in her early work *Q.E.D.* (1903), which stands for the Latin phrase *quod erat demonstrandum* ("what is to be proved"). The novel was published posthumously as *Things As They Are* (1950). *Q.E.D.* treats lesbianism openly and its narration is linear; the novel is thus far from Stein's later works, which employ a heavily experimental style and only refer to lesbianism in a coded way.

After dropping out from Johns Hopkins in 1902, Stein lived in New York and London and in 1903 she joined her brother Leo in Paris at the studio at 27 rue de Fleurus, which became the writer's permanent home for the following three decades. Leo and Gertrude soon began to buy paintings by avant-garde artists such as Gauguin, Cézanne, Picasso, Braque, and Renoir, thus starting one of the most remarkable private collections of twentieth-century art. Picasso also became a close friend of Gertrude's and was the painter of her well-known 1906 portrait. Their friendship lasted from their first meeting at the Autumn Salon of 1905 until the writer's death 40 years later. In 1907 Stein met her lifelong companion, the American Alice Toklas. Toklas was a music student at the University of Washington in Seattle and a friend of Gertrude's brother Michael and his wife Sarah. When Toklas visited Europe, she was invited to stay at the Steins' apartment and was introduced to Gertrude. Toklas soon moved in permanently to the deterioration of Stein's relationship with Leo, who moved to Italy in 1913.

Stein's first major work was *Three Lives* (1909), a collection of three stories, each about a different working-class woman, including an African American, living in the Baltimore area in Maryland. The author claimed to have been influenced by Flaubert's *Trois Contes* and by Cézanne's painting *Portrait of Mme Cézanne*, which Stein had bought for her private art collection. According to Stein, Cézanne's mode of composition was characterized by a revolutionary technique that put equal emphasis on all elements in a composition. *Three Lives* is Stein's attempt to apply this democratic pictorial style to literary prose and subject matter. Contrary to the author's later works, *Three Lives* employs simple and repetitive diction. Centering on an African American woman, the novella "Melanctha" is the most relevant of the three for gay and lesbian popular culture as it features a lesbian subplot, which involves Melanctha's seduction by Jane Harden. Several critics have also pointed out that Melanctha's ensuing relationship with the African American doctor Jeff Campbell retains queer overtones. They read Campbell as a masculinized projection of Stein. Stein's disappointing relationship with Bookstaver still haunts the three narratives, in which the writer depicts the difficulty of establishing strong bonds between women.

Stein's following works were much less accessible and more experimental in style than *Three Lives*. Although published only in 1925, the epic novel *The Making of Americans* was largely written between 1906 and 1908. The novel chronicles the parallel histories of the Hersland and Dehning families. With *The Making of Americans*, Stein tried to liberate the genre of the novel from the moral and stylistic legacies of the Victorian era. The author clearly positions herself as an outsider rejected from American society who has had no other possibility but to expatriate. The short pieces collected in *Tender Buttons* (1914) blur the boundaries between poetry and prose, displaying a complex Cubist mode of composition. The language of *Tender Buttons* can also be interpreted as forming a lesbian code, where words referring to everyday objects such as pencils and boxes acquire an allusive erotic meaning. Lesbian themes are evident also in Stein's poems which often taken the form of a conversation between the author and Toklas. Both *The Making of Americans* and *Tender Buttons* were important works in the development of a modernist literary tradition and, to a certain extent, can be considered forerunners of postmodernism. Yet, because of their little accessibility and their avant-garde style, they met with limited commercial success and with critical ridicule. Their radical challenges to ordinary grammar, syntax, and semantics were often cited by critics as evidence of the author's inability to achieve literary seriousness. The writer was described as engaged in a process of automatic writing that demanded no conscious creative agency. Stein was frustrated by her inability to reach a large readership and the difficulty of finding a mainstream publisher for her works prompted her and Toklas to start their own publishing house.

At the outbreak of World War I, Stein and Toklas were in London to sign a contract for a British edition of *Three Lives,* and the war forced the couple to stay in Britain longer than expected. Stein and Toklas then spent a whole year in Spain, and, upon their return to France in 1916, they actively started to help with the war effort delivering supplies within the American Fund for French Wounded program. After the war, Stein's Parisian salon began to attract famous American expatriate artists such as Ernest Hemingway, Sherwood Anderson, Zelda and F. Scott Fitzgerald, Ezra Pound, T. S. Eliot, and Carl Van Vechten, who became one of the keenest promoters of Stein's work. It was during these years that Stein coined the famous phrase "The Lost Generation" and became the chief animator of the literary and artistic avant garde. In the first decades of the twentieth century, Paris emerged as the capital of modernity and international modernism. Stein's weekly gatherings played a key role in the development of this innovative literary and artistic movement. In the Paris of the 1910s and 1920s, Stein and Toklas also found a nurturing cultural and social milieu for their lesbianism. The French capital became well known for being also the underground capital of same-sex desire. In particular, thanks to the movements for women's liberation and to the growing social emancipation enjoyed by women, lesbianism acquired unprecedented visibility.

In spite of her inability to reach a large American audience during the 1920s, Stein was known to the American public thanks to reports on her Parisian salon and her friendship with artists. In her later work *Everybody's Autobiography* (1937), Stein complained that she was more familiar to the public as a social celebrity than as that literary genius that she hoped to be. The dichotomy between Stein's social and cultural influence on modernism and her commercial failures was finally resolved in 1933 with the publication of *The Autobiography of Alice B. Toklas.* The book radically altered Stein's reputation as an eccentric and difficult author, making her a popular writer and finally giving her that commercial success in her country of birth that had always eluded her. *The Autobiography* became an instant bestseller, it was selected by the Literary Guild and was serialized in the prestigious *Atlantic Monthly.* Departing from literary Cubism, Stein employed a more accessible and colloquial style to depict her relationship with Alice Toklas. After thousands of pages of experimental writing, Stein produced a gossipy memoir of her life in Paris narrated through the voice of Toklas. In spite of its title, *The Autobiography* retains Stein's life as much as Toklas's at its center. The book does not explicitly define the two women's relationship as a lesbian one, but makes no secret of the deep affection and commitment that Stein and Toklas felt for each other. *The Autobiography* is one of the very first positive depiction of a same-sex domestic arrangement in a bestselling book. Successive generations of Stein's scholars have dismissed *The Autobiography* as a work of little substance. Yet, the book, with its salacious and witty comments on the world's leading intellectuals, effectively launched Stein's commercial career. Her publisher immediately demanded a sequel, *Everybody's Autobiography*, which appeared in 1937. Its title points to the radical experimentation that, in spite of the plain language and colloquial style, Stein was carrying out with the autobiographical genre: one person's autobiography can serve as another's when it is liberated from the contingencies of either person's specific life experience. The autobiography of Alice B. Toklas may well function as the autobiography of Gertrude Stein.

Thanks to the success of *The Autobiography*, Stein and Toklas were catapulted to literary and social fame in the United States. In 1934 they were invited to the United States for a six-month cross-country lecture tour, which culminated with a reception at the White House and dinners with Hollywood personalities. During the tour, Stein also had the chance of seeing a production of her opera *Four Saints in Three Acts*, originally written in 1927, which contributed to establish her popular success. The oeuvre, with music by Virgil Thomson, sparked debates partly because of its all-black cast.

As Stein and Toklas returned to Paris in 1935, they found Europe overshadowed by the fascist threat. Both women were Jewish, so friends encouraged them to move back to America. Yet, they decided to stay in France, where Stein began to meditate on her sudden literary success, her identity and her American reception in *The Geographical History of America* (1936) and in the essay "What Are Masterpieces" (1940). The couple's situation became more precarious as Nazi troops occupied France and World War II escalated. Although Stein and Toklas lived in Bilingen, an area of France left unoccupied by the Germans, during the war, their status as Jews and, after Pearl Harbor, as enemies put the two women in serious danger. Yet, also thanks to the influence of Stein's French translator, Bernard Faÿ, who had been appointed director of the Bibliothèque Nationale by the puppet regime of Vichy, Stein and Toklas made it safely through the war. When American troops liberated the area around Bilingen in 1944, Stein's home became a gathering place for soldiers who could thus find a piece of America abroad. The world conflict had a clear impact on Stein's works. In her novel *Mrs. Reynolds* (1941), the writer describes the life of Mrs. Reynolds and her husband during an unnamed war between two dictators who are clearly modeled on Hitler and Stalin. After the end of the war, Stein and Toklas returned to Paris, where Stein wrote her war memoir, *Wars I Have Seen* (1945), which was published to great commercial and critical acclaim. Stein's many plans, including the composition of more librettos for operas by Virgil Thomson, were cut short by the first symptoms of illness in 1945. The following year, the writer was seriously ill and was taken to the American Hospital in Neuilly. The diagnosis confirmed that she had inoperable cancer. Stein died on July 27, 1946, and was buried in the Paris cemetery Père Lachaise. Toklas survived her by more than 20 years.

In her works, Stein revolutionized literary genres and language, trying to subvert the conventional associations that readers attach to specific words. Her characteristic repetitive style also attempts to create a so-called continuous present, which Stein considered the main feature of modernity. Although she mostly referred to lesbianism in a coded way, Stein's centrality in gay and lesbian culture should not be neglected. Throughout her works, Stein created an erotic imaginary that enabled her to write on topics considered taboos by her contemporaries.

Women in Stein's circle, for example, could detect that she used the word *cow* to mean "orgasm" and were thus able to read her story "As a Wife Has a Cow: A Love Story" with this double entendre in mind. Stein's erotic imaginary deserves careful scrutiny from queer critics so that the writer's iconic and personality status can finally be complemented with the establishment of her reputation as a serious innovator both in terms of literary technique and gender representation.

Further Reading

Benstock, Shari. *Women of the Left Bank: Paris, 1900–1940.* Austin: University of Texas Press, 1986; Caramello, Charles. *Henry James, Gertrude Stein, and the Biographical Act.* Chapel Hill: University of North Carolina Press, 1996; Dickie, Margaret. *Stein, Bishop, and Rich: Lyrics of Love, War and Place.* Chapel Hill: University of North Carolina Press, 1997; Gilmore, Leigh. "A Signature of Lesbian Autobiography: 'Gertrice/Altrude.'" *Autobiography and Questions of Gender.* Shirley Neuman, ed. London and Portland, OR: Frank Cass, 1991; Ruddick, Lisa. *Reading Gertrude Stein: Body, Text, Gnosis.* Ithaca, New York: Cornell University Press, 1990; Souhami, Diana. *Gertrude and Alice.* London: Pandora, 1991; Stimpson, Catherine R. "Gertrude Stein and the Lesbian Lie." *American Women's Autobiography: Fea(s)ts of Memory.* Margo Culley, ed. Madison: University of Wisconsin Press, 1992; Wineapple, Brenda. *Sister Brother: Gertrude and Leo Stein.* New York: Putnam's, 1996.

STIPE, MICHAEL (1960–)

The lead singer of American rock band R.E.M. and filmmaker Michael Stipe is well known for his distinctively brooding lyrics and for his social and political activism. His singing style has been described as mumbling, and Stipe pushes it to such an extent that the lyrics become at times indecipherable. As a political activist, Stipe took a firm stand against the Iraqi war and campaigned for the election of Democrat John Kerry in the 2004 Presidential election. R.E.M is usually considered one of the most liberal and politically correct groups in the United States. They have helped to raise funds for environmental, feminist, and human rights causes. "Idealism," Stipe argued in a 2003 interview (Sturges, *Independent* online), "has been the springboard for almost everything I've ever done." Yet, in spite of his political commitment, he has never particularly liked to answer questions about his sexuality. In the early 1990s, however, rumors about his homosexuality began to circulate and some people, always on the watch-out for the next **AIDS** celebrity, even hinted that he was HIV-positive. Stipe was forced to become more open about his sexuality, although he did not immediately identify himself as gay.

Stipe was born on January 4, 1960, in Decatur, Georgia. During the singer's childhood, his family moved often due to his father's job as a career military officer. Stipe grew up in several American military bases and he also spent several years in Germany. He attended high school in Illinois, and in 1978 he enrolled at the University of Georgia as an art student. At college he met Peter Buck, Mike

Mills, and Bill Berry, who all shared his interest in alternative music. All four students never completed their degrees, preferring instead to pursue a career as rockers and founding the band R.E.M. Their first single, "Radio Free Europe," was a huge success with college radio stations and helped them to get a recording contract with IRS Records. Their first full-length album was the critically acclaimed *Murmur* (1983), which *Rolling Stone* magazine chose as Album of the Year. This was only the first of a long string of hits which brought the band to sell more than 50 million copies of their albums worldwide. From their underground beginnings, the group spectacularly made it into the mainstream signing a first contract with Warner Brothers for $10 million and re-signing with the same label in 1996 for $80 million. Over their 20 years together, R.E.M have become one of the most successful groups in the history of rock and experienced an unusual longevity. Singles such as "Losing My Religion," "Shiny Happy People," and "Leaving New York" are classic contemporary ballads. R.E.M. reached the peak of their career in 2007 when they were inducted into the Rock and Roll Hall of Fame. Critics have assigned the band a pivotal role in the transition from post-punk to alternative rock and their influence can be heard in the music of Nirvana, Pearl Jam, and Radiohead. Stipe's lyrics, as well as his impetuous way of performing them, which markedly contrasts with his personal reserve, have been instrumental to the group's fame. Christopher Farley (2001, *Time* online) has qualified Stipe's lyrics as "characteristically erudite and elusive," superficially "random," but really aiming for "Proustian resonance."

Michael Stipe (second from left) with R.E.M. at the MTV awards. Courtesy of Photofest.

Since the late 1990s, Stipe has also been active as a film producer. He has founded two film companies, C-Hundred, based in New York, and Single Cell Productions in Los Angeles. Stipe's companies produce independent, arthouse releases such as *Velvet Goldmine* (1999), the Academy Award-nominated *Being John Malkovich* (1999), *American Psycho* (2000), and the controversial *Saved!* (2004), which explored the thorny issues of religious faith and sexual identity.

In spite of the media curiosity about his sexuality, Stipe eluded questions about his private life for a long time. He argued that he refused to categorize his sexuality and held that it was indecipherable, later specifying that he enjoyed both female and male partners. Yet, in the late 1990s, Stipe became more open about his queerness or at least he was forced to be by the persistent rumors that described him as gay: "I felt forced to talk about my sexuality, my queerness, just because I felt like I was being looked on as a coward for not talking about it, and I abhor that. I thought it was dead obvious to everyone all along—I was wearing skirts and mascara in 1981, on-stage and in photo-shoots. All the lyrics I have written, for the most part, with a few exceptions, are really gender unspecific" (VH1 profile, 1998). In a 2001 interview with Christopher Farley of *Time*, Stipe described himself as a "queer artist" and said that he had been "in a relationship with an amazing man." Yet, in a 2004 interview with the British newspaper *The Independent on Sunday* (McLean 2004, online edition), the singer denied that the *Time* interview was a coming out piece and that he felt frustrated because of what he described as his constant outing by the British press: "Somebody wrote that I have been outed by the UK press more times than Frank Sinatra sang 'My Way'! It just seems that every time there's a slow news day, I get pulled out of the closet again." Stipe maintained he had started to talk frankly about his sexuality openly to people beyond his family and friends in 1994: "I was on the cover of *Out Magazine* in 1995. I've been pretty frank about my sexuality for the better part of ten years, publicly, and privately since I was a teenager. Did it provoke some phenomenal change in my writing? No!" Stipe has also been critical of the media for giving credibility to the rumor that he had AIDS: "I wore a hat that said 'White House Stop AIDS.' I'm skinny. I have always been skinny....I think AIDS hysteria would obviously and naturally extend to people who are media figures and anybody of indecipherable or unpronounced sexuality. Anybody who looks gaunt, for whatever reason. Anybody who is associated, for whatever reason—whether it's a hat, or the way I carry myself—as being queer friendly."

The rising parable of Michael Stipe and R.E.M. shows that it is still possible to combine political commitment with commercial success.

Further Reading

Farley, Christopher John. "Michael Stipe and the Ageless Boys of R.E.M." *Time.* May 14, 2001. http://www.time.com/time/arts/article/0,8599,109715,00.html (accessed on September 8, 2007); McLean, Craig. "Angels in America." *The Independent on Sunday.* November 14, 2004. http://findarticles.com/p/articles/mi_qn4159/is_20041114/ai_n12762937/pg_3 (accessed on September 8, 2007); Sturges, Fiona. "Who Are You Calling an Elder Statesman?" *The Independent.* October 20, 2003: features section, 2–3. http://findarticles.com/p/articles/mi_qn

4158/is_20031020/ai_n12720664 (accessed on September 8, 2007); VH1 Behind the Music profile of R.E.M first aired on December 6, 1998.

STREISAND, BARBRA (1942–)

The Jewish-American actress, singer, and film director Barbra Streisand has become one of the biggest gay icons in twentieth-century popular culture, second only to Judy Garland. Her choice to embrace her ethnic difference rather than seeking to hide it, her determined rise from poverty to stardom, and her challenge to the limited standards of beauty of the Broadway and Hollywood industries have made Streisand an appealing personality for the gay community. Throughout her long career, Streisand has constantly refused to conform to the standards set for her by mainstream society. Streisand has also spoken in favor of gay rights, stating that they are not to be regarded as so-called special rights, but simply as civil rights which gays and lesbians should be able to enjoy like everyone else.

Barbra Joan Streisand was born on April 24, 1942, in New York City to Emmanuel Streisand, a high school English literature teacher, and Diana Rosen Streisand. Her childhood years were characterized by economic and emotional hardships as Barbra's father died of an epileptic seizure when she was just 15 months old. Streisand's mother had to take care of the family and she found a job as a school secretary. She also married a car salesman named Lou Kind. Barbra felt neglected by her mother and did not get on with her stepfather. The artist has repeatedly confessed that the privation of her youth led her to strengthen her determination to succeed and to improve her life. Her remarkable achievements started at an early age indeed. When she was 16, she graduated with honors from Erasmus High School in Brooklyn. Streisand did not attend university and tried instead to find work as a musician. In the late 1950s, she sang in nightclubs and bars, changing her first name, but leaving intact her surname, which, for many, sounded too Jewish. This exemplifies well Streisand's defiance of mainstream standards of acceptability, an attitude which made the artist popular with queers.

Barbra Streisand in Sidney Pollack's *The Way We Were* (1973). Courtesy of Columbia Pictures/Photofest.

Success finally arrived in the early 1960s and it came not for her acting, as she had always wished, but for her singing. After a few years spent singing at the Greenwich Village's Bon Soir Club and in off-Broadway productions, a Broadway producer signed her for the part of Miss Mamelstein in *I Can Get It for You Wholesale*. Opening in March 1962, the show ran for nine months and consolidated Streisand's image. Columbia Records produced two albums for her in 1963, the first of which won her first Grammys, including Best Album and Best Female Vocal. In spite of the political turmoil of the decade and Streisand's progressivism, the artist's repertoire from the 1960s does not contain references to the political situation. Streisand chose mainly to sing cover songs, often written before World War II. She was particularly fascinated by Fanny Brice, the *Ziegfeld Follies* star of the early decades of the twentieth century. Her musical nonconformity was instrumental to her success. Her albums sold well and, thanks to her knowledge of Fanny Brice, Streisand landed the leading role in the 1964 Broadway musical *Funny Girl*, which was based on Brice's life. Four years later, Streisand got the same part in the film adaptation of the musical and won the Academy Award for Best Actress, a prize she shared with Katharine Hepburn for her performance in *The Lion in Winter*.

The 1960s and the 1970s were full of successes for Streisand. *People*, released in 1964, became a top-selling album and earned the artist another Grammy. The popular and critical acclaim reserved for her albums also led to several television specials. After the Oscar for *Funny Girl*, Streisand also launched a career as an actress, starring in important if not always successful musicals such as *Hello Dolly!* (1969) and *On a Clear Day You Can See Forever* (1970). After these two musicals, Streisand tried her hand at comedy with *The Owl and the Pussycat* (1970) and *What's Up, Doc?* (1971). The artist proved that her acting abilities could sustain her in a diversity of genres when she starred in Sydney Pollack's drama about McCarthyism, *The Way We Were* (1973), which earned her an Oscar nomination as Best Actress. Her performance of the title song was also a phenomenal hit. Streisand returned to the musical genre with *Funny Lady* (1975), where she starred again as Brice, and *A Star Is Born* (1976). In spite of the differences between all these films, Streisand's film persona is often built in contrast with the rugged good looks of the male leads such as Robert Redford in *The Way We Were* and Kris Kristofferson in *A Star Is Born*. As the filmic narrative begins, Streisand is subordinate to the male characters. Her awkwardness is contrasted to Redford's self confidence, and her obscurity is opposed to Kristofferson's stardom. However, as the narrative develops, Streisand's characters emerge as the truly gifted ones and the male leads go into decline, becoming her shadow both in terms of personality and career.

In the 1970s, Streisand began to include pop hits on her albums, which, like the early ones, continued to sell well. During the decade, however, she decided to stop performing live following a death threat and attacks of stage fright. She only returned to live concerts in the 1993, when her tour sold out after a few hours from its announcement and was deemed by *Time* the music event of the century. Finishing the 1970s as the most successful American singer of the decade and as one of the top-grossing female stars at the box office, Streisand also began to work behind the camera in the 1980s and the 1990s. She directed *Yentl* (1983), *The Prince of Tides* (1991), and *The Mirror Has Two Faces* (1996), all of which received awards and nominations. After a long period away from the screen, Streisand made a major comeback with the hugely successful sequel to the comedy *Meet the Parents* (2000), *Meet the Fockers* (2004). Although cast in a supporting role as Ben Stiller's overbearing mother, Streisand's performance was central to the movie's success.

Throughout her career, Streisand has always taken her audiences and critics by surprise, refusing to be pigeon-holed into a music or film genre. She has also consistently rejected uncritical conformity to standards defining what is acceptable and what is not. She has always emphasized, rather than downplayed, what differentiated her from the mainstream. This aspect of her personality was clear in the artist's stance in favor of gay and lesbian rights. On gay marriages and gay parenting, for example, she stated that "[t]here is no one 'perfect' model on which all family structures can be based. If we surveyed human history, we would see representations of every type of possible social arrangement. There is no 'standard' to which all families must adhere to. The idea that anyone can impose their image of what a 'normal' family should be on others seems absurd to me. We all come from different backgrounds, cultures, and traditions and have different understandings of what a family looks like" (Wieder 1999, *Advocate* online). Declarations such as this, together with her iconoclastic attitude, have made Barbra Streisand a favorite with the gay and lesbian movement.

Further Reading

Andersen, Christopher. *Barbra: The Way She Is*. New York: William Morrow, 2006; Dennen, Barry. *My Life with Barbra*. Amherst: Prometheus Books, 1997; Edwards, Anne. *Streisand: A Biography*. Boston: Little Brown & Company, 1997; Riese, Randall. *Her Name Is Barbra*. New York: Birch Lane Press, 1993; Santopietro, Tom. *The Importance of Being Barbra*. New York: Thomas Dunne Books, 2006; Spada, James. *Streisand: Her Life*. New York: Ballantine Books, 1995; Wieder, Judy. "Interview with Barbra Streisand." *The Advocate*. August 17, 1999. http://www.highbeam.com/doc/1G1-55316114.html (accessed on October 25, 2006).

SYLVESTER (1946–1988)

African American singer and drag performer Sylvester was one of the most talented figures of the 1970s and 1980s disco music. He contributed crucial songs to the disco songbook as well as ballads which proved his versatility as an artist. Sylvester represented the gay black roots of mainstream disco. According to Anthony Thomas (1995), he helped the gay black subculture to re-appropriate the disco impulse. With his music, particularly the super hit "You Make Me Feel (Mighty Real)," the singer emphasized the link between gay sexuality and the disco beat. His work, together with his insistence not to be butched up by producers, paved the way for the acceptance of drag performers like **RuPaul** into the mainstream of popular culture and was influential for many gay and straight singers such as Prince, **The Village People**, Bette Midler, and Jimmy Sommerville.

Born Sylvester James in 1946 (although 1944 and 1947 are sometimes given as his years of birth), the artist grew up in a bourgeois family in Los Angeles. His grandmother was the blues singer Julia Morgan, who exposed the child to African American music from an early age and encouraged him to sing. Sylvester entered the choir at the Pentecostal Palm Lane Church of God and Christ in South Los Angeles, where he was immediately noticed for his distinctive and powerful voice. The child was in great demand as a gospel singer in Los Angeles churches and at gospel conventions in California. His childhood and adolescence, however, were not happy ones, plagued by a difficult relationship with his parents and a growing awareness of his homosexuality. His education was irregular and he increasingly felt constrained in Los Angeles. In 1967 Sylvester moved to San Francisco, the city that would come to be associated most closely with his successful career. There he re-invented himself and felt free of family ties. He started to perform in drag clubs, inspired by the figure of blues singer Billy Holiday, but he also continued to sing gospel in churches. In addition, he joined the experimental theater group The Crockettes, whose revues soon became a successful part of San Francisco's **camp** subculture of the early 1970s. However, after a disappointing debut in New York, the group dissolved in 1972.

After his experience with The Crockettes, Sylvester contemplated a solo career, but formed instead his Hot Band in 1973. The group signed a contract with Blue Thumb Records. Sylvester fronted the band in drag as a glamorous diva. The Hot Band, which also included future *Weather Girls* Izora Rhodes and Martha Wash, released the LP *Lights Out* and two more rock-oriented works, securing a cult following in San Francisco. However, it was a chance encounter with former Motown producer Harvey Fuqua that allowed Sylvester to reach a much wider audience. Recognizing his promising talent, Fuqua persuaded the singer to go solo and sign with Fantasy Records. His first album, *Fantasy* (1977), failed to attract considerable attention, but his second one, *Step II* (1978), gave Sylvester international fame. Born out of the collaboration with remixer Patrick Cowley, *Step II* marked the artist's shift towards disco music and made Sylvester an icon of the genre. The songs "You Make Me Feel (Mighty Real)," originally a gospel piece, and "Dance (Disco Heat)" instantly became dance hits and, with the years, acquired a long-standing reputation as dance classics. Within the gay community, "You Make Me Feel" has also come to be considered a sort of international anthem. As Jake Austen (1997, Roctober online) has claimed, "You Make Me Feel" locates the disco as the place where gayness could be openly expressed; the artist's falsetto "voice describes the ecstasy of the disco, the love, passion and lust he feels for his partner on the dance floor, and the orgasmic intensity of the experience as a whole." *Step II*, which was awarded three Billboard Disco Forum awards, was followed by *Stars* in 1979, and, in that same year, Sylvester was named Best Male Disco Act by *Disco International Magazine*. He also appeared in the Bette Midler's vehicle *The Rose*.

Sylvester and Fuqua released together three more albums, including the double live-recorded *Living Proof* (1979), but they eventually split over the producer's concerns that the artist's outrageousness and excessive disco style were not well-suited to the 1980s. Sylvester then signed a contract with Megatone, the label of his friend and collaborator Patrick Cowley. His first album with Megatone, *All I Need* (1982), included another dance classic "Do You Wanna Funk?," which gave a more aggressive treatment to the themes already explored in "You Make Me Feel (Mighty Real)." The song was a great hit and set the standard for the future Hi-NRG music. Two more albums followed for Megatone, *Call Me* and *M-1015*. The latter became a particular hit with gay audiences and includes the explicit "Sex." However, Sylvester's collaboration with Cowely was cut short by the onslaught of **AIDS** as Cowely was one of the first showbiz personalities to succumb to the virus.

When his contract with Megatone expired, Sylvester finally landed a contract with a major record company, Warner Brothers, for his upcoming album *Mutual Attraction*. In 1986 he also fulfilled one of his long-standing dreams, that of singing with Aretha Franklin for her album *Who's Zooming Who?*. Working for Warner gave the artist the wealth of technical and financial resources that he had always hoped for. However, he was unable to take full advantage of them as he was diagnosed with AIDS. The artist spent his last months working to raise awareness about the illness and made his last public appearance at San Francisco Gay Pride Parade in 1987. He was particularly concerned that the virus was still thought of as a white male disease. He found that the black community was still so far behind in getting information about HIV although the virus had hit African American men particularly hard. His decision to go public about his status was motivated by the urge to give other people the courage to face the virus. He died on December 17, 1988, in San Francisco.

Sylvester did not simply leave a great gay musical legacy to popular culture, rather, his example as a gay man who never compromised his gayness on the way to stardom can be inspirational for many generations of queers to come.

Further Readings

Austen, Jake. "Sylvester." *Roctober* 19 (1997): http://www.roctober.com/roctober/greatness/sylvester.html; Gamson, Joshua. *The Fabulous Sylvester: The Legend, the Music, the 70s in San Francisco*. New York: Henry Holt and Co, 2005; Larkin, Colin. "Sylvester." *The Encyclopedia of Popular Music*. 3rd. ed. New York: Muze, 1998. 7: 5270–5271; Thomas, Anthony. "The House the Kids Built: The Gay Black Imprint on American Dance Music." *Out in Culture: Gay, Lesbian and Queer Essays on Popular Culture*. Corey K. Creekmur and Alexander Doty, eds. Durham, North Carolina: Duke University Press, 1995. 437–445.

T

Tewksbury, Mark (1968–)

In December 1998, Olympic swimmer champion Mark Tewksbury became the first Canadian athlete to come out publicly as a gay man. His announcement drew a great deal of media attention. Even before his official coming out, Tewksbury had lost a lucrative contract as a motivational speaker for a financial corporation because he was felt to be too gay. Tewksbury's coming out raised debates over corporate discrimination as well as over homophobia in the world of sport. Tewksbury has frankly denounced the hostile climate against queers in sports in his autobiography *Inside Out: Straight Talk from a Gay Jock* (2006). The swimmer's private and professional biography closely resembles those of other North American athletes who have come out as gay such as **Greg Louganis** and **Billy Bean**. Closeted throughout his sport career, Tewksbury has become a vocal supporter of queer causes. The athlete has been particularly active in making the world of sport more hospitable to gays and lesbians and, to this end, he has held important positions such as co-president of the 2006 World Outgames in Montreal and board member of the Gay and Lesbian Athletics Foundation.

Born on February 7, 1968, Mark was adopted by Roger and Donna Tewksbury. The family spent the first five years of Mark's life in Calgary, Alberta. As Tewksbury's father worked for an oil company, he was transferred to Texas and the whole family moved to Dallas. Tewksbury first took his first swimming lessons while in Texas and continued to train once back in Calgary a few years later. As with other gay athletes, sport represented an important emotional outlet for Tewksbury who was conscious of his sexual orientation from an early age and felt very self-conscious about it. As he tells in his autobiography, he experienced an oppressive sense of loneliness and homophobic bullying at school. Tewksbury changed schools, but his condition did not improve. The burden of homophobia proved so harsh and heavy to bear that Tewksbury considered suicide as a way out from an unbearable situation. "I would never actually hurt myself," he stated (2006, 35), "but the depths of my self-loathing and desperation in wanting to be something different than what I was pushed me dangerously close." Too honest to keep up pretending to be straight and date girls, and too afraid to establish a romantic relationship with a male, Tewksbury devoted all his efforts to swimming. In 1985 he represented Canada in the Pan Pacific Championships, finishing eighth in the 100-meter backstroke, his specialty. This first important competition marked the beginning of impressive achievements for the swimmer, who won gold in the same specialty at the next two Pan Pacific Championships and swept the silver medal at the 1991 edition. He was also a member of the medley relay teams that won gold and silver medals at the Pan Pacific Games in 1987 and 1991 and at the Commonwealth Games in 1986 and 1990.

At the Olympic Games in 1988, Tewksbury contributed to the silver medal of the Canadian relay team, but arrived only fifth in the 100-meter backstroke. Without losing his determination, the athlete managed to land a profitable contract as a motivational speaker for a corporate group that gave him the necessary financial resources to train for the next Olympic Games scheduled for 1992 in Barcelona. There Tewksbury won the gold medal in the 100-meter backstroke, also setting the new world record for the event. This victory transformed the swimmer into a Canadian national hero and earned him the cover of *Time* magazine. In addition to being inducted to the Canadian Olympic Hall of Fame, he was named the Canadian Male Athlete of the Year.

Tewksbury's fame led to advertisement deals, but also to increasing media attention due to his lack of girlfriends. Rumors of his supposed homosexuality began to surface, making the athlete more uncomfortable about his closeted status. "Someone," Tewksbury recalls (Hays 2006, *Montreal Mirror* online), "would come up to me and say, 'You're a hero, you're doing all these amazing things!' I would walk away, and I would think to myself, 'Would you still think this if you really knew me?' I felt very dishonest about the double life I was leading." After coming out to his family, Tewksbury emigrated to Australia, where, in 1995, he completed a political science degree that he had started nine years before in Canada. He was, however, back in Canada when he was given the opportunity to represent his mother country on the International Olympic Committee (IOC). This was a disappointing experience for Tewksbury, who was appalled at the corruption surrounding the administration of Juan Antonio Samaranch. Tewksbury led a vocal group of athletes, Olympic Athletes Together Honorably (OATH), who fought for the removal of Samaranch as the IOC President. Tewksbury eventually resigned from his position as Canadian representative in 1999.

At the same time, the swimmer, who had began to live his homosexuality more openly, decided to officially come out and organized to do so during a one-man show *Out & About*, whose profits would go to a Toronto AIDS hospice. The show took place on December 15, 1998, although his coming out story had already been leaked by the morning edition of Toronto's newspaper *Globe and Mail*. Since his coming out, Tewksbury has supported gay and lesbian causes. He has also invested his fame as an athlete to make homosexuality more visible in sports and fight the pernicious effects of homophobia. He has worked for the Gay Games Federation, and, after strong disagreements with the Federation's decision to award the 2006 Gay Games to Chicago rather than Montreal, he co-founded the Gay and Lesbian International Sports Association (GLISA). The association became the sponsor of the first World Outgames, which took place in Montreal in 2006. For his entire career as a swimmer, Tewksbury felt obliged to remain in the closet. Yet, he is op-timistic that things are changing. In a 2006 interview with Matthew Hays for the *Montreal Mirror*, he stated: "I see a time when someone in a team sport could come out. I think it will happen, probably in the next five years. When that barrier is first broken, it'll be a big deal. But by the third time, it will no longer be. In my day, you stayed closeted because you risked losing everything—your coach, your job, your financial backing. In 2006, being gay simply doesn't mean the same level of public disdain that it did."

Further Reading

Hays, Matthew. "Golden Girl. Mark Tewksbury's flaming new memoir reveals a slew of contradictions." *Montreal Mirror*. http://www.montrealmirror.com/2006/041306/news1.html (accessed on February 10, 2007); Tewksbury, Mark. *Inside Out: Straight Talk from a Gay Jock*. Mississauga, Ontario: John Wiley & Sons Canada, 2006.

Tom of Finland (1920–1991)

The Finnish illustrator Tom of Finland has made a fundamental contribution to the creation of a gay male erotic imagination, acquiring a large cult following and influencing the work of other gay artists such as photographers **Robert Mapple-thorpe** and **Bruce Weber** and film director Rainer Werner Fassbinder. His draw-ings exude sheer male erotic energy and offer an extreme version of masculinity. They characteristically feature muscled and well-endowed hunks who joyfully engage in sexual intercourse and orgies. Tom of Finland was not afraid of classify-ing his photographs as pornographic as they are meant to sexually arouse viewers.

Tom of Finland was born Touko Laaksonen in the village of Kaarina, Finland, on May 8, 1920. When he was 19, he moved from his native village to Helsinki to attend art school and began to develop a particular interest for erotic art. In 1940, as a result of the Winter War between Finland and the Soviet Union, Tom was drafted into the Finnish Army where he also served during the World War II. After the conflict, the artist worked in advertising as a freelance and continued to draw. He soon became a visible member of Helsinki's bohemian life, although he was always uneasy about the effeminacy of certain homosexuals. As his biographer F. Valentine Hooven has made clear (1993, 49), Tom did not fit in many post-war homosexual circles because "public gay life was, in post-war Finland, the reign of the queen." Tom's drawings reflect his yearning for masculine gay men and also react against an-other feature of 1950s society: its sexual repression and conformity. Gay men were made to feel guilty about their sexuality. To counter this tendency, Tom's drawings feature men who are positive and confident in their sexuality: "I knew—right from the start—that *my* men were going to be proud and happy men" (Hooven 1993, 88). Not surprisingly, drawings which subverted so radically the predominantly negative notion of homosexuality widespread in the 1950s were immediate hits within the gay community.

In the mid-1950s, Tom sent several of his drawings to the **muscle magazine** *Physique Pictorial*, which, under the bodybuilding cover, was really a magazine done by and for gay men. His work was enthusiastically received by the editor who chose one of Tom's drawings for the Spring 1957 issue, signing it with the pseudonym Tom of Finland. The lumberjack featured on the cover was the first of a series of hyper-masculine types that peopled Tom's drawings. More characters soon appeared in Tom's erotic imaginary, including sailors, policemen, prison guards, and leather bikers. Tom's work began to circulate in the United States, and the artist himself made regular visits to the country since the 1970s when he was finally able to give up his advertising job and work full time as an artist. Portraying as they did gay men in an affirmative light, Tom's drawings were particularly daring at a time when censorship laws were strict. They had a double function, both of inspiration for and as a mirror of the gay liberation movement. They were inspiring for the visibility that they gave to gay men and for their refusal to equate gayness with effeminacy. Yet, they also mirrored the different phases of gay liberation as they became increasingly explicit as censorship laws relaxed. While full frontal nudity is avoided in his early drawings, his later images prominently feature men with huge penises engaging in sexual acts of different types, including S-M. The men's members often occupy the center of the composition, and their unbelievable sizes signify the realm of erotic fantasy in which the characters move.

Since the late 1970s, Tom's work has been exhibited at art galleries both in the United States and worldwide, blurring the boundaries between pornography and art, popular culture and mainstream cultural products. In 1979 Tom formed the Tom of Finland Company in partnership with businessman Durk Dehner, which later evolved into the Tom of Finland Foundation. Since the artist's death on November 7, 1991, the Foundation has been responsible for keeping interest in Tom's work alive and for looking for new talents in gay male erotic art. Although the name of Tom of Finland has become synonymous with gay erotica, the artist's work has attracted controversial comments even from certain quarters of the gay community and from progressive critics. His reliance on hyper-masculine types in his drawings, for example, has been criticized as validating notions of patriarchy and racism, a reading which is often supported by calling attention to a series of early drawings featuring Nazi characters. The artist openly disavowed these early drawings, which form a comparatively small part of his large oeuvre, and stated that he was interested in Nazi soldiers not as bearers of a particular ideology but because "they had the sexiest uniforms": "In my drawings I have no political statements to make, no ideology. I am thinking only about the picture itself. The whole Nazi philosophy, the racism and all that, is hateful to me" (Hooven 1993, 30). Criticism of Tom's hyper-masculine men also underestimates the subversion of sexual roles in the artist's drawings, which often feature muscled men as the passive object of gay sex. In spite of the controversies generated by his work, Tom of Finland is an enduring icon of gay popular culture. He has contributed images of homosexuality radically different from the invisible and negative ones prevalent in mainstream society. As Micha Ramakers has put it in his book-length study *Dirty Pictures* (2000, xi), Tom of Finland "invented a (pretty butch) fairy-tale gay universe in which masculinity was held up as the highest ideal."

Further Reading

Blake, Nayland. "Tom of Finland: An Appreciation." *Out in Culture. Gay, Lesbian and Queer Essays on Popular Culture.* Corey K. Creekmur and Alexander Doty, eds. London: Cassell, 1995; Hooven, F. Valentine III. *Tom of Finland: His Life and Times.* New York: St. Martin's Press, 1993; Hooven, F. Valentine III. *Beefcake: The Muscle Magazines of America, 1950–1970.* Cologne: Benedikt Taschen Verlag, 1996; Ramakers, Micha. *Dirty Pictures: Tom of Finland, Masculinity, and Homosexuality.* London: St. Martin's Press, 2000; Ramakers, Micha. *Tom of Finland: The Art of Pleasure.* Cologne: Taschen, 1998; Tom of Finland Foundation, Official Web site. http://www.tomoffinlandfoundation.org/foundation/N_Tom.html (accessed on October 25, 2006).

TOMLIN, LILY (1939–)

Throughout her career as a stage, screen, and television actress, American Academy Award-nominated performer Lily Tomlin has demonstrated a remarkable versatility in portraying different characters from all strata of society. Although she only officially came out in 2000, her long-term relationship with Jane Wagner was never denied and Tomlin's lesbianism was an open secret. In addition, even before her coming out, the actress has consistently spoken in support of queer causes and has lent her acting talents to give more visibility to gay and lesbian themes on screen and in popular culture in general.

Born Mary Jean Tomlin on September 1, 1939, Tomlin grew up in Detroit where her working-class parents had moved from Kentucky. Her family was from a Southern Baptist religious background, but Tomlin realized at a very early age that she could never be a religious fundamentalist. The idea of adults flailing and beating their breasts was always ridiculous and embarrassing to Tomlin. While she found the Baptist milieu stifling, she loved the preaching for its theatricality. Tomlin developed a serious interest for acting while a student at Wayne State University and soon moved to New York to pursue a comedy career and study with Charles Nelson Reilly. She held odd jobs during the day to support herself and played at stand-up clubs in the evenings. In 1966 she made her first appearance on television on *The Garry Moore Show* and she then landed a part in the NBC's sketch

Lily Tomlin as telephone operator Ernestine, one of her most popular characters. Courtesy of NBC/Photofest.

comedy show *Laugh In*. The characters that she embodied for that show greatly contributed to her success and have become part of her long-standing repertoire. They included the caustic telephone operator Ernestine and the five-year-old brat Edith Ann. Ernestine, in particular, proved so popular that the telephone company AT&T offered Tomlin a contract for a commercial with her character. Tomlin refused at the time, but, decades later, she accepted to shoot two commercials as Ernestine for the video-conferencing services company WebEx. The fact that the character was still of interest for commercial purposes in 2003 is the best evidence of Tomlin's enduring popularity.

In 1971 Tomlin met Jane Wagner, who became her life partner and also her closest artistic collaborator. Her successful participation on the *Laugh In* show opened new possibilities for Tomlin's career and the actress began appearing in films too. In 1975 director Robert Altman selected Tomlin to play Linnea Reese in *Nashville*. In the film, Tomlin plays a mother of two deaf children who has an affair with the country singer played by Keith Carradine. For that role Tomlin received an Academy Award nomination for Best Supporting Actress. Throughout the 1970s, she was awarded three Emmys and a Grammy for her comedy albums and programs. These, mostly one-woman comedy shows, remained Tomlin's favorite artistic expressions and include *Appearing Nitely* (1977), *Lily—Sold Out* (1981), and the Tony-winning *The Search for Signs of Intelligent Life in the Universe* (1985), written by Wagner. Tomlin was graced with a *Time* cover in 1977 which hailed her as the "New Queen of Comedy." Although the film *Moment by Moment* (1978), directed by her companion Jane Wagner, was panned by critics and was a commercial flop, Tomlin made her major screen comeback with the comedy *Nine to Five* (1980), in which she co-starred with Jane Fonda and Dolly Parton. She has continued to collaborate with Robert Altman, appearing in his films *Short Cuts* (1993) and *A Prairie Home Companion* (2006). Tomlin has also had recurring roles in hit television series such as *Murphy Brown, Will and Grace*, and *The West Wing*.

Tomlin did not openly talk about her lesbianism until 2000 and her coming out was not as dramatic as that of other Hollywood and showbiz personalities. "[I]n most articles, most people refer to Jane as my partner or my life-partner or whatever," Tomlin explained to Ann Northrop on cable-access program *Gay TV* in 2000. "We've been around so long and been through so much and I always kind of took a lot of stuff for granted." Yet, throughout her career, Tomlin never denied her relationship with Jane Wagner and was not afraid of supporting battles for gay and lesbian rights, also trying to choose roles that suited her personal political beliefs. In her 1975 comedy album *Modern Scream*, she famously played a journalist grilling Tomlin about her film role in Robert Altman's *Nashville* and asking her how she had felt to play a heterosexual woman. Tomlin, impersonating herself, responded that she had been exposed to heterosexuals and observed them throughout her life, so that she knew how to play them. The fake interview obviously positioned the actress as not straight. In Franco Zeffirelli's film *Tea with Mussolini* (1999), Tomlin was cast in an explicit lesbian role and, in *The Beverly Hillbillies* (1993), she appeared in the same role played by lesbian actress Nancy Kulp in the 1960s TV series upon which the film is based. More important than these coded nods to the queer community have been Tomlin's efforts in supporting gay and lesbian causes. The actress agreed to participate in important movies such as *And the Band Played On* (1993), exposing the completely inadequate governmental response to the **AIDS** crisis. She has also narrated the documentary *The Celluloid Closet* (1996), based on Vito Russo's pioneering work on film representations of gays and lesbians. Tomlin's contribution to the advancement of queer rights has been openly celebrated by the Gay and Lesbian Center in Los Angeles, which has established a new performing arts center in the name of the actress and her partner: The Lily Tomlin Jane Wagner Cultural Arts Center. Proceeds from ticket sales there go to providing health services for HIV positive patients.

Further Reading

Duralde, Alonso. "Thoroughly Modern Lily." *The Advocate*. March 15, 2005. http://www.highbeam.com/doc/1G1-131280347.html (accessed on May 15, 2007): Minkowitz, Donna. "In Search of Lily Tomlin." *The Advocate* 589 (November 5, 1991): 78–82; Sorensen, Jeff. *Lily Tomlin: Woman of a Thousand Faces*. New York: St. Martin's Press, 1989.

TROCHE, ROSE (1964–)

With her films, particularly *Go Fish* (1994) and *Bedrooms and Hallways* (1998), and her work for the hit TV series *Six Feet Under* and the groundbreaking *The L Word*, lesbian director Rose Troche has made male and female homosexuality more visible in American popular culture. Her works present sexual difference in an assertive and positive light, avoiding the tormented and self-hating characters that all too often constitute the celluloid representatives of queers. As other queer directors such as **Gus Van Sant** and **Todd Haynes**, Troche has made a successful transition from her underground beginnings to quality mainstream cinema and TV, directing stars such as Glenn Close and Jennifer Beals.

Rose Troche was born in Chicago in 1964 to a family of Puerto Rican origins and grew up on the city's north side until she was in her teens. Her family then moved to the suburbs, attracted by the improvement of their social status implied in the move. Yet, the family never quite fit in the new environment. "My parents thought moving to the suburbs was a sign of success," recalls Troche in an interview with the *Advocate* (Stukin 2003, online edition), but, she also adds, "[w]e were always the family that made everyone say, 'There goes the neighborhood.'" The anxieties of suburbia, hidden under a hypocritical coat of respectability and decorum, are the subject of Troche's third film, *The Safety of Objects* (2001). Troche developed an interest in film while working part time in a Chicago movie theater and later enrolled at the University of Illinois where she majored in art history. She then stayed on as a graduate film student. While still a film student, Troche directed several short films and met Guinevere Turner, who became her partner and her major collaborator for the project that eventually became *Go Fish*.

Based upon Troche and Turner's experiences within the lesbian community in Chicago, *Go Fish* was a difficult film to make as it was almost entirely self-financed by the two artists. In addition, when the film was planned, lesbians and, particularly, lesbian

Marlee Matlin, Jennifer Beals, and Cybill Shepherd in the fourth season of Rose Troche's lesbian series *The L Word*. Courtesy of Showtime/Photofest. Photograph by Naomi Kaltman.

sexuality were still invisible in the media. Yet, when the film premiered at the Sundance Film Festival in 1994, it was incredibly well received and was soon acquired by the Samuel Goldwyn Company for its distribution. The film was a sleeper hit and proved the marketability of lesbian issues for the film industry. The narrative of *Go Fish* is unconventional, broken up by dialogues that discuss lesbian issue and even the responsibility of queer filmmakers of representing their own community on screen. The protagonists of the film's lesbian love story, Max and Ely, are filmmakers, and Max's roommate Kia teaches a women's studies class that aims to recover the obscured history of lesbianism.

Although the film made Troche an overnight sensation, her career took time to develop. Troche, who, by the end of the shooting, had split up from Turner, felt that the film was too politically correct and that it threatened to confine her to lesbian-themed projects. When promoting her next, larger-budget film *Bedrooms and Hallways*, the director complained that audiences and critics considered her "a professional queer," a fact that she sometimes hated: "*Go Fish* made me such a card-carrying member. It is, like, boring. I go into interviews for *Bedrooms and Hallways* and all anyone can talk about is being gay, gay, gay" (Feinstein 1999, *Advocate* online). Shot in London, *Bedrooms and Hallways* was also about being gay, although Troche's focus this time was on male sexuality and bonding. Contrary to *Go Fish*, Troche could count on the financial backing of a major studio and the film went on to win the Audience Award at the 1998 London Film Festival. Centering on Leo (Kevin McKidd), an openly gay furniture-maker, and his two housemates Darren (Tom Hollander), a flamboyant screaming queen, and Angie (Julie Graham), a straight woman, *Bedrooms and Hallways* is a sex farce that tries to challenge conventional and rigid views on gender and sexual orientation. The film, which, at a certain point, may hint that Leo is going straight, celebrates the fluidity of sexuality. In an interview about the movie (Feinstein 1999, *Advocate* online), Troche said she really wanted to make a film "that's genderless, without sexual identity and politics." After the militant tone of *Go Fish*, many were disappointed by the ending of *Bedrooms and Hallways*, which leaves Leo with a woman, Sally. Some critics went on as far as claiming that the film rejected queerness and celebrated the crossover to heterosexuality for commercial reasons. Troche's response hinged on the necessity to "opening up of the parameters of the definition of homosexuality. And sexuality cannot just be based on ultimately who you fuck. When I say I'm a lesbian, that's said with saying that I've had as much sex with men as with women in my life. People could say I'm a traitor, but the reason that I say I'm not is when I imagine in my mind who I'd be spending time with, and I imagine myself with a woman" (Krach, Indiewire online).

The director's third film, *The Safety of Objects* (2001), brought Troche back to the United States and to the suburban life of her childhood. Based on several stories by A. M. Homes, the film stars Glenn Close and Dermot Mulroney. It follows the events which affect four suburban families who, by the end of the movies, will find their lives are interconnected in ways they could not imagine. In her portrayal of American suburbia, Troche depicts alienation with humor and her choice to give the characters a part in each others' lives alters the sense of loneliness pervading A. M. Homes's separate stories.

Troche has also been active in quality television productions. She has directed episodes of HBO's critically acclaimed series *Six Feet Under* (2001–2005), and she is the co-executive producer and writer of Showtime's *The L Word*, a popular series about a group of Los Angeles lesbians of which she has also directed several episodes. At the time of writing (2007), the show entered its fifth season and continues to provoke debates within queer communities because of its unconventional representation of lesbianism. *The L Word* has gone beyond the mere boundaries of a television show, launching a social networking site OurChart.com and enjoying an increasing popularity on Second Life.

Further Reading

Feinstein, Howard. "Bedrooms and Cameras." *The Advocate*. September 14, 1999. http://www.highbeam.com/doc/1G1-55927488.html (accessed on June 10, 2007); Krach, Aaron. "Rose Troche Goes from Fishing to British Farce with 'Bedrooms & Hallways.'" http://www.indiewire.com/people/int_Troche_Rose_990902.html (accessed on June 10, 2007); Stuckin, Stacie. "Rose to the Occasion." *The Advocate*. March 18, 2003. http://www.highbeam.com/doc/1G1-9985 0231.html (accessed on June 10, 2007).

V

VAN SANT, GUS (1952–)

Throughout his career, gay director Gus Van Sant has displayed a remarkable versatility. He has worked on mainstream films with superstars (including Sean Connery and Robin Williams), music videos, more personal productions focusing on gay plots such as *Mala Noche* (1985) and *My Own Private Idaho* (1991), and fictionalized reconstruction of events like Kurt Cobain's suicide (*Last Days*, 2005) and high school massacres (*Elephant*, 2003). Even in his more mainstream productions, however, Van Sant has remained faithful to his unwillingness to conform; when *My Own Private Idaho* came out, he said: "I identify...with queer punks. I always fight against anything that suggests conformity" (Ehrenstein 1994, 388). Van Sant has also stated that he is interested in sociopathic people, both in his life and movies. His films explore queer and other subcultures without feeling compelled to offer positive role models.

In spite of his nonconformity, the director was born into an upper-middle-class, wealthy family in Louisville, Kentucky, on July 24, 1952. In 1970 he entered the Rhode Island School of Design. His major interest then was painting. However, Van Sant soon discovered the experimental filmmaking of **Andy Warhol** and the Beat literature of William Burroughs, both of which constitute major influences upon his own style. After releasing a series of commercials and shorts, he shot his first film, *Mala Noche*, in 1985. Set in Portland, as many other Van Sant's movies are, the story focuses on the unrequited love of a liquor store clerk for a Mexican hustler, who quickly understands that he can exploit the clerk to his own advantage. Van Sant already displays in this debut film his distinctive visual skills. *Mala Noche* won the Los Angeles Critics' Award as best independent film.

Van Sant's second feature *Drugstore Cowboy* (1989) enjoyed a wider circulation, thanks also to the casting of Matt Dillon and Kelly Lynch in the leading roles. This road movie follows a band of four junkies led by Dillon in their robberies against hospitals and pharmacies. Van Sant explores the precarious balance among the members of the gang. Among other things, the superstitious beliefs of its leader

Keanu Reeves (left) and River Phoenix (right) in Gus Van Sant's *My Own Private Idaho.* Courtesy of Fine Line/Photofest.

threatens the cohesiveness of the gang. *Drugstore Cowboy* received unanimous critical praise and featured literary legend William Burroughs in the role of a defrocked drug addict priest. The rave reviews and the many awards that the film gathered allowed Van Sant to shoot *My Own Private Idaho* (1991), which instantly became a gay cult movie. Starring Keanu Reeves and River Phoenix, the film chronicles the journey of self discovery of two male hustlers, the rebellious Scott (Reeves), born into an affluent Portland family and son of the city's mayor, and Mike (Phoenix), a narcoleptic gay obsessed to find the mother who had abandoned him as a child. In their quest for Mike's mother, the two prostitutes become close friends. In one of the film's most moving scenes, Mike declares his love for Scott, who, however, rejects him claiming that he is really straight. In the end, the two hustlers go their own separate ways. In spite of its potentially controversial subject, *Idaho* won many prestigious awards, including the Volpi Cup for best male actor (Phoenix) at the international Venice Film Festival. The ***Advocate*** commented on the film enthusiastically stating that "Van Sant establishes for queer movie goers a beachhead in their ongoing struggle for cinematic representation. Hustlers may exist in the margins of the gay world, but the love that Mike feels for Scott is central to us all" (Ehrenstein 1994, 388).

My Own Private Idaho is an imaginary place where Mike can be finally reunited with his mother and live happily with her. Yet, this typically American promise of fulfilling one's own dreams does not materialize for Mike as it never materializes for the more marginal elements of society. Because of the stress on Mike's subjectivity, *Idaho* is a post-modern pastiche of styles, ranging from clinical observations of gritty details as in a Neo-Realist movie or an early Pasolini film to dream sequences and camp musical acts. The dialogue itself echoes this diversity, combining improvisation with Shakespearian overtones. The character of Scott is based on Prince Hal, the king's son in Shakespeare's *Henry IV*, who, like Van Sant's hustler, slums it before reclaiming his proper role in society and replacing his father.

After *Idaho*, Van Sant set to work on another gay story, the biography of Harvey Milk, San Francisco's openly gay Supervisor, who was murdered in 1978. The film was to be based on Randy Shilts's *The Mayor of Castro Street* (1982) with Robin Williams in the role of Milk. However, it was never realized due to disagreements over the screenplay between Van Sant and Oliver Stone, the film's prospective producer. None of the director's following movies have treated homosexuality as explicitly as *My Own Private Idaho*. Except for *Even Cowgirls Get the Blues* (1994), starring Uma Thurman, which flopped badly at the box office and got poor reviews, Van Sant's subsequent films have established him as one of the most original directors working in Hollywood. They have been particularly appreciated for their broad range in both themes and style. With movies such as the Academy Award–winning *Good Will Hunting* (1997) and *Elephant* (2003), which won a Golden Palm at Cannes Film Festival, Van Sant has continued to focus on the lives of those considered marginal by mainstream culture. While *Good Will Hunting* and *Finding Forrester* (2000) are more traditional in their narrative structure, Van Sant has cultivated his more experimental side with a shot-for-shot remake of Hitchcock's *Psycho* (1998) as well as with *Gerry* (2002) and *Last Days*, where narrative development and dialogue are kept to a minimum.

Further Reading

Ehrenstein, David. *Open Secret: Gay Hollywood, 1928–2000*. New York: Harper Collins, 2000; Ehrenstein, David. "My Own Private Idaho." *Long Road to Freedom: The Advocate History of the Gay and Lesbian Movement*. Thompson, Mark, ed. New York: St. Martin's Press, 1994. 388.

VIDAL, GORE (1925–)

The eclectic and influential novelist, playwright, screenwriter, essayist, social critic, and political activist Gore Vidal has constantly and openly developed gay themes in his works. He has repeatedly criticized American society and political establishment for having turned the United States from a republic into an empire. Vidal has felt increasingly uncomfortable to live in the United States, and, since the mid-1960s, he has divided his life, together with his late companion Howard Austen, between his homeland and Italy. His camp sensibility and his pioneering portraits of queer characters have helped to expand the space and the visibility for gays and lesbians within American popular culture.

Eugene Luther Gore Vidal was born on October 3, 1925, in West Point, New York, the son of Nina Gore and Eugene Luther Vidal, a teacher of aeronautics at the U.S. Military Academy and future director of air commerce under President Franklin D. Roosevelt from 1933 to 1937. His parents divorced when he was 10, and his mother remarried with millionaire Hugh D. Auchincloss, although the marriage was short-lived. Auchincloss would later marry the mother of Jacqueline Bouvier, President Kennedy's future wife. Gore grew up in Washington, DC, attending St. Albans and Los Alamos Ranch School. Vidal shortened his first name to Gore, the surname of his maternal grandfather, a Democratic Senator, upon his graduation in 1943 from Philipps Exeter Academy in Massachusetts. The political views of his ancestor Thomas Pryor Gore were to influence Vidal's own positions, notably his challenge to American imperialism. In 1943 he enlisted in the Army and served in the Aleutian Islands in the Pacific. During this time, Vidal composed his first novel *Williwaw* (1946), published when he was only 21 years old. The novel was based on the author's military experience and was well received by critics. His following novels *In a Yellow Wood* (1947), *The City and the Pillar* (1948), *The Season of Comfort* (1949), *A Search for the King* (1950), and *Dark Green, Bright Red* (1950) all revolve around the quests of young men trying to find meaningful identities within the modern world.

The City and the Pillar has become a central text in queer popular culture for its frank description of homosexuality at a time when such a candid discussion was considered taboo and even offensive. Starting in the 1930s and ending with World War II, the novel focuses on Jim Willard, a professional tennis player whose adolescent crush on his best friend Bob Ford has turned into an obsession. Although Jim has sex with other men in the course of the novel, he always hopes to be reunited to Bob. The two had sex during a camping trip when they were about to leave high school. When, after many years, they meet in Bob's hotel room in New York, Bob, who by now has married, seems at first to be as willing as Jim to have sex. Yet, he is suddenly seized by panic for fear of being considered gay and starts to insult Jim. The publisher requested that the book should end with a violent death, but Vidal refused to kill off his protagonist as the homophobic tradition of homosexual suicides would have suggested. The first edition of the novel ended instead with Jim killing Bob. When the novel was revised in 1968 thanks to the more favorable cultural climate, Vidal made substantial changes to his narrative, including the ending. In the altered version, Jim does not kill Bob, but violently rapes him. His reaction is justified by Bob's insults and violent behavior.

The novel originally came out when homosexual acts were still prohibited in the United States. Its depiction of gay men differed from the usual effeminate stereotype to include more varied and nuanced descriptions. What was disturbing to conservatives and homophobes in *The City and the Pillar* was that all types of men, including married ones, engaged in same-sex activities. This threatened the safe boundaries of homosexual representation. Literary critics started to ignore Vidal's production. To make up for the declining sales of his novel, Vidal turned to writing plays and scripts for television and films. As Edgar Box, he also produced three mysteries centering on detective Peter Sergeant.

In his attempts to reach a safe place within the mainstream of American popular culture, however, Gore Vidal never forgot gay characters. His works for the theater and the cinema gave homosexuality a visibility which popular media had denied for decades. For example, his political drama *The Best Man* (1959) revolves around the blackmailing of a straight man for a homosexual intercourse. Hired by MGM, Vidal also worked, uncredited, on the script for William Wyler's *Ben Hur* (1959), and he later declared that Wyler allowed him to create a homoerotic subtext between Ben-Hur and Messala. Throughout the McCarthy's years and the Eisenhower Presidency, Vidal warned Americans of the danger in the rise of political demagogues. He also ran for Congress in a conservative constituency in upstate New York for the Democratic Party. Defeated, he nonetheless increased votes for the Democrats.

By the 1960s, Vidal had gained a reputation for being an incisive social and political commentator. His plays and collections of essays were well-received. With his characteristic eclecticism, he tried a new genre, the historical novel, to which he would regularly return throughout his career. Carefully researched, *Julian* (1964) reconstructs the attempts of Emperor Julian (331–363) to remove Christianity from the Roman Empire. While lamenting the passing of the Hellenistic values, the novel also comments on the loss of the values of the American republic. The book firmly established Vidal as a bestselling author and, in the same year, Vidal also received an award at the prestigious Cannes Film Festival and a Screen Writers Annual Award nomination for his film adaptation of his play *The Best Man*. Vidal's outspoken views on politics and society hit the television screen in 1964 when he hosted for a year *The Hot Line*, a discussion show. His connections to the Kennedy family (his stepfather had remarried the First Lady's mother) allowed him to gain an insider's perspective on the administration. In spite of his initial enthusiasm for Kennedy, Vidal was soon disillusioned as the Vietnam War escalated. His disillusionment is mirrored in his political thriller *Washington D.C.* (1967) and by his unsuccessful play *Weekend* (1968), which contained direct challenges to the Vietnam War and President Johnson, and the play closed after only 22 performances. The novel *Two Sisters* (1970) is also often read as a satire of the Kennedy Administration with its several mocking remarks on the First Lady and the celebrities surrounding her. Vidal inscribes himself in the novel as one of the narrators, and he talks explicitly about his sexuality and the freedom he enjoys away from the United States.

The novel *Myra Breckinridge* (1968) forcefully and unexpectedly returned to the themes of gender difference so dear to the author. Through camp humor and black comedy, the book follows the diary of Myra, who was Myron before a sex-change operation, a transsexual who loves to dominate and rape straight men. Myra finds her victims in her uncle's academy for aspiring young actors and actresses. Set in Hollywood in the 1960s, *Myra Breckinridge* is a powerful reflection on the influence of popular culture has on the creation of images that later come to define individual and national identities. Myra's body, for example, is an attempt to reproduce the film iconography of the 1930s and 1940s. The novel came as a shock for both critics and readers with its frank description of sexual acts and drug taking. Predictably, critics were divided. Some argued it was simply pornographic material, but their rejection could not prevent the book from becoming a global bestseller and a cult work. In his critical study on Vidal, Dennis Altman (2005) defines *Myra Breckinridge* a cultural assault on received norms of gender and sexuality. According to Altman, that single book was more subversive of the dominant rules on sex and gender than the whole series of queer theory books that theorize sexual subversion nowadays. The book was made into a film in 1970, directed by Michael Sarne and starring Raquel Welch in the title role. Actress Mae West came out of her retirement to act in it and the rest of the cast included John Huston, Farrah Fawcett, and Tom Selleck in his debut role. In spite of the stellar cast and the controversies surrounding the book, the film flopped badly at the box office, but quickly became a cult movie.

In 1968 Vidal and his sexuality were also at the center of the public attention for his participation, opposite the right-wing conservative William F. Buckley, in a series of televised debates during the Republican National Convention in Miami and the Democratic National Convention in Chicago. Broadcast by ABC television, these debates proved extremely confrontational with a reciprocal exchange of accusations between the participants. Vidal accused Buckley of being a "crypto-nazi," while the conservative retorted by calling him "a queer." Once the series was over, the arguments between the two continued with mutual lawsuits and competing versions in *Esquire.*

The years of the Nixon's presidency naturally saw Gore Vidal at the forefront of political opposition, challenging what he perceived as the president's opportunism and his sudden changes of policies. His essay "The Twenty-Ninth Republican Convention" (1968) and the play *An Evening with Richard Nixon* (1972) reflect this critical stance. *Myron* (1974), the sequel to *Myra Breckinridge*, focuses on the conflict between Myron, a typical Nixon voter, and the radical Myra, two halves forced to remain within the same body. The sequel, however, did not do as well as the first book both in terms of sales and reviews. Published five years after the Stonewall riots, the book suffered from the changes in the readership's taste and its material was not that scandalous any longer.

Since the 1970s, Vidal has developed his fiction mainly within two directions. The first is the historical novel, represented by books such as *Burr* (1973), *1876* (1976), *Lincoln* (1984), *Empire* (1987), *Hollywood* (1989), *The Golden Age* (2000), and *Creation* (1981; rev. 2002). The genre is not used by the author to achieve merely a scholarly reconstruction of past times. On the contrary, the books function as powerful commentaries on the present. For example, *1876* critiques the scandal of the Grant Administration, having in mind the scandals of the Nixon Presidency. This group of novels also uncover how power is closely linked to the media for its perpetration, from Lincoln's intimidation of the press and his use of the telegraph for political purposes to the rule of Hollywood over the nation. The second strand in Vidal's fiction displays that camp sensibility and iconoclastic humor which have become his trademark from the 1960s. *Kalki* (1978), *Duluth* (1983), *Live from Golgotha* (1992), and *The Smithsonian Institution* (1998) all mercilessly satirize American cultural, political, religious, and sexual obsessions. Vidal also continues to be involved in the cinema industry, although with uneven fortunes: he was praised for his acting in the progressive *Bob Roberts* (1992) and the sci-fi *Gattaca* (1997), but he was also involved as screenwriter in the disastrous project *Caligula* (1979), about the Roman Emperor of the same name.

Vidal's reputation seems to rest increasingly on his essay writing, which is often sparked by his outrage against the American political establishment. Vidal particularly targeted the Reagan and Bush administrations. His pieces are praised as being well researched and entertaining at the same time. In 1991 his most important essays were collected in *Writer against the Grain*, and a volume on film, *Screening History*, also came out. In 1993 his collection *United States (1952–1992)* earned him a National Book Award. It was followed by the autobiographical *Palimpsest* (1995), where the author candidly talks of his love for men; *Sexually Speaking* (2001), which collects Vidal's most significant stances against homophobia; and *Point to Point Navigation* (2006), the continuation of autobiography.

Further Reading

Altman, Dennis. *Gore Vidal's America.* Cambridge: Polity Press, 2005; Dick, Bernard F. *The Apostate Angel: A Critical Study of Gore Vidal.* New York: Random House, 1974; Kaplan, Fred. *Gore Vidal: A Biography.* New York: Random House, 1999; Kiernan, Robert F. *Gore Vidal.* New York: Ungar, 1982; Parini, Jay, ed. *Gore Vidal: Writer against the Grain.* New York: Columbia University Press, 1992; Summers, Claude J. *Gay Fictions: Wilde to Stonewall. Studies in a Gay Male Literary Tradition.* New York: Ungar, 1990; White, Ray Lewis. *Gore Vidal.* Boston: Twayne Publishers, 1968.

VILLAGE PEOPLE, THE

Although the Village People was never explicitly identified as a gay band, it targeted gay men as its privileged audience. The band produced a string of disco hits in the late 1970s and early 1980s that became lasting anthems for the gay community. The man behind the project was French gay producer Jacques Morali, who wanted to create a band displaying all the most obvious homosexual stereotypes, but that would still appeal to gay men. With its successes, the band introduced the themes, sexual innuendo, and iconography of the gay male disco subculture into the mainstream of American popular culture. Although gay audiences tired of the group as it increasingly embraced the mainstream market, the catchy tunes and suggestive lyrics of the Village People make the band one of the most important groups which emerged from the disco arena.

Morali first received the inspiration for the establishment of the band when he saw Felipe Rose dancing in an Indian costume at a gay bar in the Greenwich Village, a location that would be reflected in the future band's name. Together with his partner Henri Belelo, Morali started to audition other male singers. In the end, the band was formed and each member represented a macho type taken from gay male erotic fantasies. Significantly, the ad placed by Morali explicitly requested men with moustaches. In addition to the openly gay Rose as a Native American, the original Village People consisted of construction worker David Hodo, policeman Victor Willis, soldier Alex Briley, cowboy Randy Jones, and biker leatherman Glenn Hughes. The group's first hit was "San Francisco" (1977), a hymn to the city that was most associated with the movements of sexual liberation of the 1970s. The song celebrates this atmosphere: on the way to Polk and Castro, you feel that "Freedom, freedom is in the air, yeah." The song charted in the UK's Top 50 Single. Success arrived the following year with "Macho Man" and the two international hits

Introducing gay iconography into the mainstream: The Village People in 1979. Courtesy of Can't Stop Productions/Photofest.

"Y.M.C.A" (UK number 1/US number 2) and "In the Navy" (UK number 2/US number 3).

Although these songs became big hits and are nowadays performed at all sorts of parties, gay or straight, they have a characteristically homoerotic content, which does not need the latest sophisticated queer theories to be brought out. For example, "Y.M.C.A" states that "it's fun to stay at the YMCA," because "They have everything for you men to enjoy,/ You can hang out with all the boys." The song "In the Navy" encourages men to "join your fellow man/In the navy," "where you can find pleasure" and "search the world for treasure." Gay audiences took pleasure in the sexual innuendo of these songs and in the flaunted homosexual stereotypes of the group's iconography. Gays also took pleasure in the irony that, although mainstream culture marginalized gayness, it could wholeheartedly embrace such a group as the Village People. The U.S. Navy even thought of using "In the Navy" for a recruiting advertising campaign on television and radio. Morali and Belelo agreed on condition that the Navy helped the group to shoot the video. The Navy initially agreed and the Village People started shooting at the San Diego naval base with a war ship and hundreds of men provided by the Navy. When the video began showing and the Navy started to plan its campaign, a furor broke out over using taxpayers' money to fund the video of a pop band, and one of dubious morality at that. Although the Navy cancelled the campaign, the controversy propelled the song at the top of the charts both in North America and Europe.

The band scored more hits with "Fire Island" (1977), "Go West" (1979), later remixed by **The Pet Shop Boys**, and "Can't Stop the Music" (1980). Several of their albums went gold and platinum. It is estimated that the group has sold more than 80 million copies of albums and singles. The fame of the group peaked in 1979 when the Village People were featured on the cover of *Rolling Stone*. However, this year also represented the beginning of the group's downfall, as the disco genre with which the Village People were closely associated was itself on the decline. The fictionalized film on their origins, *Can't Stop the Music* (1980), was a notable commercial disaster and was also panned by critics. It succeeded in being nominated in almost every category of the Golden Raspberry Awards. Over time the film has acquired a devoted cult following around the world. With the end of the disco era, the Village People tried to re-invent themselves as a New Wave group with their album *Renaissance* (1981), which, however, was a big commercial flop. The group dissolved in 1986, but regrouped with three new singers in 1998, seven years after their founder Jacques Morali had died of **AIDS**-related complications.

The group continues to produce albums and has performed as opening act for sold-out tours such as Cher's 2005 Farewell Tour. Yet, it will always be best-remembered for its dance hits of the late 1970s. In an interview with the **Advocate** (Mangels 2000, online edition), the group's original cowboy Randy Jones stated that the Village People helped to pave the way for the boy bands of the 1990s such as 'NSync and The Backstreet Boys. "We're like the godfathers of a lot of those bands. We had a phrase back then. We said we were the first 'all-guy all-girl group.'" Jones and Rose are the only two members of the group who have openly discussed their sexuality and identify as gay. Rose puts down the reticence of the group to come out as gay to the climate of the late 1970s: "I don't think it was a question of no one coming out....I think at that time—the political climate the country was in—it would have been too sassy for us to be openly out like that. We probably never would have had any success" (Mangels 2000, online edition). In spite of the reticence of some members to discuss their sexual orientation in real life, rather than as a stereotype on stage, the Village People certainly contributed to the transition of several images and themes of the gay male subculture of the 1970s into mainstream American popular culture.

Further Reading

Mangels, Andy. "Playing Cowboy and Indian: Out Musicians Felipe Rose (the Indian) and Randy Jones (the Cowboy) look back on 25 years of the Village People." *The Advocate*. May 14, 2000. http://findarticles.com/p/articles/mi_m1589/is_2002_May_14/ai_85523497 (accessed on October 20, 2006); http://www.officialvillagepeople.com (accessed on October 20, 2006).

WARHOL, ANDY (1928–1987)

With his work as pop artist, filmmaker, and artists' entrepreneur, Andy Warhol became an icon of the 1960s, contributing to the countercultural challenge against conventional norms of good taste both in society and the arts. Both in his innovative artistic style and in his public persona, Warhol embraced camp and extravagant solutions, which ran counter to the traditional image of male artists. In spite of his overt gayness, however, Warhol was never a committed gay militant. Yet, he lent his personal encouragement and financial support for the careers of gay artists such as Jean-Michel Basquiat and Keith Haring. In addition, his works contain several coded references to queer subculture, which, incidentally, have been consistently played down by critics. In the pages of his *Diaries*, Warhol talks explicitly about his love of men. However, when he was asked questions about his sexuality during his lifetime, Warhol was extremely evasive. The critical assessment of Warhol has seldom taken into account the artist's homosexuality and its impact on his art in favor of the creation of a more asexual persona.

Warhol was born on August 6, 1928, in Pittsburgh, Pennsylvania, in a working-class family of Czech origins. His actual surname was Warhola and he was the youngest of three boys. His father Ondrej was a laborer for the Eichleay Corporation and his mother Julia was a folk artist. Warhol attended Schenley High School in Pittsburgh, from where he graduated in 1945, and then went on to study pictorial design at the Carnegie Institute of Technology, obtaining a BFA in 1948. The following year, Warhol moved to New York where he shortened his surname and explored the rich gay life of the city. He worked as a commercial illustrator and his sketches immediately made him a successful artist. In the 1950s Warhol's works were exhibited in galleries and reprints of his sketches were published in limited edition books. He established several important contacts in the art world, but still lacked that recognition that he had dreamed of since his childhood.

In the early 1960s, Warhol began drawing popular cartoon characters such as Dick Tracy and Popeye, but that type of imagery had already been appropriated by

Roy Lichtenstein. Success came when the artist persuaded Ivan Karp, an assistant at Leo Castelli's gallery, to view his new works. Karp was favorably impressed by a painting of complex lines of Coca-Cola bottles. Karp convinced Castelli to take in Warhol. In 1962 his exhibition of paintings recreating Campbell's soup cans and Coca-Cola bottles propelled the artist to stardom. Warhol soon attracted a devoted following of artists and assistants at the Factory, his studio in Union Square. In 1963 he developed the silk-screening techniques which became one of his artistic trademarks. This technique allowed the mass reproduction of portraits and banal objects. This appealed to Warhol who wanted to express the emptiness of American material culture as well as his detached posture as an artist. Following the suicide of Marilyn Monroe in August 1962, Warhol decided to pay her homage with a series of silkscreen variations starting from a still of the actress in the film *Niagara*. The series features strong, neon colors whose combinations change in every portrait. The same method was applied to another pop icon, Elvis Presley, and later to stars and political personalities such as Liz Taylor, Jacqueline Kennedy, and the Chinese leader Mao Tse-tung. Warhol was fascinated by the way media created celebrities or trivialized tragic events. His silkscreen portraits are ambiguous representations of the world of the rich and famous. They can be both read as a celebration of that world and as a satire of it. Warhol did not suggest any interpretation of his art. To him his works were simply meaningless.

In 1964 Warhol was asked to make a mural for the World's Fair, and he produced a huge wall of mug shots of the 13 most-wanted men from the FBI. The mural angered Governor Rockefeller, who ordered to have it painted over. From his choice of subjects, it is clear that Warhol liked to associate himself with power as well as with controversy. Queer critics have suggested that the censorship of the mural was dictated by the work's subversive and radical critique of state power. Richard Meyer (2002, 12) characterizes the mural as setting up a "circuitry…between the image of the outlaw and Warhol's outlawed desire for that image—and for these men. To put it another way, Thirteen Most Wanted Men crosswires the codes of criminality, looking, and homoerotic desire.…It is not only that these men are wanted by the FBI, but that the very act of 'wanting men' constitutes a form of criminality if the wanter is also male, if, say, the wanter is Warhol."

Warhol explained his interest in everyday objects such as Coca-Cola bottles or soup cans in terms of their symbolizing American cultural values. For example, he celebrated Coca-Cola as the symbol of American democracy: "What's great about this country is that America started the tradition where the richest consumers buy essentially the same things as the poorest. You can be watching TV and see Coca-Cola, and you know that the President drinks Coke, Liz Taylor drinks Coke, and just think, you can drink Coke, too. A Coke is a Coke and no amount of money can get you a better Coke than the one the bum on the corner is drinking. All the Cokes are the same and all the Cokes are good. Liz Taylor knows it, the President knows it, the bum knows it, and you know it" (Warhol 1975, 100–101). How serious Warhol really was in his comments is still a matter of debate among scholars. Warhol's Pop Art, with its emphasis on consumer goods, testifies to the collapse between high and low art in contemporary society.

In the 1960s, Warhol also started to produce and direct films, which are often ignored by Warhol's critics because of their frank homosexual representations. In less than a decade, Warhol directed more than 60 experimental movies. Although his filmmaking activity is an obvious outcome of his fascination with Hollywood and stardom, Warhol's films are usually described as underground, and they have nothing commercial about them. Warhol used a hand-held camera and his films had plotless development and unconventional topics including a man sleeping for six hours (*Sleep*, 1963), the act of fellatio (*Blow Job*, 1963), and the Empire State Building from dusk to dawn (*Empire*, 1964). *My Hustler* (1965) is Warhol's film where gay themes and characters are most explicitly portrayed. The story follows the sexual tension between an older sugar daddy, Ed Hood, and two hustlers, the semi-retired Joe Campbell and Hood's new lover Paul America. Paul is also Joe's object of desire as the older hustler tries to seduce the younger. The film is a rare insight into the pre-Stonewall gay community, reproducing as its does gay slang and mannerism. *Horse* (1965) has a Western setting and, decades before the major motion picture **Brokeback Mountain**, twisted the genre to accommodate homoerotic undertones. *Four Star* (1967) runs for 25 hours and is considered the culmination of Warhol's career as an experimental filmmaker. It also contains an explicit scene of two males falling in love. The most successful Warhol film was *Chelsea Girls* (1966), which enjoyed wider theatrical release than his other projects. It follows the lives of several women living at the Chelsea Hotel in New York and consists of actually two different 16 mm films being projected simultaneously, with two different stories being shown at the same time. Unfortunately, Warhol's films are seldom shown, even at the artist's many retrospectives.

In 1967 Warhol expanded his activities to music too. He started to produce the records of the Velvet Underground and designed the famous allusive banana cover of the band's first album *The Velvet Underground and Nico*. By the late 1960s, the Factory had become a countercultural Mecca for a composite crowd of aspiring artists, drag queens, hustlers, rock stars, and Hollywood starlets. Warhol was also accused of exploiting the misfits in his court to enhance his own extravagance and thus attract more media attention. On June 3, 1968, a tragic event marked Warhol for the rest of his life. Valerie Solanas, an aspiring playwright, who had founded and was the unique member of SCUM (Society for Cutting Up Men), shot Warhol several times, almost killing him. Solanas had been harassing Warhol for months due to a manuscript of her play *Up Your Ass*, which Warhol had lost. After she turned herself in to the police, Solanas declared that Warhol had too much control over her life and that he was planning to steal her work. Warhol barely survived the attack and the injuries he experienced forced him to wear a corset for the rest of his life to prevent them from getting worse. Security at the Factory became more tightly organized, as Warhol became obsessed by the thought that Solanas would attack him again. To some radical feminists, Solanas became a hero of the women's movement, although she soon drifted into obscurity and she was repeatedly hospitalized in mental institutions.

The attack had the effect of increasing Warhol's fame. He retired as director, but continued to produce many underground films which were mainly directed by Paul Morrissey and starring Joe Dallesandro. These films often portray the damaged lives of the urban outcasts and their subcultures. *Trash* (1970) was one of the most successful and, in spite of graphic scenes of sodomy and drug injection, had a wide cinematic release throughout the United States. In the 1970s and 1980s, Warhol was a superstar and his first retrospectives were held in important museums in America and Europe. He became one of the most wanted men at social events, and celebrities were prepared to pay phenomenal amounts of money to have their portraits painted by Warhol. His work continued to exhibit clear queer tones. For example, the cover of the *Rolling Stones* album *Sticky Fingers* (1971) shows a close-up of Joe Dallesandro's crotch in rather tight jeans. The series *Ladies and Gentlemen* consists of images of drag queens. His *Torso* and *Sex Parts* Polaroids (1977) explicitly depict men having sex with men.

Warhol died of cardiac arrest following a gall bladder operation on February 22, 1987, in New York City. His oeuvre and his camp persona continue to attract massive scholarly attention. His retrospectives draw thousands of visitors. Yet, contemporary critical assessments of Warhol all too often avoid the subject of his homosexuality. On the contrary, a complete appraisal of Warhol's work cannot exclude its queer inflections in the wider countercultural climate of the 1960s.

Further Reading

Bockris, Victor. *The Life and Death of Andy Warhol*. New York: Bantam, 1989; Crimp, Douglas. "Getting the Warhol We Deserve." *Social Text* 59 (1999): 49–66; Cumming, Alan. *Andy Warhol: Men*. San Francisco: Chronicle Books, 2004; Doyle, Jennifer, Jonathan Flatley, and José Esteban Muñoz, eds. *Pop Out: Queer Warhol*. Durham, NC: Duke University Press, 1996; McShine, Kynaston, ed. *Andy Warhol: A Retrospective*. New York: Museum of Modern Art, 1989; Meyer, Richard. *Outlaw Representation: Censorship and Homosexuality in Twentieth-Century American Art*. Oxford: Oxford University Press, 2002; O'Pray, Michael. *Andy Warhol Film Factory*. London: The British Film Institute, 1989; Rosenblum, Robert. "Andy Warhol: Court Painter to the 70s." *Andy Warhol: Portraits of the 70s*. David Whitney, ed. New York: Random House, 1979. 8–21; Silver, Kenneth. "Modes of Disclosure: The Construction of Gay Identity and the Rise of Pop." *Hand-Painted Pop: American Art in Transition, 1955–62*. Russell Ferguson, ed. Los Angeles: Museum of Contemporary Art, 1992. 179–203; Smith, Patrick S. *Andy Warhol's Art and Films*. Ann Arbor, MI: UMI Research Press, 1986; Warhol, Andy. *The Philosophy of Andy Warhol (From A to B & Back Again)*. New York: Harcourt Brace Jovanovich, 1975.

WATERS, JOHN (1946–)

Openly gay film director, scriptwriter, and photographer John Waters first achieved fame in the early 1970s through his extreme films starring drag queen impersonator **Divine**, including *Pink Flamingos* (1972) and *Female Trouble* (1974). These contained shocking scenes for the times such as Divine eating dog feces or killing her own child before being electrocuted. These details and plot turns earned Waters the title of "king of bad taste." Although his later films, such as *Hairspray* (1988), *Cry-Baby* (1990), *Serial Mom* (1994), *Pecker* (1998), and *Cecil B. DeMented* (2000), have been accepted by the mainstream and include international stars such as Kathleen Turner, Christina Ricci, and Melanie Griffith, Waters's early oeuvres continue to shock audiences. Commenting on the re-release of *Pink Flamingos* for its 25th anniversary, the director congratulated himself on his success at shocking three different generations of viewers. What unifies Waters's early and later films is an interest for queer characters who do not conform to accepted social norms. Although not as excessive as the characters in his early films, the protagonists who people his later comedies are, according to the director's definition, "nuts but think they are the sane ones." It is this interest in what is socially and sexually less acceptable that has made Waters a central figure in gay and lesbian popular culture, in spite of the scant presence of gay and lesbian characters in his movies. In addition, underlying all Waters's production, is a **camp** aesthetics that has made the filmmaker a popular culture icon for queers. Such a role was somewhat institutionalized when Waters guest-starred as John, a gay collector of junk pop culture memorabilia, in the 1997 episode of *The Simpsons*, "Homer's Phobia." The particular brand of camp that sustains Waters's films is the love of excess, artifice, and the unnatural. It is, as Homer describes the contents of his house and of John's store, "worthless valuable junk." This may be why Waters's films are so difficult to categorize in a precise genre.

Born in Baltimore, Maryland, where he has lived most of his subsequent life, Waters met Harris Glenn Milstead, whom he would later rename Divine, when the two were adolescents. They both clearly disliked the world of suburbia where they were growing up. Years later, talking about his film *Polyester* (1981), Waters still held to the same dislike arguing that the film was really about enemy territory and that he always felt an outsider whenever he went to the suburbs. Waters and Divine soon started to collaborate, initially making 8 mm movies such as *Roman Candles* (1966), then passing on to the 16 mm format with *Mondo Trasho* (1969), for which Waters was taken to trial and acquitted, and *Multiple Maniacs* (1970). *Pink Flamingos* (1972) and *Female Trouble* (1974) established Divine as an underground star and received a wider theatrical release than the director's first films. These early oeuvres rest on Divine's anarchic energy, which challenges standards of social acceptability, often by focusing on extreme situations such as mother-son fellatio, shit eating, cannibalism, and murder. As Waters (1981, 2) wrote in his book *Shock Value*, "I've always tried to please and satisfy an audience who think they've seen everything. I try to force them to laugh at their own ability to be shocked by *something*. This reaction has always been the reason I make movies." Waters's early movies directly stem from the days of the 1960s counterculture, when American youth was engaging in protests against the U.S. involvement in the Vietnam War and in the nation's policies of racial segregation. Usually shot with the same cast and crew, the Dreamlanders, these early films pushed gender and sexual boundaries, for example by showing explicit lesbian sex, using men to play women, and taking non-professional actors from the gay and lesbian community. In *Pink Flamingos* and *Female Trouble*, Waters combined a soap-opera style with a shocking taste for filth and grossness. As Daniel Cunningham (*Senses of Cinema* online) has written, the filmmaker's "trash imagination celebrates the marginal and excluded; his films elevate white trash above all else."

Polyester (1981) was Waters's first movie to enjoy a standard theatrical release, pitting Divine against former teen idol Tab Hunter. Divine is Francine Fishpaw, a Baltimore housewife who is abandoned by her husband and loathed by her children. The movie subverts the idealized notion of American suburban life into a living nightmare, which forces the protagonist to alcoholism and threatens to drive her insane. Through a series of surreal events, Francine will be able to change her life and regain her family. *Polyester* is a parody of the so-called women's films which were particularly in vogue during the 1950s and early 1960s. These usually centered on upper-middle-class, middle-aged housewives whose frustrations were solved by the appearance of a charming man. Waters explicitly fashioned *Polyester* after the films of Douglas Sirk, the undisputed master in the genre, even using lightning techniques and equipment from Sirk's times. Accordingly, the director moved the setting from Baltimore's working-class districts of his first films to upper middle-class suburbia. The film also used a special gimmick to emphasize the importance of smells. Audiences were given a scratch card so that they could smell what the characters smelled on screen. In the commentary released with the DVD in 2004, Waters notices with characteristic fashion that he was delighted to have the audience pay to smell shit. Although tamer and more mainstream than Waters's early films, *Polyester* made the audience closely identify with Francine, who is played by a man in drag, thus continuing the director's challenge against gender boundaries. Waters began to appear not only on the covers of specialized cinema magazines and in the local papers of Baltimore, where his early films had already reached a cult status, but also on more mainstream media. His road to institutionalization included the mayor's proclamation of February 7, 1985, as "John Waters Day" in Baltimore. As the *Sight and Sound* reviewer of Waters's 1998 film *Pecker* remarked: "The greatest irony of John Waters's career is that he has ended up loving and being loved by Baltimore, the town he initially tried to infuriate. From being the most disgusting filmmaker in the world, Waters has become something of a local hero, venerated for bringing an element of glitter into an area not known for its star-spangled potential" (Kermode 1999, 51).

Hairspray (1988) definitely signaled the filmmaker's crossover to the mainstream, although it retained Waters's characteristic inventiveness. It was the last film the director made with Divine, who died a few weeks after its release, just at a time when rave reviews and good box office results were finally making the actor a film and TV star. *Hairspray* centers on a fictitious show, *The Corny Collins Dance Show*, and its segregation of white and black dancers. The film's protagonist, Tracy Turnblad, fights equally hard to gain a place as a dancer on the show and force it to integrate. The film was a big hit and its Broadway adaptation opened in 2002, sweeping eight Tony Awards including Best Musical, Best Book, Best Original Score, Best Actor, and Best Actress. After *Hairspray*, Waters began to use Hollywood stars in his films, although their commercial success has been uneven. The fans of the filmmaker's early movies are somehow disappointed by his later efforts which are technically more refined and thematically less angry. Yet, Waters never stops looking at American society and the film industry through the sarcastic lenses of his campy humor. *Serial Mom* (1994), for example, offered Kathleen Turner an unforgettable role as Beverly Sutphin, a dubious serial killer housewife whose career flourishes when the rights to her story are sold for a Hollywood film. *Cecil B. Demented* (2000) targets more closely the film industry, focusing on the decision of young, ambitious underground director Cecil (Stephen Dorff) to kidnap famous insufferable Hollywood star Honey Whitlock (Melanie Griffith) and force her to star in his underground film. *A Dirty Shame* (2004) represented a return to the more controversial topics of his debut, although with a bigger budget.

Since *Hairspray*, Waters has also appeared in mainstream media, becoming a popular guest on David Letterman's *The Late Show*. Writer William S. Burroughs, an expert in counterculture and trash aesthetics, once called Waters "the Pope of Trash." Since his early days, however, the director seems to have changed his strategies to push the sexual and gender boundaries of American society. Once the king of bad taste who directed extreme movies, Waters has now moved to more mainstream forms of expression. In Sarah Hampson's words (2003, *Globe and Mail* online), "He is the iconoclast who has become an icon; the anti-establishment voice who has become an institution."

Further Reading

Cunningham, Daniel Mudie. "John Waters." *Senses of Cinema.* http://www.sensesof cinema.com/contents/directors/03/waters.html (accessed on August 10, 2007); Daugherty, Timmerman, and Janet Stidman Eveleth. "Disparate Disobedients: John Waters and Philip Berrigan." *Maryland Bar Journal* 29, no. 1 (January 1996): 14–18; Hampson, Sarah. "King of the Golden Age of Trash." *The Globe and Mail.* April 5, 2003, http://www.theglobeandmail.com/servlet/ArticleNews/ TPPrint/LAC/20030405/RVHAMP/TPColumnists/ (accessed on August 10, 2007); Hightower, Scott. "Charles Laughton—John Waters." *Western Humanities Review* 52, no. 2 (1998): 169–171; Ives, John G. *John Waters.* New York: Thunder's Mouth, 1992; Mark Kermode, *"Pecker"* [review], *Sight and Sound* 9, no. 2 (1999): 51; Pela, Robert L. *Filthy: The Weird World of John Waters.* Los Angeles: Alyson, 2002; Waters, John. *Crackpot: The Obsessions of John Waters.* New York: Vintage, 1986; Waters, John. *Shock Value.* New York: Thunder's Mouth, 1981.

WEBER, BRUCE (1946–)

Thanks to his commercial photographs for the advertising campaigns of Calvin Klein, Ralph Lauren, and Abercrombie & Fitch, Bruce Weber has become one the most popular contemporary fashion photographers. His homoerotic pictures are consumed by gay and straight viewers alike. Weber has contributed to make homoeroticism a marketable commodity, and his black and white photographs have blurred the boundaries between artistic and commercial photography. The men in his works are models of the all-American white boy next door. Weber's photographs for the Calvin Klein and the Abercrombie & Fitch campaigns have also made these labels an integral part of gay male culture. Yet, as the homosexual act is always kept out of the pictures, Weber's photographs can appeal to straight consumers too. His models make up an exclusively white, young, and privileged world of perfect bodies. Although the vast majority of Weber's works focuses on amateur young men, several of his portraits are devoted to the world of Hollywood celebrities. Parallel to his career as a photographer, Weber has also developed a successful career as a filmmaker, directing music videos for Chris Isaak and the **Pet Shop Boys**, as well as documentary features. Described as "a Hell's Angel duped into a health spa" or as "a mad pirate,...plundering people's souls with his lens" (Muir 2002, *Independent* online), Weber displays a persona whose characteristic beard, bandanas, and baggy shirts sharply contrast with the fashionable and polished images of his photographs.

Born on March 29, 1946, in Greensburg, Pennsylvania, Weber grew up in wealthy family. In spite of this affluent background, Weber's childhood was often a solitary one, marked by a tense relationship with his father and by the frequent absences of his parents. Yet, Weber's family had a passion for photography and Super-8 filming, and, as a result, Weber was exposed to photography and filmmaking from a very early age. His father, the owner of a successful furniture store, was an amateur photographer and would take pictures at Sunday family gatherings or shoot films of them. The photographer has traced his passion for photography to this family tradition and has credited his photographic style to the quintessentially American aesthetics of his rural hometown. However, Weber did not set out to study as a photographer. He first studied theater at Denison University, Ohio, and in 1966 he enrolled for filmmaking at New York University. Weber's interest in filmmaking is apparent in his career not only for the acclaimed documentaries and music videos that he directed but also for the cinematic style of his photography. His 1991 *Vanity Fair* supplement for Calvin Klein, for example, arranges still photographs as if they were forming a narrative. While in New York, Weber began studying photography with Lisette Model, and through her, he met the famous photographer Diane Arbus, who became a friend and a clear influence on his work. Weber once commented (Muir 2002, *Independent* online) that Arbus showed him that "being a photographer is like being a vagabond out in the world." Other influences which shaped Weber's vision of the ways in which photography should portray male bodies were Imogen Cunningham and Herbert List.

International fame came in the 1980s with Weber's advertising campaign for Calvin Klein Underwear. Weber chose non-professional models for the photographs that would make him known all over the world. In 1982 Weber photographed Olympic pole vaulter Tom Hinthaus wearing nothing but Calvin Klein briefs. The picture forces the viewer to gaze at the muscular body of the athlete, making it an erotic and idealized commodity. Heterosexual and gay viewers find themselves in the similar position of worship and admiration for a modern-day Adonis. Weber thus successfully brought gay imagery and conventions within mass-market American visual culture. It is this eroticizing of the athletic male body that constitutes Weber's revolutionary contribution to the representation of men in American popular culture. In the 1980s, his photographs also contrasted with the increasingly widespread images of male bodies devastated by **AIDS**. Weber's photographs portrayed healthy and muscular men who self confidently put their bodies on display, rather than hiding them to conceal the shame of the illness. Reading Weber's pictures against the devastating effects of the AIDS crisis partly explains their popularity within the gay community. Thanks to the success of his Calvin Klein photographs, the celebrated Robert Miller Gallery in New York began to put on displays of Weber's works. In the mid-1980s the photographer was already considered by art critic Paul Smith (1984, 126) as a "pre-eminent fashion photographer." The following year, his photographic installation *Studio Wall* was included in the Whitney Museum's Biennial Exhibition. The pictures of Hintnaus and of another non-professional model, Jeff Aquilon, firmly established Weber's reputation as a daring photographer of male bodies and made him a point of reference for future male photographers. Since the late 1980s, Weber has regularly worked for U.S. and British *Vogue*, *Vanity Fair*, and other leading fashion magazines. In 2005 he was awarded with the Lifetime Achievement Award by the International Center of Photography. On that occasion, designer Lauren celebrated his long-standing collaboration with Weber stating that "Bruce Weber is Ralph Lauren and Ralph Lauren is Bruce Weber."

In the same year, Weber debuted in filmmaking with his first film *Broken Noses*, a documentary about boxer Adam Minsker to whom the photographer also devoted *The Adam Book* (1987). In 1989 Weber obtained an Academy Award nomination for his documentary on jazz player Chet Baker, *Let's Get Lost*. Weber's collaboration with the Pet Shop Boys started in 1990, when the photographer directed the video for the single "Being Boring." The result was costly and controversial for the time, as the video showed a wild party involving a varied group of people and the display of male nudity, although tame by contemporary standards, was enough for MTV to ban it from the United States. Six years later, the photographer teamed up again with the British pop duo for the video of "*Se a vida é*" from *Bilingual*. In 2002 Weber directed another Pet Shop Boys video, "I Get Along," from the album *Release*. Weber's most personal film creation was the autobiographical *Chop Suey* (2001). In this eclectic documentary, the photographer sheds light on his imagination suggesting that the perfect world of polished bodies that he often portrays in his pictures was all that he was denied when growing up. Talking about photographing high school wrestler Peter Johnson and his friends in the shower, Weber's voice-over reminisces about his own adolescence: "I wanted to be one of those kids padding around without a care in the world but I couldn't. I'd be swimming all day in the country club and my mom would tell me to shower for and dress [there] for dinner but I told her I couldn't. The locker-room would be too crowded at that hour and it seemed to me that every guy in the Midwest would be in that locker-room showering and dressing for his six o'clock date. Instead I'd wash at the washbasin wearing my underwear and a towel." His concluding remark on the episode is telling: "We sometimes photograph things we can never be" (Muir 2002, *Independent* online).

Both Weber's photographs and music videos clearly suggest gay sex, but never display it explicitly. Most of the photographer's pictures are set in an all-male world where physical contact between men is prominently showed. The sentimental engagements of the men in Weber's photographs are often ambiguous. Such ambiguity displaces explicit homosexual desire, yet it also makes the viewer's gaze complicit in homoerotic situations. Even when Weber portrays wrestlers, the viewer wonders if their behavior and attitude are more suggestive of a sentimental relationship than of a fighting match. The photographer's masculine ideal, renewing the Arcadian combination of athleticism and sentimentality, has helped to permeate American popular culture and mass-marketing advertising with unmistakable homoeroticism.

Further Reading

Hainley, Bruce, and David Romanelli. "Shock of the Newfoundland: Bruce Weber's Canine Camera." *Artforum International* 33 (April 1995): 78–81; Kismaric, Carole, and Marvin Heiferman. *Talking Pictures: People Speak about the Photographs That Speak to Them*. San Francisco: Chronicle Books, 1994; Leddick, David. *The Male Nude*. New York: Taschen, 1998; Muir, Robin. "All Is Finally Revealed." *The Independent on Sunday*. March 31, 2002. http://www.highbeam.com/doc/1G1-84287954.html (accessed on March 16, 2007); Official Web site: http://www.bruceweber.com (accessed on March 16, 2007); Smith, Paul. "Bruce Weber's Athletic Fashion." *Arts Magazine* 58, 10 (June 1984): 126–127; Weber, Bruce. *Bruce Weber*. New York: Knopf, 1988; Weber, Bruce. *Hotel Room with a View*. Washington, DC: Smithsonian Institution Press, 1992.

WHITE, EDMUND (1940–)

Edmund White occupies a central position in contemporary gay and lesbian literary culture. His fiction and nonfiction writings have often focused on gay characters, personalities, and themes. His best-known work is the semi-autobiographical trilogy composed of *A Boy's Own Story* (1982), *The Beautiful Room Is Empty* (1988), and *The Farewell Symphony* (1998). The books chronicle the different stages in the development of a gay consciousness from the pre-Stonewall era to the post-**AIDS** crisis. White has also openly discussed his own HIV-positive status since his diagnosis in the mid-1980s.

Edmund Valentine White III was born in Cincinnati, Ohio, on January 13, 1940, into a middle-class and relatively wealthy family. When Edmund was seven, his parents divorced and, together with his sister, he followed his mother to the outskirts of Chicago. As he recounts in his autobiographical writings and in his essay "Out of the Closet, Onto the Bookshelf" (1991), White was conscious of his homosexuality from an early age and spent his adolescence trying to find positive role models. White loved to read so he looked for volumes that could clarify his confusion about his sexual identity. Yet, in the 1950s, he could only find books which vaguely hinted at homosexuality and treated it as something to condemn. White's education started in the racist South and continued in the more liberal and integrated district of Chicago, where he had moved after his parents divorced. After attending the traditional Haven Intermediate, White also attended the prestigious Cranbrook boarding school in Michigan. Throughout his school years, White was encouraged by his mother to develop his literary talents, and during this time, he put together a first collection of poetry and an unpublished novel. His mother was, however, less supportive of his son's sexuality, and White was subjected to psychotherapy to try and cure what was perceived as his deviant sexuality. This experience would be the basis for the satirical critique of American society's reliance on standard notions of gender, class, and race in *A Boy's Own Story* and *The Beautiful Room Is Empty*.

White enrolled at the University of Michigan, Ann Arbor, to study Chinese. He attended university in the early 1960s, when the oppressive climate of the 1950s was giving way to the more liberating and liberated milieu of the next decade. A diverse coalition of queers, civil rights activists, and feminists was starting to challenge the patriarchy embedded in institutions administered by predominantly straight white men. From his graduation in 1962 to 1970, White worked in New York at the publishing group Time-Life. In the city, White witnessed the blossoming of gay and lesbian cultures and, at the same time, the backlash against homosexuals that followed their increasing social visibility. White's first two novels *Forgetting Elena* (1973) and *Nocturnes for the King of Naples* (1978) document the power of the closet within pre-Stonewall gay communities, while his *The Beautiful Room Is Empty* chronicles how gays and lesbians increasingly came to reject marginalization. *The Farewell Symphony* brings in a third phase of gay and lesbian life, the post-AIDS crisis.

In the late 1970s, White began to acquire the status of spokesperson and cultural critic of the gay community with the publication of *The Joy of Gay Sex* (1977) and *States of Desire: Travels in Gay America* (1980). Both works treat homosexuality as a cultural and social phenomenon. The latter volume, in particular, offers a survey of the different American gay communities. White's popularity within New York's gay circles continued to grow, and he came into contact with important artists such as the photographer **Robert Mapplethorpe**. He also started to teach university courses in literature and creative writing, becoming the Executive Director of the Institute for the Humanities at Columbia University in 1980. In that same year, he co-founded the Violet Quill, an organization which gathered several gay writers including Christopher Cox, Felice Picano, Andrew Holleran, and Robert Ferro. These writers would meet regularly to discuss each other's works.

It was, however, the publication of *A Boy's Own Story* that catapulted White into international literary fame. Focusing on a Midwestern boy's increasing awareness of his homosexuality in the 1950s, this semi-autobiographical novel became a best-seller and challenged American notions of manhood and masculinity. *A Boy's Own Story*, for which White was presented with the Award for Literature from the American Academy of Arts and Letters, parodies cherished American institutions and exposes the racism and homophobia underlying them. White continued his narrative of the formation of a gay consciousness in the pre-Stonewall days with *The Beautiful Room Is Empty*, written largely on a Guggenheim Fellowship. In an interview to the *Advocate* (Perry 1994, 38), White stated that the novel was about "a different type of oppression than the one we are threatened with now, but still similar." The writer conceived *The Beautiful Room Is Empty* as his most militant book, a response to the homophobic backlash caused by the AIDS crisis. As White himself admitted, during the days of early gay liberation, he was not interested in writing positive role models for gays and lesbians. Yet, with the advent of the AIDS crisis and a recrudescence of homophobia, "gay culture is in danger of being wiped out and, certainly, gay rights are in danger of being suppressed." Thus, White considered his books "as a sort of bulwarks" against these tendencies.

White has divided his life between his native America and Europe, where he has spent long periods of time in France. His passion for French culture and literature is evident in his non-fiction projects, which include studies on Jean Genet, Marcel Proust, and the Parisian travelogue, *The Flâneur*. The biography of Genet, published in 1993, is particularly consistent with the fictional project of *A Boy's Own Story* and *The Beautiful Room Is Empty*. Like the two novels, White's study of the French writer is an in-depth look at a gay life, focusing on the intersections of race, class, and sexuality in the intellectual biography of Genet. White is not solely concerned with Genet's literary production, but also with the author's political contacts with African American and Palestinian political militants. The biography, which earned White the prestigious National Book Critics Circle Award, also argues that any analysis of Genet's oeuvre cannot avoid the issue of the author's homosexuality. The French government officially recognized White's significance for French culture in 1993, making him a Chevalier de L'Ordre des Arts et des Lettres.

Although *The Beautiful Room Is Empty* indirectly responded to the AIDS crisis, White explicitly analyzed the impact of the virus on the gay community with both the collection of short stories *The Darker Proof: Stories from a Crisis* (1988) (written with Adam Mars-Jones), and *The Farewell Symphony*, which brings to an end the trilogy begun with *A Boy's Own Story* and *The Beautiful Room Is Empty*. As with the first two volumes, *The Farewell Symphony* is semi-autobiographical in nature and updates White's project to narrate a gay life in depth during the age of AIDS, in which many of the writer's friends and lovers succumb to the virus. *The Married Man* (2000), which builds upon White's relationship with the French architect Hubert Sorin, also returns to the impact of AIDS upon gay life, composing a moving elegy for the dead lover. The book was awarded the Ferro-Grumley Award from the Publishing Triangle.

White has often been taken to task for his emphasis on sexual promiscuity in his depictions of gay life. His critics find that this emphasis on casual sex portrays the gay community as desolate and barren, and its members as incapable of developing meaningful relationships. The *Gay Times* reviewer of *The Married Man* (Lovatt 2000) also objected to the choice of still writing yet another tragic story where one of the lovers dies of AIDS. These charges stem from White's central role within gay culture, a role that gives him the status of spokesperson for an entire community, putting on the writer, whether or not he is willing to bear it, the burden of representation. Yet, while White partly conceives his novels to be "bulwarks" against the recurrent outbursts of homophobia that characterize American society, he considers political correctness to be just as constraining for his artistic imagination. His writings are pleas for a hybrid culture that defies standard distinctions along gender, racial, and class lines.

Further Reading

Barber, Stephen. *Edmund White: The Burning World*. London: Picador, 1999; Bergman, David. "Edmund White." *Contemporary Gay American Novelists*. Emmanuel Nelson, ed. Westport, CT: Greenwood, 1993. 386–394; Cowan, Paul. "The Pursuit of Happiness." *New York Times Book Review* (February 3, 1980): 12–13; Lovat, Simon. "Compassion Fatigue." *Gay Times*, March 2000. 258: 70; Official Web site http://www.edmundwhite.com (accessed on September 10, 2007); Perry, David. "Authors: Edmund White on Gay Writing." *Long Road to Freedom: The Advocate History of the Gay and Lesbian Movement*. Thompson, Mark, ed. New York: St. Martin's Press, 1994. 338; *The Review of Contemporary*

Fiction. Vol. XVI, n. 3. September 1996. Issue devoted to Edmund White and Samuel R. Delany.

WILL AND GRACE

NBC's Emmy Award-winning series *Will and Grace* was one of the first TV shows to focus on the life of a gay man, Will, a New York lawyer. For eight seasons starting in 1998, *Will and Grace* offered to American audiences gayness without mediation or coding. Two of the central characters, Will and his friend Jack, explicitly identify themselves as gay. Many of the show's jokes refer to gayness so that there is no need of particularly intellectual queer readings to understand what the show is all about. Yet, many gay and lesbian viewers have asked whether such an explicit representation of homosexuality is, in the end, liberating or simply entertaining. How far has the phenomenal success of *Will and Grace* been construed on its challenge against televised stereotypes of gays and lesbians? Or is such success eventually built upon the show's reliance on those very stereotypes? What remains undisputable is the hit status achieved by *Will and Grace*, which, after its debut in September 1998, gained viewers steadily and was soon included in NBC's *Must See TV* bill. Although its ratings declined during the sixth season, the show was the second-highest-rated sitcom from 2001 to 2005, second only to *Friends*. During its run, *Will and Grace* won 16 Emmys.

Will Truman (Eric McCormack) is a gay New York lawyer who shares his flat with his best friend Grace Adler (Debra Messing), a Jewish interior designer. Will and Grace's circle of friends include Jack (Sean Hayes), a campy aspiring actor, and socialite Karen Walker (Megan Mullally), who is employed as Grace's assistant. The series follows their lives, their relationships, and their conflicts. Although Grace gets involved romantically with other men, her main love interest seems to be Will. The two were together in college before Will's coming out. Will's private life has been somewhat limited by his friendship with Grace, a fact that has angered many gay critics who have described the character's life as almost celibate. The character

The cast of *Will and Grace*: Megan Mullally (Karen), Eric McCormack (Will), Debra Messing (Grace), and Sean Hayes (Jack). Courtesy of NBC/Photofest.

of Jack also has attracted criticism for his stereotypical flamboyance. According to Melinda Kanner (2003), the openly gay characters on the show make homosexuality acceptable and mainstream and prevent any possible queer and subversive interpretations. *Will and Grace* portrays homosexuality through the reassuring conventions of the situation comedy genre, reducing its potential for controversy. Queer critics have also pointed out that the show likens homosexuality with lack of masculinity and obscures the larger social and political movements with which the characters are connected.

Andrew Holleran (2000, 65) has pointed out that gay audiences tend to identify and sympathize with Karen, rather than with Will and Jack. Following Holleran's line of argument, Melinda Kanner (2003) emphasized that Karen is the only genuinely queer presence. She is the toughest and most flirtatious character on the show and, as Kanner and Holleran note, capable of out-doing any gay quotient established by the openly gay characters. Contrary to the actors playing Will and Grace, who have firmly established their heterosexuality, Megan Mullally, who embodies Karen, has explicitly talked about her bisexuality and her friendship with many gay men.

The relationship between the characters of Will and Grace blocks any possibilities for Will to have a fulfilling private life. The two characters resemble in many respects a heterosexual couple, in spite of Grace's marriage and boyfriends. The fact that Will, who is consistently less successful than Grace in finding a love interest, is openly gay does not subvert the heterosexual image that the couple projects. His homosexuality is affirmed more through verbal than behavioral evidence. Contrary to Will and Grace's apparent conformity to an heterosexual model, Karen disregards all norms of social acceptability and this, together with her overt sexual behavior, is precisely the source of her queerness.

Because of its explicit handling of homosexual characters and themes, *Will and Grace* has been repeatedly hailed as offering the most groundbreaking TV treatment of gayness by a mainstream network. Its success helped to pave the way for more gay-themed programs in mainstream networks, both in terms of fictions such as **Queer as Folk**, and reality shows like **Queer Eye for the Straight Guy**. Yet, such success came at a prize as the series ignores, or at best marginalizes, the most relevant political debates for the gay and lesbian community. The final episode finally shows Will in a quasi-stable relationship with his partner Vince and the two even have a son. Yet, for the entire eight seasons, the political struggles of gays and lesbians to achieve same-sex marriages are neglected, a fact that, together with Will's celibate status for much of the series, risks reinforcing the fundamental stereotype of homosexuals as unable to commit to long-term relationships.

Further Reading

Castiglia, Christopher. "'Ah yes, I remember it well': Memory and Queer Culture in Will and Grace." *Cultural Critique* 56 (Winter 2004): 158–188; Holleran, Andrew. "The Alpha Queen." *The Gay and Lesbian Review Worldwide*. Summer 2000: 65; Kanner, Melinda. "Can *Will and Grace* be queered?" *The Gay and Lesbian Review Worldwide*. July 2003. http://www.highbeam.com/doc/1G1-104329367.html

(accessed on September 10, 2007); Mitchell, Danielle. "Producing Containment: The Rhetorical Construction of Difference in *Will and Grace*." *The Journal of Popular Culture*. Volume 38, Issue 6 (November 2005): 1050.

WILLIAMS, TENNESSEE (1914–1983)

Although American playwright, poet, short story writer, novelist, and essayist Tennessee Williams, a central figure in twentieth-century American literature, only wrote explicitly about homosexuality in his later oeuvres, his whole production is characterized by an in-depth focus on, in the writer's own words, "the crazed, the strange, the queer" (Adler 2006, *Literary Encyclopedia* online). Since his very first plays, where his homosexuality remained hidden, Williams was interested in representing people who live differently from mainstream society and who are misfits because of their sexual, racial, or ethnic identities. According to Williams, theater is a powerful medium to unlock and light up "the closets, attics, and basements of human behavior and experience" (Adler 2006, *Literary Encyclopedia* online). To uncover the repressed sides of human conduct, Williams combines realistic insights into his characters' psychology with a poetic use of language and a heavy reliance on stage symbolism. No matter how late he was in coming out from his own closet, Williams's interest in opening up theater to behaviors which were considered as deviant in the conformist American society of the 1940s and 1950s earned him a central place in gay and lesbian popular culture. For example, gay director **John Waters** (2006, ix) explicitly acknowledges Williams's influence on his own work, going as far as claiming that the dramatist saved his life and soon became a virtual "childhood friend." As Waters recalls (2006, x), Williams was "joyous, alarming, sexually confusing and dangerously funny." Thanks to Williams's books, Waters discovered that he could neglect society's rules and stop worrying about fitting in: "there was another world that Tennessee Williams knew about, a universe filled with special people who didn't want to be a part of this dreary conformist life that I was told I had to join" (Waters 2006, x). The centrality of Williams in Waters's life is representative of the dramatist's centrality in the lives of an entire generation of gay men, although the playwright has often been taken to task for his conflicting feelings about his own sexuality. Several critics have defined Williams's perception of his own homosexuality as marked by a deeply ingrained and internalized homophobia. Contemporary gay and lesbian popular culture has nonetheless appropriated some of Williams's classic plays such as *A Streetcar Named Desire* (1947), which was turned into *Belle Reprieve* (1991), a gender-bending show, by the joint efforts of the gay troupe *Bloolips* and the lesbian artists of the *Split Britches*. Spanish gay film director Pedro Almodovar put a production of *A Streetcar Named Desire* at the center of his Academy Award–winning masterpiece *All About My Mother* (1999).

Born Thomas Lanier Williams on March 26, 1911, in Columbus, Mississippi, the dramatist had a childhood characterized by ill health and the frequent arguments of his parents. Tennessee, a nickname later given to him for his Southern accent, had a particularly conflicted relationship with his father. His family moved to St. Louis in 1918 and the writer always expressed his dislike for this city. This was where Williams wrote his first short stories. Although he enrolled at the University of Missouri at Columbia, his father forced him to return home to work with him as a shoe salesman. Yet, Tennessee did not give up his artistic inclination and studied both at Washington University and the University of Iowa, where he received his only formal education as a playwright. Williams graduated in 1938 and, in the same year, wrote his first play *Not about Nightingales*, an overtly political drama set during a prison hunger strike led by a poet. Although far from his later plays for its explicit political message, *Not about Nightingales* introduced many recurrent themes in the dramatist's oeuvre, such as human loneliness, the outsiders' sufferance, the need to establish communal bonds in the face of an ever-increasing dehumanizing society. *Not about Nightingales* was the only play by Williams to receive a Broadway production in the 1930s.

After graduating from Iowa, Williams moved to New Orleans where he continued to write plays and had his first homosexual experiences. It was also during these years that Thomas adopted the nickname of Tennessee. The first official recognition came when Williams won a Group Theater award for his one-act play *American Blues* (1939). This allowed him to find an agent, Audrey Wood, who would remain with him for the best part of his career. He was also able to secure a grant from the Rockefeller Foundation to attend John Gassner's playwriting seminar at the New School for Social Research in New York. Williams's life in the early 1940s was marked by his frequent travels to Europe and by the meeting of his long-time partner Frank Merlo. Yet, these were the years of a family tragedy that left an enduring and painful sense of guilt on Tennessee: his beloved sister Rose was forced to undergo a prefrontal lobotomy, which supposedly should have cured her of dementia.

Critical and commercial success came with the Broadway production of *The Glass Menagerie* (1944), where Williams introduces another central theme in his dramatic output: the nostalgia for a genteel, agrarian South of quasi-mythical dimension. The play focuses on the Wingfields, an impoverished Southern family living in a tenement. Deserted by her husband, Amanda, a domineering and manipulative mother, tries to find a suitor for her crippled daughter Laura with the help of her son Tom, whose artistic ambitions are

Paul Newman and Elizabeth Taylor as Brick and Maggie in Richard Brooks's screen adaptation of Tennessee Williams's play *Cat on a Hot Tin Roof*. Courtesy of MGM/Photofest.

frustrated by his job in a shoe factory. Tom also acts as the narrator of the play, re-calling the events roughly a decade after they took place, and once he has, like his father did before him, deserted his mother and sister. The play is thus configured as Tom's attempt to overcome his guilt. All the characters live in a world of their own, trying to cope with their own loneliness: Amanda has constructed a Southern belle past for herself, Laura has withdrawn in her collection of little glass animals (symbolizing her own frailty), while Tom lives in a parallel world of celluloid ad-venture and literature to prevail over the frustration of his menial job and his clos-eted homosexuality to which only coded references are made. *The Glass Menagerie* is rich in autobiographical references. Tom's guilt towards his mother and sister reflects that of the author for having been unable to prevent his sister's lobotomy. Laura's physical handicap mirrors the mental distress of Williams's sister, while Amanda's aggressiveness and ambition for a genteel life echo those of the author's mother. The play also presents complex layers of symbolism, which will become the distinguishing feature of much of Williams's future literary productions.

Williams's next play, *A Streetcar Named Desire* (1947), won a Pulitzer Prize and definitely consecrated its author as a central figure in American drama. Set in the French Quarter of New Orleans, the play opposes Blanche DuBois, a representa-tive of the decaying Southern nobility, to the working-class Stanley Kowalski, an American of Polish descent who has married her sister Stella. Stella has been happy to leave behind all social pretension in exchange for the sexual satisfaction that she has found in her down-to-earth husband. When Blanche arrives in the Kow-alskis' household, the conflict with her brother in law, who considers her a threat to his relationship with Stella, immediately explodes. In the tragic denouement, the tensions between Stanley and Blanche will lead to Blanche's rape and mental insan-ity. While being taken to a mental asylum, Blanche delivers one of the most famous lines in twentieth-century American theater exclaiming that she has "always de-pended upon the kindness of strangers." Just as Tom is in *The Glass Menagerie*, Blanche is haunted by her past, which, in her case, is directly and explicitly related to homosexuality. Shortly after marrying, Blanche discovered her husband in bed with another man, and she confronted him, voicing all her disgust. Deeply ashamed, he committed suicide. Blanche has been unable to work through her sense of guilt and start a new life until she meets Stanley's gallant friend Mitch. Yet, this brief moment of happiness soon crumbles as Stanley reveals to Mitch that Blanche has had many sexual partners in her past, including a teenage student. This last event led to her dismissal as a schoolteacher. While, at the beginning of the play, Stanley may be seen as a hero fighting against social pretension, by the end of *A Streetcar Named Desire*, it is clear that, no matter how vain Blanche is, the author's sympathy lies with her.

A Streetcar Named Desire aptly illustrates some of the problems that gay readers might have with Tennessee Williams's pre-Stonewall plays. While homosexuality is mentioned, it is hardly represented on stage and remains a haunting presence, usually linked to characters who are dead. At the same time, *A Streetcar Named Desire* offers intriguing possibilities to subvert a literal reading. For example, the text is rich in gay slang. In addition, its central character, Blanche DuBois, has been read as a man in drag since her major features are excess and theatricality. After the success of *A Streetcar*, Williams started the 1950s with three less popular plays: *Summer and Smoke* (1948), *The Rose Tattoo* (1950), which received a successful film adaptation earning Anna Magnani an Oscar for Best Actress, and *Camino Real* (1953), a complex drama which focuses on the portrayal of a repressive society, probably modeled upon the investigations of McCarthy and the House Un-American Activities Committee. During these years, Williams also published his most daring short stories; texts that, because they reached a much smaller audience than his Broadway plays, afforded him more freedom of experimenting with overtly homosexual themes. According to many gay critics, stories such as "One Arm," "Desire and the Black Masseur," "Hard Candy," and "The Mysteries of the Joy Rio," rather than the author's plays, should constitute the point of departure for queer readers of Williams. While describing graphically gay sex, these short stories still reflect the predominantly negative attitude of 1950s American society towards homosexuality, often linking it with death and bowel cancer.

From the mid-1950s to the early 1960s, Williams was again at the center of critical and commercial success. He obtained his second Pulitzer for his play *Cat on a Hot Tin Roof* (1955) and in 1962, he was featured on the cover of *Time* as the world's greatest living dramatist. *Cat on a Hot Tin Roof* replicates the association between homosexuality, guilt, and death encountered in *A Streetcar*. Brick, a former football star, and his sensual wife Maggie live in the same room occupied by Jack Straw and Peter Ochello, the two gay lovers who founded the plantation now run by Brick's father Big Daddy. As Blanche, Brick too suffers from guilt, which he tries to quell with heavy drinking, directly related to homosexuality. His friend Skipper confessed to him once his sexual desire for him, but Brick rejected him, causing Skipper's suicide. Contrary to Blanche, Brick is conscious that Skipper's desire may well mirror his own and is horrified by the possibility of being branded as queer. In a central scene of the play, Williams reverses the usual dynamics of father-son confrontations over homosexuality. Here it is Brick, the son, who is horrified by his father's acceptance of homosexuality. Big Daddy, who was raised by Straw and Ochello, is dying of cancer, a disease usually associated with gayness and sodomy in Williams's fiction. Brick's confused feelings about his sexuality also make him unable to have sexual intercourse with his wife, who is particularly anxious to give Big Daddy a grandchild. In spite of the association of homosexuality and death throughout most of the play, *Cat* ends with the privileging of gayness over heterosexuality as it is Brick and Maggie who will inherit the plantation, not Brick's brother Gooper and his fertile wife Mae.

Williams's string of successes continued with the controversial screenplay for Elia Kazan's film *Baby Doll* (1956), which provided Carroll Baker with a career-defining role, and with the plays *Suddenly, Last Summer* (1957) and *Sweet Bird of Youth* (1959). The former centers on Catherine, another female character who, like Laura in *The Glass Menagerie* and Blanche in *A Streetcar*, experiences a similar fate to Williams's own sister. The play is set in the majestic New Orleans conservatory of Catherine's cousin Sebastian Venable, a gay poet, whose violent death Catherine has witnessed. Sebastian's domineering mother, Violet, tries to have Catherine lobotomized to prevent her from telling the truth about Sebastian's death by cannibalization at the hands of a group of Mexican rent-boys. Violet wants to protect her son's image as an asexual poet and cannot tolerate that he should be associated with homosexuality. As in *Streetcar* and *Cat*, homosexuality in *Suddenly, Last Summer* is not seen on-stage and is linked to a dead character.

Williams's fame is mainly the result of these plays and their successful film adaptations. *The Glass Menagerie* was first adapted in 1950 by Irving Rapper with fine performances by Jane Wyman as Laura and Kirk Douglas as the gentleman caller. It was then remade by Paul Newman with Joanne Woodward playing Amanda in the late 1980s. *A Streetcar Named Desire* was directed by Elia Kazan in 1951, launching Marlon Brando's career and providing Vivien Leigh with one of her most interesting roles. Richard Brooks directed the adaptations of both *Cat on a Hot Tin Roof* (1958), starring Paul Newman and Elizabeth Taylor, and *Sweet Bird of Youth* (1962), with Newman and Geraldine Page in the leading roles. Joseph L. Mankiewicz adapted *Suddenly, Last Summer* in 1959 with an all-star cast including Katharine Hepburn, Elizabeth Taylor, and Montgomery Clift.

After *The Night of the Iguana* (1961), Williams was unable to recapture the success of his plays from the 1940s and the 1950s. The death of his long-time partner Frank Merlo in 1963 caused the dramatist to suffer from severe bouts of depression. Williams became increasingly dependent on drugs and alcohol, and he himself nicknamed the 1960s "my stoned age." He kept on writing and prolifically so, but many of his plays failed to attract critical and commercial attention. In later plays such as *Small Craft Warnings* (1970), *Vieux Carré* (1977), and *Something Cloudy, Something Clear* (1981), Williams treated homosexuality more openly than in his earlier texts. Yet, his homosexual characters are often self-loathing, a feature that has angered many gay critics. The author also candidly spoke about his own sexuality in his autobiographical *Memoirs* (1975) and in his novel *Moise and the World of Reason* (1975). Williams died on the night between February 23 and 24, 1983, at the Hotel Elysée in New York, choking on the cap of a medicine bottle.

In spite of the failures of his later years, Tennessee Williams is firmly established as a central figure of modern drama. His plays are among the most often revived in the history of modern theater. While he did not use his writings to further an agenda of gay and lesbian liberation and was often reticent about his own sexuality, Williams helped to introduce in American theater characters whose lives do not conform with the norms of social acceptability. As John Waters recalls in the introduction to Williams's *Memoirs*, the dramatist showed to a whole generation of gays and lesbians that an entirely different lifestyle, far from the conformist milieu of the 1940s and 1950s, was possible. "My place in society," Williams (Waters 2006, xiii) has pointed out, "has been in Bohemia."

Further Reading

Adler, Tom. "Tennessee Williams." *The Literary Encyclopedia*, 2006. http://www.liten cyc.com/php/speople.php?rec=true&UID=4738 (accessed on January 14, 2007); Bigsby, C.W.E. *A Critical Introduction to Twentieth Century American Drama, II: Williams, Miller, Albee*. Cambridge: Cambridge University Press, 1994; Clum, John M. *Acting Gay: Male Homosexuality in Modern Drama*. New York: Columbia, 1992; Clum, John M. "Something Cloudy, Something Clear: Homophobia in Tennessee Williams." *Displacing Homophobia: Studies in Gay Male Literature and Culture.* Ronald Butters, John M. Clum, Michael Moon, eds. Durham, NC: Duke University Press, 1989. 149–167; Leverich, Lyle. *Tom: The Unknown Tennessee Williams.* New York: Crown, 1995; Roundané, Matthew, ed. *The Cambridge Companion to Tennessee Williams.* New York: Cambridge University Press, 1997; Savran, David. *Communists, Cowboys and Queers: The Politics of Masculinity in the Work of Arthur Miller and Tennessee Williams.* Minneapolis: University of Minnesota Press, 1992; Spoto, Donald. *The Kindness of Strangers: The Life of Tennessee Williams.* New York: Ballantine, 1986; St. Just, Maria. *Five O'clock Angel: Letters of Tennessee Williams to Maria St. Just, 1948–1982.* New York: Knopf, 1990; Waters, John. "Introduction." *Memoirs.* Tennessee Williams. New York: New Directions, 2006. ix–xiv; Williams, Tennessee. *Memoirs.* With an introduction by John Waters. New York: New Directions, 2006.

WONG, B. D. (1960–)

Chinese-American actor B. D. Wong is best known for his unforgettable performance in the title role of David Hwang's play *M. Butterfly* (1988). That role made Wong the only actor to have won the Tony Award, the Drama Desk Award, the Outer Critics Circle Award, the Clarence Derwent Award, and the Theater World Award for the same performance. Wong has since developed a career as a character actor on TV and film and has also taken part in Broadway productions. Although Wong did not consider himself fully out until he gave an interview to the ***Advocate*** in 2003, he never publicly denied his homosexuality. Since his coming out, he has supported gay and lesbian causes and has vividly narrated the experience of becoming a father in his moving memoir *Following Foo* (2003).

Born Bradley Darrell Wong on October 24, 1960, in San Francisco, where he also grew up, Wong is a fourth-generation Chinese-American. Following his high school graduation, he went to New York to study acting and start his career. While in New York he took roles in dinner theater and in off-Broadway productions. However, his career did not take off until he moved back to Los Angeles as part of the cast of the Jerry Herman–**Harvey Fierstein**'s musical ***La Cage Aux Folles***. Although Wong was not out at the time, he did not eschew gay roles. Challenging the coyness of actors to accept to portray queers, Wong accepted the role of Song Liling in David Hwang's *M. Butterfly* for his Broadway debut in 1988. Hwang's play deconstructs Puccini's *Madame Butterfly*, turning the orientalist stereotypes of the Italian opera upside down. Song Liling masquerades as an opera diva, but is, in fact, a male spy working for the Chinese government. Unaware of her real gender, the French diplomat Rene Gallimard falls for her, and Song uses this relationship to extract important secret information from him. With his multiple award-winning performance, Wong convincingly embodied the fluidity of gender implied in the play. Song complies to the Western stereotypes that construct Asian women as submissive and meek, and Asian men as effeminate, only to challenge these stereotypes as the play progresses. Yet, as John Deeney (1993, *Melus* online) has pointed out, the play dramatizes the foibles of both East and West: "The West is taken to task for its patronizing and mistaken attitudes of masculine superiority over a feminine

East which is weak and helpless to resist. The East, on the other hand, is implicitly criticized for its complicity in sustaining this stereotype by reproducing images of the delicate, the dainty, the subservient, the polite, and the apologetic." As the only actor to win five prestigious prizes for the same performance, Wong clearly made the most of this complex role.

The actor starred as a gay man in two important productions for the queer community. He was Kiko Govantes, the lover of activist Bill Kraus, in the 1993 HBO movie *And the Band Played On*, based on Randy Shilts's study on the spread of HIV in America and the indifference that characterized the official response to the virus. Wong also joined the cast of the New York Shakespeare festival's production of the play *A Language of Their Own* (1995) by gay Singapore writer Chay Yew. The piece evokes with lyric language the loneliness of four men considered outsiders by society for their ethnicity, sexuality, and HIV status. In spite of the few roles available for Asian Americans on the big screen and on TV, Wong has developed a solid reputation as a character actor. He was Margaret Cho's brother in ABC's *All American Girl* (1994–1995), the first sitcom on a network channel to focus on the Asian-American community. He also had recurrent roles in the series *Oz*, where he played an idealistic Catholic priest who provides spiritual counsel for the inmates of a maximum security prison, and *Law and Order: Special Victims Unit*, where he was a forensic psychiatrist. On the big screen, he has appeared in mainstream films such as *Father of the Bride* (1991) and *Jurassic Park* (1993). Wong lent his voice for the character of Captain Li Shang in Walt Disney's *Mulan* (1998) and *Mulan II* (2004).

Wong has also taken part in Broadway and off-Broadway productions such as Irving Berlin-Moss Hart's *As Thousands Cheer* (1998), Clark Gesner's *You're a Good Man, Charlie Brown* (1999), and the **Stephen Sondheim** musical *Pacific Overtures* (2004), a disillusioned reflection on America's 1853 mission to westernize Japan. In 2004, he also directed his first film, *Social Grace*, an independent comedy about the romance between an Asian-American woman and a

B. D. Wong in his multiple award-winning performance as Song Liling in David Hwang's *M. Butterfly*. Courtesy of Photofest.

Caucasian male. In a 2003 interview in the *Advocate* (Bernstein 2003, online edition), Wong explained that he'd taken a long time to officially come out, because he feared what the impact of being Asian and gay might have had on his career: "I went into this business knowing I faced a fairly long list of limitations. Being Asian-American was one. Adding the fact that you're gay is career suicide. At least that's how it felt." His public coming out coincided with the writing of the book *Following Foo*, where the actor narrates the difficult birth of his premature twin sons (via a surrogate mother) and the death of one of them in 1999. Since his coming out, Wong has been a prominent supporter of gay and lesbian battles and has spoken on the importance of not letting other people define one's own identity: "Labels can affect your ability to be yourself.... You find yourself conforming to everyone else's ideas of who you are" (Bernstein 2003, *Advocate* online). Being the one who defines his own identity is an ongoing struggle for Wong, one in which both his Asian-American descent and his gayness play a fundamental role.

Further Reading

Bernstein, Fred. "Baby Comes Early, Daddy Comes Out." *The Advocate*. June 10, 2003. http://www.highbeam.com/doc/1G1-105367669.html (accessed on October 29, 2006); Deeney, John. "Of Monkeys and Butterflies: Transformation in M. H. Kingston's Tripmaster Monkey and D. H. Hwang's M. Butterfly." *Melus* Vol. 18, No. 4, Asian Perspectives (Winter, 1993). 21–39. http://www.highbeam.com/doc/1G1-14878604.html (accessed on October 29, 2006); Wong, B. D. *Following Foo: The Electronic Adventures of the Chestnut Man*. New York: HarperEntertainment, 2003.

BIBLIOGRAPHY

Aaron, Michele. *New Queer Cinema: A Critical Reader.* New Brunswick, NJ: Rutgers State University Press, 2004.

Adams, Stephen. *The Homosexual as Hero in Contemporary Fiction.* London: Vision Press, 1980.

Avena, Thomas, ed. *Life Sentences: Writers, Artists, and AIDS.* San Francisco: Mercury House, 1994.

Baker, Rob. *The Art of AIDS.* New York: Continuum, 1994.

Barrios, Richard. *Screened Out: Playing Gay in Hollywood from Edison to Stonewall.* London: Routledge, 2005.

Benshoff, Harry. *Queer Cinema: The Film Reader.* London: Routledge, 2004.

———. *Queer Images: A History of Gay and Lesbian Film in America.* New York: Rowman & Littlefield Publishers, 2005.

Benstock, Shari. *Women of the Left Bank: Paris, 1900–1940.* Austin: University of Texas Press, 1986.

Bergman, David. *Gaiety Transfigured: Gay Self-Representation in American Literature.* Madison: University of Wisconsin Press, 1991.

Brett, Philip. *Queering the Pitch: The New Gay and Lesbian Musicology.* London: Routledge, 1994.

Bronski, Michael. *The Pleasure Principle: Sex, Backlash and the Struggle for Gay Freedom.* New York: Stonewall Inn Editions, 2000.

Bronski, Michael, Christa Brelin, and Michael J. Tyrkus, eds. *Outstanding Lives: Profiles of Lesbians and Gay Men.* Detroit: Visible Ink, 1997.

Burston, Paul. *A Queer Romance: Lesbian, Gay Men and Popular Culture.* London: Routledge, 1995.

Butler, Judith. *Gender Trouble: Feminism and the Subversion of Identity.* New York: Routledge, 1990.

Butters, Ronald, John M. Clum, and Michael Moon, eds. *Displacing Homophobia: Studies in Gay Male Literature and Culture.* Durham, NC: Duke University Press, 1989.

Chauncey, George. *Gay New York: Gender, Urban Culture, and the Makings of the Gay Male World, 1890–1940.* New York: Basic Books, 1994.

Ciasullo, Ann M. "Making Her (In)Visible: Cultural Representations of Lesbianism and the Lesbian Body in the 1990s." *Feminist Studies* 27, no. 3 (Fall 2001): 577–608.

Cleto, Fabio, ed. *Camp: Queer Aesthetics and the Performing Self—A Reader*. Edinburgh: Edinburgh University Press, 1999.

Clum, John M. *Acting Gay: Male Homosexuality in Modern Drama*. New York: Columbia, 1992.

———. *Something for the Boys: Musical Theater and Gay Culture*. New York: St. Martin's Press, 1999.

Creekmur, Corey K., and Alexander Doty, eds. *Out in Culture: Gay, Lesbian and Queer Essays on Popular Culture*. Durham, North Carolina: Duke University Press, 1995.

Crimp, Douglas, ed. *AIDS: Cultural Analysis/Cultural Activism*. Cambridge, MA: MIT Press, 1988.

DeAngelis, Michael. *Gay Fandom and Crossover Stardom: James Dean, Mel Gibson, and Keanu Reeves*. Durham, NC: Duke University Press, 2001.

De Cecco, John, Dawn M. Krisko, and Sonya L. Jones, eds. *A Sea of Stories: The Shaping Power of Narrative in Gay and Lesbian Cultures*. Binghamton, NY: Harrington Park Press, 2000.

de Jongh, Nicholas. *Not in Front of the Audience: Homosexuality on Stage*. London: Routledge, 1992.

D'Emilio, John. *Sexual Politics, Sexual Communities*. Chicago: University of Chicago Press, 1998.

Doty, Alexander. *Making Things Perfectly Queer: Interpreting Mass Culture*. Minneapolis: University of Minnesota Press, 1993.

———. *Flaming Classics: Queering the Film Canon*. New York: Routledge, 2000.

Drake, Robert. *The Gay Canon: Great Books Every Gay Man Should Read*. New York: Anchor Books, 1998.

Duberman, Martin, Martha Vicinus, and George Chauncey, Jr., eds. *Hidden from History: Reclaiming the Gay and Lesbian Past*. New York: New American Library, 1989.

Dyer, Richard, ed. *Gays and Film*. London: British Film Institute, 1977.

———. *Now You See It: Studies on Lesbian and Gay Film*. London: Routledge, 1990.

———. *The Culture of Queers*. London: Routledge, 2002.

———. *Heavenly Bodies: Film Stars and Society*. London: Routledge, 2003.

Ehrenstein, David. *Open Secret: Gay Hollywood, 1928–2000*. New York: HarperCollins, 2000.

Faderman, Lillian. *Surpassing the Love of Men: Romantic Friendship and Love between Women from the Renaissance to the Present*. New York: William Morrow, 1981.

———. *Odd Girls and Twilight Lovers: A History of Lesbian Life in Twentieth-Century America*. New York: Columbia University Press, 1991.

Feinberg, Leslie. *Transgender Warriors: Making History from Joan of Arc to Ru Paul*. Boston: Beacon Press, 1997.

Fuss, Diana, ed. *Inside/Out: Lesbian Theories, Gay Theories*. London: Routledge, 1991.

Gever, M., J. Greyson, and P. Parmar, eds. *Queer Looks: Perspectives on Lesbian and Gay Film and Video*. New York: Routledge, 1993.

Gill, John. *Queer Noises: Male and Female Homosexuality in Twentieth-Century Music*. London: Cassell, 1995.

Hadleigh, Boze. *Hollywood Gays*. New York: Barricade Books, 1996.

———. *Sing Out: Gays and Lesbians in the Music World*. New York: Barricade Books, 1998.

Hanson, Ellis. *Out Takes: Essays on Queer Theory and Film*. Durham, NC: Duke University Press, 1999.

Hooven, F. Valentine. *Beefcake: The Muscle Magazines of America, 1950–1970*. Cologne: Benedikt Taschen Verlag, 1996.

Horne, Peter. *Outlooks: Lesbian and Gay Sexualities and Visual Cultures*. London: Routledge, 1996.

Hubbs, Nadine. *The Queer Composition of America's Sound: Gay Modernists, American Music, and National Identity*. Berkeley: University of California Press, 2004.

Jones, Sonya L., ed. *Gay and Lesbian Literature since World War II: History and Memory*. Binghamton, NY: The Haworth Press, 1991.

Jones, Therese, ed. *Sharing the Delirium: Second Generation AIDS Plays and Performances*. Portsmouth, NH: Heinemann, 1994.

Kaiser, Charles. *The Gay Metropolis. The Landmark History of Gay Life in America since World War II*. Fort Washington, PA: Harvest Books, 1998.

Kaplan, E. Ann, ed. *Women in Film Noir*. London: BFI Publishing, 1998.

Leong, Russell, ed. *Asian American Sexualities: Dimensions of the Gay and Lesbian Experience*. New York: Routledge, 1996.

Lilly, Mark. *Gay Men's Literature in the Twentieth Century*. New York: New York University Press, 1993.

Loughery, John. *The Other Side of Silence. Men's Lives and Identities: A Twentieth-Century History*. New York: Henry Holt & Company, 1998.

Madsen, Axel. *The Sewing Circle: Hollywood's Greatest Secret: Female Stars Who Loved Other Women*. New York: Carol Publishing Group, 1995.

Mann, William J. *Behind the Screen: How Gays and Lesbians Shaped Hollywood 1910–1969*. New York: Viking, 2001.

McLellan, Diana. *The Girls: Sappho Goes to Hollywood*. New York: St. Martin's Griffin, 2000.

Meese, Elizabeth. *(sem)erotics theorizing lesbian: writing*. New York: New York University Press, 1992.

Meyer, Richard. *Outlaw Representation: Censorship and Homosexuality in Twentieth-Century American Art*. Oxford: Oxford University Press, 2002

Murphy, Timothy F., and Suzanne Poirier, eds. *Writing AIDS: Gay Literature, Language and Analysis*. New York: Columbia University Press, 1993.

Nelson, Emmanuel S., ed. *AIDS: The Literary Response*. Boston: Twayne Publishers, 1992.

———. *Gay American Novelists: A Bio-Biographical Critical Sourcebook*. Westport, CT: Greenwood Press, 1993.

Pollack, Sandra, and Denise D. Knight, eds. *Contemporary Lesbian Writers of the United States: A Bio-Bibliographical Critical Sourcebook*. Westport, CT: Greenwood Press, 1993.

Reynolds, Simon, and Joy Press. *The Sex Revolts: Gender, Rebellion and Rock'n'roll*. London: Serpent's Tail, 1995.

Ridinger, Robert B. Marks. *An Index to the Advocate: The National Gay Newsmagazine, 1967–1982.* Los Angeles: Liberation Publications, 1987.

Robinson, Paul. *Gay Lives: Homosexual Autobiography from John Addington Symonds to Paul Monette.* Chicago: University of Chicago Press, 1999.

Russell, Paul Elliott. *The Gay 100: A Ranking of the Most Influential Gay Men and Lesbians, Past and Present.* New York: Birch Lane Press, 1994.

Russo, Vito. *The Celluloid Closet: Homosexuality in the Movies.* Revised Edition. New York: Harper, 1987.

Sarotte, Georges-Michel. *Like a Brother, Like a Lover: Male Homosexuality in the American Novel and Theater from Herman Melville to James Baldwin.* Garden City, NY: Doubleday, 1978.

Schwarz, Christa A. B. *Gay Voices of the Harlem Renaissance.* Bloomington: Indiana University Press, 2003.

Signorile, Michelangelo. *Queer in America: Sex, the Media and the Closets of Power.* New York: Random House, 1993.

Smith, Richard. *Seduced and Abandoned: Essays on Gay Men and Popular Music.* London: Cassell, 1996.

Summers, Claude J. *Gay Fictions: Wilde to Stonewall.* New York: Continuum, 1990.

———, ed. *The Gay and Lesbian Literary Heritage.* London: Routledge, 2002.

———, ed. *An Encyclopedia of Gay, Lesbian, Bisexual, Transgender, and Queer Culture.* http://www.glbtq.com.

Thompson, Mark, ed. *Long Road to Freedom: The Advocate History of the Gay and Lesbian Movement.* New York: St. Martin's Press, 1994.

Tyrkus, Michael J., ed. *Gay and Lesbian Biography.* Detroit: St. James Press, 1997.

Walters, Suzanna Danuta. *All the Rage: The Story of Gay Visibility in America.* Chicago: University of Chicago Press, 2003.

Waugh, Thomas. *The Fruit Machine: Twenty Years of Writings on Queer Cinema.* Durham, NC: Duke University Press, 2000.

Weiss, Andrea. *Vampires and Violets: Lesbians in Film.* London: Penguin, 1992.

White, Patricia. *Uninvited: Classical Hollywood Cinema and Lesbian Representability.* Bloomington: Indiana University Press, 1999.

Whitely, Sheila, and Jennifer Rycenga, eds. *Queering the Popular Pitch.* London: Routledge, 2006.

Wittig, Monique. *The Straight Mind and Other Essays.* Boston: Beacon, 1992.

Woodhouse, Reed. *Unlimited Embrace: A Canon of Gay Fiction, 1945–1995.* Amherst: University of Massachusetts Press, 1998.

Woods, Gregory. *A History of Gay Literature: The Male Tradition.* New Haven, CT: Yale University Press, 1999.

INDEX

About the Author

LUCA PRONO is an independent scholar who teaches English in Italy. He has contributed chapters and entries to many Greenwood reference books.